DO

THE RISE, FALL, AND REDEMPTION OF KEVIN CHILES

KEVIN CHILES
with **Richard Ray, Esq.**

Copyright © 2019 by Kevin Chiles and Richard Ray, Esq.

All rights reserved.
Published by Don Diva Global Media, New York.
dondivamag.com

For permission requests, contact the publisher at tc@dondivamag.com.

Ordering Information:
Special discounts are available on quantity purchases.
For details, contact the publisher at tc@dondivamag.com.

Printed in the United States of America

Paperback ISBN: 978-0-578-67912-9
Hardcover ISNB: 978-0-9791710-8-6
eBook ISBN: 978-0-9791710-7-9

Cover Design: Pen 2 Pen

CONTENTS

FOREWORD BY RICHARD RAY	iv
PREFACE	vi
GENESIS OF A HUSTLER	4
EVOLUTION OF A HUSTLER	28
COLLEGE DROPOUT	40
HUSTLE HARD	55
D.C. ON ARRIVAL	70
C.R.E.A.M.	82
LET THE GAMES BEGIN	95
LORD OF THE FLIES	110
NEW YORK, NEW YORK	124
BALLIN	134
THE STREETS ARE ALWAYS WATCHING	146
DEAR MOMMA	160
LEVELS OF DARKNESS	173
DOWN BUT NOT OUT	182
CAN'T STOP THE HUSTLE	203
THE HITS KEEP COMING	213
BIPOLAR STATE OF "THE LIFE"	231
ARREST	240
PREPARING FOR BATTLE	268
FIRST TRIAL	283
2ND TRIAL & PLEAS	297
PRISON	313
HOME SWEET HOME - SORTA	334
FOLLOW THE LEADER	341
STILL DODGING BULLETS	359
EPILOGUE	371

FOREWORD BY RICHARD RAY

I met Kevin Chiles in 1985. It wasn't a particularly memorable introduction for him, and that theme continued on several other occasions we crossed paths for the remainder of the '80s. His brother, Tony, and I started as classmates at Columbia University in the summer of 1985 and remain good friends to this day.

I was aware of Kevin's tribulations and trials and the creation of *Don Diva* magazine while he was doing his bid. I had been practicing entertainment law for over ten years when Tony reached out in late 2003 to see if I could help *Don Diva*. He told me Kevin was getting out of jail shortly, and I agreed with no hesitation.

So, in early 2004, I met with Kevin and Tiffany and began serving as counsel for the brand. Kevin and I developed an almost immediate friendship. Even then, it was evident that he was a man that had many intimate relationships yet, still maintained some distance with people. I had once been told I was the world's only living heart donor, so I could empathize with someone who may have had emotional intimacy issues.

I began to fashion myself a writer after I took some time and penned a fictional novel titled *Thicker Than Blood*. Afterward, I would occasionally mention that he needed to tell "his story" outside of just *Don Diva*. The brand continued to grow exponentially under his and Tiffany's direction. Yet, I still felt like his story was deserving of an audience delivered through the silver screen. For a number of reasons, I don't think Kevin ever felt the timing was right for such a project.

The Hot 97 interview with Funkmaster Flex in September 2017, changed our narrative. This isn't to say he was still convinced, because he wasn't. However, if only to pacify my persistence, we embarked on daily, three-to-four-hour conversations, for months, on every nuance that shaped his life. I took copious notes, and a story was forming, but it was apparent Kevin was still not fully sold.

As our conversations continued, it became clear that we had even more in common than realized. We truly lived parallel, if not divergent lives. I was intimately familiar with life during the Crack Era. Though I maintained my academic pursuits, I was never far from the realities that were taking place in the streets. I could see his comfort and confidence in the process grow daily, and it became obvious when he was fully on-board.

Kevin is a hustler, and once he was all in, I could see him putting other, existent money-making ventures on hold to immerse himself in our project. This became both of our passions, and it was therapeutic, as well. As time went on, we developed a syncopated rhythm within our differing styles. We were so in tune that whole chapters could be delivered from shorthand conversations. Outside editing was welcomed to help flush out story developments that we may have glossed over because our easy understandings may not have always been clear to a reader. The result is a project we share with pride.

We are both unsure but optimistic as to how this book will be received. What we do know is that it was written with honesty and hope. Kevin's story is entertaining, educational, and serves as a cautionary tale.

Hopefully, it will be equally inspiring.

PREFACE

It is often said that in cases of accidents or grave danger, one's life flashes before their eyes. I have been in life-threatening situations before (unfortunately more times than should be counted). While I understand and agree with the sentiment, nothing compares to the levels of introspection on that first night of incarceration, especially when faced with the possibility of never returning home again.

I had never been previously incarcerated for more than a night or two, but knowing many who had, I often heard what that first night behind bars entailed. Every sight and sound is magnified. Most importantly, that initial clanking of the bars combined with declarations of "Lights out" leads to introspection.

I came to prominence in what is known as the Crack Era in New York City. Part of what made the time so fascinating (beyond pure nostalgia) was the larger-than-life characters that embodied Harlem, New York, and the entire country. My story is my own. However, it would not be complete or as interesting without the cast of characters that influenced my life and the culture of the era.

So here, I share my story-- an eventful life with several chapters still to be written. Do not let the sometimes-colorful commentary blind you from the cautionary lessons to be learned.

1
GENESIS OF A HUSTLER

The Bronx is considered the founding home of Hip Hop. Yet, before every urban kid having dreams of escaping the hood using two turntables and a microphone, most aspired to leave through hoop dreams or selling drugs. It didn't feel like there were many other available options for achieving the "American Dream."

New York City was particularly rough in the 1970s. In 1975, the city was facing an economic crisis in which it was nearing bankruptcy. Essential city services like garbage pickup were held up. You can only imagine how much less urgent it was for the city to address the issues in predominantly Black and Hispanic areas like much of the Bronx. So much of the Bronx was littered with dilapidated and abandoned buildings. The landscape looked like war-torn Beirut. In the summer of 1977, the city experienced a 25-hour power Blackout, which led to widespread looting and panic. Between the financial crisis, Blackout, and high crime rates throughout the city and its subways, nearly a million residents fled the nation's largest metropolis by the end of the decade. The concrete jungle was seen as being in irreversible decline, and people wanted out. The hopelessness that many New Yorkers felt was exponentially higher in forgotten areas like the Bronx, Harlem, and much of Brooklyn.

This was NYC in the 1970s, a city that served as the inspiration for glorified, lawless movies like Fort Apache: The Bronx, Death Wish, and The Warriors. If you look at photos of the city during this time, it was grimy with piled-up garbage and graffiti everywhere. The Hudson River was a cesspool of germs and bacteria that set the tone for the place. People were really trying to "Escape From New York," after the city seemed to lose its signature aura of "greatness."

Black and brown communities in the city were also inundated with drugs and rampant addiction issues, most notably from heroin use. The movie SuperFly was fictitious. However, individuals like Nicky Barnes and the Council (along with other notable figures) flooded minority neighborhoods with the help and strategic design of the Mafia and crooked cops.

This was the backdrop of my youth. The pressure and despair that my family felt would inevitably shape my basic instincts to survive and my yearning for so much more out of life. This was my reality. This was my New York.

For many, the "American Dream" is a fundamental equation of education plus hard work equaling or leading to success. Immigrants were, and still are, drawn to America because of these promises of hope and prosperity. It is true. America is and can be a land of opportunity. However, for the generations of minorities hampered by racism and a lack of resources, that basic equation of success did not apply so readily.

Both of my parents were born and raised in Asheville, North Carolina. They grew up during the reign of Jim Crow in the South and witnessed the spawning of the Civil Rights Movement. The Civil War unofficially abolished slavery, but inhumanity towards blacks persisted in the form of rampant discrimination. The struggle for social justice and civil rights that took place in the Deep South during the 1950s and 1960s left an indelible impression on my parents as it did for much of the country.

My mother, born Barbara Jean Duckett, and father, Tony Chiles, dated during high school. My mother was an extremely bright woman who did well in school. My father, on the other hand, by his own admission, not so much. He was a great athlete and excelled in multiple sports, but his love of basketball is what he was primarily known for. My father told me that if it weren't for my mother, he literally wouldn't have made it out of high school.

During their senior year, my mother became pregnant. Her parents, Juanita and Hubert Duckett, weren't too happy with the situation or my father. My father had aspirations to play college basketball (as some of his classmates, not nearly as talented had done). However, my maternal grandmother didn't have it. Back then, they didn't play those games. They called them "shotgun weddings" for a reason. You paid for any mistakes you made, and you were going to be held accountable. My father was expected to marry my mother, get a job, and take care of his family.

They graduated that June, and five months later, on November 7, 1966, Kevin Dewane Duckett was born. My birth name was indicative of the displeasure my maternal grandparents still festered towards my father. My parents were eventually married shortly after my birth, and Kevin Chiles officially became my name.

The responsibilities that come with marriage and raising a family forced my father to abandon any hopes of playing college ball. That first year out of high school, my father only managed a few different odd jobs making very little money, but it beats a blank. He told me that he had an Aunt Bay that had migrated to New York City. She was one of the first residents of the then-new St. Nicholas Housing Projects on 129th Street and 8th Avenue in Harlem. He had visited her a couple of times and stated he really didn't like New York. Many Southerners were migrating north during that time to different cities like New York and as far west as Los Angeles. They hoped for better lives, believing they were leaving behind the prejudice and racism of the South.

My mother's parents also found themselves in New York City shortly after my birth. They ended up living about a mile further downtown on 8th Avenue from Aunt Bay's apartment. They ended up on the second floor of a tenement walkup two blocks from the entrance to Central Park at 112th Street. This was a mere coincidence because my father said that the respective families really didn't have much of a relationship before migrating to NYC. My grandparents were accompanied by my uncles Tit and De De, as well as my aunts Betty and Diane, leaving us behind.

Less than a year later, my father felt New York possessed better opportunities than Asheville and moved us up to the city too. Initially, we stayed with my grandparents, but the living arrangement proved temporary. We moved five blocks away to 117th Street and 8th Avenue.

The building was really run down, and the living conditions were less than ideal, mainly because my mother was now pregnant with my brother. Finding somewhere else to live took on a sense of urgency.

We were only on 117th Street for a couple of months before my brother, Tony Chiles Jr., was born on January 3, 1968, at St. Luke's Hospital. Shortly after his birth, we moved to the Highbridge section of the Bronx on 169th Street and Ogden Avenue.

Highbridge encompasses a series of five to six-story walkup tenement buildings. We moved into our fifth-floor, one-bedroom pad. Apartment 5D accommodated our family of four with my parents' queen-size bed, along with our bunk bed in the single bedroom. The apartment was sparsely furnished at first with the little there was that was likely given by others. Over time, my mother was able to finance a new couch and chairs, which were then covered in plastic to ensure their longevity. The walls were covered in red velvet wallpaper.

When we first moved to the Bronx, there were still a handful of Caucasian families living in the neighborhood. The buildings were initially decent compared to what we had just come from in Harlem. You could see that the building had once been nice with granite stairs and subway tile flooring. I am not sure exactly how long before the White flight took place, but within a couple of years, the landscape changed, and there weren't any White families around. In turn, the landlords increasingly gave less of a shit as the demographics of their tenants changed.

***

My father was a marginalized Black male that had been raised in the Deep South. He grew up in poverty and was regularly beaten by his mother, who ridiculed him for not doing well in school. My paternal grandmother was only 14 years old when she had him, no more than a child herself. I am sure any amateur psychologist could infer that some of the beatings might have been the result of him looking like the father he never knew. In reality, he had vision problems that made it difficult for him to learn during those times, and it went undiagnosed well into adulthood.

Once he moved to New York, life was not necessarily that much easier for an uneducated Black man in the 1960s and 1970s. My mother was very patient with him, being supportive, and dealing with his shortcomings. Early on, he worked a variety of jobs delivering various products throughout the Garment District before moving on to construction. When he was working, he provided. The work inconsistency, however, was more real, and we were all primarily dependent on my mother. She worked for NYNEX, the phone company (also known as Ma Bell). Her job was steady, but paying the bills and feeding two growing, active boys put a strain on her financially and psychologically.

Society may have marginalized him, but my father was undeniably the man of the house. Right or wrong, what he said was law. He had the physical appearance of a heavyweight prizefighter. He stood 6'2' and weighed 220 lbs. With a broad-shouldered, athletic, muscular build. As a kid, he was intimidating without having to say much. A menacing look in our direction was enough. He was far from lazy but continuously weighed down by the lack of opportunity. He dealt with it but was increasingly frustrated. This led to him, at times, having displaced aggression towards my mother as well as my brother and I.

My mother was secure in that she knew he had a good heart. However, immersed within his own frustrations, he never really seemed to consider the additional burdens he bestowed upon her. It took very little to set him off, so we all often danced around him, avoiding anything we thought would light the fuse. Unfortunately, we were not always successful.

There were times when my brother and I would be in our shared room and hear my parents fighting, both verbally and physically. The physical altercations clearly weren't fair fights because my father was eight inches taller and at least 80 pounds heavier. We couldn't clearly understand what they were fighting about. If I had to guess, they centered on him not being home, and my mother questioning him about having affairs. She was complaining about him not doing what was needed around the house but having time for other nonsense.

My brother and I were happy when our father wasn't at home. We didn't have to worry about the arguing or him putting his hands on her. I felt completely helpless in not being able to do anything. What I do know is whatever the issues were; it had nothing to do with my mother. All she did was go to work and take care of us to the best of her ability.

***

I went to Public School 11 for grades one through three. Although the school was only across the street from my house, walking there on my own gave me a sense of independence. Growing up in the Bronx, none of us ever sat around talking about being poor. In all honesty, I didn't grasp our plight because everyone in my neighborhood resembled us in varying degrees. So, it all seemed reasonable. We were resourceful kids and created fun from virtually nothing. We played from sunup to sundown. Some of our favorites were; Red Light Green Light, Hot Peas and Butter, Tag, and Skullies in the street while the girls Jumped Rope and played Hopscotch.

During the summer months, all you needed was a makeshift funnel from an old can and the fire hydrants, which we called "Johnny Pumps." We played until the fire or police department would come and shut us down. Their reasoning was the usage caused the water pressure to be low, so in the event of a fire. We only cared about the benefits we got from our ghetto waterpark on those stifling days stuck within our concrete jungle.

We would build go-carts from items thrown away in the garbage. Shopping carts would supply the wheels, wooden milk cartons for the seats, and a two by four for the body. A hammer and some nails are all it took. When we were too small to play on the real basketball courts, we would play basketball using the fire escape attached to the front of my building as the hoop. In the house, we would assemble a basketball hoop made from a wire hanger hung on the closet door along with a sock we'd use as the ball. Ghetto ingenuity knew little bounds, and minimal resources proved to be the mother of inventions. My Bronx neighborhood was all I knew, and it was special to me.

There was a feeling of community. As the saying goes, it takes a village to raise a child. Those sentiments rang true in these kinds of neighborhoods. It wasn't odd for your parents' friends to reprimand you if they caught you out of pocket. Actually, it was expected. There was no such thing as back-talking to your parents or any adults in the neighborhood. Helping older people upstairs with their packages and going to the store for whoever asked you was the norm. "Yes, Sir" and "Yes, Ma'am" were how you addressed adults. You better not get caught cursing because whatever adult heard, you would pop you in the mouth before you could even think about apologizing. My parents stressed having manners and being respectful to our elders. My neighborhood almost had a small-town feel amid a city of eight million.

I attended P.S. 126 for grades four through six. It was on 166th Street and Ogden Avenue, a couple of blocks from where I lived. I had the responsibility of dropping my brother off to school first on 167th Street and Nelson at the Annex that housed his grade; then I'd continue on to my school, which was just two blocks from there. After school, I'd go back and pick him up. He understood that he'd better not move until I got there, and we'd walk home together. This was required of me every day. Part of my adamance toward my brother staying put was the fact that I had been hit by a car shortly before. Thankfully, I was not hurt, but the incident scared me. I never told anyone what happened. It would have resulted in an ass whipping and limiting of the newfound liberties I had been gaining.

I was what was commonly known as a latchkey kid. I was mainly on my own, and usually in charge of my brother's care from the time school was out until my mother returned from work. We were required to finish our homework before we could even think about going outside. We were only allowed to play in front of the building or within earshot of my mother's calling. Over time, the distance was extended.

There were benefits that came along with being responsible and unsupervised to a degree. Now, I was able to go to other parks in the area to play. By this time, I developed into a pretty good basketball player. I'd venture to the local park a block away on 168th Street and Ogden Avenue as well as Nelson Park on 165th Street, where the competition was a lot better.

In these parks, the older guys ran the main court, while us little guys would be relegated to the side courts. We would play 21, or 3-on-3 until they allowed us to have the court. There would be instances where they only had nine players, needing one more, and I'd get picked up to play with them. This helped to build my confidence and give me the experience of playing at a higher level. I always handled my business and fared well. I took to the challenge, and over time, the older guys took to me. They would often send me to the store to get them juices or snacks to have after playing, and I got to keep the change from the errands.

Some of those older guys who used to send me to the store hustled over on 170th Street and College Avenue on the Eastside. I was uncertain what their hustle was initially before I came to understand it was heroin. I was barely leaving the stoop, but their clothes, money, and girls, along with them seemingly not having a care in the world, left an impression on me. This all occurred up until I was ten years old or so. The guys were but teenagers themselves. It was at this early stage I could identify the neighborhood shot callers and determine who was who. It was an education I didn't even realize was taking place.

***

For years, our routine included visiting my grandparents on the weekends in Manhattan. It was a different world from the Bronx. I just remember how crowded the streets felt, and it seemed like people were everywhere. I don't remember anything like that in the Bronx except possibly on Fordham Road. My head felt like it was on a swivel, taking in all the activity. Our neighborhood in the Bronx was nearly all residential, but in Harlem, I saw businesses everywhere. There were beauty parlors, barbershops, clothing stores, and every other kind of business imaginable. Everyone appeared to be in a rush, and there were tons of people selling goods on the streets. The sensory overload was intense, especially as a child. I can remember my mother holding my hand tightly early on during these excursions.

These visits were the first time that I saw a dope fiend. That area in Harlem, especially off 116th Street and 8th Avenue, was the epicenter of New York's heroin epidemic. Even without a full understanding of what was going on, what I saw was indelibly inked in my mind. I'll never forget the imagery of grown men standing but nodding like they were asleep. They looked like they were going to fall, but right at that moment, they'd come to and get their composure, only to nod back out again.

My grandfather was a handsome guy, smooth and well-dressed with a couple of gold teeth. He'd regularly keep a late model Cadillac. One I distinctly remember was yellow with whitewall tires that were always clean and shiny. I don't remember what he did for a living, but I do remember him selling alcohol after hours and on Sundays. He was one of the first entrepreneurs/hustlers I ever met. He knew that people loved to drink, and when the liquor stores closed, he was the only store open, leaving them nowhere to go but to him.

My grandmother, on the other hand, was a Hellraiser. She enjoyed her cocktails, but they sometimes got the better of her. That's when you'd needed to stay out her way. She wasn't one to bite her tongue, and anyone was fair game if they got on her bad side. Early on, my father could attest to that fact. My recollection of her was that she was a loving person who spoiled and always catered to me. At the time, my brother and I were her only grandchildren.

***

Besides the time we spent with my grandparents, I spent every moment outside of school playing basketball. When school was off, I was out there literally all day. Part of this was simply for a love of the game. However, an almost equal part of staying out so long was the refuge basketball provided in having to spend as little time as possible in our cramped, overcrowded apartment, usually overrun with tension and aggression. Of course, growing up in the hood is laced with irony. One drawback to looking to the parks and streets to provide a sanctuary is those same streets are often what we needed the most protection from.

One winter day, when I was either ten or eleven, highlighted how precarious life in the Bronx could be. A little snow on the ground was not enough to dissuade us from shoveling off the court to play. So this particular dreary, drizzling day was definitely not enough to keep a handful of us from occupying the blacktop off of 168th Street and Ogden Avenue for hours. Once I was done, before traveling the block to get home, I stopped to get some candy. The bodega was run by a Hispanic couple. On this day, the wife was behind the counter, and the husband was in the aisles. As I approached the counter to pay, two armed men burst in declaring it was a stickup. It was probably not coincidental that I was the only customer in the store. The husband and I were quickly ushered into the back bathroom. We were told that no one would get hurt if we just stayed put.

I could hear one of the gunmen yelling that "it wasn't enough." I assumed it was about the cash-on-hand, but the wife's retorts were mostly indecipherable. I recollect that the place served dually as a convenience store and illegal numbers spot, so it being targeted made sense. The husband looked at me and told me to stay in the bathroom with the door closed. He then reached down and pulled out a pistol he had holstered around his ankle. He slowly opened the door and began stealthily creeping out. Seconds later, I started hearing gunshots. I was startled, unable to see and unsure of what to do, so I stayed quiet in the bathroom. Moments later, the door swung open. It was the store owner, escorting me out of the bathroom. One of the gunmen was lying motionless in a pool of blood on the floor.

Many of the specifics were a blur afterward. However, I remember not having any discernible emotions or feelings about seeing my first murdered body. The 44th Police Precinct was only about three blocks from the park and store. I cannot recall if they were already on the scene by the time I came out of the bathroom, but they took me to the precinct where I remained until my father was able to come a short time afterward. This would not be the last time I saw extreme violence in my neighborhood.

The bodega served as a central memory in my childhood besides serving as a robbery/murder scene. In many neighborhoods like ours, the local grocer or bodega would often extend credit to families to make it through to payday. First, you would roll up pennies and other change to pull together whatever could be mustered. When that ran out, credit would typically be extended for a carton of eggs, milk, and bread. The loan was for basic necessities, along with the occasional cold cuts of spiced ham and cheese. This was never anyone's favorite, but it was relatively cheap and sufficed.

I remember my canvas Pro-Keds or Converses would be worn until they had holes in them, which matched my socks. I would fold my tattered socks inside my sneakers, putting cardboard in my sneakers to reinforce them and provide support to extend their life.

In the winters, my hands and feet would be freezing. That was my norm, and it wasn't something I gave much thought to beyond merely trying to stay warm. It was quite a few years before I realized this wasn't an issue for most of America because they had adequate clothing to protect them against the elements. Broadening your horizons and gaining perspective has a way of shedding light on things we once otherwise thought were typical in the hood.

Even though my mother worked tirelessly, it seemed like she just couldn't get ahead. We lived literally from paycheck to paycheck just getting by, if that. I hated seeing her despondent and stressed. I just picked up on her energy, and the frivolity of basketball began to take a backseat to the needs of helping her. Adults often fail to understand how intuitive kids are to stress and problems within households.

Since I was the oldest, it would be me helping my mother carry the grocery bags up the five flights of stairs to our apartment. I'd do the same with the laundromat, running errands, or just going to the corner store. When the garbage had to go out, it would be me taking it down the five flights of stairs and around the corner of the building where it had to go. I'd better not look in any way like I had a problem with any of this either. Honestly, I didn't enjoy any of it, but I readily did whatever I could to make the load a little lighter for my mother.

I started packing bags around the age of ten in the local supermarket. I also offered to carry the bags for women and older people up the tenement walk-ups. The stairs were so much more tolerable when I got paid to climb them. I may have only made $20 - $30 on Saturdays and Sundays, but that money I would give to my mom really made a difference, mainly when it came to food.

One of my next hustles was selling and delivering the Sunday paper. I would buy a stack, sell them, then run back and buy more as needed. I usually sold them for their cost-plus tips. Sometimes, I was lucky enough to occasionally swipe some if I caught the truck dropping them off early in the morning. They would be thrown on the sidewalk in front of the variety stores before they'd open, allowing me to grab a few if I got to them early enough.

My contributions were helping, which meant my mother no longer had to ask for credit as often from the corner store. I could also see the relief to her pride. Words were not exchanged, but I knew how much that little bit of money helped her, and the lessened stress was noticeable. I now also had, literally, a few bucks in my pocket for the first time, and I liked it. I was hooked to hustling because of how much of a difference I knew it made in my family's life.

I started collecting baseball cards and comic books in grade school. Comic books were an escape from my reality. I would envision becoming a superhero, but more importantly, a life outside of my present circumstances. "Collecting" is a convenient term considering my means of attaining comic books. Packs of baseball cards were cheap to buy. You could quickly add to your collection with a game called flipping, which essentially just meant matching cards or colors. You might start with 25 or so and leave school with all your pockets filled if luck was on your side for the day. In the course of playing the games, you might acquire your favorite players or rookie cards of future Hall of Famers in pristine condition, which went up in value each year. I acquired players like Hank Aaron, Reggie Jackson, Robin Yount, Don Sutton, and Thurman Munson, to name just a few. We didn't necessarily know the value when we were kids, but I had always heard stories of how valuable baseball cards could be. Today, I have a substantially valuable collection built on my days flipping and collecting in the Bronx as a kid.

We had heard the same stories about the potential value of comic books, particularly early and first editions of new series. My newfound economic bounty of a few dollars every week meant I could actually buy some of the latest comics that came out, including the first Star Wars issue. The already high valued ones, sold mostly at comic book conventions, were clearly out of my economic reach. However, I wasn't going to let a little issue like affordability deter me from collecting valuable issues. This would all become easier as my freedom to travel increased.

***

Due to a lack of junior high schools in my immediate area, once I graduated from sixth grade, I was forced to attend one on the other side of the Bronx. Junior high would be where I would be reintroduced to James "Fojo" Cusar. He and I had met each other a year earlier playing ball against one another in middle school. He was the best guy on his P.S. 73 team. I was awarded the MVP trophy at P.S. 126.

I had to travel an hour each way back and forth to school. I would get on the bus in front of my building on 169th Street and Ogden Avenue and take it to its last stop near Yankee Stadium. I'd then transfer to another bus that would take me across town to 161st Street and Park Avenue on the Eastside. I would get off and walk four blocks to 164th Street and Teller Avenue, where P.S. 145 Arturo Toscanini was located.

It was the furthest I'd traveled by myself to school. I didn't find it overly challenging because it's what all of us had to do, and it quickly became my regular routine. With that came more responsibility and the trust of my parents, knowing I was able to move about confidently.

In the comic books, I saw advertisements mentioning different conventions in and around the city. I had never been to one and often wondered what they were about. With my ability, confidence, and freedom to travel beyond my immediate vicinity, I decided I would go to one.

My mother always had concerns about me traveling and my whereabouts, but my father consented to me venturing out. The funny thing is, he really didn't know how to travel on mass transportation other than the couple of places he frequented.

I found my way to one of those conventions in Midtown, Manhattan with my brother in tow. One of my requirements for going anywhere outside of school was that I had to take my younger brother with me. My brother and I are only fourteen months apart. Instead of ever having any type of sibling rivalry, from my earliest recollections, my brother always looked up to me. He could see my basketball skills and soon followed suit. He could also see how my hustling at the grocery store helped him and the family. As strange as it may be to say, from the earliest stages, my brother always trusted me. We have a strong bond... still have, though it has almost always gone unspoken. So, it wasn't hard to enlist him as a wingman on my comic book capers.

My parents were none the wiser. Sometimes there was a fee to get into the conventions. I don't specifically remember the amount for entering that first one, but knowing myself, I found a way around it, sneaking us both in.

These conventions were a predecessor to the comic-cons of today. They were smaller venues but still crowded nonetheless with kids everywhere, of all ages and ethnicities. This dynamic was fertile grounds for the distractions I needed to do what I was doing.

You didn't have to be a comic book expert or connoisseur to be able to determine the most valuable editions at comic bookstores or conventions. They were all carefully vacuum-sealed and placed in a less accessible manner to convey their status. My brother would serve as the decoy or distraction for my sticky fingers. The five-finger discounts were responsible for helping me amass a really valuable collection by the time I was 12 years old. I was able to secure First Editions like Spiderman or Ironman, as well as books in which characters like Silver Surfer were introduced.

This would be one of the rare and last times I would ever have my brother participate in any type of illicit activity. My role as a big brother and protector was to keep my brother out of harm's way. I did things and provided, so my brother never had to put himself at risk or veer off the straight and narrow.

Money was always tight at the house, but at some point, I knew the comics represented more than just collector's items. I don't recall exactly how it came to my attention. I probably overheard an argument of some type between my parents concerning a need for money. My small contributions to my mother were always welcomed, but she never actually asked for anything.

So, I'm sure my mother and father were quite surprised when I said I could probably help get the money needed. His surprise was likely muted and measured to a degree when I mentioned that I needed his help in pulling it off. I told him I had collected a bunch of comics and that some of them were probably really valuable. I actually knew this for sure because I had a price guide that determined value based on the condition of the comic book. I needed him to go to the comic book convention so the vendors would not question where or how I attained them. Or, try to rip me off.

We took a handful from my collection and went to the convention. This one took place at the Hotel Pennsylvania located directly across from Madison Square Garden. I don't remember the exact amount, but I think the comics sold for around $2,500 to $3,000. I could tell my father was surprised, yet never once did he ask how the hell, I had $3,000 worth of comics at 12-years-old. What was clear is that I wasn't going to see a dime of that money. My father held it. I'm sure he gave some to my mother for bills, but I also recall him using part of the money to buy DJ equipment.

***

Music was always an integral part of my family's life, especially my father's. I am sure he dabbled prior, but once he secured the DJ equipment and speakers, it became his hustle and by default, our family hustle.

My father was DJ Tony Rome. He would put a large speaker in the window during the warmer weather weekends for the benefit/detriment of the neighborhood. We would also take to the neighborhood schoolyards, throwing what was called park jams, running electricity from the streetlights.

Besides my brother and I, the Tony Rome Crew, consisted of Chris, Ant-Man, Lil Dice, Don Q, Ron Dew, Handsome, June Brown, Wayne O, Crawford, Carmelo, Reggie, Marvin, Stretch, Cedric, Carl, Vincent, Russell, Raynard, Joey, Stacks, and Lil Stacks. Everyone had varying roles from DJs, to emcees to security to just being part of the crew. They were a close-knit group that stills keep in touch to this day.

Eventually, this transformed to house parties in our apartment where all the furniture would be moved into the bedroom, and he would charge admission of a couple of dollars. We might have up to 40 or 50 people over at a time. My brother and I would spin first, catering to the younger generation immersed in the new and burgeoning Hip-Hop scene. My brother was DJ Tony Rome Jr., and I was DJ KC or Kansas City Kev. This lasted until I began high school when I started losing interest, and other things had my attention. My father continued DJing and even providing or renting the equipment to others as well.

***

By now, my after-school basketball play was mainly taking place in Nelson Park on 166th Street. This is where my game was solidified, and I met most of my basketball peers, many of whom went onto becoming elite players in the sport. James "Fojo" Cousar was already a friend, and there we met Mark Felder. The three of us would pick two other people to complete our five. Me and a handful of friends went wherever the competition was. We never ventured too far, mostly other neighborhoods in the Bronx within walking distance. I believe having those experiences early on gave me the confidence to move beyond my area and later throughout the city. Basketball was everything growing up for most in my neighborhood. Your skills on the court could earn you respect and a reputation. The competition daily was so intense that it eventually led to numerous Division I college players coming out of Highbridge. They included brothers Cornbread and Troy Truesdale, who I recall as the first from our neighborhood to play Division I ball. It also included two NCAA stars and eventual NBA players, Walter Berry of St. John's and John Morton of Seton Hall, as well as streetball legend Master Rob.

There was such a storied history of basketball lore growing up in the Bronx and NYC overall. We all knew it could potentially lead to a college education, if not a career in the pros. NBA Hall of Famer Kareem Abdul Jabbar was just across the bridge in Dyckman. The Bronx was home to Nate "Tiny" Archibald. Streetball legends such as Earl "The Goat" Manigault, Joe "The Destroyer" Hammond and Pee Wee Kirkland made basketball easily the most intoxicating path for any NYC youth to follow out of their bleak surroundings.

I initially played for Intercession coached by Mr. Black. Intercession was a Church in Harlem with a full-court gymnasium in its basement that took up nearly a whole city block on 155th Street between Broadway and Amsterdam Avenue. This often meant leaving home on Saturday as early as 8:00 or 9:00 in the morning via bus and not returning until late in the evening. My brother went to practice because played on the super Biddy team, which was the ten-year-olds while I played Biddys, which were 12 and under. Our practices were usually on the same day an hour or so apart on opposite sides of the gym. Even with the early morning rise, we still had to do our chores. This was all part of the learned conditioning of doing what I had to do in order to do what I wanted to.

My reputation as a basketball player grew as I played in the Biddy, Midget, and Junior leagues. I was called on by various coaches to play in tournaments throughout the Bronx and Harlem. I was introduced to the elite organizations like Riverside Church and the Gauchos. I played in tournaments at the Rucker, City Wide, and Each One Teach One in Manhattan. Some of the kids I met playing ball, I would end up hustling with later.

Basketball is where I first learned to identify fear as a kid. When it was crunch time, you would have to show what you were really made of. I remember the look in individual players' eyes, including my teammates, that indicated they would panic under pressure and turn the ball over. Choking is the term we used to describe it. In other instances, they just wouldn't want the ball at all. I excelled in those moments. Honestly, I lived for them. My ability to see people and things for what they were was a sort of sixth sense I would eventually understand I possessed.

Instincts are called instincts for a reason, and when they are telling you something, nine out of ten times, they're right. It's when we go against them that we live in regret. Trusting those natural instincts came in handy throughout my life.

***

Eventually, our time in Highbridge would come to an end. Our living conditions had become deplorable. Everyone I had grown up with moved away. My best friend, Chris Mack, and his family had gotten an apartment over on the Eastside on Park Avenue and 159th Street in a newly constructed development. We were one of the last families to leave. Chris had moved into Highbridge on 168th Street and Plimpton when I was about 12. He was from a large family of six brothers and five sisters. We initially bonded in the park across the street from our own apartments. Our families essentially adopted each of us. We immediately became close friends, and it was rare to see one of us without the other. Chris always had my back. No matter how crazy my schemes were, Chris still held me down.

We had been living there for about eight or nine years, and things had just continually gotten worse. We had roaches and mice that lived with us like rent-paying tenants. Heat and hot water were sometimes luxuries we couldn't afford. In our last winter, we went without heat for weeks on end. My mother had to boil water just for us to take birdbaths and used the oven to attempt to heat the apartment. This was the result of living conditions at the hands of slumlords in the Bronx.

The building had become all but abandoned, with many of the apartments vacant. Break-ins were becoming a norm, and a telltale sign of their occurrence was when the lights were out on a floors' hallway. When the lights were replaced, you could see their pattern of placing aluminum foil over the outside of people's peepholes to further prevent any detection.

The landlord had walked away from the property, leaving the tenants that were left to fend for ourselves. That last winter, there was one of the worst yet not having hot water or heat. As you can imagine, the deteriorating conditions had an adverse effect on the mood and personal dynamics within our home. It just increased the stress and tensions within our family, and something had to change. By the time the weather was breaking, my mother had made provisions for us to move.

Going into my ninth-grade year, we moved to Soundview, a neighborhood at the western edge of the Bronx. More specifically, we moved to the Clason Point section at 521 Commonwealth Avenue in the Academy Gardens Apartments. For years, my mother had been working towards getting a Section 8 apartment. It was like hitting a housing lottery, but I recall that it took a while to take place, and they made her jump through a bunch of hoops to secure it. Section 8 helped by paying a portion of the rent, which allowed us to move into an apartment that she wouldn't usually be able to afford based on her income. Even then, if there were changes in your financial circumstances, it could make you ineligible. One of the ironies is that getting a raise could cost you more in the long run.

At the time, I was only vaguely familiar with this part of the Bronx. A few friends and I had been brought there by one of the hustlers from my neighborhood, to play against some kids up there on a wager with another hustler. We just played and then went back home after winning. That's all I really knew about the area. What I did know was it had to be better than where we were.

Academy Garden was a renovated, gated housing development that took up a whole city block. It had two entrances with security on both ends that required non-residents to be announced before entering. It had all new appliances, playgrounds, grass walkways, and trees. On the surface, it appeared to be heaven coming from what we had just endured.

It was not very long before I realized that looks can be very deceiving. When I went to the store, I realized that we were smack dead in the middle of a drug den. The corner of Commonwealth and Randall Avenue was called Cozy Corner. I remember my mother and father getting into it with him, arguing that she didn't investigate the area well enough.

Even with this being our new reality, the living conditions were still far better than where we had just left. It didn't take long before we all got acclimated to our new surroundings. My mother usually just entered from the opposite side of the complex to avoid what was going on. I wasn't overly bothered by it, myself. I was more intrigued than anything.

***

By the time I got to high school, organized basketball had taken a back seat to my hustles. I still played, but my motivation had changed. There was a basketball organization called the Trotters based out of the Bronx run by twin brothers, Richard and Raymond Taliaferro. I played for them in the 8th and 9th grades. These teams in New York preceded what is more commonly known today as traveling AAU teams. There were no corporate or sneaker sponsors back then. It was either generous individual benefactors or people like the Taliaferros who figured it out otherwise.

My friends and I gravitated towards them because of the many perks they offered. They had professional-looking uniforms, which included home and away jerseys with matching shorts. We had pull-away warm-up suits and sneakers. We were also given duffle bags to carry our gear, which was all customized with the Trotters logo. We traveled to different cities to play games. In our eyes, it was what we imagined NBA players felt like. The emblazoned gear we carried around represented bragging rights of our prowess on the hardwood, and it was recognized by others throughout the Bronx. This may seem commonplace to many of you reading this today, but at the time it was almost unheard of.

While we proudly rocked the Trotters gear, uniforms, duffle bags, and trips did not exactly come free. The Taliaferros were not independently wealthy, and all of us kids were relatively poor, so there were no direct fees charged to be on the team. Instead of registration fees, there was a fundraising component attached to being on the team. We were expected to sell raffle tickets to raise money to support things like our travel, hotels, food expenses, and uniforms.

The Trotters had four teams from as young as ten (Biddys) up until 14 (Juniors) with 12 on each team for a total of 48 players. Our raffle sales quota was $25 a day, three to five times a week when we were home. When we were on the road, our quota doubled or even tripled. We might travel someplace every other month. As you can imagine, for a poor kid, traveling to play basketball was a dream come true.

We may have sold raffles throughout the year, but the drawing only took place once, annually, around Christmas. It was supposedly held on Randall's Island, which is obscurely located, just off the borough of Manhattan separated by the Harlem River, from Queens by the East River and Hells Gate, and from the Bronx by the Bronx Kill. Randall's Island is known for housing psychiatric institutions and cemeteries with no public residences. As a kid, I had no idea where this was, and obviously, in hindsight, neither did the people buying the raffles. The raffles stated the winner need not be present at the drawing. I quickly realized it was a scam after the first year. There was never any mention of a winner or even a drawing.

It didn't seem like anyone noticed, or maybe they just didn't care. We surely didn't. However, once I realized what was going on, I managed to find a way to take advantage of the program. I was able to capitalize because, along with several others, Raymond specifically took a liking to me. Initially, I wasn't sure as to the reason why beyond I was one of the best players. Nevertheless, the favoritism allowed me to have access to the raffles we were selling.

There were tens of thousands of raffles printed in boxes in his apartment. I began to steal them, initially selling them and just keeping all the money. My coveted post was standing outside the Bryant Park Library on 42nd Street. I started to give them to my brother and my friends from my neighborhood that I had brought onto the team. We'd evenly split the profits while also maintaining our quotas. This went on for some time. We did the same thing when we traveled to other states and cities. Wherever we went, we sold raffles. After a while, we began to realize the games we played were little more than pickup games versus any kind of organized league.

Eventually, there came a time when I realized why I was being shown favoritism. A few teammates and I were out with Raymond in the Bronx at a store called Jewman. We all openly called it that, including its owners, because there was no other name known for the store. It was famously known for what would later be called urban and Hip-Hop fashion. It was a store owned by an older Jewish couple before their kids took over.

The wife was really aggressive, not one to allow easy browsing, and the husband was always perched above us, looking over his store on his ladder. It was filled with an eclectic assortment of trends. It was a small spot, with a line always outside because they would only let ten or so in at a time. There was no real order to it. Something in the store one week might not be available the next.

Raymond was there buying the team peacoats. He began explaining his relationship with some of my teammates and why they had some of the "extra" things they had and how I could have all those things as well. I had an idea of where he was attempting to go with the conversation but played dumb, making him spell it out. He went on to say that it really wasn't sexual but being intimate to my level of comfort. I listened to him, not saying anything one way or another in an attempt to avoid my contempt being so blatant. It didn't really matter because I already made up my mind that I was outta there. When the team got back to Raymond's house, I gathered all my stuff, plus what I knew was going to be the last set of raffle tickets I was going to have access to. I informed my brother, Fojo, Chris, and his brother Ant-Man of what happened, and that it would be our last day as Trotters.

Unbeknownst to me, this type of scenario was probably being played out throughout the city. Two nationally renowned AAU squads from the Bronx (Gauchos) and Harlem (Riverside Church) had wealthy, Caucasian benefactors that were either accused of sexual improprieties with kids. And, in the case of Ernie Lorch of Riverside Church, indicted for sexually assaulting minors. Lorch's case was never actually adjudicated since he was deemed physically and mentally unable to withstand trial. Rumors around these and other organizations persisted for years. In hindsight, it all makes too much sense. Most of the kids on these teams were poor and many from fatherless households. Many were not able to stand up for themselves. They did not have anyone in their homes to protect them from the predators that acted like much-needed father figures.

Poor kids are the perfect target for pedophiles, because who was ever going to believe them anyway? Unfortunately, too many boys and girls have been preyed on by the very adults that were supposed to be role models, mentors, and protectors. Thankfully, I was not susceptible to this type of manipulation, and my brother and I were spared what others undoubtedly endured.

Leaving the Trotters made basketball take an even further backseat in my priorities. Maintaining and making money took precedence in my life. Yankee Stadium was what divided the Westside from the Eastside in the Bronx. I lived a stone's throw away from the stadium on the Westside up on the hill. A bunch of the kids from my area went to Yankee Stadium, hustling to make a few bucks. My friends consisted of myself, Dexter, Lil Jon, Dinky, and Chris. We did everything from scalping tickets to running scams to pickpocketing. Many would've called us hoodlums.

I began working as a helper to a guy named Chauncey, who had a souvenir stand outside of the stadium. He was about seventeen or eighteen. I was thirteen, still unable to get any kind of regular job because legal working papers were not granted in the city until age 14. Chris started out with me about the same time, but because he was a little older, he was able actually to get a job selling souvenirs at the stadium. As much as Chris and I developed a long and storied history of hustling, even our earliest experiences were indicative of his ability to square up when he saw fit and work regular jobs.

I made about $50 to $75 per game, helping Chauncey two hours before the game and an hour or so after. Eventually, I started to meet some of the kids scalping and realized there was way more potential to make money doing that than as a souvenir helper. Since I was so young, people would often just give me their extra ticket(s), assuming I was standing outside trying to get into the game myself. If they did not give them to me, they usually sold them to me below face value to try and recoup some of their money.

I got a map of the stadium seating and learned the value of the tickets I secured. In a week-long Yankees homestand, it was reasonable for me to net $300 to $500. This not only beat souvenir helper money, but keep in mind a summer youth employment job paid about $1.35 an hour at the time. People in those jobs were barely netting $150 bi-weekly for 35-hour work weeks and not much more than $600 for the entire summer.

2
EVOLUTION OF A HUSTLER

Once I got to high school, my hustle increased. School was never difficult, but now, the only subject I cared about was the economics class not being taught. Reading, writing, and arithmetic were relevant only to an extent. I needed to figure out how to add and multiply my money, as well as read any information that helped me achieve those goals. Everything else was simply extraneous noise. Choosing a high school was more about my level of comfort than it being best suited to give me a better future.

I attended Graphics Art High School, then known as Printing. It was located on 49th Street in the Midtown, Manhattan area known as Hell's Kitchen. I felt comfortable because Chris was joining me along with a few older neighborhood guys already attending.

Many kids worry about being hazed or bullied in school, but in New York, the stakes were far more perilous. There were wolf-packs, that seemed to go to school for no other reason than to prey on the vulnerable. One of those groups was a gang out of Brooklyn called the Decepticons. They gained notoriety for savagely robbing kids of anything of value. Knowing people gave me a degree of relief that I wasn't going to be an easy win for anyone. However, that threat still didn't stop us from carrying a shared .25 pistol along with the box cutters and knives we kept throughout high school.

I considered having to bring the weapons a necessity. New York City, on a whole, was rough-and-rugged, and kids robbing other kids for their items was pretty commonplace.

A bus and two different trains lead to a ninety-minute one-way commute. When I finally reached 50th Street and 8th Avenue, I would have to walk two additional blocks to 10th Avenue. Those two blocks were where the drama was most concentrated. They could feel like miles, especially if I was running late.

You stood a better chance of dealing with them if you were on time and happened to run into friends to walk with. However, in those instances, when you were late and had to trek those long blocks, alone, it was hell. Honestly, it probably made more sense just to turn around and go back home instead of taking the chance.

Although that may have been the most difficult part of my travels, it didn't mean you didn't encounter other places where you'd get robbed along the route. One day I was on a bus, probably four or five stops from home. I was sitting down, and a dude was standing over me. I didn't pay him much attention because personal space issues were something you learned to live with riding mass transit. I was wearing a sheepskin coat, British Walkers on my feet, and a pair of Cazal's on my face. As the bus came to a stop, the dude snatched my glasses and ran. Instinctively, I jumped up and ran after him. He dropped my glasses about a half-block later and kept running. We must've made a scene because the bus hadn't pulled off. I jogged back where the bus driver and a few passengers asked if I was alright before we continued.

Looking back, I realize it could have been different, as it was for my brother. He was close to home at a parochial school known for its academics and athletics, instead of the treacherous terrain. I wonder if I had chosen a school with an upper-echelon basketball program, how different my future might have been.

In Printing, I was easily one of, if not the best, players in the school. I had no desire to play other than in my required gym class and intramurals, where I would dominate effortlessly. Hoops gave way to the grind. I felt I had to hustle to continue to take care of myself as well as help my family.

Kids were merciless to those who didn't keep up with the trends. We all lived in similar housing projects and tenements, but limited, tattered or worn gear set you up to be ridiculed. At that age, most of us developed our self-worth from our ability to stay up-to-date with the latest fashions. I liked dressing nice and enjoyed all the compliments from my friends and the girls.

The hood always had its own sense of style. Before it being labeled "urban wear," there were trends made up by young New Yorkers who embodied the evolving street culture. Traveling all over the city to get limited-edition sneakers wasn't uncommon for us that considered ourselves to be fly and always fresh to death. I would go as far as Sneaker Circus on Pitkin Avenue in Brownsville, Brooklyn, because they were one of the only places in the city that had the suede Super Pro-Keds. I'd cop overlaps, teardrops, and gabardine pants and the straight-legged Lee's, with matching knits shirts. I bought British Walkers and Playboys at Florsheim Shoes and went to KP Kong which were both a short train or bus ride in Harlem. Jewman was right in my backyard. My hustles allowed me to keep up without burdening my parents

The academic part of school was relatively easy. My mother never stressed my academic future. My father would only intervene for disciplinary reasons, and my mother had chosen to stop involving him. I remember him being particularly volatile during that period. I had pretty much figured out what was necessary to stay off the radar. This kept everyone off my back and allowed me to move about with little issue.

It took me a minute to understand the lay of the land at Printing, but eventually, I developed a little weed hustle. I'm not sure how obvious my activities were. The reality is that because of my other legal hustles, no one, including my parents, had any real reason to suspect that I was doing anything out of pocket. I was just a nickel and dime dealer anyway. I had been essentially taking care of myself for some time; no one was giving too much thought to the source of my money at this point.

***

Around my junior and senior years in high school, I started a juggling act that would follow me well into adulthood. I was going out with two girls simultaneously. There was Gina from Fort Greene, Brooklyn, and Yvette, who was from Harlem. I was much faster than Gina. She was a good girl. I might have even been her first, but Yvette had me beat like Usain Bolt racing a kid.

Around this same time, Chris and I increasingly began hanging out with my Uncle Glen, known on the streets as "Kid." He got the nickname from some of the older hustlers as recognition for being one of the youngest getting money. He dropped out of the eighth grade and got started at 15 after being put on by his stepdad, who was in the drug game.

He was married to my mother's sister, Diane. My aunt Diane was the youngest. Initially, I was only around him when I babysat my cousins. My aunt always looked out and, until I got older, I was around them more related to her. Over time, my relationship with Glen developed to the point where I affectionately called him "Fat Man," years later, when he began to gain weight. He wasn't that big beside a bit of a Buddha's belly, but considering I wasn't much more than a buck sixty soaking wet, my perspective may have been a bit skewed. He was 13 to 14 years older than me. Our increased time together would profoundly shape the direction and course of my life.

I watched during my childhood as Aunt Diane and Kid moved up like the Jeffersons. They went from living in an apartment in Harlem on 112th Street between 8th and 7th Avenues to a row house in the Gun Hill section of the Bronx to a luxury apartment in Yonkers to buying a house in Willingboro, NJ, about two hours outside of New York in 1977.

The Willingboro house was on a golf course with a pool in the backyard. There were mopeds and luxury cars in the driveway. Kid was the only person I knew who embodied the "American Dream." He had accomplished all these things by the age of 24. In 1981, he purchased a bigger house closer to New York in West Orange, New Jersey, which was only about 30 minutes outside of the city.

The West Orange house additionally had a pool table and other tabletop games along with arcade-style video games, including Pac Man, in the basement, and an office. Compared to where I lived, visits to his house were like going to a resort. He was in the city nearly every day, and we began spending a little more time together. Kid had several luxury cars and always had pockets full of money. He had a few businesses and real estate holdings.

However, I became aware that the primary source of his income came from the heroin trade. I make the statement so casually because if you were Black or Latino from New York City (as well as most other urban areas across the US), it was highly likely that you had someone in your family who was either using drugs, selling drugs or both. Drug issues in minority communities are a microcosm of the struggles and lack of opportunities that those areas have endured for generations. Organized crime had strategically decided to inundate the Black community with narcotics, and the bleak realities of life within those communities made people receptive to both the escapism and economic opportunities that drugs provided.

During that time, many of the dealers often got high on their own supplies. It was the way most of them socialized, and it was openly acceptable. Although Kid was relatively young, he followed suit and routinely snorted both coke and heron. Perhaps because he never used a needle, I never looked at him as a dope fiend.

While I never judged Kid or viewed him as having an addiction, no doubt seeing someone you are around so closely routinely using drugs ultimately has a profound effect on you. It either makes it easier for you to follow in their path or work harder to do the opposite. I am not even sure any of this was ever conscious thinking for me, but perhaps all of that time with Kid served as a greater influence than I realized for my never engaging with drugs as a user.

The reality is that Kid did have an issue with drugs. He was a functioning addict, and it was hard for others to ignore, including himself. I recall one time when I was around ten or so when we visited him and Aunt Diane in Willingboro. My aunt picked us up to spend the weekend, but on the return trip home, my uncle scared us all to death throughout the nearly two-hour drive back. He began falling asleep while he was driving. My mother was constantly waking him in a panic. At one point, he asked her to drive, knowing she had never been behind the wheel of a car in her life. We all felt like we barely made it home to the Bronx.

He dropped us off and went about in a matter of fact manner that indicated this was his norm.

There were times when he and I were together. He'd nod-off at traffic lights, and I'd have to nudge him awake. I remember thinking he'd fall asleep and kill us. My fears were well-founded because of the earlier incidents, so when I first started driving for him, it was more by default and self-preservation than a job.

When I finally suggested he let me drive so he could rest, it was a welcome request. I would drive him to the location he'd ask and park. It was usually in the evening going into the late night. What was supposed to be right back; would often turn into me spending the night in the car. I would get concerned because hours would go by. I didn't know what to do. I didn't even know what apartment he'd gone into or even who he was going to see.

When he would come down in the morning, he would have to knock on the window to wake me up. I'd open the door, and he would get into the car laughing saying how the time got away from him and not much else. After a short while, he began asking me to drop him off, so he gave me his pager, the car, and told me he'd page me when he needed me. That was cool for me because now I wasn't just sitting in the car for endless hours. I had the ride and wouldn't be spending the night in it parked.

I was showing him how reliable I was and gaining his trust. He wouldn't pay me set amounts, but it was never less than $300 - $500 a week. He didn't have to give me anything because the access to his cars would have been payment enough. At first, I was using the free time running around hanging with my friends, just fronting and getting girls. Depending on the time, I would go up to the Bronx and get into things. If it was early enough, I went and played basketball. You could imagine the looks I received from my peers jumping out of a brand-new luxury vehicle with a pager and a pocket full of money.

During this time, I had not yet graduated to selling cocaine. However, people were taking notice of me in the neighborhood and assuming I was doing more than I was. Some older guys asked if I had any coke. For some reason, I said I did even though it wasn't true. I told them I didn't have anything on me at that moment, but I'd get back. They told me they were looking for half grams and grams. That's when I came up with the bright idea that I was going to get some coke.

I knew what my uncle was doing. At least I believed I did. So, I found my way into having a conversation where I asked if I could buy some powder from him because I had people who'd asked, and I wanted to make some money. He told me how he didn't want to have anything to do with what I was considering because of my mother and, of course, my aunt. He didn't want to be responsible, because if something were to happen to me, he'd never be able to forgive himself. For the moment, I left the conversation alone and continued driving him around.

There came a time, not long afterward, when he began asking me to accompany him upstairs on his runs. Once upstairs, I would sit in another room while he took care of his business. On one of these occasions, I got restless after a long while and walked into the room he was in. He had fallen asleep counting money at a table covered with heroin. Some of the money had fallen out of his hands onto the floor, and the rest was just about. I picked up the money, counted it, and put it into piles of a thousand. I don't remember how much there was, but it was more money than I had ever seen. When he came out of his stupor, he realized what I had done, and he came to have a conversation with me. He wasn't upset. He was more so digging what I had done and the way I did it. He knew how much money it was supposed to have been, and he was aware that every dollar was accounted for, nicely stacked, in some order.

From that point on, our relationship changed. We had already been close, but I think he saw something in me that he respected. I started seeing more regarding who he actually was and how things really worked. He started taking me with him when he had to meet his Italian connect. I wouldn't sit in on any of their meetings, but outside of a restaurant, or wherever the meetings would take place.

The more confident he became with me, the more access I had to see what a drug dealer of his stature did. Much of the time was spent moving in and out of bars in Harlem, like The Oasis, The Seville, and Flash Inn, to name a few. His generation hung out and did much of their business inside of these smoke-filled, dimly red-lit bars. I gained an interesting perspective seeing all the open cocaine and heroin use by the stylishly dressed men and women who frequented the various establishments.

He began introducing me to everyone as his nephew. One of those people was his lieutenant Norman. The introductions alone carried some weight because of the respect they all had for him. I had no idea what an introduction into that lifestyle meant, in any capacity, but I would learn to embrace it, soon becoming close with Norm as well.

I received some unintended benefits from getting close to Kid and Norman. One night I was driving around with one of their lady friends who worked for them. Norman had become my de-facto uncle as well and asked me to drop him off then take her home. An otherwise uneventful ride quickly got interesting when she began talking to me about the type of girls I was messing with. She went on to describe them as kids with little experience who didn't know what to do with a real man or how to treat him. Not long after conversing, we found ourselves at a hotel. She was about ten years older and one of the sexiest women I had ever laid eyes on. She was brown-skinned with a curly afro, an amazing smile, and the perfect pair of full lips. Her body was flawless. Nice-sized breasts and a tapered waist with a beautiful, round Black woman's behind.

She talked and taught all the while, showing me how a man was supposed to be treated intimately and sexually. She took control of the situation, taking her time, and teasing me. Seeing how inexperienced and thirsty I was, she exploited my willingness to do anything. Her comfort with her own sexuality and sensuality was in marked contrast to the encounters I had up to this point. I had been having sex, but what I was feeling was in stark contrast to those experiences. This was my *50 Shades* training. She was erotic, masturbating and talking to me, asking if I was enjoying myself. She occasionally tasted herself, telling me how good her pussy smelled and tasted. The emphasis was put on taking her time and the mutuality of us enjoying the experience.

I was turned out in the process. She kissed, licked, and sucked every part of my body, paying close attention to those spots she noticed caused me to moan and squirm. She instructed me on how she liked to be touched and made love to but equally like to be fucked. She was the kind of super freak a young man only dreamt about or saw in pornos, especially at 18. She got all into my head, growing my imagination, and lessening my inhibitions.

After that experience, I stepped up my game, becoming a pleaser knowing it would be reciprocated. From that point forward, there was little with women I was unwilling to try. Most importantly, she told me that honesty was the best policy when delving into the minds, hearts, and souls of women. She told me to always give a woman a choice to accept me for the person I was and that I'd be surprised at their choice. I began to do exactly that giving them a choice instead of trying to run games and lying. The drama that comes with lying is a job in and of itself, and I have always had an aversion to this type of mental and emotional labor.

I was never again going to be the boy I once was, and I was hardly complaining about this fact. I became a fixture around my uncle and his associates. I would be the only sober person in a room, so my perspective on the things I would see and experience changed. I'd come to learn that drinking, doing drugs and sex went together for many.

It happened sort of organically that I was propositioned to have sex with one of the women. Most of the men seemingly couldn't be bothered. I'm guessing this being their norm played into that fact along with the adverse effects that prolonged exposure to drugs and alcohol had on erections way before Viagra was a reality. That, of course, wasn't the case for me.

I was young, full of energy and stamina, qualities that were very desirable for a high, horny woman. The men that were high wanted to lay back pretty much and be served by a woman. This is where the void came in. The one I was more than happy to fill. The women would perform the requested act, satisfying the men, and then be left hanging.

I'd become "The Equalizer" that balanced the situation and added to their high and sexual experiences. There were times when I wasn't around that I would be requested. I'd get the page and be told, "listen, nephew, I need you to get down here and come fuck the shit out this broad." I became part of their entertainment. And in the immortal words of Bill Wither: "I want to spread the news that if it feels this good getting used...Oh, you just keep on using me until you use me up."

There was one woman who I really came to like. Her name was Ava, and she was beautiful, with an insatiable sexual appetite. We would fuck for hours, and both still want more. At some point, we started hanging out outside of those situations. On one occasion, she said that she wanted me to get someone else to come hang out with us. I had known a couple of fast girls in my teen years that had extended their generosity to me and some of my friends. These occurrences never happened nearly as much as we'd desire them to and never so easily. I was arranging the tryst before Ava could finish asking. Ava was a young man's fantasy. She made her needs understood, and the drugs went hand in hand with her pleasure.

Bartering sex for drugs was almost commonplace within these settings. We thought nothing of it, and it seemed more like a form of foreplay then it did anything seedy. It made the woman more desirable and lessened inhibitions. Perhaps, because cocaine wasn't easily accessible, its value was perceived higher, and it allowed these types of easy interactions. Initially, even as cocaine was becoming more available with my generation, it still had the acceptability of just being viewed as a party drug.

It wasn't until much later, when cocaine and then crack became part of the fabric of the landscape, that it took on a darker, dirtier connotation. Then, you would see women selling themselves for hits. This wasn't about cocaine as part of the sex, but the addiction to the drug, being so overwhelming that sex became currency. Unfortunately, once that happened, the desirability of the women seeking crack for their addiction was significantly less. Part of that was the physical toll the drugs took on people's appearance.

***

When I again approached Kid about buying drugs, it was received differently. He hesitantly agreed. I was way more mature from when I first asked, though it had literally only been a couple of months. I had shown him that I was reliable and responsible. I initially only got a quarter of an ounce, and I always paid for my work upfront. I am sure he could see an inevitability to my path and gave in more than assuming he was corrupting me in any way.

Kid frequently took Chris and I to restaurants. Admittedly, this was not something I was really used to beyond the occasional fast food and Chinese spots I frequented. When he went shopping, we got gear, too. We were able to afford our own clothes, but Kid put us on with bigger purchases than we would have normally even thought of splurging on for ourselves.

I gravitated toward my uncle for several reasons. The first was that I dug his style. Old school hustlers are some of the most interesting and charismatic figures. Plus, besides being family, I just liked him. It also wasn't lost on me that there were many benefits from being in his company besides eating good and shopping excursions. His tutelage became the most formalized part of my education during my last years of school, without any direct lessons taught. It was akin to the tales of the old-time hustlers and Mafioso being groomed to take over positions by just constantly being around the heads of the organizations.

We never had one specific conversation on how to sell drugs or be a drug dealer, but I picked up on how to lead and treat people by watching his interactions with his lieutenants and crew. Consciously or not, I watched how he moved and business decisions he made. I took notice of his ownership of real estate and legitimate businesses. He could see I cared about being fly and had ambition. Kid looked out because he liked my company, and he probably understood his tutelage was appropriate for the direction I was going in, with or without his input.

My father was a strong presence in my life, for both positive and negative reasons. However, by this time, I was hardly spending much time at home. Though every teen boy ultimately thinks of himself as a man, on some level, they all crave positive interactions with men. This is perhaps a universal sentiment, but holds especially true for Black and Hispanic boys, particularly if they have not had present or strong male figures in their lives. Kid provided substantial guidance during this formative, adolescent time.

3

COLLEGE DROPOUT

After high school, I enrolled at Bronx Community College. I was still hustling but continued with school in part because it made my mother happy. Ironically, after never having played ball for my high school team, I heeded the calls of the coach to try out for the junior college team. I came out and with little effort, made the team.

There was a player named Derrick Campbell on the team. He was from Queens, and we quickly became close. He was doing some hustling as well, and we began hanging out. He knew Fat Cat and suggested I get him samples from my uncle to bring out to Queens. Nothing ever came of it, but he was someone, like me, trying to figure it out.

Derrick was a pretty good ballplayer who was being recruited by several Division I schools. In the course of coaches coming out to scout Derrick, I began to get noticed as well. Derrick got an offer for Northeastern University, and we began discussing the idea of attending together because they were showing some interest in me as well. Eventually, coaches from Northeastern convinced me to join Derrick in Boston.

My time at BCC was also noteworthy because of a few relationships that I formed. One of the most important was meeting Albe. He was just one of the many colorful characters that entered my life during these formative years. Albe was a couple of years older and had his own coke hustle. At some point, our conversations progressed to us doing business.

My drug business was mainly selling half grams and grams of cocaine. Cocaine was probably the most expensive I've ever known it to be during this time. In the early-to-mid '80s, it was upwards of $50,000 a key. I was buying anywhere from seven to fourteen grams weekly. At $50 a gram, my purchases were $350 to $700 in total. Since the price of coke was so high, one of the ways I was able to maximize my profits was by adding cutting agents like procaine and menita. I was able to buy those at smoke shops, which were common.

While the goal was to stretch my profits, you couldn't cut it to the point that it would lose its potency. People still needed to get high from it. I started dipping my pinky finger in the coke and tasting it, waiting for the freeze or numbness as a gauge of how potent or good it was. This was even the litmus test I used when I eventually copped outside of Kid. The funny thing is, I did this having seen it done as a means to test it. I thought that I knew what I was doing. Years later, I would realize how foolish that test was because, at some point, they started selling a cutting agent that would give your tongue the same reaction without there being any actual cocaine.

I packaged my product in what was called "pyramid papers." It was paper with a waxy sort of consistency. The ends would fold inward, locking the drug in the center. Most of my customers were referrals. I had a pretty good business making somewhere around $1,000 or so a week. During that time, I'd give most people the drugs in advance and they'd settle with me when they got paid, which was usually every two weeks.

Another guy on the basketball team was an East Indian kid named Mark. He had a job working at a hospital while at BCC where he had access to syringes. Dope fiends labeled syringes back then as "works," and before them being free and widely available to addicts, they were harder to get and cost $5 apiece. Mark sold me the syringes at 0.50 cents per.

My mother's younger sister, Aunt Betty, worked in Arnold's Variety Store on 115th Street and 8th Avenue. They sold everything from sandwiches and burgers to works on the side. I approached Old Man Arnold once I knew I had access to getting the syringes and asked if he had any interest in them. I would sell them to him for $2 a pop. I bought whatever Mark was able to get, usually two or three hundred at a time, and sold them as fast as I got them.

Around this time, Aunt Betty was dating Luv Bug Starski. Several years older, he was one of the prominent figures in Hip-Hop's early days as a DJ and rapper. I knew who he was from his records that were being played on Mr. Magic's Rap Attack, one of the only shows on the radio dedicated to Hip-Hop. There weren't very many Hip-Hop records on the radio then, making him and his songs a pretty big deal. Starski ended up being my biggest referral in the world of Hip-Hop, leading me to serve many of the more known MCs and DJs of the era.

Starski introduced me to Kurtis Blow and his DJ, AJ Scratch, at one of the shows at the iconic Disco Fever in the Bronx. The Fever was considered one of the notable spots in Hip-Hop's early stages, featuring the likes of Grandmaster Flash and is noted for being the venue of Run-DMC's first show. Starski was performing, and I accompanied him. I began doing business with all those guys regularly. There was absolutely no stigma attached to it in that scene, with it being done regularly in the open. There was a time when Kurtis Blow was short on money and asked me would I take a check. I didn't have a problem with the idea of it because my mother worked at a bank, so getting it cashed was the least of my concerns. The funny thing about this story was that the check bounced. We straightened it out, and Kurtis and I remain cool to this day

My balancing act continued with my dealing and schooling. The basketball season at BCC wasn't particularly noteworthy, and as for school, it was what it was for me. Before I knew it, my freshman year came and went. I matriculated to Northeastern University for my sophomore year. My mother, Aunt Diane, and Kid drove me to school. The culture shock supplied by Boston was only part of the reason I was on the phone to NYC daily, having handed over my business to Chris. I was truly living a Jekyll and Hyde lifestyle. I was physically in Boston, enrolled in school, but I was otherwise still in a New York state of mind, constantly checking in and trying to handle any issues that arose.

I was used to the segregation of New York City. It was as much based-on economics, as it was on race. Boston's racism was much more overt, and my brief stay resulted in me changing up some of the more explicit ways I spoke. In New York, I had used the words "nigga" and "bitch," so often growing up, you would have thought I had stock options in their use. However, upon seeing people's reactions to my speech patterns in a climate in which I already knew, I was constantly judged and stereotyped; it made me take stock. I intuitively took those words out of my vocabulary and cursed much less to rarely, at least publicly.

My stay in Boston ended up being brief as the pull of NYC won over Beantown and college. The fact that I ended up having to sit out the year, from playing basketball, did not help. Who knows what could have happened had I been more patient at Northeastern and put my focus into ball? We were coached by Jim Calhoun, who later went on to win three national championships at the University of Connecticut. Additionally, Reggie Lewis, from Baltimore's legendary Dunbar High School, was a teammate before he went on to become a Boston Celtic great before an untimely death at the age of 27.

However, my focus was not on school, to begin with, and with basketball being delayed for a year, getting back home was just much more compelling. So, after a few months on campus, I called up Chris and had him come get me. I never looked back. I was embarking on a much different path, as I was set to immerse myself in hustling fully.

***

Here, I was a little over 16 months out of high school in early October of 1984. I was about a month shy of my 19th birthday, and I was back home in New York with college life firmly in my rearview. I was at a crossroads as to what to do. I resumed the business that Chris had been handling but knew I could do much more without faking the pedestrian lifestyle, restrained by being a student.

I settled in at my aunt's and uncle's place. I did not stay at their Jersey home, but one of the properties they owned in the Bronx that had several apartments and two storefronts. One of the storefronts was L & N Deli that was named after my first cousins Lamont and Nechelle. It was in the Bronx on 213 Street and White Plains Road. The other space was a pool hall for a short time before it was rented out and became a real estate office. On the main floor, there were two apartments. The one I occupied was attached to the deli directly behind it and had access from the apartment into the deli.

Uncle Norman was there as well, occupying an apartment above the deli directly facing the front with a street view. He caught a drug case and was out on bail. He eventually skipped out on his bail altogether when he blew trial as well as his sentencing. On the run and laying low, Norman served as a proactive mentor to my budding career, giving up constant game and insight along the way in an unrestricted way that was different from Kid's.

Shortly after getting back, while Chris and I were trying to figure things out, he mentioned that he enrolled in the Army. This caught me completely off guard. I remember trying to get him to change his mind. Chris was always more practical and level-headed. I was always the one cutting corners, coming up with some kind of hustle to get rich, and I'm sure Chris looked at the Army as the smartest, most stable move.

He had met a girl one night while we were hanging out at Skate Fever off of Jerome Avenue in the Bronx. They had only been dating for a couple of months when he asked her to marry him. Chris was all in and ended up having a ceremony, which I helped pay for. We all looked sharp in our tuxedos, and while I was happy for my dude, it was bittersweet knowing his celebration came with changes. We had been getting a few dollars, but Chris didn't want this for his future. When his enlistment was finalized, he was off to the Army with his new bride in tow. I didn't understand Chris' move or way of thinking. Going into the military was like taking a square job times a hundred. His departure left a significant void. Everything I did to that point was always somehow inclusive of him. His leaving was an emotional setback, but it did little to deter my focus on getting money.

***

My brother was a senior in high school at the Bronx Catholic school, All Hallows. Since I was back home, I was able to attend many of his games. One night, after parking my car, I got out and could feel someone quickly approaching. Before I could make out who it was, I had a gun pointed at me. I didn't have time to think. I just reacted by pushing the gun away, and it went off. I could hear several additional shots as I was running away.

I ran into the park toward 161st Street, where I exited on Walton Avenue. I felt fluid running down my body and initially believed it might have been blood. It wasn't until I was clear of danger that I checked myself and realized it was only sweat.

I walked back up Walton Avenue to the school, went inside, and watched my brother win his playoff game on their way to winning the state championship, never mentioning I had been shot at that night. That was the first time, but it wouldn't be the last. Unfortunately, the tension with my father was probably a contributor to me missing that title game in Niagara Falls.

The uneasiness between my father and I had increased upon my return, and my independence and ever-increasing hustling status made our presence around each other strained. It had been several months since I had spoken to or physically saw him.

That summer, during a basketball tournament, my father oversaw, sponsored by Academy Gardens, we fought. I can't really classify it as much of a fight because I never threw a punch. I had a team of guys that I brought from Downtown who were running other teams out of the park. We hadn't even come close to losing a game. My team was scheduled to play that day, and as some issues arose, I felt my father said something that wasn't favorable towards my team. It felt like he was hating on my guys. It was not the first time I felt this energy from him. At this point, I was on my own, so I didn't pay it any mind. He overheard me telling some of the guys what his issue was and apparently didn't like what I said. He wasn't a fan of our showmanship, and new school versus old school ideals collided.

He walked over to me and asked what I had said. I repeated it, and he just started swinging on me. I was definitely caught off guard. I sensed his anger, but his actions weren't justified. His reaction was clearly about more than the words said at that moment. I'm sure they were a manifestation of many things, including my longtime independence and how well I got along with my mother. She was increasingly independent of him, in part because of my help. It all came out that day.

He hit me several times, and I sort of just blocked his punches protecting myself. I couldn't find it in myself to swing back. After a couple of punches, he must have caught himself and stopped. I looked at him with contempt in my eyes and turned, walked off, jumped in my car and pulled off.

I was raised to respect my elders, especially my parents. At that moment, it wasn't deserved. It had been years of torment and anguish for my family, especially for my mother. Through it all, she never uttered one bad word about him to my brother or me, but this was the straw that broke my camel's back. Things would forever be different between my father and me, and it would be years before we'd speak again.

My brother had his own issues with Mad, but he still went on to receive numerous Division I scholarship offers to play ball. Instead, he chose to attend an Ivy League institution (which technically does not offer athletic scholarships) on an academic ride, essentially. Any disappointment my mother may have felt towards my choices was erased by my brother's decision to attend Columbia University. The financial support I was able to provide helped ease that disappointment, as well.

***

I was still dating my high school sweetheart, Gina Taylor, who lived in Brooklyn. Gina was very shy, and reserved when we met. She became pregnant around the time of Chris' departure, and that lent to some of what I was also dealing with at the time.

In the daytime, I worked at L&N, usually until my aunt arrived in the afternoon. The wages from the job were what they were, but my pay was supplemented by basically living in the apartment behind the store rent-free. Kid used the apartment as well, but more times than not, the apartment was where I laid my head at night.

In the evening, I ran the streets with my uncle while also tending to my clients. I was also hustling on the block going hand-to-hand on the corner of Nelson Avenue and 165th Street in the Bronx. There, I stood under a canopy in rain, sunshine, sleet and snow selling dimes and twenties of cocaine and then crack. Dexter and Eric, two childhood friends from the area, were running with me at that time.

When we first started slinging, most of our customers were my peers. Cats may have bought to sniff, but what was becoming equally as popular were "coolies." As opposed to being unskilled laborers from China or Asia, these coolies were cocaine mixed with the tobacco in cigarettes. At some point, our clientele expanded and changed. It was becoming older, and instead of coke, there was an increasing demand for crack. The coolies that people smoked were replaced by "woolies," which was crack mixed in with weed. The escalation that occurred was organic but noticeable. Yet, no one analyzed it much in the beginning; we just took notice that the growing demand meant more money.

I didn't have any fear or concerns about anything I was doing in my old neighborhood. Looking back, I can blame my ignorance on a lot of my choices. There came a time when the inevitable occurred. Eric was out one night and got robbed by Jeff To The Left. That was his street name. We all knew who did these kinds of things and I am unsure why I was so surprised when he told me. I guess it probably had something to do with the fact that we felt comfortable since we felt like we knew everyone on our block.

I was now confronted with what to do in return. Before then, we regularly scrapped, of course, as most of the kids in these types of neighborhoods come up doing. However, dealing with this was going to be different. Jeff was several years older than us. He was known throughout the neighborhood for doing stick-ups and robbing gambling games.
Something I never understood, though it's a commonplace in the hood, is how guys got robbed by someone they knew and just let it ride. I wasn't going for this. Eric and Dexter looked to me to have all the answers. I knew I had to do something because this wasn't going to become the norm. I told them that I would handle it.

I rapped with my Uncle Norman. He was someone who always gave me sound advice. He told me what I already knew: that I was going to have to lead by example and handle the situation. He reminded me that this is what came with the territory, and if I wasn't ready, then maybe I should consider another occupation. He handed me a revolver and asked me if I knew how to use it. I'm sure he already knew the answer was no. Why would I? The only time I had handled a gun prior was in high school when we all shared that .25 automatic. I might have shot it a time or two, but that didn't make me an experienced gunman.

He gave me a crash course on its use. Then he grabbed another gun, tucked it in his waist, and I followed suit, mimicking his move. After that, we were in the car heading to the block in search of Jeff.

I remember contemplating what I'd do when I saw Jeff. I'm not certain if I was scared or anxious, but there was an undeniable adrenaline rush with the unexpected anticipation. Uncle Norm was so cool that I don't remember us doing too much talking during the ride. When we arrived, it was already dark outside, so we had that in our favor. We went to a couple of places where we knew he hung out but didn't find him that night.

It would be days before I would run into Jeff. He knew me as a kid that played basketball from the neighborhood and had somewhat of a kinship with my father. When I saw him, I wasn't strapped. But I approached him and made him aware of the situation. Jeff surely wasn't afraid of me, but he had respect for me and more so for my father. Mad was known to take no shit and for his many fistfights on and off the courts. Jeff had no idea I had anything to do with Eric, and had he known he would've never done it due to whatever he felt towards me.

I didn't get the couple hundred dollars back, but I felt the outcome ended better than me having shot or killed him over that little bit of money. I would've justified shooting him based on principle, but in not having to do it over bullshit money, I avoided the potential repercussions that could have occurred. At least for the moment, disaster was avoided. It was one of my earliest lessons in assessing value and consequences to my actions.

Even if it was subconsciously, I knew I needed further tutelage, so I continued driving around with my uncle while he handled his affairs. Our paging system allowed me to tend to my business checking in on my people. You can only imagine how a teenager in NYC in the early '80s could benefit from having unsupervised access to different new luxury vehicles and a pager (which only doctors and guys like my uncle, originally, had) for a few hours every day. Initially, the pager only directed a user to a service when they received a message. Shortly after technology improved, and though the names were almost interchangeably used, beepers were developed where a direct number was given and visible. This new development in the technology allowed us to add codes to the phone numbers that could range from 911 if an emergency, or numbers to distinguish who an individual may be.

I had purchased a used Delta 88 right after high school. It reminded me of the OJs my friends and I used to rent. OJs were large late model cars like Cadillacs, Buick or Oldsmobile that we would hire for the day with a driver. My car was cool, but compared to my uncle's 7 Series BMW and Audi 5000, the difference was night and day.

One night after closing the store, I got fresh and got up with a couple of my friends. We made our way across the bridge to 155th Street in Harlem. The Rooftop was located between 8th Avenue and the FDR Drive across the streets from Rucker Park, the baseball fields, and The Polo Grounds housing project. Willie (of Willie Burger) had originally owned the spot before Gusto bought and took it over. Gusto was a hustler himself who was some years my senior and knew the lay of the land in Harlem with a pulse of what was going on.

We walked up and immediately were taken aback by the line outside. It was a Wednesday night, which happened to be known as "Ladies' Night." This wasn't the summer, but a normal school night in early October. The line of mostly teens outside could rival any downtown club on a Friday or Saturday night. That was just the beginning of the show as the pageantry displayed by young hustlers began before you even entered the doors.

There was no valet at The Rooftop. Most people parked at their own risk in the more deserted areas under the FDR. Yet, for a few, there seemed to be reserved spots for all the kitted, customized vehicles on the oversized sidewalks that existed on the Southside of 155th between 8th and the FDR drive. Guys would pull up, pay someone who had blocked off the sidewalk spaces, and walk right past the large lines right into the club.

I knew a few people on the line, so the time passed, but I was still having difficulty with the feeling of being regular and having to stand in line while watching so many others get VIP treatment. I was getting money, too, but no one knew-- yet.

Guys my age or just slightly older pulled up and walked in like they were ghetto superstars. From the line, especially when the doors opened, you could hear the DJ shouting out who was in the building.

Let me take a second and explain The Rooftop a little better. It was actually a skating rink, which is why there were so many young people in the building. However, at 11:50 PM, the DJ, Brucie B, would start the countdown to let you know that skate time would be ending. By midnight, The Rooftop turned into a full-fledged club. The place was filled with hustlers, trendsetters, and assorted characters from Harlem and the Bronx. All the cute and popular girls had little cliques with colorful names like the "Go Girls" and "Gucci Girls." All of these people were intermixed with regulars because of the skating rink component. I say regular, but there was no denying that The Rooftop had energy reserved for teens and young adults already committed to a faster way of living.

The first night I was taking it all in. I told myself at that moment that I was going to be the man before it's all said and done. It didn't take long to figure out the surroundings. The DJs, Brucie B and DJ Hollywood, made it easy by shouting out everyone you should know. It was part of Brucie B's hustle. He recorded every night and sold recordings from weeks prior as mixtapes for $10 a pop. All the hustlers took special interest and bought multiple cassettes, especially when they were name-checked on the productions. It was all part of establishing a reputation.

Within a couple of months of my initial visit, I would end up buying multiple tapes from Brucie B after my first shout out. I paid $100, letting him keep the change. I let him know there was plenty more where that came from. That gesture got me extra shouts moving forward.

DJs became part of the landscape for Harlem through that time period. Many notables such as Kid Capri, Ron G, Dowop of Bounce Squad, and many others became known for selling mixtapes, and one of the prominent places you could cop these mixtapes (if not from the DJs themselves) was with Rock and Will. Rock and Will worked out of a variety store on 124th Street and 7th Avenue that sold all the happening mixtapes. The tapes became so valuable that we had custom carrying cases for them.

The Rooftop was where I first became aware of many of the generation's top hustlers, including Rich Porter, Alpo, Travis, Jason, Azie, and LA. All the young hustlers inevitably hung out there, talking shop, chasing girls. Most importantly, it was a place to post up and be seen. The only other places that really rivaled The Rooftop for my generation's places to see and be seen in Harlem in the summer was the Kings Tower tournament (also known as Foster Projects) which was located between 115th and 112th and Lenox and 5th as well as the 139th St Lenox Ave park, where a basketball tournament was held, and later the Entertainers Basketball Classic at Rucker Park. These were iconic venues for the times.

That first night, at The Rooftop, was also the night I met a girl named Reika. One thing I have come to recognize is that I can pick the movers and shakers out of a crowd. That was only one of the reasons I honed in on Reika. She was one of the prettiest and most popular girls in the place. I noticed her within minutes of arriving, but it was only when I saw her alone by the cafeteria that I got up the courage to approach her. She still had her skates on and was a bit sweaty, so I offered to buy her something to drink. She gave me the twice over before accepting my offer. We were only able to talk for a few minutes before her friends made it clear that her social obligations were more pressing than the new guy.

That night I, declared to myself I had to have her. We didn't get a chance to exchange numbers, but even in our brief interaction, I got enough information to figure out where I might run into her again other than The Rooftop.

Reika lived in the Polo Ground projects with an aunt. She often hung out around 152nd Street and 8th Avenue with her girlfriends. She wasn't exactly hard to get to or out of the way, and I made it a point to run into her. After I did, I gave her my beeper number, and she said she would use code 155.

Another night after The Rooftop had let out, we were talking on 152nd Street just getting to know each other. I had to drop someone off, so our conversation was brief. I told her to beep me next time she was free. I said my goodbyes and headed further down 8th Avenue. On my way back uptown, I decided to double back the same way, hoping I might run into her again even though it was already past 3:00 AM. To my surprise, she was still outside talking with another girl named Kim. I pulled up asking why she was still out there. She said she was waiting on her girlfriend, Lisa, who had gone off with some dude. I was sensing there wasn't something right about her story as if perhaps she was just avoiding going home, so I asked if they wanted to come hang out. They both jumped in the car and we headed back to the Bronx.

I'd come to find out from Reika what was going on. She told me that when she was 2 years old, she lived in Brooklyn with her mother and her boyfriend. One night while upstairs at the babysitter's house with her older brother and sister, they came back downstairs to their apartment. The door was wide open and when they walked in, they found their mother and her boyfriend lying in pools of blood from multiple gunshots. They both died from their wounds. I probably knew Reika a few weeks before she revealed that she had a baby who was nearly a year old and that she was only 15. From the time of the tragedy until I met her, she had been living with different family members and when she was 14, she had gotten pregnant, which led to her being put out and sent to foster homes for pregnant teens.

My relationship with Reika quickly developed even though I was technically still in a relationship with Gina, who was probably in her first trimester of pregnancy. I'm not sure what I was thinking. I was only a month shy of my nineteenth birthday and the reality is I probably just wasn't actually thinking. My life was moving faster than I was able to process.

I met Reika in October of 1984. I remember her planning a first birthday party for Pop later that month and me buying him a bunch of toys. He didn't have any capacity to understand or appreciate the gesture, but I will never forget seeing the look in Reika's eyes. Her appreciation for the gifts she and Pop received left their mark on me. He was actually named Carlton Lamont Carter after his biological father with Reika's last name. Further evidence of my youth and immaturity was that I probably didn't realize this fact till years later, just accepting of us calling him exclusively by a nickname that stuck, and never really needing further explanation. The dynamic between Reika and I was unique. We both clearly filled voids for each other and while I have no doubt Reika would have been okay in life had we not met, her circumstances clearly appealed to that side of my development that included being a provider and taking care of the people I cared about.

One day, Reika and Pop were hanging out with me, driving around in the Bronx in the vicinity of Yankee Stadium on the Grand Concourse. I'm not certain what the conversation was about, but it led to us arguing. Before I realized what had happened, Reika jumped out the car, ran across the street and disappeared around a corner. I pulled over, giving her a minute to reappear figuring she would come back shortly, but she didn't. I ended up taking Pop to my mother's apartment. I believe it was a day or so before I heard back from her. I should've realized then that I probably was in over my head, especially with all I had going. While my mother was sympathetic to Reika's situation, she was less than enthusiastic about the idea of me dating a girl with a young child while having a baby on the way.

However, once they were introduced, my mother just took to Reika. They eventually got along better with each other than they did individually with me. My mom loved Pop immediately and, in many ways, she looked at Reika as the daughter she never had. She encouraged her to go back to school and was instrumental in Reika getting her GED and taking care of her own affairs, such as setting up a bank account which allowed Reika to receive money and benefits that had been going to her aunt instead.

I am a hustler by nature, yet that nature is clearly cultivated by my desire and need to take care of those close to me. Unlike my mother and unborn son, Kevin Queron Taylor, who would come into the world in May of 1985, Reika and Pop were not my responsibility. I could have walked away before things turned serious, but once those decisions were made, the added responsibility to care for and protect them definitively drove my hustle.

***

Shortly after Gina's pregnancy, it was becoming clear that we were not on the same page. Our youth and my ambitions were probably a bad combination to begin with, but the relationship showed increasing signs of strain daily. I was experiencing life at a rapid pace and my changes did not match with the person Gina first met and who she still remained. I gave her money throughout her pregnancy in anticipation of our son's birth, but I was not prepared or focused to fit into an ideal and the expectations she probably had.

Within a few weeks of Kevin's birth in Kings County Hospital in Brooklyn, I began to realize that our son did not have many of the perceived necessities we had discussed and thought the monies given were supposed to take care of. It was not about the money, but Gina didn't give me any explanation and that dismissiveness was enough to allow me to distance myself. I genuinely loved Gina, or at least as much as I understood and was capable of loving at the time. I can look back now and see the foolish pride and immaturity, but within it all, while I didn't allow myself to grow with Gina, I never neglected my connection or responsibilities to our son.

4
HUSTLE HARD

I built up the spot in the Bronx, using mostly guys I grew up with and trusted. The crack phenomenon/epidemic was really in its relative infancy in 1985. I don't specifically remember one moment where it all changed. It was more like a growing coke business became organically redefined as customers grew in both numbers and frequency, and instead of wanting the powder, they wanted it ready made and cooked.

For the uninitiated, crack, in its purest form, had been around. The vets that cooked and smoked cocaine prior to the epidemic it became known called it freebasing. The water-soluble method of heating the cocaine removes alkaloids, which gave it its optimal purity. Inhaling it gave users the best experience. The high is more intense than what comes from snorting or even injecting. The basic distinction between freebase and crack was the addition of baking soda, which changed the chemical components, and made it slightly less pure, but still highly addictive. Over the years, wannabe ghetto chemists started adding all kinds of crazy chemicals like ammonia and other cleaning solutions thinking it would make the drug even more addictive. In most cases, it just made people lose their minds faster.

I ramped up the quantity to meet with the increasing demand and the next thing you knew, I had 24-hour shifts. The basic economic laws of supply and demand were in play. Besides being young and relatively inexperienced overall in the drug game, crack was an entirely new and different learning curve for all of us.

I had never cooked cocaine turning it into freebase or crack. I remember when I first tried to cook it based on a conversation I had with an individual. He explained it to me and made it seem so simple. Following what he said, I put the cocaine in a Gerber's baby bottle jar filled with the water minus the baking soda and, in a timely manner, it all evaporated and was gone. Although it was only a couple of grams, I realized I needed to find someone who knew what they were doing.

Fatman knew a woman who was a noted cocaine chef. They may have hung out freebasing and that's how he knew of her talents. She lived on 126th Street in a brownstone between Lenox Avenue and 7th Avenue. I paid her to cook it up for me until I learned how it was done. I was still hanging out with my uncle on occasion, though that started to naturally decline as I began focusing more on growing my own business. It had nothing to do with our bond and relationship. My apprenticeship just gave way too much bigger aspirations now.

Apparently, my ambitions and come up were starting to become noticeable to others as well. Two of the first young cats on the scene that took notice of me and became friends were Jason and Travis. They had already been friends before I met them. Jason was the catalyst, making the first move. I believe I popped up on his radar because of the different cars I was driving. This is when I first started going to The Rooftop and driving my uncle's cars. I owned a late model Audi that I had actually purchased from my uncle. It was one of his least expensive cars. Jason was one of the young dudes I'd noticed as well. He kept himself fresh, and he was one of the few who was driving during that time. He had a French-manufactured, luxury, white Renault, which was all hooked up with a custom kit. Both our personal cars had all the bells and whistles on them.

I'd come to find out Jason was sharp and very observant. He figured I had something going on and aimed to find out what it was exactly. Not long after meeting, we started hanging out. He talked about a crew called the Shack Crew that he was down with along with Travis and, if my memory serves me correctly, I want to say it included music producer Teddy Riley and some others that don't presently come to mind. They hung out in the vicinity of 116th and 118th Streets and 7th Avenue. He took me on what I will call the "Harlem Tour." We went to just about every block that he knew of where young cats like us were getting money.

THE CRACK ERA

I wasn't born and raised in Harlem and wasn't as familiar with it as he was. My lineage came from my grandparents living there and several aunts and uncles migrating from the South. We went from Uptown as far west on the hill to 157th Street and Amsterdam Avenue, where Jason pointed out dudes like Duwop and John John, who had spots where I witnessed long lines of people copping drugs. I wasn't sure of the relationship or even why he lumped those two together. As the years would pass, it just seemed like when one was mentioned, the other was. We went as far east as First Avenue in 100s. He mentioned Rich Porter, Azie, Alpo, T-Money, Big Dave, Darryl Bonds and Spencer (the last two mentioned, I happened to have gone to high school with). He gave me the rundown on anybody that was somebody that he knew. I realized right out the gate how informed he was. We discussed doing business together and making some things happen.

I was a quick study. I learned the landscape and continued in my quest for dominance in this lifestyle, coined "the Game." There were a lot of young cats getting money during this time. I'm not able to mention them all because it would change the direction of the story. Those I tend to mention were the catalyst for many getting put on, no different than myself.

Around this time, Uncle Norman introduced me to his nephew, Nappy Red, who was about my age. Red was from Harlem, and he was always fresh every time I saw him. It was easy for me to identify him as someone who was on the fast track. Besides his hustling, Red just naturally stood out. He was 6'2" with naturally red, nappy hair. He was solidly built, with a reputation for being nice with his hands. Red was working for an older hustler that had an around-the-clock spot on 135th Street between 7th and Lenox Avenues. Red was working 12-hour shifts seven days a week. The spot was packed at certain times of the day and night. You would have thought they had a license to sell crack with the conspicuous full-time lines outside.

I vaguely remember being a kid in the Nicky Barnes, Guy Fisher days of open-air drug markets in Harlem and seeing lines of fiends leaning and nodding on blocks. This was during New York City's really rough stretch when the city had particularly given up on places with predominantly minority populations. These were well past the days of Harlem's fabled renaissance. The fiends blended in with the overall dirt and decay of abandoned buildings and vacant lots that so much of Harlem had come to embody.

This was one of my first times seeing anything like this as a young adult and being able to comprehend what it represented. In so many ways, Harlem is a self-contained entity. I remember thinking there was no way the police didn't know what was going on. They had to be allowing this to take place as some strategy. Either they were getting paid, or they just let it happen because they thought it was contained to a few areas, and they couldn't be bothered.

I don't remember how much Red told me the spot was clocking per shift, but I knew there was a way to capitalize on its good fortune. I went to a smoke shop downtown in Greenwich Village that sold all kinds of paraphernalia and duplicated the exact packaging they were using from the size of the bottles to the color of tops. I packed my work with the idea to infuse my product through the spot. Red was making a straight salary of approximately $1,500 a week. I suggested we do a 60/40 split on everything we mixed in. So, on every thousand dollars, that would be an additional $400 a day for him which meant an additional $2,800 a week.

I told Red my idea, and he was with it. Honestly, it didn't take a whole lot of convincing since it just made sense. That first day, he paged me after a couple of hours to say the $1,000 worth of work was already gone. This wasn't only a windfall for Red, but me as well. The timeframe of making money so easily and quickly dwarfed the $2000 a day or so that I had to split with my guys over 12 to 24-hour shifts in the Bronx.

I was hooked and Red, and I just kept increasing the amount of our work we would slide into his shift's traffic over time. At our height, we might have put in $10,000 a day, which, of course, eventually diminished the spot's numbers. We had a few months' run before it was detected. Red never got directly busted because there were multiple workers and multiple shifts, but his entire shift of workers was eventually fired. His increasingly extravagant lifestyle was starting to exceed his salary during this short run, including the copping of two or three new cars and a noticeable jewelry collection. His spending probably did not help deflect suspicion from the spot or Red.

The money was great, but it was when Red's shifts were over that the real fun began, as my coming out party was officially in session. Whenever he got off his shifts, we would pull out one of our cars or go back-to-back doing the Harlem circuit. Red had a Volkswagen Jetta and Toyota Supra, and he always had his cars match his hair color. I was driving an Audi Quantum and 325e BMW. We customized all of our cars from the sound systems and interiors to kits on the exteriors and the rims, which were mandatory on every vehicle.

The circuit included various spots in and around Harlem like beauty parlors, barbershops and car washes that were epicenters for being seen. Harlem popped 24/7. The finest girls from all five boroughs would walk the streets of Harlem, looking to catch that hustler who would make their ghetto dreams come true. This was many years predating the Internet, but if the right people saw how you were moving, you could go "Uptown Viral" in a matter of hours, and when you were young like we were, there was no point in getting money if no one knew about it.

Red had an apartment on Convent Avenue near City College in a section called Sugar Hill. He had decorated his crib with all the latest styles and furnishings, and the place became our hub. There was a boosting crew lead by a guy called Sneaker Man. Red and his crew were his biggest customers, and with Red and I being essentially the same size, Sneaker Man and his crew effectively started boosting for me as well, making staying fresh almost hassle-free. Standing out became our norm, and that included our new jewelry. Dookie rope gold chains, crosses, and gold nugget bracelets and rings were vital elements of the required drug dealer starter kit, and we wore our uniforms well.

I was only a little over a year out of high school, and Red was still finishing up his GED program during the first six months of our partnering. We would pull up in our whips at lunchtime or after school and post up at different high schools. Julia Richman on 67th Street, Brandeis on 84th Street and Columbus Avenue, as well as Campus on Convent Avenue in Harlem, were our favorite stops. On nice days, we would park our cars and walk uptown from 125th Street to 155th Street and Rucker Park, over to the park on 139th Street and Lenox Avenue and back. This gave us the opportunity to see, feel and touch the people all the while collecting girl's phone numbers and dapping up the homies. They were becoming used to seeing us driving by hitting the horn and throwing up peace signs.

We made going to the different beauty shops throughout Harlem part of our tour. We paid for the hair appointments of girls we had met, sometimes paying for all the girls in the shop in a way that everyone saw us making a spectacle of it. The conspicuous displays of throwing money around lead to your name ringing, and the more girls seeing this and talking, the bigger your reputation grew. The word was out, "I may not have been a trick, but I definitely was one to treat."

Harlem had these designated areas where you could make an impression within a 30-block radius. Everything was or could become a spectacle, including the knots of cash in your sweatpants pockets. There was pageantry in pulling out cash to pay for anything, even at the local bodega. We were accessible at the car wash where all the hustlers congregated, or sneaker stores, in the skating rinks, as well as the gambling spots. We looked for any reason to go into our pockets and pull out knots of cash.

I looked forward to getting fresh and going out of the house every day. It was like being a performer in the midst of creating a "brand," well before the term was so commonly used. The excitement and the energy I felt was second to nothing. Our lives were daily movies within multiple genres, from the erotic tales to gangster flicks to dramas to comedies. No two days were ever alike, but we dressed the part of featured performers every day, even if we didn't have an exact script for the day's events. It was like improv theater, but we weren't looking for laughs, rather respect and adulation. The more girls you had talking about you, the more relevant you became and the closer to the unspoken goal of becoming "that nigga."

I know how juvenile and even misogynistic this may sound, but everything we did, beyond taking care of our business, was related to trying to make ourselves appealing and impressive to girls. The fairer sex absolutely motivated all the extras, the flamboyant swag, style, fronts, cars, jewelry, and cash during these times. They were not only our aspired trophies but the biggest callings of our success, especially if you treated them well.

Girls were a great motivator and prize. It wouldn't be overstating our reality to declare that they were directly or indirectly the reason so many guys hustled. It's the peacock syndrome where we made ourselves stand out apart from the rest to become more attractive. In your late teens and early twenties, the formula is relatively simple. Nice cars, clothes, and a pocket full of money were enough to do the trick. Of course, there are different levels to everything, and the level of your hustle and fronts was a barometer to the types of girls that were within your reach. Along the lines of the exclusivity of the girls was the different levels of one's preferences and proclivities. Everyone has their thing(s) that they are into. I was just lucky enough to have found mine relatively young to really enjoy it.

Our reputations were cemented by the company of the *baddest* girls we kept and how well we treated them. This eventually meant buying clothes, shoes, furs, in some instances paying rents and, for those special girls, even cars. The more exclusive a girl was, the more she was treasured and desired. We were unapologetic misogynists. I hustled hard, and I played harder. What was the point of getting this money if I couldn't fully exploit it to have the things that made me happy and gave me pleasure? Beautiful girls did just that for me. The juvenility of all of this isn't lost on me, but I was a selfish teen with a high sex drive and plenty of money. I wasn't going to pass on these options for no other reason than I was gluttonous. Eventually, that energy and reasoning in my dealings with girls transferred to a realization that I didn't expect to live long enough to have regrets, so there was little chance of me denying myself anything, let alone the company of beautiful women.

Adolescent men dominated the headlines of the subculture of the time. However, girls were undeniable, if less heralded, co-stars. Their impact both behind the scenes and as the era's undisputed muse cannot be argued or understated. For many, like myself, it started with wanting to help our mothers and grandmothers, to graduating to wanting to impress (and even possess) the flyest and most attractive girls of our generation.

I hustled hard and partied harder, even while being in a relationship. If you dealt with me, this is what came with my lifestyle. I didn't think this made my woman any less of a woman for dealing with me on those terms. I believe they accepted and respected that I kept it real, in part, because I put emphasis on my lifestyle, as well as the dangers and short-term prospects of my life.

I was relatively respectful and very generous. If you wanted to reap the full benefits of being one of my girls, you simply had to understand there was a price to pay for it. I knew what I had to offer financially and intimately and tried to make sure it was always a mutually beneficial situation. If it wasn't beneficial to her, there was never any coercion or manipulation on my part to get them to stay or change their minds.

Unlike the older hustlers before us, we were essentially kids without much guidance or experience, and everything was on-the-job training. None of us had ever had any real money and barely knew others who did to emulate. The most distinct and obvious difference between the two generations was age. The average heroin dealer in his apex was in his late thirties to forties, whereas the crack generation was led by a bunch of teenagers and early twenty-year-olds. What the older generation had over these younger guys was simply wisdom and life experiences, which made a world of difference. When they were our age, they apprenticed or started on the bottom and worked their way up. Our trajectory and learning curve, in being bosses as teens, was foreign to anything that they had experienced.

The older generation wasn't photo-friendly. They saw the concept of pictures holding their money and guns as possible evidence the government would try and use against them. They also stressed that violence, especially when it came to murders, was bad for business and only to be used when necessary. Clearly, my generation did not understand or ignored most of those lessons.

I was luckier than most in having my Uncle Kid as a baseline to follow. We were getting money and wanted reps. That was part of the Harlem way before the word "swag" was ever invented. At our age, there was no reason to get all this money and no one knew. "Incognito" was an old-timer selling drugs still living in the hood because he was too scared to attract attention. It was part of our youthful bravado and foolishness that eventually contributed to our destinies. Instead of being on the low, we proudly wore the H (Hustler) on our chests.

If nothing else, our ignorance and short-sightedness were genuine. In accepting "The Life," one of us expected to live past our twenties, so we celebrated the immediacy of the here and now, unrepentant to the bullseye our lavishness brought from predators in the game or the police. We were clichés for becoming self-fulfilling prophets to our tragedies, but what more could be expected from juveniles and young adults living a fast life with resources beyond their imaginations.

Keep in mind; a top ten NBA Draft pick was making little more than $300,000 - $400,000 a year in the mid-1980s, numbers me and some peers easily exceeded in a month- in cash, with no off-season or agent (and, for most, no IRS) taking a cut. We blazed a trail. Hip-Hop was gaining traction as an art form. Our popularity and money were far outpacing any recording artists' pay. We were the images they would come to rap about. We drove the cars they aspired to have and dated the girls they fantasized about. Hip-Hop is built on street cred, and the only ones, at the time, that had certified authenticity in that realm were us young hustlers, and none of us were picking up any microphones, because no one would risk the pay cut.

***

My initial run with Red was short. It was about a year or so, but I was officially hooked at this point. Getting money and the rep that was being carefully cultivated was almost as addicting as the product the fiends were being served. My addiction may not have held the physical component of drug dependency, but psychologically, the pull may have been just as strong if not even stronger.

This is not about me minimizing drug addiction but rather pointing out how strong the pull of real money and power was to poor kids that aspired to have nothing more in life. Suddenly it was not only attained but in numbers that far exceeded our initial limited imaginations. Once there, it was all-consuming and, in the beginning, it looked like it wouldn't stop. Outlaw ghetto entrepreneurship was real and thriving in New York and throughout the nation, if you were willing to take risks and put in the work.

After Red got fired, we went into business for ourselves. I was the one with the access to an actual connect, plus our arrangement just worked, so it was in both of our interests to continue a partnership. We opened our spot on 134th Street and 8th Avenue. We split it up into two crews (his and mine) for two 12-hour shifts. He had the day shift in part because he had worked a day shift previously and I had no issues with him picking it. No two days were ever alike. Sometimes, his shift made more, sometimes mine did. Red's crew was comprised of his brother and cousins. I started initially with Eric and Dexter. That didn't last long for one reason or another. I had been hanging out with John Rutledge and his brothers ever since John's days at the spot on 136th Street. John was the oldest of five brothers that were all relatively close in age. Besides his hustling proficiency, John had a reputation as a thorough dude. All the brothers had that reputation to a degree. One thing was sure, if you fought one Rutledge, you were fighting them all, and that genuine closeness made them a formidable force, even as teens. John worked in the spot with Red, but as time went on, John and I got tight. He told me his brother Breeze could handle the roll, so Breeze took over as a manager running my shift.

Breeze was the second oldest of the brothers. He was the pretty boy. Unlike the reputations of his other brothers, Breeze was a lover, not a fighter. However, don't let the light-skinned, hazel-eyed, Creole, pretty boy looks fool you. He handled his business. We hung hard. Breeze was always the cat who had a get rich*er* scheme. He would deadass pitch getting on a plane and going to Colombia to find and meet up with Pablo Escobar to get a direct connect. Breeze was an idea guy. Between his outlandish schemes and ideas, he had a great sense of humor. No matter how serious he was, it was always comedic. Breeze was always solid and a good dude who handled our business in the spot with no issues.

Red remained in the profitable grind of our spot while I began to branch out when other hustlers started approaching me. Part of the positive side of your name ringing in the streets is that it presents countless new business opportunities. The word was out that I had the hookup, and my fronts and all the talk in the streets trumpeted my success. I started wholesaling to other hustlers in the city in addition to the revenue from the spot Red and I shared. The wholesaling component to my hustle eventually got pretty big.

There came a time that the building on 134th Street that Red and I were pumping out of got condemned and shut down by the city. It was an abandoned building the city-owned. The powers-that-be had given up on places like Harlem so it didn't take much to get a locksmith to put up metal doors and locks on city-owned property. During the 1970s and '80s, first under Ed Koch and then David Dinkins's direction, 60% of the land in Harlem was owned by the city. Slumlords had walked away and left a majority of the buildings in decay. With the increase in drug usage, these were considered the dark ages of Harlem. We cut into a Con Edison worker to get electricity. It didn't take too long for the spot to get too hot. We were making upwards of $40,000 to $50,000 on some days between the two shifts.

After our spot was shut down, we parted ways. Red and I never really did any other business together after that. We stayed friends up until his untimely death, in Virginia (RIP Nappy Red) less than a year later. His passing came as a surprise, especially since he was not normally known to do business out of town.

Even with the successful wholesaling I was doing; I eventually started getting other spots in and around Harlem. One was on Lenox Avenue and 128th Street in a building nicknamed Castle Grayskull due to its appearance resembling the animated TV show. Another was up on Bradhurst and 153rd Street. They were being run by Breeze and Troy Rutledge, all overseen by John, who had become my new counterpart in our drug business.

A new spot in a 24-hour period eventually made, on average, $30,000 a day. Twenty thousand dollars for a kilo turned into $50,000 broken down, minus 40/60 splits I shared with workers because they were family. Most others were doing 30/70 splits. This meant a return of $30,000, netting me $10,000 on every key being sold through our spots, which were all doing about three keys a week. Plus, outside of the spot, I started giving $1,000 packs (or G Packs) with a 60/40 split. The simple math is I got back $600 for every G Pack. I was also consigning out ounces to ½ eighths and eighths of a key to select new guys wholesaling outside of my stable spots.

Troy was the next to the youngest of the Rutledge Brothers. He was solid and not particularly outspoken. He was only about 13 or 14 when we first met. Troy had a temperament that was always middle-of-the-road. Like his brothers, he was also not one to play with. Troy had a maturity that was way beyond his years. Of all his brothers, he was the calmest of the bunch. He didn't fool with just anybody, but when he did, you could bet your life on him having your back. Troy and I had a special relationship uniquely different from the other brothers. I can't put my finger on what it was specifically, but we just got each other without a whole lot of words being spoken.

My relationship with John continued to develop, and we became great friends, even being known as cousins. In hindsight, he filled a void with Chris' absence, but it was genuine nonetheless because John was such a good, solid dude. He became my closest confidant.

In 1985 I moved Reika and me into a luxury high rise building on Prospect Avenue in Hackensack, New Jersey. I was 19 and Reika was 16. My mother put the apartment in her name but never resided there. Reika and I assumed the roles of brother and sister, and no one ever questioned us outwardly, even with our 1-year-old son, Pop, in tow. I'm not sure what our neighbors thought. I was hardly there, and for the most part, Reika seemed to avoid any awkward situations with the neighbors who were undoubtedly curious as to our story.

Reika was my woman, but in all honesty, besides being young, we were still getting to know each other, and that learning curve didn't come without bumps and bruises that undoubtedly made us both question our choices.

There was this older hustler by the name of Jack, who was one of the last of the heroin kingpins in Harlem. Jack was getting a lot of money, and he had a thing for young girls. What I remember about him was that he and some of his guys held court in Dapper Dan's. I believe that he may have had something to do with some ownership in Dan's boutique.

He had a son by this young girl named Theresa. I came to meet Theresa sometime in the fall of 1986. I was uptown on 8th Avenue close to the Rucker, and she pulled up on me in a 190 Mercedes Benz with a couple of her girlfriends. She clearly knew who I was, but I had no idea who she was. She said, "Hey, Kevin," smiling. Random girls knowing me wasn't overly surprising due to the fact I was making it my business to be known. What caught me off-guard more was what she was driving and her matter-of-factness in acknowledging me. Theresa asked me to pull over. Had this been anywhere else, or even a certain time of night, I would have found that to be an unacceptable request, but it was early afternoon, and I was quite comfortable where I was and what was going on. I pulled over and jumped out of my BMW.

When she jumped out of the car, I realized the minimal first glance I got did her little justice. She was beautiful with long, dark, straight hair down near the middle of her back. She had this Indian thing going on, a nice shape, and a smile to go with it. My first question to her was, "How do you know me?" She might have replied something to the effect, "Who doesn't know you?" I smiled and said to myself, "Good answer. A great way to stroke my ego." She was clearly flirting with me.

It wasn't long after that the conversation's true intent revealed itself. She told me that her man, Jack, was getting at my girl Reika. She went on to say a bunch of things, but basically, she felt one good turn deserves another. I wasn't aware of anything she was saying, but regardless of what it was, I was with getting to know her better. As for Reika, I would soon get to the bottom of that, but at this moment, I was going to close this deal. I started seeing Theresa regularly. She was super cool, sexy, and her motivation made the time we spent together interesting, to say the least.

When I confronted Reika on the matter, she told me that Jack had taken her and her friends out and that he was trying to give her all kinds of gifts. She gave the standard denials to that question asked by guys to their girls when confronted about this kind of shit.

Jack ended up going down on a big case some months later, on February 2, 1987. James "Jack" Jackson was arrested on charges of conspiracy to distribute and to possess with intent to distribute heroin. Jackson was identified as the head of a ring responsible for distributing heroin in Manhattan, the Bronx, Bridgeport, Connecticut, Boston, and Washington, D.C., according to then-U.S. Attorney, Rudolph Giuliani. The indictment charged that Mark Reiter, a member of the Gambino crime family, supplied heroin to James Jackson. Mr. Reiter, who also faced drug charges in Brooklyn with Gene Gotti, brother of reputed Gambino boss John Gotti, "was a major heroin distributor operating at a very high level with organized crime." The Gambino group was considered the nation's strongest Mafia organization. Jack would soon flip and cooperate with the government against Mark Reiter and Gene Gotti.

***

During this period, as money was flowing in on a consistent basis, I began to question legitimate businesses because they appeared to be as corrupt as mine. I was spending money fast, and there was no way that these "legitimate" entities such as car dealers and others did not know someone as young as me, spending cash, was not engaged in illicit activities. Yet, they did not care. It's difficult to expect me as a teenager and young adult to have any real kind of moral dilemma to selling drugs when it became increasingly clear that nearly everyone was corrupt on some level if presented with enough money as temptation.

Much has been written and documented about the "Cocaine Cowboy" era in Miami in the 1980s. It has been argued/speculated that much of Miami's economy and its ever-increasing skyline of high-rise buildings were built upon the foundation of money laundering and the cocaine economy. Nothing quite that dramatic took place in Harlem and New York City, but if there was ever any positive to the destruction ensued by the crack epidemic, it was the economic infusion that did exist in most of New York's most economically depressed areas for its most forgotten citizens.

The drugs, during the time, absolutely spread a destructive path. Generations felt the effects of addiction, death, violence, and long-term incarcerations that affected families for years afterward. It is hard to see much upside of the Crack Era, even as I write about a time period memorialized and glamorized by so many. I get it. America, like no other place, celebrates gangsters and outlaw societies. From the Wild West to the Capone Prohibition, to the Mafia to the Cocaine Cowboy/Crack Era, America embraces and is fascinated by outlaw culture because it is far more relatable to what the average American can identify with over the more rarefied and unfamiliar paths of the Carnegies, Mellons, J.P. Morgans or a Donald Trump.

The positive economic effects of the era extended well beyond people being able to buy boosted goods at a discount or purchase TVs and VCRs on the cheap from a crackhead. Families were being fed and clothed. Some people and families never had cars or taken a trip finally having the means and opportunity. Much of the money was contained and spent in the hood. Grocery stores, cleaners, restaurants, car washes, clothing stores, barbershops and beauty shops flourished. None of us ever benefited from any trickle-down effects of Reaganomics, but the community benefited from the money being made and spent during the era. It all came at a cost. Yet, for underserved and forgotten demographics already living in Hell, the money flowing offered a brief respite. The era didn't turn the neighborhoods into Hell. That Hell already long existed. The money was too intoxicating, and while it came with a price, none of us were going to turn it down.

5

D.C. ON ARRIVAL

My reputation grew with my name ringing in the streets. All my stunting and antics proved fruitful. Business was good, but not so good to be able to turn down new and prosperous opportunities. My friend Albe, from Bronx Community College, and I stayed good all this time and continued doing business. At some point in 1985, Albe ventured down to Washington, D.C., and made a connection with some guys that were doing their thing.

An eighth of a key was $2,500. I saw Albe go down to D.C with an eighth and come back in one day with $5,500 to $6,000. Albe had gone to D.C. with work I provided, and within a week, he went from flipping a couple of eighths to having money for a key for his re-up two trips later. This was all I needed to see. I accompanied him on his next trip and brought two-eighths of a key on my own.

Keep in mind I didn't know anyone in D.C. beside Albe introduced me. I was long on courage and imagination, but short on perspective. I had little understanding to know any better of all the potential dangers in pioneering so far away from home. I came back two days later with $12,000, and that was strictly wholesaling. I was selling nothing but ounces for $1,500 apiece. Albe had someone whom he was selling, and they bought as much as we brought down. After doing this a few times, the initial buys got bigger, and his contacts also put us onto other buyers, who collected a percentage for their efforts.

In 1985-86, the streets of New York City and D.C. were not yet flooded with cocaine or crack. Cocaine was still relatively difficult to get, and even those in the trade did not have direct and consistent connects. The consistency of my access to product would always be one of my greatest assets in the game.

Cocaine, more specifically crack, was a younger guys hustle. At that time, a key of coke might cost $25,000, and you might make 2 or 3 points (thousands) wholesaling it on a quick flip. A key of heroin might cost $180,000, but you would make at least double from it, depending on its purity. Even wholesaling it, you could make $15,000 to $20,000 on a quick flip. Crack was a different hustle with different rules (or lack thereof), and most of the more established guys, like my uncle, preferred the lane they knew.

Heroin was my uncle's primary business, and he had a serious Italian connect. He only really had coke for personal and partying usage. My uncle was a great hustler. He had achieved sustained success in The Game. I'm sure if he had foreseen the promise and my future success, he probably would've made provisions to supply me. Part of the routine that may have made the older hustlers like him successful may have also played a part in his reluctance to see beyond his circumstance and look at something new. He was comfortable and didn't foresee how big I would get or how relatively easy it would have been to make money from me. If my uncle had continued to supply me, I probably would have never looked elsewhere. The points on my run alone would have pushed him way past comfortable to wealthy. Instead, as I grew my business, I outgrew being able to cop from him.

***

Harlem is considered predominantly black, but even then, the Dominicans were a staple on the Westside, particularly on Broadway from 135th Street till you reached Washington Heights. The Dominicans had the Colombian connects, but they didn't have the same retail distribution outlets as we did. It wasn't unusual for them to run up on guys like me at places like the car wash, restaurants, or wherever if they thought we were getting it. This sounded simple for me, but in reality, a solid, consistent coke connect was not that easy to find. Looking the part of a successful hustler did have benefits. Though detriments would undoubtedly follow, my initial focus was solely on capitalizing on the fast-moving events that embodied my life.

On one occasion, a Dominican guy sought me out. I knew he had work and an introduction was set up. He was from Broadway in the 130s, and the meet took place in a gym.

Upon being introduced, I told him what I was capable of doing. We discussed prices and incentives if I moved a certain amount within a particular time frame. Although we initially met up in Harlem, when I went to do business, we met up in the Bronx in an apartment he had near the Jerome Park Reservoir off of Sedgwick Avenue not far from where my mother lived.

We started doing business, and things were good. Our business relationship was growing as well as our developing personal relationship. Not long into our dealings, he caught a case though I wasn't certain of all the particulars of his situation. I had gotten cool with him and one or two of his guys, so when I reached out, they told me about the incident, and they would get back to me once they got things figured out. Things like this were commonplace, so while it was a setback, it was only a minor one. I had been dealing with a few different connects and usually dealt with whoever had the best price.

At some point, his younger brother, Juan, reached back. We met and talked about getting back to business. I started dealing with Juan, and the prices and product were pretty good. We would meet up alone in different places throughout the Bronx dropping off and picking up.

There was one time when I had to meet up with Juan that stood out. I had some money I owed him, and he told me to meet him downtown on Broadway and 95th Street. When I arrived, I parked and walked to the location we were to meet. The first thing I saw when I got there were a bunch of guys who I knew. One was T Money and a few other local hustlers from Harlem. Unbeknownst to Juan, I had a problem with this. Though I was cool with many of them, I wasn't good with these guys knowing my business. I dapped everyone up and pulled Juan to the side. We spoke for a few minutes then walked to get money. I pulled my car up to his, made sure our surroundings were good then passed him the money. I dapped him up and told him we'd catch up. That was the last time we did business. I'm not sure if we ever discussed what my issue was in greater depth, but we nonetheless remained friends.

I then met another Dominican guy named Pascualito. I don't remember how I met him, but I'm certain we were introduced. This occurred shortly after I got home from college and was just figuring out my thing.

Pascualito lived in a small one-bedroom apartment in the area of 183rd Street in the Washington Heights section of Manhattan. I would call Pascualito before I arrived so he could have my product ready, and I could just cop and go. If I needed the coke right away, I would have him cook it for me for convenience. Usually, he would have what I was buying on-hand. However, as I began coming more frequently, there were times he would not have everything in place when I arrived. In these scenarios, I would hang out until he finished cooking, or his connect brought the product I needed. Just by happenstance one day, his connect, and I arrived at the same time. I had never met or saw this person prior. If he did come by when I was in the apartment, I stayed out of sight in the room and only heard them speak in Spanish.

This was an awkward occurrence for both of us. We were both attempting to move inconspicuously. I was moving with the money, and the connect had the work on him. We walked up the stairs, me first and him right behind. I could tell he was the connect because of his disposition, and I'm sure he assumed the same about me.

We arrived at the floor and uncomfortably knocked on the door, waiting for it to open. When Pascualito opened the door and saw both of us, he ushered me into the bedroom. They handled their business, and immediately after I copped, I headed out. To my surprise, when I attempted to leave the building the connect was in the lobby waiting on me. He approached me, but we had a little difficulty communicating. His English wasn't that good, and my Spanish was just as bad. I did the minimum to pass Spanish in high school, not realizing how handy it could be in my future. I understood enough to know that his name was

Mario; he was giving me his number to call and deal directly with him the next time.

That was the break every hustler lives for, and things after that would be forever different. Mario had asked about me, wanting to know why Pascualito wasn't taking more product in advance to alleviate the issue that was becoming a normal occurrence and inconvenience.

I would make that call the next time I needed to cop. I was told to meet him in the Dyckman section of Washington and Inwood Heights. I met him in a nice, quiet building off the last Manhattan exit of the West Side Highway before going into Riverdale. When I entered the apartment, I was greeted by Mario and Janice, who he introduced as his wife. Mario was Colombian. Janice was Dominican but spoke English well and translated.

The business took place without issues, and this became my new situation. Pascualito reached out to me several times to see what was going on and if I needed anything. I told him I was good and after a couple of calls, he got the message. It wasn't long before Mario, and I discussed taking additional work on consignment due, in part, to how fast I was moving product. Mario and I discussed the terms of our new arrangement. He asked a bunch of questions about my family and where I lived. I knew what this was all about, so to make the process move along, I took him to my house and showed him a couple of spots in Harlem I had. I felt that this would allow him to see my setup and generally make him comfortable. I had no concerns about doing this because it was done as good faith and I never had any intentions of running off on the connect and putting my family in harm's way.

I had everything to gain by doing this. I knew the more comfortable he was, the better our working arrangement would be. After all, I had met his wife and knew where he laid, so I looked at the mutuality of my openness as a key to building our relationship. Doing this did exactly what I desired, and immediately after that, I started getting consigned work.

THE CRACK ERA

As our relationship grew over the years, I was invited to family dinners as well as social outings. I was a fixture around him and his family and even got close enough to start dating one of his nieces. She was beautiful, and I had to catch myself in that situation and step back to not risk our business relationship in any way due to hurting someone's feelings. Whatever I bought, he would match allowing me to expand and grow my business. This allowed me to wholesale at a good price. As a sign of appreciation during the holidays, I'd often gift him and Janice with jewelry, furs, and cars. I had a direct Colombian connect, and though my relationship with Mario was my mainstay and endured throughout my run, droughts in New York or just convenience sometimes led me to use other connects as well.

***

In D.C., we ended up at the Branch Avenue Motel in Maryland directly across the street from the Iverson Mall in Temple Hills, alongside Sam's Car Wash. This was a rundown motel that felt like it was going to be condemned any minute. We stayed there just long enough to get the business done, and we rolled back to the airport to New York. This was the only landmark I knew at the time, near Albe's people, so I stayed there. Before too long, Wise (also known as Arnold), who was Albe's half-brother, and Crusader Rob, who I also originally met through Albe, were in D.C. as well.

Rob got his nickname as a youth from the older cats for doing stickups and robberies in his South Bronx neighborhood. His reputation was already certified by the time I met him. He was cool with Albe and we hit it off. I'm not certain what their relationship was built on. One thing that drew me to Rob was that he was always composed under any circumstances. He was well-read and a sharp dude. His disposition was such that gave you the impression he was not someone you wanted to have a problem with. As our relationship grew, it became obvious that his efforts and energy would be better served hustling than in the *taking* game. With his reputation, he already had one component most hustlers needed to address -- collecting money. Most people would have never dared to not pay Rob.

Wise was from the Boston Road area, which was almost the furthest point you could go in the Bronx before you hit Mt. Vernon. We called it "The Valley." Wise had a reputation for scrapping in school and running with the tough kids. Wise did this thing, barking like a dog when he got excited to get his point across. This unnerved those not in the know and even scared some who knew him. He was aggressive and brolic, so you felt his presence. He was good-hearted and very loyal, but in an instant could become your worst nightmare. Overall, Wise was just a solid dude.

I was constantly jumping on the New York to D.C. air shuttle with drugs and coming back the same or next day with money. Before the mid to late 1990s, you could buy airline tickets in cash, without identification. The Trump Shuttle from New York to D.C. only cost a hundred bucks round-trip. It was an hour from wheels up to wheels down. In the beginning, I'm sure people assumed we were just college kids. With institutions like Howard University and Morgan State in and around the nation's capital, we went unnoticed, hopping in and out of the airports frequently. I'd strap Ziplock bags of crack around my waist, the sleeves of my coat, and pockets.

The relatively easy flips made me take a closer look at the time and resources of having spots in New York. You can potentially squeeze every last dime out of a package breaking it down to maximize your profit. This still didn't match the money I could make taking my show on the road. Plus, spots require more effort and are labor and time-intensive. Already having a steady wholesaling component of G packs, eighths and quarter keys made me value the freedom of not being tied down by a New York spot. Running spots was increasingly challenging, anyway, because of all the growing competition over ever-shrinking real estate.

When I tell you, it felt like everybody was selling crack on their block or a part of a crew selling crack, I am hardly exaggerating. It was the gold rush minus having to travel out west; just stand on a corner and retail small amounts that you were able to easily purchase or get *hit-off* by someone. It was *Ghetto Entrepreneurship* at its best and worst. The blocks didn't only get hot in New York City; they were getting crowded as hell along with all the gimmicks like 2-for-10s and even 3-for-10s that eventually even went as low as $2 bottles for what was originally sold as 10s or 20s. This was due to all competing for that all mighty dollar.

The time consumption was even worse. Packaging was labor-intensive. If it took two hours to package 20s or dimes, it would now take four to six hours to package the same amount of work. You also had to factor in having to store twenty to thirty thousand bottles at a time.

I never sold smaller than $10 bottles in New York City, but I could see the trend spiraling downward. Additionally, that fight for profitable drug real estate was becoming increasingly violent and stressful, which was making less sense with smaller profit margins and increased competition.

There were several instances where we had to deal with encroachment, and other BS and shots were exchanged. Once, someone set up shop in one of our buildings, and in the course of shooting out the locks on the doors with a machine gun, one of our guys was hit by friendly fire and had to go to the hospital. Those violators quickly moved out of the building, but those scenarios were becoming too common of occurrences.

In contrast, the smallest increments I sold in D.C. were 50s, which still served as a wholesaling component to the locals. The locals could usually break them down, re-package, and double their money. A kilo broken up into $50 grams could be packaged up as fast as an hour and held a greater profit margin. One thousand grams made us $50,000 on every kilo, with a key costing $20,000. In addition to the straightforward return, other increasing benefits came from holding down spots in D.C.

I went from barely knowing how to cook crack to be a master chef. I started out cooking grams at a time using the baby Gerber bottle. I graduated to a coffee pot, then to a bigger pot, and ultimately to a stewing pot in which I was able to cook hundreds of grams at a time. I could eventually cook a whole key in less than a half-hour, and if you were nice with it, you'd have extras. Extras were what occurred if your timing was just right. When cooking the coke with the baking soda, there was a small window in which if you whipped the coke as it was turning to oils at just the right time when adding the cold water, it would come back with more. If you cooked 250 grams mixed with 125 grams of baking soda, you could easily come back with 300 plus grams, giving you an extra 50 plus grams of the finished product. That would give you almost 250 additional grams per kilo. The profit on 250 grams was minimal $5,000 wholesale and as much as $10,000 when I ran it through one of my spots. When you're moving as many keys as we were, that extra $10,000 on top of the normal profit from the joints made it worth being a top chef. Every two keys were a brand-new Rolex or a new car. That's what's considered extras.

Another thing that was very important when moving so many joints was the discarding of the packaging as well as the clean up afterward. I would clean up thoroughly then secure the trash that I was disposing of. I always chose places that weren't associated with me, such as random garbage cans in front of buildings along my travels. I treated the kilo wrappings like a *hot* pistol. A lot of people didn't realize that those wrappings alone could be used as evidence to prove the number of kilos you were moving. I had heard of cases being built on that alone without the person ever actually busted for physically having any drugs.

Ironically as the trend was to lower prices or come up with sales gimmicks, in D.C., we just continued wholesaling, and our numbers increased in the weight sold. In New York, all the gimmicks left dealers essentially competing for the direct business of crackheads. My method in D.C. of wholesaling streamlined my business model and the dealers welcomed my entry-level prices, fast delivery, and better profit margins.

This is what made D.C. so appealing to me in 1986. After a few months going back and forth, I started to talk to my crew about D.C. and how the situation was mushrooming into something much bigger.

***

In the course of going down for a few months through our mutual friendship with Albe, Rob and I started to get tight. Our stays at the Branch were not always uneventful, and I will never forget one specific time when the cops busted into the room. They commanded me, Albe and Rob, to put our hands on the wall and stated if we removed them they would shoot. Rob defiantly turned around and took his hands off the wall. It was one of those defining moments where I realized he was just a different kind of dude. We laugh about it to this day. Luckily no harm came to him or us since we never kept work in the rooms we actually occupied.

Having alliances with thorough dudes, like Rob and Wise, lent to my confidence to pioneer in places where I otherwise had no familiarity. Most people never left their blocks to hustle, yet I was willing to set up shop, literally, in someone else's backyard. All of this was done without really being able to look at someone else's blueprint on how to navigate such a move. Once that decision met with some success, the commitment to D.C. was fully in place.

I initially brought down John, Breeze, Troy and a few others. I didn't initially close the New York spots, but the transitioning had begun. Around the same time, Rob brought in his mob of Tim Sally, Juice, Beef Strow, Greg, Tony, and his brother. Wise also brought in his crew of Ben, Ari, Dexter, Terry, and a few others. We were all initially separate entities, intertwined by Albe, but our new cohesiveness helped us to quickly outgrow the Branch.

That single room eventually turned into ten rooms at a Ramada Inn in Oxon Hill, Maryland, right on D.C.'s border. It was a far better spot than The Branch. As my D.C. presence multiplied, I would stay for days, leave, go back to New York with money, return with more work and never check out. Those days quickly turned into a couple of months.

I am not sure what the hotel staff or management thought about our presence besides fuller occupancy and cash-paying customers. One day, I took a look at the throngs of loud and wild teens all under my direction and knew that we needed a change of program. The spot was getting hot, so we had to switch things up.

Some guys started to develop relationships within D.C. Initially, we would pay the rent for the mothers of girls we were seeing so we could have places to stay outside of the hotel. These situations served to camouflage the overwhelming testosterone presence as well as hide the

D.C. ON ARRIVAL

drugs, guns, and money. Paying their bills, food, rent and more also served another purpose. By helping locals, we were looked at less as marauding invaders and more as part of the community, even beloved to those that we were helping. Around this time, Rob and I got our own apartment, but I never lost sight of the importance of ingratiating ourselves into our new communities instead of appearing to just take over.

Now that we were situated more comfortably, and no longer were under the scrutiny of coming in and out of the hotels, we were able to put a structure in place to maximize the potential goldmine we knew was in front of us. I would give my crew the work in eighths of kilos on up. The amount they could get at one time depended on how fast they moved. Usually, it ranged in half kilos. I would gross $15,000 for the half and $30,000 for the whole kilo. My cost might have been $20,000 per kilo, allowing me to net $10,000 a kilo, headache-free-- no cutting, bagging, etc. They would then take it to the block and make anywhere from $5,000 to $6,000 on an eighth of a kilo, making from $20,000 to $24,000 per a half kilo. After paying me, they'd walk away with $5,000 to $9,000 for themselves on a half a kilo, which most of them were moving easily in two days.

Despite the obvious ridiculousness of us running around so wild, young, and deep in the Ramada, I still consider the timing of our moving out as divine intervention rather than any kind of smarts. It wasn't long after we moved out of the hotel that we started to hear of multiple crews getting run up on by the police and clipped in those same hotels.

We were kind of the first crew from New York to come into D.C. heavy. There were a few cats from NYC already there, but we set up our own camps quickly. During my many trips back and forth on the shuttle from New York to D.C., I repeatedly ran into Billy Guy, a childhood friend who was now was hustling in Baltimore. My history with Billy Guy dates back to our childhood in the Bronx. I came to know him when my squad challenged kids from other areas to be kings of the basketball courts. Billy was from Sedgwick Avenue, a stone's throw from Roberto Clemente State Park. Roberto Clemente had an indoor basketball court, along with all the newest sports equipment and an outdoor pool. The amenities were the first of its kind in neighborhoods like ours.

Billy also spent time as a kid in my neighborhood because we had a common friend in Rodney who lived down the block from me on 164th Street and Ogden. Rodney would become Billy's lifelong crimey. They would spend decades behind bars as co-defendants and comrades. These coincidental run-ins on the shuttles re-invigorated our friendship, and Billy would become a staple in my life afterward.

6

C.R.E.A.M.
CASH RULES EVERYTHING AROUND ME

Cars were easily the first and most obvious calling card of a hustler's success. They were customized from the radios to the seats to exterior body kits. It probably took longer to customize them than the time we actually kept the cars. Customizing was a way to stand out. Harlem was known for its car culture and young cats getting money were copping heavy.

Albe bought his Mercedes 190E with cash in '86. Albe was a resourceful dude, and his buying first made the process less intimidating for me. I had purchased two used cars previously. I bought my first car in PA and another from my uncle directly. Albe took Rob and me to his people, the first time I purchased a new whip from the dealership. I bought my first 3 Series BMW, and Rob purchased a 300 Benz. Based on my stature, I could have picked a larger, more expensive car, but being thin-framed and a buck sixty-five, I probably picked a car that fit me physically more than anything. Rob was 6'2", 190 lbs, and probably picked based on his size as well. Once this was done, I quickly outgrew the car and any intimidation to the car buying process. We didn't mind paying what we knew to be premiums for the purchases.

The individuals we dealt with made the purchases comfortable. They didn't ask any questions and that's exactly what we desired. We were naïve until it was quickly dispelled that we didn't need introductions and intermediaries. Car shopping was one of the few times we were positively profiled. We looked like drug dealers and literally had bags or sneaker boxes full of money and the letters (H) hustler or (D) drug dealer emblazoned on our chests.

***

Eventually, aside from wholesaling quantity, I didn't hustle in New York full-time. Coming back to New York with money was like being home from the NBA in the off-season. I didn't have to be on my game and could enjoy many of the fruits of my labor once I was back. I still had to deal with family, but I didn't have the same business headaches, leaving more time and energy to stay fly and spend money.

Now, every time I was back in New York, my perspective on the landscape changed. As I would drive around, I saw where guys were getting money, and I was easily able to identify the scene. I also knew what it all entailed, especially the work that went into it that now seemed so laborious. I was getting that out-of-town money, which was way different. I still sold work to a bunch of people in New York, but that wasn't so arduous. It was mostly cash and carry, so I had no issue with that.

I can't even lie or pretend like I wasn't feeling myself. I was feeling powerful-- invincible even. Me, Rob and my dudes felt like we were on top of the world. I remembered not too long prior, we had talked about being on top, and now, here we were. As far as I was concerned, there wasn't a close second to us as far as crews went. Our aura was giving it off from the way we dressed to the jewelry we wore to the cars we drove. I considered us the Bosses of Bosses and that theme would continue throughout my run.

During this transition, Rob and I started hanging out more in the city. Our partnering also came about because Albe started falling back from coming to D.C., just accepting points on the moves.

As D.C. kept growing over the next year, both in business and the number of people (most whom he didn't know) I think Albe was just more comfortable being less involved. Plus, as good a dude as Albe was, he always had funny style relationships with women, and it would not have surprised me if his being out of town so much was causing friction at home, contributing to his falling back. Nevertheless, his absence didn't stop the momentum.

He was more comfortable serving as our go-between for my New York connect. Albe's heart wasn't into the everyday hustle as much as it was into gambling, so it was a good fit for him. I think D.C. just got too big, too fast. He saw it as more of a headache than it was worth. Gambling was probably his true calling and had less risk to him. This model, of course, only works as long as lady luck is on your side, and Albe happened to be having a good run. Even when he wasn't, he always had me and Rob and all our fronts as backup. Throughout it all, he stayed trustworthy and reliable. He was the only person I let deal with the connect when I wasn't around.

It had been almost two years since Chris headed off to the army. We stayed in touch through it all. His tour had taken him out of the country to Germany, and he eventually was deployed back stateside in Kentucky. Shortly after getting back, John and I jumped on a plane and headed down to see him. Neither John nor I had ever been to Kentucky. The flight from New York's LaGuardia airport to Kentucky was just over an hour. We rented a car and were off to catch up with Chris. This would be the first time Chris and John met. I gave Chris a little background and brought him up to speed on my current status in more detail than could ever be discussed over the phone. We all went to get something to eat at a steakhouse with some of his Army buddies and further catch-up. He told me how life in the Army had been up until that point and his plans now that he was back. Chris stated that he needed to get some transportation to get around and get himself acclimated.

John and I noticed gun shops everywhere while we were driving to the restaurant, and we asked Chris how hard it was to make purchases. He confirmed there was a ton and said all you had to do was go in and buy them. I believe he mentioned there was a limit on how many you could buy at one time, but he had friends that would buy for us as well if needed. We spent most of the day hanging out, just kickin' it. We had a flight that evening heading back home, so before John and I headed back to the airport, I reached in my pocket and gave Chris around six or seven thousand dollars. It was for the motorcycle he mentioned wanting and some pocket money to get himself whatever else he needed. I let him know there was plenty more where that came from. I told him whatever he needed just let me know and we dropped him off and headed back to New York.

A couple of weeks went by, and I looked up and saw Chris was back in New York. He had rented a U-Haul truck and went AWOL. Temptation got the best of him. However, he didn't come back empty-handed as he bought an arsenal of weapons back with him. We discussed his choice of going AWOL, and I told him I didn't think it was a good idea. He wasn't trying to hear anything I was saying. When he left for the Army, our hustling was lightweight at best. We were getting a few dollars, but nothing worth making a life decision over. Much had changed since he left, and he could see I was playing the game at a higher level than he could have ever imagined. He wanted in. He was ready to get to the money.

I was initially concerned about Chris's decision. However, that was the reality. Ultimately, I was just happy to have my friend back home. I also accepted another less obvious benefit to Chris's return. Through military training, he developed a special skill set. He understood weapons and was able to clean and break them down, ensuring they were in good working order, potentially preventing them from jamming or misfiring. I saw this as a tactical advantage over any of our unforeseen adversaries.

I wanted to limit Chris's exposure when he initially came back home. However, he didn't have it. While I may have moved my people that managed our NY spots to D.C., we still supplied the people who took over those spots. Chris then took over the duties of overseeing those various spots as well as many of the other wholesaling clients I had throughout the city.

With Chris back, and business consistently growing, life was good. So, when I was back in the city, many nights were often spent in hot spots all over the city like The Rooftop and The Red Parrot. One night Breeze and I were uptown hanging out when Rob contacted me. He told me to come through The Red Parrot, where he and his crew were hanging. It was a virtual who's who of young hustlers from throughout the city. The Red Parrot was in Midtown, right off the West Side Highway and 57th Street. Its central location made it accessible to all the boroughs. This centrality led to interesting dynamics that highlighted some of the distinct differences amongst NYC's five boroughs.

***

KRS-1 best described some of the nuances between the boroughs on his classic album *Criminal Minded* in a song called "The Bridge Is Over,". One of the lyrics was, "Manhattan keeps on making it; Brooklyn keeps on taking it; the Bronx keeps creating it, and Queens keeps on faking it." I'm certain the last statement might not hold true, but keep in mind this was a response to a rap battle being had by KRS-One and MC Shan that incorporated the two boroughs labeled "Bridge Wars." However, the point is that reflected within NYC's five boroughs each had its own identity.

Although the Bronx and Manhattan, specifically Harlem, are minutes apart from each other from a certain vantage point, the differences between them are night and day. The people, the fashion styles, mentalities and, simply put, the culture have distinct differences.

If I had to say, and most would agree, the Bronx and Brooklyn had reputations for being the two roughest boroughs during those times. Brooklyn may have edged out the Bronx only since there are twice as many people that populate the borough. Violence and robberies were commonplace throughout the city. Once you become accustomed to these things, if you ventured out beyond your borough, you just moved about accordingly, knowing how to handle yourself with an awareness of your surroundings. With all due respect to Staten Island, it didn't come on most of our radars until years later when the Wu-Tang Clan came out. All these geographic reputations came to light when guys were behind bars. Dudes from Manhattan may have a reputation for making money and being fly but were not necessarily known for being the toughest.

***

From Harlem, I jumped on the highway and headed downtown to catch up with Rob. By the time we got there, they had been there for some time and already made some connections with chicks they planned on spending the rest of the evening with. We rapped some before Rob told me they were heading out. I told him we were staying a little longer to see what we could come up on. He asked if I was good, and I said I was. He said by "good" he meant did I have a gun on me. My response was I didn't because I knew he and his people were there. We went out of plain sight, and Rob passed me his joint. Everyone else with him was still strapped. I dapped everyone up, and they rolled out. If we didn't all move as one, we at least made sure we were all good all the time.

***

In late 1986, Crusader Rob was implicated and wanted for questioning for a shooting in New York that resulted in someone's death. He was not immediately arrested, and there was no initial warrant, but when the police stopped by some of his last known addresses and places he frequented along with his parents' house in the Bronx, he realized he had an issue. He didn't feel inclined to voluntarily wait around for them to return or go to the precinct on his own.

We had been moving along smoothly and in the midst of our D.C. run a drought for "work" descended upon New York. We would later understand that the cocaine supply to New York would dry up for various reasons, from major drug busts to a multitude of other reasons. Those things just happened without much notice or explanation, but our impatience wasn't going to just let us sit around when we thought there was an actual solution to our problem. *Scarface* starring Al Pacino had come out in 1983 and had left such an impression on the drug culture that I went with seven or eight people to Miami in 1986, assuming it was the answer to our problem. I wasn't sure what we were going to actually do once there. We didn't have a contact person or a specific destination. We arrived with over a hundred thousand dollars. We took our dope boy swag, jewelry and went straight to South Beach and Coconut Grove, looking for a connect.

I cannot lie. We expected to see a Tony Montana on every corner or club, but it was not nearly as easy as the movie portrayed. There was a hesitancy from the Miami Latins to do unintroduced business with the New York dope boys. We eventually met someone who took notice of us and said he could hook us up. We ended up in the predominantly Black section of Opa Locka at a car wash owned by a guy named P-Man Sam. Sam was a well-connected dude in Miami. He and his Colombian partner Roberto were owners of a club called the Base Station in Miami. They had a direct Colombian connect. We may not have found our Tony Montana, but instead found someone who knew one of his proverbial "cousins," and this worked for us.

Sam pulled our coat about the guy who had been taking us around, saying he was trying to set us up, and we were lucky that we ended up meeting him. Sam gave us the once over and could quickly tell we were the real deal. We talked with him for a couple of hours before Sam took us by his house, which happened to be the nicest in the neighborhood. From the gated entrance, you could see fountains and columns leading into the house. The rest of the houses on the block were ok but nothing like his. We copped three keys from Sam, got back to our hotel, enjoyed Miami for a couple of days before we strapped the work up, jumped on a plane and went back to NYC.

With a drought, the goods were sold before we landed. It was $20,000 to $25,000 for a key in NY before the drought-hit. The price had almost doubled in the city if you were even able to get anything. We had copped the keys for only $17,000 in Miami. Even at that price, we only made the initial purchase of three keys because we didn't have a concise game plan for transporting much more back that first time. We were freestyling, and there was a large group of us. A few strapped on the goods, and we flew out. We needed to work the kinks out, and once we did, things were good. We would occasionally fly, using Fort Lauderdale instead of Miami International, but ultimately chose the train as our standard method when we did use Miami.

Miami always had cheaper prices than New York, but I also always had to weigh the risks and rewards of making a few extra thousand per kilo versus the convenience of going to Washington Heights and the increased risk of any losses because of the distance to transport. The necessity and even greater profits left by droughts in New York made these decisions easier to make. We went back and forth several times during the droughts and for years to come, but only really when needed.

There were times I might go ahead of Rob. If he was coming in right after, I would leave the rental car for him at a designated place and put the keys to the car on the tire so he could pick it up and move right on. This was usually done with the hotel still open and room keys left as well, so there was no new checking in and out till he was done. Everything was seamless, and this all added to our attempts to stay under the radar coming in and out of these hotels, a lesson learned from D.C.

Reika was in her ninth month of pregnancy, and I ended up missing the birth of my son, Kevin Dewane Carter, in February 1987 during one of these trips to Miami. He was my second (biological) born and my second to be named Kevin as well. Though I still provided and was active in my other son's life, my strained relationship with Gina led her to call our son by his middle name, Queron, instead of his birth name, Kevin. I assumed his being called Queron wasn't just a disassociation from me but even a way to further avoid having to call my name out. I even followed suit and called him Queron, as did her immediate family. This all played a role in naming my firstborn with Reika, Kevin, as well. Like Queron, Kevin didn't take on my last name, in part, because it made it easier for both women to continue receiving whatever government aid or insurance that was available without the complexities of having to explain the different last names of mother and child.

I got hell from Reika and my mother for missing Kevin's birth. My family always came first, but my dedication to my hustle was unmatched, and paper won over sentimentalities, especially knowing she was in great hands with my mother. Our situation in D.C. was so profitable that when the drought-hit, there was no way I was going to lose the momentum we had built up, and if that meant I needed to be in Miami, then I was there.

We always made it a combo trip, usually bringing some girls we either knew or were trying to get to know. The trips to Miami usually included me, Rob, Chris, Albe, and two or more of the Rutledge brothers. On the return trip, someone would be taking the train because increasing word of people getting busted flying made it time for that change. Chris ended up riding back with one of the chicks on the train on this particular trip, and I flew back with the brothers. He didn't get back on schedule, and I started to worry. Eventually, the next day I finally heard from him, but the news wasn't good. He was arrested in D.C.

As the train stopped in D.C., the police entered with drug-sniffing canines. This was all "random" in the sense that they weren't looking for anyone in particular or tipped off. The D.C. corridor on the trains, planes, and Interstate-95 was increasingly treacherous with the police aware of the routes and methods many of us were making up and down the East Coast. They openly profiled Black and Hispanic youth and used the weakest probable cause to search people. It was a numbers game, and the police assumed if they violated enough freedom of movement, it could all be justified by the few busts it would ultimately yield.

Chris did not have the bag in his actual possession or anywhere near his sleeping car. However, he made the mistake of leaving his ID in the bag with the four kilos, which they found in one of the overhead compartments. I felt sick. He was just getting his feet wet and had only been rocking for nine months since going AWOL from the Army. The date was April 7, 1987. He was the first in my crew to get busted and more so by the Feds. He was never granted bail, in part because he was from New York and got busted in D.C. Plus, his AWOL situation finally caught up with him, so there was no chance he was going to be released.

I was in New York, and Rob was in D.C., so he took the initiative and got Chris's lawyer. Despite or because we hired prominent D.C. lawyers, he ended up getting 48 months on a plea deal. The irony to him getting busted is it literally could have been any of us. We barely knew the girl and damned near did "rock, paper, scissors" for the opportunity to ride back and party with her on the train, something we had done several times prior. Chris's L happened because he won. She was arrested with Chris, but he copped to ownership, so she was released and avoided jail time.

Going to Chris's arraignment in D.C. with Rob was one of the most difficult experiences for me up to this point. I could see the despair in some members of his family, who were like my own, and the reality that my best friend was not going to come home for a while was starting to hit home.

The hearings may have also had an indirect effect on Rob as well. The police were being persistent in looking for him in places he was known to frequent in the Bronx and Harlem. I had been living in a luxury apartment building in Hackensack, and we knew we needed to give Rob a little more distance from that stress. I put Rob on with my realtor, who found him an apartment in the same building, two stories above me. Initially, I didn't think much of it and figured New Jersey was a good place for him to lay low.

As upset as I was by Chris's situation and setback, it didn't stop the show. I might have even felt inclined to go harder, with the added obligation to fund his defense, help his family, and ensure I was financially strong enough to handle any future problems as well. This meant pouring my energies into an increasingly profitable Washington, D.C.

Most of my crew had already been with me in either the Bronx or Harlem. D.C. welcomed us because we had the cheaper work. Rayful Edmond, one of D.C.'s biggest dealers, was initially copping from NYC dudes before he started getting work from a Cali connect. At first, the relationship with D.C. and NYC was great. We would see each other, sell work, and party to an extent. We hung at all the happening spots amongst all of D.C.'s top dealers. Chapter 3 was the D.C. equivalent to the Rooftop. We went to the concerts at Constitutional Hall and various Go-Go events throughout the city. We also tore the malls up making our presence felt with our numbers and conspicuous spending.

We were easily identified at first because of our different dress and slang, but we quickly got with the program and began blending in acting the part of a local. I integrated my crew into the landscape where we were speaking and dressing like the natives. Three things stood out in every town that outwardly marked the differences between New Yorkers and locals: the way people dressed, the type of music (even if still within the

Hip-Hop genre), and each town's distinctive slang. Guys in D.C. wore the taller 40 Below Timberlands, while New Yorkers usually wore the construction Timbs. There were different nuances like that in every city.

Initially, we brought our custom cars and big jewelry down from New York, flossing and stunting, but soon realized that attention wasn't in our best interest. We would occasionally floss hard when a show or some sort of big event was occurring, but by this point, we realized that notoriety came with heat, so we cautiously did this only in those instances. Just enough to make our presence felt. We either bought hoopties or paid for women's cars down there. It was worth the investment because we had cars registered locally, usually by older women who were more than grateful for our contributions. Having New York plates would have stuck out for all the wrong reasons, so they were out of the question. We were deep, but initially, there was no conflict. The conflict didn't occur until a few years later when resentment, jealousy (over women), and territorial issues contributed to an NYC versus D.C. environment.

Initially, we were in Southeast D.C., which had a suburban feel of mostly low-rise housing developments and single-family homes. If there were housing projects, they were only like four or five stories. I never remember feeling uncomfortable whereas Northeast and Northwest D.C. were more densely populated like the rest of the city. The tranquility didn't last long, however. What we liked about the neighborhood and its suburban feel eventually is what made it so much more perilous because its wide-open landscapes and desolate areas lent to things getting real aggressive fast.

When New Yorkers from Brooklyn, the Bronx, and Harlem visit any area that has low rise buildings, row homes or single-family homes with tree-lined sidewalks, we look at it as the suburbs. It didn't matter if it was urban or predominantly Black if it wasn't densely populated and didn't have high rise housing projects or obvious tenements, it was the burbs and viewed as safe. We looked at Queens that way to a certain extent. The treacherousness of that landscape during the time, including some notorious characters that it spawned like Supreme, Prince, Fat Cat and Pappy Mason, should have taught us better, but it did not. For many that came from the city with me, traveling to Southeast D.C. visually didn't pose a threat.

It was never quite that peaceful, but in the beginning, our presence in SE D.C. was relatively conflict-free. We were initially welcome, with proverbial open arms. We supplied a product difficult to attain at better prices than they were otherwise used to. That led to guys in SE D.C. getting money. Plus, we came in peace, so everyone was happy in the beginning.

While I was primarily in SE, our reach in D.C. continued to spread like germs. Wise and his crew started to gravitate to N.E. D.C. in an area known as Paradise. The name spoke for itself due to the amount of money made there.

The symbiotic relationship grew in part because of the mutual respect between he and I. It was simply understood, since Wise headed his crew and he essentially deferred to me, his crew became part of my crew by proxy and mine his, creating a stronger, solid unit.

At some point, instead of them having to go back and forth to NY to cop and bring it back down to D.C., I made it worth his while to cop from me. I made myself an invaluable component to his success, and in return, he held me down. My relationships worked because I was a boss dealing with bosses and that included a similar relationship with Rob. I never made people feel like they worked for me but with me. I tried to enhance where they may have fallen short, and there was mutual respect garnered from that. Those were my relationships across the board.

Wise caught a couple of cases over the years. One was for an alleged murder in D.C., but he wasn't convicted on any of those cases. He became part of the Usual Suspects in murders and such in part based on reputation. He spent some time in jail for many of those cases but never convicted for anything. A lot of his crew ended up doing long stretches for murders, kidnappings, and such.

As D.C. was humming and the money expanding, none of this was lost on anyone within my sphere. Mark, known as Black, was with me from the very beginning. When I first started hustling in the BX with Dexter and Eric, Mark lived around the corner on Ogden and 164th Street. Mark played on my basketball team with some of the other neighborhood kids I sponsored and coached. He was originally friends with my brother, and only about two years younger than me. They went to school together, playing basketball at All Hallows. Because of the proximity of his house to where we were hustling, it was a great location to stash the work. After graduating from high school, Mark continued his education and went off to Marist college. I drove him to school to get him settled.

By this time, my hustling had grown. I was moving and shaking in Harlem as well as D.C., so he was quite aware of what was what. I remember him constantly calling me asking if he could come to D.C. with me. I looked at him like a little brother and always tried discouraging him against it in the same way I did with Tony. I often hit him off with money to keep him from wanting. He was seeing and hearing so much about how big we got in D.C. that he just continued pressing me. Finally, he took it upon himself to jump on a shuttle and come to D.C., hoping his presence would make a difference. In the end, persistence overcame resistance, and he quickly became a fixture in D.C. It didn't take him long before he was running his own crew, bringing Jack, Beanie, Barris, and a gang of the neighborhood dudes down with him. Mark followed the blueprint to the letter while implementing some of his own ideas and personal flair.

Breeze and Troy were already there and by this time, had really figured things out and were flourishing as well. They had people under them with their own teams, and everything was going smooth. Their attention to detail enabled me to keep moving without having to micromanage and after Mark came down, the machine was nearly fully operational. Rob and I were coming back and forth to New York at least twice a week if for no other reason to not let the money stack too crazy. At this time, we were probably bringing back a couple of million dollars a month, and we still hadn't even hit our peak, yet.

7

LET THE GAMES BEGIN

Chalk this up to irony, but getting money in this time was not nearly as difficult as figuring out what to do with it all. You can only hide the money in so many places, and lacking a Wharton degree in money laundering, like so many on Wall Street, it wasn't always easy to figure out what to physically do with so much cash. I was the definition of new money. I tried not to go through my money like I was allergic to it. I did the best I could with little guidance. I spent, in part, because I thought the money was never going to end and partially because of the inevitable words of ignorance-- why not?

It was that time again. Spring 1987 was my unofficial second year in the game in Harlem. While I may have thought I was doing it the prior year, by this time, I had it worked out; the year before, I was getting my feet wet. Red and I were running around, and now, a year later, I was fully immersed in The Game. I had been getting plenty of money, and my reputation as one of the top guys on the circuit was cemented.

Capitalism was in high gear. Everyone took our money, no questions asked. From car dealers to jewelers to furriers to realtors, no one was beyond approach. The streets kept score and certified you. It didn't take more than an hour to purchase a car with cash. However long it took to count the cash, that's how long the transaction was, outside of getting the appropriate insurance paperwork. After that, you just drove off the lot with your temporary tag taped to your back window. Many of the cars never lasted beyond the 30 to 60 days on the temp tag because we often flipped them to each other or our connects. Rarely did I ever keep cars past six months.

Once purchased, we took the cars immediately from the dealerships to customizing shops to get them completely modified. The customization raised the value on the street and the flip to another hustler but gave zero value to its Kelley Blue Book assessment. Ghetto economics are totally different from corporate calculations. I learned this lesson the hard way when one of my cars was stolen. I realized all those customizations meant zero to the insurance company. Yet, when flipping the cars to other hustlers or connects, I always got great value for the money put in. If I paid $30,000 for the car but got two keys at a value of $40,000, it was a win-win for both sides. Other hustlers were willing to pay the premium because of the immediacy of getting a finished product as opposed to having to duplicate and the time it took to get it done. It was all about instant gratification and showmanship.

So much of what made the crack era unique was our youth and competitive natures. We treated hustling, almost like an athletic competition. We all vied for Harlem's top spot. In early 1987, Azie Faison was at the top of the food chain and was feeding many of the young hustlers from Harlem like Rich Porter, Alpo, Jason, Travis, Darryl Barnes, Spencer, T-Money, Twin and a bunch of others. They operated out of Azie's spot on 145th Street. I can't say if they considered themselves a crew, but they all were loosely affiliated. My crew and I viewed them as the opposition; whether we were even on their radar at that moment or not.

There wasn't any real beef, just spirited competition. We were all quick to acknowledge others getting money, but we were determined to make our presence felt and understood. Perhaps, we even had chips on our shoulders from feeling overshadowed by the reputation of Harlem hustlers. Besides the Rutledge Brothers, me, Albe, Billy Guy, Crusader Rob, Wise, and Black Mark were all originally from the Bronx. Harlem guys had a reputation for getting all the money. It wasn't called "Money Making Manhattan" for nothing. We just tried harder to get noticed and make our mark. At times, unsure how but determined to acquire an intangible crown.

There was only going to be one crew crowned "King of the Streets," and I was determined that we would be that. I wasn't originally from Harlem, but having spent more time there, I was intoxicated by its energy and drawn to it, eventually making it home base. Harlem was the unquestioned epicenter, and the recognition I was seeking was only going to come from being the best on the biggest stage. Madison Square Garden is called "the Mecca" for all of basketball, and we looked at Harlem as the equivalent when it came to hustling.

So, that summer, we all went all out and copped cars, showing out. The nature of these rivalries was youthful bravado at its most ostentatious. It was about being fly and one-upmanship. It was relatively light and led to the initial party atmosphere of the era. While our rivalries were perhaps over the top, no one was complaining. We entertained the masses, and many lived off the benefits of our efforts, particularly the women in our lives.

John had just copped a yellow 944 Porsche, but even before he had a chance to break it in, I was behind the steering wheel, giving it the once over. I had never driven a Porsche before, so I was putting it to the test to see what all the hoopla was about. In making the rounds in Harlem, I ran into Rich, who had recently been released a year earlier from a short stint he'd done, I believe on a gun case. We hadn't had much of a relationship before him going to prison, but at this point, we were cool with one another. He quickly got back in position and had a couple of cars. One happened to be a Porsche. We got to talking about the cars, and Rich made the clear distinction between his 24-valve, or turbo model, and what I was driving. It was kind of funny to me because those distinctions did not initially have any meaning or importance.

It was clear Rich's fanaticism with cars was unmatched. He was pre-ordering his cars and customizing them faster than the rest of us. He was a true car enthusiast, often reading Car and Driver. He understood the distinctions in engines and how fast cars went when all I wanted to know was how fly it looked while I was going slow. His knowledge did make me step my game up. The competition heated up, especially in the warmer months, from April through September. The summer became an unofficial car show where a goal was to show how many fly and exclusive cars you could bust out in that period. There was no official prize, but bragging rights were priceless.

In 1987, Rich and Alpo both had convertible BMWs. Beside Rich's Porsche, Alpo and Azie had 7 Series BMWs as well. Once I first started seeing ridiculous money in 1987, I started copping cars like a sneakerhead buys Jordan's. I would minimally have at least four to five cars I personally owned and used on any given day. I would park my cars at multiple garages throughout Harlem, and as I was making the rounds, I would pull into a garage in one car and leave out with a different car.

I cannot even recall all the cars I owned during this time period, because I went through so many. Besides the convertible, Red Benz, which was cold, I had quite a few different models, almost all customized. While I had multiple cars already, I had to find another convertible to shut the summer down. It took a minute, but I eventually found an exotic car dealership in Queens on Northern Blvd. that imported cars from all over the world for an exclusive customer base. I don't even remember how I found it, but the guy had several one-of-a-kind custom joints in the showroom. One that caught my eye was a hybrid between a 190 and a 300 Mercedes convertible. The 190 was only a four-door while there were 300 coupes. This hybrid was essentially a concept car and left me with one of the only 190 coupes in America. I paid $70 grand cash for the car. It had all customized emblems from Mercedes.

The day I purchased it, I remember driving from Queens and Long Island with the top down. At the time, while you had to manually drop the top on BMW convertibles, mine was automatic, and this was a distinction that I knew everyone would see. I can still recall the excitement I had, not being able to wait till I got to Harlem so everyone could see this one of a kind show-stopping, a convertible coupe with the custom rims to match, beige saddle-stitched leather interior, four headrests, and woodgrain dashboard and doors. There were only two like this in the country, and Rob had the other one in blue, copped from the same dealer a couple of weeks after I bought mine.

I can still recall that late March day vividly, from what I was wearing to the brick mobile phone in the car. Everything was properly in place for the optimum spectacle because I had further customized it for another $10,000 to $15,000. By this time, I was certified, no blue check needed. This was all a precursor to Instagram and social media. Yet, by the end of the day literally all of Harlem had heard about the car. This particular car was so crazy that whenever I ran into someone, no matter who, they gave it up. There was no hating, only props. I remember every time I drove past someone, it was like I was moving in slow motion in a movie scene. I could see their heads turning, and being able to read the words come out their mouths saying, "What kinda' car is that?"

However, my excitement with the Red Benz was short-lived. Part of why I could never really enjoy the car was the fact that Chris got busted shortly after its purchase. Additionally, weeks after that, only the third or fourth time in the car, I got stopped and arrested up in the Bronx on Story Avenue in Soundview.

New York City had created an auto crime division. With all of the money and new cars flowing through the hood, there were a lot more car thefts. Additionally, there were crews that had developed the hustle of selling stolen Lexus, Mercedes, and BMW from out of state lots or dealerships for $5,000 - $6,000. They were called "tag cars." They had hookups in the Department of Motor Vehicles in New York or Jersey who illegally supplied plates and registrations for the stolen cars that would turn up as valid in a standard search by the police. It was just another reason to use questionable probable cause to stop and harass us.

So, when the Bulls stopped me, I was in the car with Shavar and Dexter. I didn't initially give it much thought because none of us were riding dirty. I pulled out the insurance card. I was still riding with the temp tag, so I didn't have the real registration yet and quickly realized my ownership info was all in German. Despite my assertions, since they couldn't decipher the info, they just locked me up.

I was handcuffed and before he pulled out my identification, he asked me if I was the New York Mets star pitcher Dwight Gooden. I am not sure if he was trying to be funny or just talking shit, but one of them took some pleasure in jumping in and riding off in my car while I was taken to jail.

This would be the first time I personally used a high-profile lawyer like Murray Richman for my defense. The hire was some dumb shit. I greatly overpaid in using such a prominent drug and Mob lawyer since the car wasn't stolen and I didn't actually commit any crime. You could chalk it up as part of the theatrics of hiring such a high-profile attorney on even BS, especially since the case was just dismissed.

However, the dismissal of my case didn't end my dilemma. I still had to retrieve the car that was impounded. I paid cash for the car but put it in the name of a girl who happened to be on public assistance. I had to get a notarized letter from her saying that she permitted me to pick up the car. After that, literally every time I drove the car for the next two weeks I got pulled over. The car was too hot. It had to go.

There was a place called Formula 1 on 57th Street and 11th Avenue. Formula 1 was a high-end customization shop and dealership. Most of its clients were major drug dealers, as well as professional athletes. I used them several times to customize my cars before and had a relationship with the owner. I asked him if he was interested in helping me sell my car. He agreed that I could leave it there to sell on consignment. They ended up putting the car in the showroom window visible to everyone entering and exiting the West Side Highway off 57th Street.

The car didn't immediately sell. I was going back and forth to D.C., which had a crazy car culture and competitions of their own. One of my dudes in D.C. I was dealing with had shown Rayful Edmond a picture of the car and told him I was trying to sell it. Rayful decided he wanted to buy it. I took the car out of the dealership and drove it one block to a garage before I put it on a carrier to ship to D.C. and put it in a storage unit there. I think I agreed to sell it to Rayful for eighty thousand dollars. The next day my dude called me to say the car was impounded. He couldn't resist taking the car for a joyride as soon as it touched down in D.C., and he was subsequently locked up. I had to hire a lawyer for him and to retrieve the car. Once I got it back, I immediately shipped it back to New York. I ended up selling the car myself to a connect for four keys. After lawyers and impound fees, I probably broke even. Crusader Rob ended up selling his blue version to the connect as well for essentially the same reasons.

I was hardly the only one with fly cars. My crew all had brand new, customized whips that made us stand out. Besides the blue Benz similar to my Red Benz, Rob had a 7 Series BMW, and a custom 300E Mercedes with sheepskin seats. Billy had a 5 Series BMW and Mazda MVP. Wise had a Durango and 5 Series BMW. Mark had a Chevy Blazer and convertible BM. John had the yellow Porsche. Albe had a 190 Benz and a BMW. Chris was a Nissan man with the 300Z, Maxima, and PathFinder. Breeze was only about 17 when he got a brand-new Maxima. He didn't have a license when he purchased the car and had to be chauffeured everywhere since he did not even know how to drive. Troy somehow upstaged him with a new Honda with BBS rims at 15.

Some of you may be asking why the young New York hustlers of the time weren't buying Ferraris and Bentleys? Of course, I'm sure someone may have, but the landscape in New York didn't lend to us buying those particular brands back then. First off, we were young and most of us looked at Rolls Royce and Ferrari as the cars rich, middle-aged White men drove. Those brands didn't have the same swag in the streets then that many rappers later gave to them. In 1988, a brand-new Rolls Royce was about $150,000 and a Ferrari about the same. It was well within the means of myself and a few others to cop. However, like I detailed with the red Benz, none of us as late teens and early twenty-year-old could stand the heat that cars like that brought. Predating rappers getting real money and car dealers leasing expensive cars like that, there were no legitimate guys in the hood with that kind of money anywhere near our age, except for Mike Tyson. Who could explain how we were driving the cars we were driving, let alone Lambos and Bentleys within New York City at the time?

Besides cars, access to apartments was something that my crew was starting to amass. We had apartments that served as stash houses, some for weapons and money, some for product. We had places that we just hung out in. One afternoon in early 1987, I got a beep from either Troy or Breeze Rutledge. When we spoke, I was asked to come to one of these apartments we had. This particular one was on the Eastside of Harlem on 116th St and 5th Avenue. The call was hurried and not particularly specific. I knew they needed me to come by, but he didn't exactly make it seem like it was an emergency. I could tell it was important and that I needed to come through. I was with Rob when the page came in. If I would have sensed there was a problem, I would have brought him with me, but instead, largely because of his looming legal situation in New York, I told him not to worry, and I would get back up with him later.

It probably took me about 20 or so minutes to get to them being right across the bridge in New Jersey. When the door opened and I entered the apartment, I was shocked to see Breeze and Troy were handcuffed. The lack of urgency and panic from the call made me not only leave Rob behind, but I walked in the apartment naked, leaving my gun in the car. They were still just teens, and there was another guy there who was unrestrained. I knew him from my old neighborhood in the Bronx. He was the cousin of a girl Chris was dating. There was an opened, emptied safe in the middle of the floor along with a TEC-9 semi-automatic weapon and paraphernalia were strewn about.

So many thoughts started racing in my mind, including trying to figure out if they were forced to make the call and how they were able to make it. Before I could get any answers or figure anything out the guy started hurriedly talking. Basically, he was trying to say that he didn't know the people he brought were going to do what they did.

As I was trying to make some sense out of this crazy scene, Breeze jumped up, still handcuffed, and attempted to grab the machine gun that was lying on the floor. This led to a chain reaction, with the guy trying to grab it out of Breeze's hands. Instinctively, I joined in, and we all continued scuffling for control of the gun. In the course of wrestling for the weapon, I was able to get the clip out by pressing the release on the weapon. When the clip popped out onto the floor, the scuffle momentarily froze. Before any other move was made, Breeze just turned and bolted out the door, still handcuffed.

After that, the guy attempted to explain to me what happened. I stopped him mid-sentence and said, "Hold on, stay right here. I'll be right back," concerned where Breeze was going and what was to come from him bolting out the door. Before I could even talk to or attend to Troy, I started grabbing whatever guns and paraphernalia were left in the apartment; worried Breeze might bring attention or the police back to the crib. When I exited the building, there was no sign of Breeze. I put the items in my car, then went to a payphone at the corner and beeped John. When we talked, I told him about the incident and what he needed to bring to tend to Troy. When I returned to the apartment a short time later, the guy was gone.

We surmised that they had been set up by friends or acquaintances of this dude. We were never able to get to the bottom of who those people actually were. Sometime later, before one of his trips to D.C., Breeze said he saw the dude that stayed behind, trying to explain the situation, in the Port Authority Bus Terminal in Times Square, but he was never able to catch up to him outside that instance physically.

Around this time, I met a kid named Shavar. It was in Harlem while I was still supplying blocks that I once ran. He was a young cat, around 14 or 15. He hustled on one of these blocks. Shavar approached me, asking to get down. He told me what he was moving on the block and how much better he could be doing if he kept work constantly. I took a chance on him, giving him work on consignment. We had an apartment in the Grant Houses on the second floor. The Rutledges had grown up in the same building on the eighth floor. The first day I met Shavar, I gave him $1,000 worth of work, and a couple of hours later, he was done. I then doubled what I gave him, and he was done later that day.

The next day, he came to the apartment about mid-afternoon and said someone tried to rob him on a block that we pretty much ran. Shavar, John, and I strapped up and immediately went to the block. Upon arriving, we all jumped out of the car with Shavar heading in the direction where he thought the dude might be. I knew most of the people on the block and was trying to get some info on my own when a couple of minutes later, I heard shots ring out. Soon after, I saw an unfamiliar guy running towards me with his gun drawn. He didn't initially realize I was with Shavar, and I squeezed off first. Our eyes then locked, and we started firing at each other as he was attempting to gain entrance into a building. Somehow, I slipped avoiding gunfire and ended up on the ground, initially unsure if I was hit.

We were right on 8th Avenue and 133rd Street, and the police precinct was a couple of blocks away on 135th Street. I felt someone grabbing me. It was John helping me up, and I realized I was good. We ran in the direction of the car which we had parked on 132nd Street. A young guy I knew named Little Scotty, who lived right there in the St. Nicholas Projects, told me to throw him the *hammer*. I tossed him the gun as I was jumping into the car. As we pulled off, I saw Scotty run into the projects. The sound of the sirens grew near, and we just got out of there.

I started getting updates relatively quickly from the block. Scotty informed me dude shooting at me had been hit, but he wasn't certain of his injuries, and the police were everywhere. Sometime after that, I got a 911 page from someone about Shavar. He was in Harlem Hospital, having been shot in the thigh and leg. I barely knew him 24 hours, and here I was in a gunfight related to him. However, I liked the kid. I dug his energy, and he had a big heart. After he was released from the hospital, Shavar became a fixture around us. Shavar ended up getting really close to Troy Rutledge; I believe in part because Troy was laid-back and level-headed as well as being around the same age. Yet, with such different personalities, I never fully understood the depth of their friendship.

A couple of months later, there was another shooting involving Shavar, where someone was killed. Shavar was wanted for questioning in that incident, and he went on the run. He came to me for some guidance in that situation. I ended up taking him in to stay at my New Jersey apartment with Reika and me until I could figure things out.

He was perpetually restless. Having to stay in the house just wasn't in his DNA. We didn't live in the hood, and there was nothing for him to do. He couldn't drive and was essentially limited to the very few suburban blocks surrounding our building. Reika was only about 16 years old with a toddler, so you can imagine how his pent-up energy was consistently getting on her nerves. After about a month, I ended up taking him down to D.C. with me to get him out of the house.

***

Business continued to grow and was running relatively smoothly when, in 1987, a guy named Sickle and his crew went down. They were primarily based out of the Drew Hamilton Projects on 143rd between 7th and 8th Avenues. Sickle had a bunch of businesses on 7th Avenue in the 140s. He was the last of the older school heroin generation, though he and his crew dealt in coke, too. Many of the guys down with him were my friends and peers while Sickle was older. So, when his crew got taken down by the feds, it impacted all of us, for some time.

When something like that happens, everyone gets low for a minute trying to figure out what was happening and who's who to a degree, out of fear. Many individuals had gotten knocked prior, but this was the first sweep of a crew of my peers, and we were all forced to take notice.

However, after some time elapsed, instead of quitting, we ended up justifying why they got caught and how it wouldn't happen to us. We rationalized how we were different and wouldn't get caught up the same way they did. We naively and falsely believed that we would do it better than they did. The reality is that we were lying to ourselves. If you hustle long enough, your number will come up. You continuously hustle, and jail or death are your only certainties-- lessons the youthful don't learn soon enough.

In late August of 1987, the streets blared the headlines before the news could. Azie Faison was in critical condition. He ultimately survived being shot multiple times while three others in the apartment lost their lives. Azie was probably the first prominent member of that Rooftop class to be victimized by the dark turn of our lifestyles when he was nearly killed after being set up by his sister's boyfriend. The incident should have served as a wakeup call to us all that the good times had been replaced, but instead of fleeing or quitting, we adapted. We were immersed in the Game and the money, and besides being slightly desensitized to violence, we were willing to fight fire with gunfire.

Early the next morning, I became aware of what happened to Azie. I knew who he was and he knew who I was. We had only had a few interactions personally, one not of a good nature. Nevertheless, the news of what happened to him was very concerning.

Up until this point, for me, things had been pretty much all fun and games. Don't get me wrong, I knew of people getting robbed, individuals running off with packages, and the occasional murder of someone, but nothing this tragic or violent.

***

Besides my arrest for the red car, I had largely avoided jail. I went to visit a few of my guys, including Chris during his stretch, but I had never even been to Rikers Island until I went on a visit to see Shavar. We all knew about Rikers, and a few of my friends had spent time there, but I didn't know what to expect. I parked in a designated area and because Rikers is literally on an island, we were transported to the jail on a bus. Even as a visitor, you couldn't help but feel that this wasn't the place to be. It was dirty and dingy even back then, and you were left with no other impression than this was jail.

The New York murder case that I had let him lay low for, first in Hackensack and then in D.C., had finally caught up with him. He hadn't been in D.C. long before trouble found him. He got into a situation with someone over allegedly being disrespectful toward the person's mother, who I believe may have been a customer getting high off crack. The guy caught him slipping late one night on the block and shot him. While in the hospital recovering in D.C., I was able to visit him. It was discovered he had an open warrant in New York, and shortly after, he was arrested, handcuffed to the bed, and detained. Once healthy enough, he was extradited to New York. I was able to retain an attorney for him, but he was still denied bail at his arraignment. He was then sent to an area in Rikers that housed juveniles while awaiting trial. I was able to visit him there.

On Rikers Island, things were no different. Shavar was being Shavar, putting in work. He was affiliated with multiple stabbings and developing quite a reputation. Scotty, who I had thrown the gun to, had recently been arrested for murder himself and was being housed in the same unit with Shavar. On one of our visits, Shavar told me Scotty was having some issues and had been robbed of his sneakers and other items. Shavar asked me about Scotty saying he had been throwing my name around in there and asked me, "What's good with him?" I said he was my little man and to look out for him. Shavar said he would straighten it out because he didn't realize he was family.

Shavar hooked up with a kid named Hector and another named Daddy. Both were from Spanish Harlem, and the three began running together in Rikers. Shavar trumpeted my name and our exploits in Harlem and D.C. and earned himself some clout. His time on Rikers Island ended up serving as a recruiting camp.

Shavar and Hector both ended up beating their respective cases. Daddy got released shortly after, as well. It didn't take long for Shavar to make his way back down to D.C. sometime in late 1987 with Hector and Daddy. He had a different perspective on things and a coke connect through Daddy. I would find out that allowed him greater independence outside of me as well.

He came down before we had a chance to discuss the situation. I didn't get any notice before his coming down. When I saw him, we talked, and I told Shavar he needed to be easy and chill. "When you were last here, you had that situation, so you might want to think this through before anything." Yet, when I turned around, there were like 15 juveniles in D.C. under his control. It was clear that he wanted to be his own boss or head a crew and I understood what he was not wise enough in that moment to understand: what being a boss fully entailed. It had been less than two years, and he had been shot twice and beaten a murder case. My love for him never stopped, and I could see the inevitability of his situation, but at the same time, I knew his destiny though he was unable to see it himself. His newfound independence gave me some distance that was probably favorable to me. He never stopped being my guy even as he became more independent. His allegiance and loyalty to me never wavered.

Jail began to become an enduring thorn in our crew's existence, and shortly after Shavar got out, in September of 1987, the police task force finally caught up with Rob in our building and executed a warrant for his arrest. The theatrics from his arrest was the talk of the neighborhood, and it didn't help that a handful of the building's residents associated him with me. I already felt eyes from Shavar's short stay only weeks prior, so I knew it was time to move. Apartment living and lots of (nosey) neighbors were not for me or my lifestyle. Rob's arrest couldn't have happened at a worse time, about five months after Chris's arrest on the train in D.C.

They initially took Rob to the local jail in Hackensack, awaiting his extradition to New York. In the first few days, I remember receiving a call from Rob saying he needed new sneakers. Despite the heaviness of his situation, I remember us laughing at the fact that someone had the guts to swipe his kicks while he was sleeping. I just said to myself, for their sake; I hope he doesn't find out who did it. I also remember being informed by Rob that he and his crew had devised a plan to break him out of jail.

Rob had spent some time in Rikers, and in-state penitentiaries up North on a prior bid, so that local jail must have seemed like Mayberry, a little town jail to him. What was nearly as crazy as the escape plan was the fact that I could see the plausibility of it all. We were just so brazen/delusional/dumb/brave that our lack of respect for law enforcement and outlaw mentality made NWA's "Fuck the Police" seem like a nursery rhyme. The plan never actually got hatched, though, because they ended up moving him to New York quicker than expected.

We hired a top-notch lawyer for Rob. After several months of legal maneuvering with hearings and motions, the case against him must have started to show considerable weakness. In August of 1988, after about ten months in Rikers, Rob was able to secure $50,000 cash bail. I was able to help him get out immediately. After about a year, Rob went to trial and beat the case because there were no credible eyewitnesses against him. That acquittal precipitated his full-time move to D.C. afterward.

A couple of months later, I purchased a 4-bedroom, bi-level house for $400,000 in Hillsdale, New Jersey, within Bergen County. The house had no neighbors to its left and was located at the end of the block. I totally remodeled the house, putting in a pool and basketball court and enclosed it with a fence for more privacy. It easily became the nicest house on the block. I lived there for about two years until my expanding family and status outgrew it.

1987 was such a good year, financially, I remember John and I going to one of the garages and grabbing a Jeep Wrangler I had. It was New Year's Eve, and we decided to take the top off. It was early evening, but the temperature must have still been hovering in the 30s. We had on our furs and made the rounds throughout Harlem. The customized sound system blasted "Eric B is President." Rakim's intro to "Make 'Em Clap to This" was enough to create a party at every stop we made. Fuck giving out turkeys; we were throwing out thousands of dollars to any groups of people we came across. We were in a good mood, and the festivities didn't end there, because later that night, I remember bringing in 1988 in a custom tuxedo with much of my crew. It was either Peter Shue or Miguel's annual black-tie event held at the Omni Hotel in midtown. It was a nice way to end the year.

8

LORD OF THE FLIES

At this point in 1988, our numbers in D.C. were aggressively expanding. There were nearly a hundred people, directly and indirectly, linked to us, and because of this, the dynamics eventually changed. We got comfortable, and that did not always serve everybody well. Guys made D.C. their home, and many others started having pseudo-families there. It's one thing to come in, fuck around, and pay some girl or her family's rent. It's another to have babies with the girls from the area, many of whom may have already been someone's baby's mother. This contributed to having guys that one time peacefully tolerated us to now have feelings about our presence.

Some also got comfortable with bringing D.C. guys up to New York, where, inevitably, the D.C. guys were able to make connects on their own as coke and crack became more widespread throughout the country. We were no longer the only game in town, and our presence started to equal more competition and less cooperation to the locals. However, what really changed the landscape and dynamics of the relationship between New York and Southeast D.C. was the recklessness of some of the youngins' that came down initially through me. They grew to uncontrollable factions on their own even as they maintained allegiance to me. What made them uncontrollable was that there were now sometimes five and six degrees of separation to the new guys and me versus the one or two from my original crew and their initial people.

The problem was they lacked structure, foresight, and accountability. Often, they got locked up or killed before ever figuring anything out. Not to put it all on them, but like what was simultaneously happening in NYC, these individuals brought a lot of heat due to unnecessary violence. Within my clique, there was a true structure with order and a hierarchy.

THE CRACK ERA

We moved in precision and with a purpose — one for all, all for one. We were a very tight, insulated crew and this is what kept us all safe from foes as well as law enforcement.

The crack generation got rid of all drug protocols. Previously, you had the manufacturers of heroin in Asia who essentially went through wholesale distributors a.k.a. The Italian Mafia. The Mafia had established distribution centers/retailers, a.k.a. Urban Blacks. Whether it was cultural or language barriers, Asians never really went directly to Blacks to distribute heroin. It could have also been importing issues that bonded the Asian manufacturers and the Italian Mafia, but that's how heroin was essentially distributed.

Cocaine distribution initially started the same. However, as Colombian drug cartels started to see America's appetite for cocaine and expanded the market, initially through Dominicans, at some point, they realized they didn't need the Italian Mafia to distribute its products.

While they didn't have direct access to the Black distributors at the time, that cowboy and outlaw mentality is what allowed these independent guys to run up on guys like me and offer the product direct. They needed us as much as we needed them, and all of a sudden, that protocol and pipeline that had dictated how drugs were essentially distributed in America was gone, and now it was like a flea market. If you wanted to open a spot or lived on a block, you could open up shop.

The break-in this protocol also had a byproduct in that it created anarchy, renegades and increased violence within the generation. Violence, kidnapping, and murders always existed in the drug game, but back in the day with Nicky Barnes, Guy Fisher, and even my uncle, people knew that they were robbing an organization. Within those organizations, the Mafia was usually seen as a party in protecting its distribution network. So, guys had to pick and choose who to rob carefully and, even then, immediately knew the consequences.

Once that order was gone, it was a lot easier to rob individuals. Guys felt like they were just taking off their peers. Couple this with the brazenness of youth. There were no rules, and as unsupervised kids are prone, they just didn't really fear the repercussions. It was like *Lord Of The Flies* on steroids.

All of this was nearly simultaneously taking place as the AIDS epidemic was ravaging our communities as well, particularly with the intravenous heroin users... The communities were being hit in so many directions. It was like looking up and constantly going, "WTF?"

The renegades didn't have a long-term strategy like we did to be able to see D.C. as a real business. And by long-term, I mean beyond them trying to get money for the day or to purchase a car or jewelry. Age and immaturity surely were contributors as well. I was only 19 when I hit D.C., but many of these individuals were more prone to unnecessary violence than business. I was young, but they were younger-- some as young as 14-years-old. That fact in itself did not normally strike me, but on occasion, it would hit me how ridiculous our overall youth was. One of those short-sighted situations occurred with a guy that came down to D.C. through his affiliation to Bugalou Rutledge.

Bugalou was the middle of the Rutledge brothers. I met him when he came home from juvie. He was thorough and already established with a reputation equal to his brothers. He was always in and out of Spofford, but when we moved, he moved. His popularity was more due to him and John being known for one-punch knockouts robbing people in their neighborhood. I had only recently been introduced to him, and he brought with him a whole crew of adolescents that were eager to get money.

Bugalou had not been with us long enough to fully understand the structure of our program in D.C. I believe Shy was a Five Percenter from Queens that Bugalou probably met in juvie. I had been introduced to Shy and had my reservations about his energy, but he seemed cool. At some point, I was made aware he came down to D.C. by himself and had like an eighth or two that he moved in a day. When I started having conversations to see what was going on, he was gone. He came back down a second time with several guys while I was out of town. One of them was alleged to have been held against his will and made to work the block for Shy. I was told they all came down on the train, forcing this individual to carry the drugs and weapons while they sat in view of him. When they arrived and got situated, they all went out to the block and set up shop. At some point, the guy got from under Shy and ran to the police to allege he had been kidnapped. When the police came back to the apartment they were occupying, there was like a half a key of crack and a couple of weapons recovered in the search. Shy and his crew was arrested. Shy ended up getting sentenced to 22 years. The others got 18 and 17, respectively. Only being in D.C. for the second time, their experience was short and ended tragically.

Shavar's presence, along with many of the others, helped to contribute to the climate getting dark. They were making the whole situation different, and that wasn't good for business, longevity or self-preservation. Shavar and his crew of adolescents changed the whole energy of SE D.C. even though his actual run wasn't long. In October 1988, less than a year from his Riker's release, Shavar, his brother Kurt and another co-defendant, Lamont, all juveniles, caught murder cases, and each ended up being sentenced to 25 years to life. Hector and Daddy were both killed in D.C. along with a host of others during their run.

Shavar always showed me respect and stayed loyal to me. I loved him. He was a good kid with the heart of a lion, but I had to distance myself. Shavar's presence in my life, as much as it made sense, I knew it made no sense if that makes any sense. Shavar was like the Tasmanian Devil. Shavar could best be described as Joe Pesci's character, Tommy, from *Goodfellas*. He was a whirlwind of chaos, and as much as I loved him, I knew he had the potential to be my downfall. Much of his and his crew's actions could have been placed on me under the RICO Act. He put you in harm's way, but by the same token, there was no better person to have in your corner if you were put in harm's way.

Shavar stayed in jail for that case until being released in February of 2010. His brother Kurt was released in August 2010. They did over twenty years after being sentenced as young teens. Most of his crew down in D.C. have been long deceased. In prison, Shavar was diagnosed as bipolar and schizophrenic. He may have always suffered from such ailments, but besides it never being diagnosed, it was a different time. Regular people were not diagnosed as such in the 1980s and 90s. We just called people like Shavar wild, crazy, or bugged out with no understanding that there may have been something deeper beyond their actions. At the very least, he was young, brash and quick to never let shit pass lacking either the judgment or will power to control his path.

In 1988, at 24.4 killings per 100,000 residents, D.C. ranked only behind Detroit (at 24.7) for the most murders in the United States. New York City was tenth on that list at 11.5 slayings per 100,000 residents. New York's actual number of murders was actually greater than D.C. because of the larger population. In fact, during the "Crack Era," NYC saw nearly unprecedented numbers of murders. In 1984, there were 1,784 murders in New York. In 1985, there were 1,683; 1,907 in 1986; 2,016 in 1987; 2,244 in 1988; 2,246 in 1989; and all-time high of 2,605 in 1990; 2,571 in 1991; 2,397 in 1992; 2,420 in 1993; 2,016 in 1994; and 1,530 in 1995. By comparison, there were 630 recorded murders in New York in 2016.

During this time, Jule Rutledge made it down as well, even though he was only about 14. Jule wasn't initially allowed to work, but it was almost easier to manage his wild spirit by having him near us rather than unsupervised back home, however rational that was. There was so much overflow money that after a short time, he was able to make money simply by being around and then put to work.

One night, while running a spot on 9th Street SE & Yuma, some dudes came to the door that Jule didn't recognize. The spot was fortified to a degree, but they started trying to kick in the door. He had enough time to grab the money and work, then jumped out the back window and got away. In another instance, at the same spot, the police raided it. Jule again went to jump out the window, but this time he wasn't as fortunate. The two-story fall led to him fracturing his arm causing permanent scarring to his ring finger and pinkie. He was arrested and taken to the hospital to deal with his injuries. Jule gave them a D.C. address and an alias and was released to a woman he claimed was his caregiver due to him being an adolescent.

After those two incidents, Jule figured out a way to keep his $1,500 a week shift minus the aggravation and pitfalls. He showed hustling acumen way beyond his years because he got another kid to work the shift for him for $500 a week, freeing up time to make other money and stay out of harm's way.

***

When Rob started spending more time in D.C., particularly after beating his case, it became like home. Rob already had his mob down there, and when he brought his brother Rudy down, it solidified it. I knew Rudy but didn't have much of a personal relationship with him outside of his being Rob's younger brother. Rudy turned into one of many that went missing in D.C. I remember Rob and me discussing the situation and how crazy the conversation was for me. It was one of those times when I couldn't make heads or tails of something and didn't know what to say.

We looked everywhere that he was known to stay and spoke to everyone we thought would have an idea of his whereabouts. This went on for weeks till we came to terms that something tragic had to have happened to him. We never found Rudy; may he be resting in peace. We were having some issues with some dudes there, and some back and forth was going on between us. We believe Rudy may have been a causality of that, but honestly, it could've been several things. As you can imagine, his loss had a domino effect that impacted the lives of many in D.C. which fractured alliances and calm. Rudy's death only compounded things and caused our presence to become even more aggressive towards anybody or anything that didn't sit right with us.

There were so many people now loosely associated with us that I probably didn't know half of the people at some point claiming me or our organization. There were loose sets, and not everyone was 100% down with or loyal to me as far as copping exclusively from me. If I didn't come with the work fast enough, they would get it from someone else. I could have taken issue with this if I was power tripping, but I chalked it up to the nature of the times. I wasn't exclusive to my connects, so I understood that guys had to do what they had to when it came to getting money. I was moving fast. Everyone was moving fast during the time, and if I wasn't readily available to give someone work, I couldn't expect them to not eat.

The reality is that everyone was evolving through this experience. Instead of stifling this and feeling the need to keep people under me, I readily encouraged my crew to expand. The bigger they got, the bigger I became. So many were dependent on me, seeing others more independent eased my burden, if ever so slightly.

Growing so fast does not come without complications. Early on, we realized that we weren't going to keep being able to jump on and off planes with work. We had gotten wind of a few instances where people had gotten caught taking the shuttle into D.C. We then started to use different people, we placed on buses from Port Authority and trains from Penn Station in New York to D.C.

This worked for a time before it got hot like the planes, but not before we took a couple of hits. There were two instances where young ladies who helped transport got popped. One was Reena. She was initially one of Rob's people, but by this time, we all became super cool. She and her girl Brenda were regulars around us and often hung out and traveled with us. The other was a girl that Mark used that I was less familiar with and had really no dealings with. We took care of their legal bills, and in Mark's case, he looked out for the girl throughout her several-year bid. Both girls stood tall, and we tried as best as we could to reward them for their loyalty by trying to make their circumstances as bearable as possible before, during and after their incarceration. While you never get used to people getting busted, essentially for you, it leads to really mixed feelings. We all know the risks, and while it is important to make sure your people are represented and taken care of, you build up a shield in understanding that the show must go on. It sounds callous, but everyone who signs up for The Life understands this is just a mantra we all live and abide by.

These incidents were happening more in general, so we had to adjust. We figured that our chances on the road made the most sense. There were hundreds of thousands of civilians going up and down the highway every day. Our odds favorably increased on the road blending in with traffic moving at 55 mph versus public transportation where you were eyed and profiled much easier.

THE CRACK ERA

The only problem with that potential solution was finding people who fit the bill of being able to blend in. John and I discussed our dilemma, and he mentioned a friend of his named Norman who knew a couple of guys from his projects with licenses that might work. Having a license at the time was such a big deal, it had stood out to Norman. In our crew, me and possibly Rob were the only ones who had a driver's license. Everyone else around me was the same age or younger, and I don't believe even had ID. The driving age in New York was 18, and with public transportation and poverty being so common, most New York City teens just didn't run out to get a driver's license at the first opportunity.

Ideally, an older person would've filled the bill, but it wasn't like we had that at our disposal, so we had to work with what was available. No one with a bit of sense or maturity would have had anything to do with the craziness we were engaging. Knowledge was a burden, and ignorance was bliss, and the money wasn't going to just make itself. A true testament to youthful stupidity.

John introduced me to the guy with the license. His name was H.R., which stood for Hungry Rob. I never knew what the "hungry" stood for and don't believe I ever asked. H and his family were originally from South Carolina. He was a good old country boy and knew quite a bit about cars and fixing them.

We propositioned him with what we needed from him, offering him $1,500 a trip. Before I could get the whole plan out my mouth, he stated he was in. Maybe that's why they called him Hungry. The crazy thing about this time period was that everyone I knew was riding around without a license and didn't think twice about it. Honestly, I know a lot of people who made the trip back and forth to D.C. dirty, with no license, never concerned about the consequences. Today, that alone might get you locked up, but back then, you could get pulled over without any form of ID. If the car didn't come back as stolen, it was more than likely you would just get a warning or a citation. I don't believe anyone gave a damn about or paid the citations, which were given solely on the information you verbally provided to the police. You know the adage about the blind leading the blind? Well, the equivalent is juveniles leading other juveniles with no true sense of the consequences.

Even using the cars, we had to conceal the drugs somewhere. At first, we loaded the car with a bunch of luggage. Having the proper paperwork would be the first line of defense if stopped. If it went beyond that, we made sure we had the right story supporting the travel so they would not want to search the luggage. We did this for some time, successfully, before we started to hear of incidents of others getting pulled over and violated. Some claimed being pressured to sign a consent allowing officers to search the car. Even if consent wasn't given, they'd harass you and keep you on the side of the road for hours threatening to have the K-9 unit come.

Armed with these evolving developments, we continued to try and stay ahead of the cop's familiarity with our methods. We opened the door panels on the front and back of the vehicle placing the drugs in a hollow area. We became aware of this opportunity from seeing the doors off when the guys who put our sound systems in ran the wiring. We then, at some point, approached a guy at a tire shop that we often used. We constantly had to change flats or bent rims on our cars. We had a conversation with him about putting the drugs in our spare tires and offered a hefty price for him to do so. We would put the tire back with its covering, and for added measure, place all the luggage on top. Additionally, we would place the packaging with coffee grinds for what we understood would throw the scent off to a K-9 if stopped.

Over time, we had several drivers, most initially through their contacts and affiliations with John. There was John's Uncle Johnny and cousin Lester, who for the most part, was used by John and Norman on their respective runs out of town in Virginia. Walter was also used as well by John and I. Walter was from St. Nicholas Projects along with Norm and H. Uncle Johnny was actually best suited for the role. He was in his forties as opposed to a teen like the others and fit outside of the profile. However, he had other responsibilities and was not always available.

John, H, and I continued to try and come up with creative ways to transport the drugs. Unfortunately, most of these innovations came about because of trial and more so error of someone getting busted. I can recall the time I had just purchased a brand-new Jeep Wagoneer, temp plates still on it. This particular time, Bugalou packed the car. He had done it several times prior, but he must have been a little careless because when John got stopped by the police, part of a Ziploc was visible outside the door panel.

The absolute irony to this story is that one of the only times John didn't run from the cops, he got busted. I hired a lawyer for John. The car was titled in someone else's name other than his, and that partly contributed to his defense, that he was not the owner and thus unaware of what was in the vehicle. Besides, this was his first offense, so he was granted immediate bail.

After the bust, John was just different. He went through the motions of going back and forth to court for about a year before going to trial and eventually beating the case, but before his acquittal and even afterward, John was just not the same. Initially, I thought the stress and pressure from the pending case were the main contributors to John falling back so hard. However, he just laid lower and lower, even after the acquittal. He hustled less and stayed home a lot more. John was always a different guy, prone to being laid back, so spending more time at home with his wife and kids wasn't a stretch initially. However, those moments significantly increased. He was still around, just not to the same extent, and I would pick up the slack for him.

***

H was the most consistent and reliable transporter. He was a real road warrior. Since H's license and paperwork were already in order, it led to a natural progression that he would be asked to do much of the driving with work. I use the word "transporter" to make it easily identifiable to a reader, but these were not disposable entities but friends and relatives who filled a role that was probably most suitable to their personalities. As it turns out, long stretches on the highway were his calling evidenced by the fact that he is a long-haul trucker to this day. However, before H squared up, he was my main transporter and unfortunately, those constant long stretch runs he made for me did not come without issues.

The first occurred on October 2nd, 1988. The story of this arrest took on epically comedic proportions for how bad it actually could have gone for H besides being busted for an eighth of a kilo in a car that he honestly didn't even know existed.

The drugs that were found were part of the packaging from a previous run that H didn't even realize was still in the car. There had been an issue on his previous run of the work being short like an eighth a key. H didn't know anything about the short and gave up what was packaged and in place. Evidently, when it was packed in a Ziplock bag, the eighth must have dropped in the process of being taken out of the car and just went undetected with whatever other junk that had been lying around in the trunk.

H got caught with an eighth of a key, but, there were seven kilos hidden in the car. The cops were so satisfied with what they found that they never realized there was a real bounty they were missing out on. When I got the word of his arrest, me and Rob were in Alexandria, VA awaiting his arrival. H spoke in code, but what he made apparent was that they found a small amount of drugs in the car that he wasn't certain of how it got there. We rushed up there to the court in New Jersey to bail him out. However, besides getting him out of jail, we were equally pressed to retrieve the car and the seven keys.

There was at least $200,000 in unfound coke in the car. The car was in H's father's name, and with seizure laws not being as strict at the time, we knew there was an opportunity to recover it all. In court, we told H's attorney that his father needed the vehicle for work and the attorney explained what we needed to do to get it back. Once H's arraignment was over, we hurried to both get him bail and retrieve the car, which Rob and I did, immediately taking it down south to D.C.

The craziest part of the story may have been H avoiding carrying a minor across state lines charges. H had been seeing this young lady named Stacey, and she'd been accompanying him for a minute. He had been dealing with her and was convinced she was of age. However, when she was being processed, it was discovered that she was only 16 years old, mind you H wasn't but 19 himself. This totally caught H by surprise.

THE CRACK ERA

She was ultimately released to her mother without charges filed. H never knew, and the fact that she had the fake ID is probably the only thing that stopped H from catching a case for statutory or transporting a minor across state lines. The final punch line is that either right before or right after the bust, H found out his unknown, underage girl was pregnant with his child.

Approximately five or six months later, H got caught again on the same turnpike route. This time, they found the seven kilos in the car. He was traveling with Breeze, Walt, and Karen, who would years later, become his wife. It was probably silly to have so many in a "dirty" car, but H and I had made this run so many times in different vehicles, we were just way more comfortable riding dirty than we should have been. The stretch of road on the New Jersey Turnpike came to be known as "Cocaine Alley." Between exits 1-3 of the turnpike, the highway narrowed down to two lanes on each side from its usual 4-6 lanes on each side. The narrower lanes made it easy for the state troopers to sit on the side and actually look into profile each passing car. This didn't fare well for the hundreds of men and women that were now using the turnpike as part of their drug transport route.

The trooper that busted him this second time was the same one that arrested him and Stacey earlier. He vaguely seemed to recognize H, but he definitely should have remembered him because he was in the same light blue station wagon. The only explanation to the trooper not truly recognizing H or the car was probably related to the volume of cars he was pulling over in this narrow stretch of road. Obviously, we weren't going to risk the station wagon being caught a third time, so we unceremoniously put it to bed. After bailing out on that first case, H never returned to court and had that case hanging over his head upon this arrest. He used a different, fake ID, and the trooper didn't recognize him even though he did ask him, "Don't I know you?"

This was before traps in the car being used, so even though the trooper didn't recognize H once backup was called, they came equipped with screwdrivers and drugs were found. I bailed everyone out and got them all attorneys.

Technology had not yet caught up to our lying abilities, evidenced by the fact I was able to bail H out twice within months from the same jail. Because he used an alias on the New Jersey cases, they didn't immediately catch on. The previous charges still didn't show up on this bust, so he was still able to get bail again. Those two situations alone cost me a couple hundred thousand dollars, between bailing them all out, appeal bonds, lawyers and the lost drugs. While that is not a small amount, that number pales in comparison to the hundreds of times we managed to get work through without being compromised, making it the most viable form of transporting despite these two incidents.

Even after the two busts, H remained in the game. I'm sure he stayed in part out of loyalty and in part because, like for all of us, the money was just too good to walk away from. In fact, my drivers were able to make extra money in D.C. I might have a driver wait around D.C. for a run. While waiting, they might ask that instead of paying them in cash, I pay them in work. So, instead of giving them say $2,500, I might give them an eighth of a key. They would then take that eighth and either, with permission, put it through one of the guys' blocks, like I once did with Red, or take the work themselves and occupy the block during an unoccupied time frame. We were tight like that as a unit, even if you were not directly affiliated with a particular group of guys. I was the lynchpin to the cooperative, and at the end of the day, we were all united to make money and deal with any potential issues should they arise.

At my height and for several years after, I was netting around $300,000 a week, with the bulk of it coming from D.C. and the rest from my wholesaling back home. I was in my early twenties, and you really couldn't tell me anything. My entire family was well taken care of, and there didn't seem like anything was unattainable for me.

The world seemed to be ours, and honestly, there appeared no end in sight. Everyone down with me was getting real money, living in homes and condos, driving luxury cars, rocking the latest fashions and jewels, living the high life. They were all bosses in their own right. I wouldn't say we mastered the art of selling narcotics, but we were the '98 Chicago Bulls at our peak performance with a sustained run, on our level longer than any other crew or organization out of New York at the time.

However, like every sports fan can attest to, every dynasty comes to an end, and we would be no different, even if we didn't necessarily see it coming.

9

NEW YORK, NEW YORK

There is a difference between being a hustler, hustling, and getting money. I was a hustler with the ability to get money and not limited by my hustle. This is not to say that others in my generation were not true hustlers, because undoubtedly some of them were. However, whether they lacked the tutelage or foresight, most limited their hustle to selling narcotics.

The old-time hustlers prior invested in Harlem and had all kinds of real estate and businesses. They dabbled in everything from travel agencies, bars, restaurants, grocery stores, and hardware stores. In the end, these investments would contribute to sparing me a life sentence in prison. It was every hustler's dream to legitimize him or herself, put their families in safe living environments, give their kids increased educational opportunities and provide a better quality of life. If it wasn't the goal, then I'm not sure why you're doing what you were doing.

I opened BOSS Sneakers in 1988. It was directly across the street from the legendary AJ Lester. Anybody who was getting real money shopped at AJ's, not only throughout Harlem and the Bronx but all of NYC and beyond. Back then, cats were still clean, and the casual Jordan's and sneaker culture had yet to take over. We still dressed and wore shoes and AJ Lester's was where me and all of my crew still went to get right. There were only a few places you could even get the type of high fashions from with Layton's located in Midtown, but AJ's location usually won over in its favor. It only made sense to have a store directly across from one so prominent.

BOSS Sneakers was located on 8th Avenue between 125th and 126th. It was the heart of Harlem. 125 was Harlem's main commercial district. It was essentially the capital of Black America. The reason I opened it up was purely pragmatic. Every time my crew came out of the house, we made it a point to be fly with the newest sneakers matching our outfits. I looked at my crew alone and figured if every one of them bought from me, I could have a profitable business. In fact, we probably easily did over $15,000 in sales for our grand opening, primarily from my friends and other hustlers, if nothing else out of respect and curiosity.

It was always subtle but loud at the same time. "If I'm not the Boss in the game, then who?" It was like a subliminal rap line way before the subliminal was being done, on a street level. By this time, we were well-known and established in the streets, and that definitely lent to my energy on the subject. Many questioned the high-profile nature of the name and the business. I get the criticism to a point, but for me, the business was not just about profiling and establishing a front. It was a real business intended to make money on its own. This was one of the lessons I learned from my uncle and his peers using their business model.

There were a few guys, but for the most part, none of my peers shared my old school mentality in having businesses. There were three guys who come to mind that eventually would have legitimate businesses. One was Carlos Ortiz out of the Bronx, who had a barbershop/beauty parlor he had on the corner of 155th Street and 8th Avenue on the downtown side of the street above a grocery store. Then there was Unique Wainsworth Hall, who had Mecca Audio, a music shop that sold the latest mixtapes and different accessories on 8th Avenue in the 150s. Unique was also a promoter of sorts. He had a venue on 157th Street where he threw parties and had some of the pioneers of Hip-Hop billed early on in their careers and allowed them to perform at a time when there were no other outlets that allowed these artists to showcase their art.

Leon Blue, Jr., who was from Brooklyn had a jewelry business in the city owned Mart 125 directly across from the Apollo Theater. The Mart opened in 1986 to move the vendors off the street to give a better outward appearance and provide affordable rents to street hawkers. There were very few black-owned businesses outside of these circumstances. Blue called himself the Black Man's Jeweler. Both Carlos and Unique would catch drug cases out of town that would lead to life sentences. Carlos' case was in Baltimore and Unique's in Virginia. Blue ended up getting about 17 years with a case out of Brooklyn.

I would occasionally have conversations with friends about businesses and matters outside of hustling, but most weren't receptive to new things. I remember being with Rich and Alpo on 7th Avenue between 127th and 128th Streets at the car wash one day, just doing our usual chopping it up while our cars got detailed. It was one of the makeshift setups that began popping up all around Harlem, where guys started hand car washes from little more than a bucket and some sponges. These were usually outside barbershops and beauty parlors. They had a captive audience, and a fresh cut went hand in hand with a pristine whip. I was trying to sell them on the idea of getting life insurance being a drug dealer. It just so happens that my brother had an internship selling life insurance. I advised all the guys who were with me to buy policies. When you think about it, who needs life insurance more than a drug dealer? Nevertheless, they laughed at the idea, it being too far-fetched for them. I am not saying I was smarter than any of my peers, but for whatever reason, when things were brought to my attention, and they made sense, I was able to analyze the money and circumstances beyond purely what the streets were offering.

***

Sometime in late 1988, BOSS Sneakers got broken into. The cash register was pried open, though minimal cash was kept overnight. There was a bunch of sneakers thrown about in the basement, where most of the inventory was kept, and for the most part, that was the extent of what was done.

It all seemed like a lot of effort that went into climbing through the roof of the two-story building to break in only to have taken a few items. I wasn't particularly surprised because, as one of the only young hustlers with an actual business, I knew that most probably assumed it was just a front for us to run or stash drugs.

Just a few weeks earlier, the police had run into the store and arrested Artie and a couple of the neighborhood teenagers who hustled in the area. The teens were friends of his who were in the store shopping, and the police claimed that one of them had made a sale shortly before entering the store. It wasn't a big deal, but Artie, an employee and still just a teen himself, was arrested along with the others. The police closed the store and took him to the 28th Precinct literally two blocks from the store. My mother was made aware of what had happened, and she went to the precinct and retrieved the keys to the store. She was told Artie would get released shortly on his own recognizance.

When Artie got out, he mentioned that the police told him that they knew we sold drugs out of the store and they believed a drug dealer owned the store. We absolutely never sold or stored drugs or money at the store.

The cops are always the last in on any hood rumors, so knowing that they believed this only validated what we knew: the rumors were out there and being spread. This explained what the individuals were looking for and why so much effort went into the break-in. Those same streets that spread the rumors contributed to why it didn't take long for us to find out who had broken into the store. Plus, we were "those guys" in the neighborhood and had gained favor with the locals.

Troy and I were driving around in the area of Manhattan Avenue in the 120s. It was mid-afternoon, and Troy spotted the individual who we had been told had something to do with the break-in. In that instance, I didn't think about anything but whooping his ass. There was no plan, and before we could devise one, my emotions had gotten the best of me. I jumped out of the car and approached the dude, telling him I knew he broke into my store. I didn't wait for a response, swinging first and daring him even to fight back. I'm not certain of what he was attempting to say amid my blows upon him. It didn't matter because I wasn't trying to hear anything.

I didn't think I was getting satisfaction from my efforts, and before long, I felt Troy swinging and making a connection that floored the dude, then we began stomping him out. At some point, I regained my composure, probably because Troy was saying, "We're good, we're good." We walked off, got back into the car and went about our business as usual.

Looking back, it was something comical Troy and I laugh about to this day.

***

Selling drugs on a major level was a full-time gig as it were, and when you were committed to everything else that came with the fast pace of living "The Life," most did not see beyond the immediate. We lived our lives in dog years. To say that it was fast-paced undersold the drama and events that one day could and did hold. Add on that either our lives or freedom in the streets had such a low-term expectancy and you could further understand why so many in my generation never planned for the future. This included not buying real estate and establishing legitimate businesses.

John was definitely different than most guys in the street, and it became clear that he saw life beyond hustling. He was a mixed cocktail of contradictions, always calm amidst the craziness, but irrational at the same time. He was a street dude that also probably could have cared less about the street life. He was a paradox in that he was a homebody, but with a fiery spirit. He was cool to be around, but with one glaring flaw: he drove crazy as fuck.

John had this uncanny knack as if he had been practicing his entire life, in having the ability to drive from the east side to the west side and throughout Harlem without ever stopping for a red light. He made a game of having all the lights synchronized and rarely ever lost. John was also known for his epic, Hollywood-style car chases with the cops. He had at least a half dozen that I can recall, and never got caught.

One day, he was with Uncle Norman, preparing a car to go out of town. Uncle Norm had nothing to do with what we were doing, but he was just hanging out with John that day. When he described the story, the first part always started with him comically saying John almost caused him to shit on himself. They got eyed by the police on Convent Avenue in the 120s. Uncle Norman was still on the run, so combined with the work, John just took off. They were about ten city blocks from the West Side Highway but were able to make it there despite the police pursuit. Once on the highway, John was flying, even tapping other cars' bumpers to move them out the way. They were headed north, and he made it all the way up to Dyckman, the last exit in Manhattan. Once off the highway, to the right is the furthest northern entrance to the Cloisters and Fort Tryon Park. He had enough distance between himself and the cops to pull over and park while still being pursued. They simply walked out of the park's end toward Dyckman. Later that day, John borrowed a dog and returned to the Cloisters. He acted like he was walking the dog till he reached the undiscovered car which he had left. He was able to retrieve all the work in the car.

Another night, with Troy, he was being chased by the NYPD up the Harlem River Drive on Manhattan's eastside heading north. He was driving at speeds in excess of 100 mph and eventually began traveling across the George Washington Bridge, headed into New Jersey. He was still being chased by several cars, but halfway across the bridge, he slammed on the emergency brake, did a half donut and U-turned across the medium, heading back into the city. He made it back down the West Side Highway in Manhattan leaving the police behind.

On another occasion, John, Rob, and I were in Midtown Manhattan heading up Madison Avenue after coming from seeing Tito, the jeweler in the Diamond District on 47th Street. As was his usual, Rob was speeding and driving recklessly in the rain. I remember telling him to chill and slow down, which only incited him to drive faster weaving in and out of traffic, banging on the steering wheel, telling me to shut up. Before you knew it, we hit the back of a bus. I don't remember much after that because I was knocked unconscious after hitting the windshield. This was before you'd get a ticket for not wearing a seatbelt, so we never wore them. We were close to 114th Street and 5th Avenue.

I vaguely recall Rob and John pulling me out the car from the rain into a church, laying me down while awaiting the ambulance. Someone must have called the store to say I was in an accident because Reika came to the church. I was concussed and, in a daze, but what I partly remember, and was told, was she had on an older jacket she must have hurriedly thrown on. As I was trying to process everything in my haze, I asked her if I had been dreaming and how many kids we had while trying to figure what year it was. The old jacket she had on made me ask if we were broke. Clearly everyone had jokes about the incident. My injuries were limited to the concussion and lots of broken glass all in my face, but luckily, I was okay.

Almost all of us have some kind of car story related to John. I recall H telling me about John borrowing his GTI Volkswagen. He never thought anything about it until he was driving in Harlem several days later and came upon his car, tireless, situated on blocks. John never mentioned anything about the car or returning it, and under the circumstances, H just let it slide as if it never happened, and the car never existed.

Aside from epic car scenes and some of his eccentric antics, John was a very simple guy who didn't care much for all the hoopla hustling brought the rest of us. I remember damn near making him move to New Jersey, buy cars and jewelry. He didn't need the fronts like the rest of us. That's something that I truly admired about him. He wasn't the typical hustler. Staying home and watching TV or just vibing to his music would have suited him as long as he was comfortable. But when he did hustle, he did it well. He was thorough, on-point, and beyond trustworthy in running our operation.

***

Albe was always good for putting me onto new things. Albe introduced me to one of the guys he grew up with in the Bronx. They both rode unicycles as kids, and his friend, somehow, took that skill set and ended up working in Vegas for the world-famous magicians Siegfried & Roy as an opening act. I had never been out to Vegas until 1988 when Reika and I went out. We were front row and center. I had never seen a magic act, but I can't lie, I really enjoyed the show. Neither Reika nor I were big gamblers, and Vegas lacked the entertainment and dining options it has today. So, after a few days at the hotel, I was restless and suggested we go to Los Angeles. I was glad to take the personal time to spend with Reika, and though I didn't know anyone in LA, we jumped on a plane, rented a car and checked into a Beverly Hills hotel.

I was seeing dudes in Rolls Royce "getting it." LA left a real impression on me. It was a real eye-opener seeing that other places were getting real money. I loved LA so much I came back with my guys a week or two later. We booked ten suites in the Beverly Hills Hilton, which were at least $300-$400 a night. It was my brother, Billy Guy, Rodney, my Uncle Kid, Wise, John, Breeze, and Mark.

Back then, there was no universal swag. Every geographic area had their own thing, and there wasn't television or the Internet to show what each region was doing. However, we left little to doubt. Cats out there could tell we were doing it. Uncle Kid had family out there, and we initially leaned on them to familiarize ourselves with the surroundings and making introductions.

We had a caravan of the *flyest* rental cars, tons of money, and draped heavily in jewelry. It didn't take us long to meet some of the West Coast's finest. The girls took to our New York swag, and we began wilding. I am sure we were novelties compared to what they were used to, but none of us were complaining about being used. We were tricking off, engaging in orgies, and just really getting it in. We were in Los Angeles for ten days, and at some point, amidst the high-profiling and tricking, we managed to come up for air and went to Disneyland and Magic Mountain, Roscoe's, Venice Beach and shopping on Rodeo Drive. We went to all the hot spots to eat and party, always winding back in Beverly Hills for the freak show.

Our high-profile visibility did not go unnoticed beyond the girls. At some point, someone stepped to us, and we ended up with a West Coast drug connect. The gang culture in LA was real, and we were made aware of this. It was so different to us coming from NY. We never had any problems while we were there, but we knew not to sleep on our surroundings even though pleasure was our primary purpose.

***

I had so many different connects throughout my run. My life has always been about juggling multiple relationships, including women. Connects never really got broken off, just sometimes I went harder with some based-on convenience and pricing. LA was cool as far as a connect, but the distance didn't always make it convenient, and I had less confidence in the transport part than using something local or as sweet as I had it coming from Miami, St. Thomas, and even New York. LA was used only if everything else was dry. The first group trip to Cali was our version of a corporate retreat, meant to energize my crew, get focused, and take our game to the next level.

I also made time to get in some adult time with Reika. Most places we traveled to were a first for both of us. The Bahamas, Aruba, Cancun, Mexico, and St. Thomas were some of my favorite haunts. She went on unlimited shopping sprees regularly just because. I found myself always overcompensating when it came to Reika. I really loved her, but by all accounts, I could've been considered a creep. I justified my ways because it was me every day risking life and liberty for this lifestyle that I conveniently laid out for her comfortably. That thinking is also what lent to me treating those other women in the way that I did because a lot of them did things for me that I didn't ask of her, more specifically putting in roadwork on planes, trains, and automobiles. So, I justified those expenditures as being deserving. In my mind, all the scenarios made perfect sense, and I was being fair all across the board.

Getting on a plane to travel was always my thing. Steven Monsanto owned a travel agency on 146th Street and 7th Avenue. Steven was a hustler with many real estate holdings all over Harlem. I was introduced to him by my Uncle Kid. I ended up developing my own relationship with him and Ernie, who ran the travel agency. Ernie was my guy. All I had to do was come in, and he'd put trips together for me. Most times, I had no idea or destination in mind, and he would recommend destinations that he'd either been to or one of his customers had come back from and given great reviews. Wherever there was something fun, I tried to make it a point to go. You didn't even need real identification to fly domestically or even to some countries back then. Remember, there were no ID requirements or systems tracking you on a national level so if you got busted in one place, it was easy to leave and just to go to another, multiple times.

Part of my thing was sending my new prospective girlfriends in telling them to holla at Ernie and tell him I sent them. He knew exactly how to get me right, all the while making that perfect impression, I was looking for to close the deal. I'd show up sometime later, pay my tab, and grab the envelope with all the tickets and vouchers needed for my weekend getaway with that special Ms. Right Now.

During all the hecticness of my life, I always made time to purge and spend time with the family. I took them on family trips to Disney World, SeaWorld, Sesame Place, water parks, and other amusement parks. We pretty much hit all the popular family attractions on the East Coast. None of these experiences were a part of my childhood. I was experiencing them all for the first time, like my kids and family were. While I probably didn't get the same experience out of it as they did, the satisfaction of being able to spend the time and provide these types of luxuries and material items to my family was priceless to me at that time.

Me, Reika, and the kids all had furs and the latest fashions from many of the luxury brands along with customized Dapper Dan gear. I supplied cars to all my family and loved ones not in the game. I had multiple sets of jewelry, and if they weren't specifically customized, they were at least matching; the watch with the bracelet with the rings with the chain and medallion. Tito in the Diamond District was the guy everyone used before Jacob the Jeweler or Raffaello. If you bought sets, a Rolex was like $20 to$30k and $75k to $100k per set; iced out Mercedes, BMW or Jesus pieces sets ran you a good piece of change and of course, buying jewels for all the assorted women in your life was not for the light of pockets. The ridiculousness of all the spending, especially on disposable $1,000 plus furs for kids that might be lucky to have them for that season, was lost on me.

BALLIN

Once you do something innovative or different than the norm, inevitably everybody asks about it. I was personally shopping on the regular in D.C., Baltimore, and all along the East Coast. Since I had my own store, I would often talk with other store owners who sold similar clothes and sneakers. The styles that were popular in New York and hard to get were often easier to acquire in other states, particularly if that style was less popular in that city or state. So, I would work out deals with other store owners.

Fila was big in D.C. during the late '80s to early '90s while Sergio Tacchini was big in New York. I would trade with D.C. vendors. They would order the hard-to-find but in-demand items for me, and I would do the same for them. I purchased from the likes of Guess, Pelle Pelle, Nike, Woolrich, Timberland, etc. Manufacturers put limitations on how much of a certain product boutique store customers could purchase. This was a strategy to suppress competition from some of their bigger stores in a market as well as control supply and demand. Bartering between store owners was our way to get around that to a degree. Fila was prone to be much more attentive to selling me product in NYC where they were not as popular, and I then essentially traded them to the D.C. vendor who could move them easier. You had to be resourceful to survive in that kind of climate.

During this same time period, before Air Force 1's became a Nike staple, they were hard to get in New York in different colors. However, in Baltimore, and specifically a sneaker store in the Mondawmin Mall, they were plentiful in colors that you couldn't get in NYC except at one or two stores that had limited options like Jewman or KP Kong up on Broadway and 145th Street Before BOSS Sneakers, Jewman was noted for having exclusives that were hard to otherwise find in the city. Everybody getting money Uptown and the Bronx would come through Jewman, copping at least 15 to 20 pairs at a time for a person or crews. While Jewman was noted for its exclusive styles, it was also known as a spot that didn't treat non-regulars or unknown cats well.

Jewman became known for stickup dudes robbing cats of their purchases either in front of the store or around the corner. The guys carefully picked their vics. It was never something I or my crew ever had to worry about at this point, but you would hear the stories of guys getting got for their goods.

***

I would go to D.C. loaded with narcotics then come back with money and my store items. The exclusives always flew off the racks of my store. Most stores out of the city were eager to do business with me because they profited in my drive to have these types of exclusives. I remember buying two hundred pairs of exclusive color women's Reebok 5411's from a New Jersey store that was going out of business. I sold them all quickly at a profit to the women in Harlem. I would go to the outlets in Pennsylvania and cop manufactured short-run Timberland boots and Woolrich coats in styles that no one had seen in New York. We also had a couple of guys doing custom silk screen and airbrushed clothing, t-shirts, sweatshirts, and more in the store.

Cash Ruled Everything Around Me, so I had never really given much thought to credit cards. The concept of a credit card was for those who didn't have money and essentially needed to finance their lifestyles. I had pockets full of cash, and no doors were closed to me. By this time, everyone took my money with little to no questions asked. My mother advised me on the use of credit and credit cards. She emphasized that because I was doing business, using them could have its advantages as well as helping me establish credit, so she set me up with an American Express corporate card.

I started extending the card to my guys, which in hindsight probably wasn't very wise. I did it in part to help because of our extensive traveling, car rentals, and hotel stays. I also did it because, as the head of my crew and first to get put on to lots of things, I always felt it was my obligation to share my resources and even limited knowledge. American Express allowed you to have as many platinum corporate cards as you were willing to pay for. I had a card in my name as well as in the name of one of my aliases. Chris eventually had the same.

Additionally, Reika, Mark, and Billy Guy had access to the cards and a few others that contributed to their ridiculous monthly usage. I remember having to go to the American Express travel office downtown off of 42nd Street and 6th Avenue and routinely making cash payments of $50,000 - $60,000 on the corporate card. I would make some of the payments with checks out of the store's corporate accounts while the other cash payments would be made by each of us related to their portion of the bill.

The Amex eventually got good to my guys, and though they would pay their portion of the bill, it ballooned to $100,000 or more in some months, with half of the bill usually being mine. The ridiculousness of my payment history would eventually cause me some concern. I had many guys on the card, but consistent payments of $100,000 made me uneasy from how it might look from the outside. I know they had no issues taking our money, but as the saying should go, "Anything you do can and will be used against you," especially when the payments were significantly made in cash.

Besides using the card for purchases, I remember us using Western Union in ways that would surely get you locked up if tried today. I would occasionally receive wires of just under $10,000, avoiding the banking law that would require filling out paperwork from time to time from people. The larger sums sent usually had to be picked up from the location on 42nd Street and Broadway because the Midtown location was typically the only one that had that kind of money on-hand. However, Billy Guy regularly sent and received $10,000 to $15,000 via Western Union using it as his personal bank account. Try that today, and you might as well either report directly to jail or cop to an IRS case. I guess we were just beneficiaries of the lack of technology that exists today to keep track of such things and the fact that money laundering laws were not then what they are today.

Spending money is, of course, the fun part. I had multiple safety deposit boxes. A few years into my run, I spent as much to not have to overly save and still attained liquid multi-millionaire status. Stacking cash is not nearly as easy as it seems. It comes with all kinds of logistical concerns, including security issues, and spending freely was a naive and easy way to alleviate some of those issues.

I literally shopped every day and never went without treating at least five to six people and usually bought 15 of everything in various sizes. My spending, of course, wasn't limited to just shopping. I paid multiple rents in multiple cities to my home to have a dozen cars all paid in cash, and of course, all my business expenses.

Some of the spendings came in non-tangible forms that were all part of the high life of being young, rich and with an endless cash flow. This included going to the prize fights. More specifically, Mike Tyson fights, which were balling extravaganzas. We had grown up hearing the stories from the old-time hustlers about the spectacle that was Ali-Frazier I in 1971 at Madison Square Garden. Years later, guys reminisced about the night as if it were yesterday, dressed to the nines from head to toe and accompanied by the finest women.

None of the Tyson fights approached the drama of "Fight of the Century" status like Ali-Frazier, but Mike had a box office appeal that brought all the hustlers out. Mike was our age and a street dude. He was from Brownsville and hung out with my guys Lou, Jesus, and Domencio regularly. I was introduced to Mike by Lou and would occasionally run into him randomly, chasing women in the same circles. By randomly, I mean to be in the same Harlem elevator on a Tuesday afternoon going to see girls on separate floors. After being introduced by Lou and Mike frequenting the store, he would suggest we hang out, but you always needed some time to prep for hanging out with Mike.

His realness was largely that he was someone just like us. Most of us looked at Mike, and I am sure he saw himself in that light as well, as someone who, if he hadn't become heavyweight champ, would have been a hustler. He spent like us, flaunted his wealth, and was a visible staple in the hood. This was all part of the appeal of why hustlers from the generation were so drawn to him. That, and the one-hitter quitter and unabashed bravado that captivated us all and wasn't limited to the ring. Mike was quick to chin check dudes in the street as evidenced by the beating he gave to heavyweight contender Mitch Green one early morning outside Dapper Dan's. So, when Tyson fought in Atlantic City in the earlier stages of his career and then Las Vegas, his fights became must-see events.

The Tyson fights became like unofficial Hustler's outings for NYC and beyond. It was where cats from D.C., LA, Detroit, Chicago, and elsewhere came to show out. Every town was represented well, but I have to give it up to the guys from Detroit for standing out the most with Chicago a close second. Let's just say you couldn't miss them because they were different. New Yorkers probably thought of ourselves as being smooth, so we might not have taken the chances with yellow, red, and green gators that they proudly rocked. They were loud in every sense of the word. They weren't going to not let you know they were in the building.

We got a chance to size each other up in a non-aggressive way. Each Area had its own style and presence, and I got to see firsthand how different some of those guys were even as we shared some similar traits. We were all in a competition where not only did we not know the rules, we weren't even sure of the prize, yet we all came out knowing we were competing. Call it the Hustler's way, but like guys in the NBA, we recognized the eliteness of the company we kept and what it took to get to our respective levels.

It was like an updated Ali-Frazier at the Garden. Pimps and their stables were out in full effect. Hustlers of all types came in full-length furs, jewelry dripping on crews, and the women that accompanied us and bankrolls on full display. Some used these exhibitions as an opportunity to make new business connects while others were satisfied with the recognition from a simple head nod. These events were always next level spectacles and a big part of the culture.

The fights may have been premier events nationally, but nothing was bigger in the summer in NYC than The Rucker, aka The Entertainers

Basketball Classic. It was always one of Harlem's premier destinations. Located on 155th Street directly across from The Rooftop and the Polo Grounds housing projects, the games were easily one of the designated places to see and be seen in all of Harlem.

Early in the EBC's existence Greg Marius, who was the visionary behind creating the tournament, was still working the kinks out. He didn't properly calculate the monies from the team entry fees he charged to see the tournament through to the end. He fell short on a few occasions and reached out to me to assist him in closing the seasons out. I gave Greg the money to pay for the trophies, referees fees, and anything else needed so he was able to maintain the tournament. A few years later, he hooked up with Gusto, the proprietor of The Rooftop, and formed a partnership that gave him the stability he needed to run and maintain the EBC long-term.

Every year, leading up to the summer, top streetball players from the Bronx and Manhattan would come by the store, asking if they could run with me in the tournament. Leonard Fulton coached my team. He was a guy who had come to have a strong and positive reputation in the city's basketball community.

I had younger traveling teams I sponsored that also won multiple "Chips" with players that would go on to be notable, both locally and nationally, in different age groups. Guys like brothers Mike Boogie and Tip Dog, along with God Shammgod, went on to become streetball legends and a few would make it to the NBA. They were coached by Norman, who I met through John. I usually chartered a bus and of course, covered all the hotels, meals, and various expenses for any trips.

Besides good coaching, guys campaigned to play for me because of all the perks. My Rucker team, BOSS Allstars, may have only been local, but it easily cost me several thousand per game. I gave my older guys cab money to and from the games and supplied everyone with new kicks. After the games, I took the whole team and usually their chicks out to eat at some of the city's finest restaurants. It was normal to pay the elite players when chasing championships, but I gave extras that most didn't. At dinner, they had my ear and, an explanation of a need or two later, I was giving each guy a couple of hundred bucks which was par for the course for just being on my team.

The team had Malik Sealy who was still in high school at Tolentine who later starred at St. John's and then the NBA along with college stars John Morton and Daryl Walker of Seton Hall, Chris Brooks of the University of West Virginia, and streetball legends Terminator, Malloy "Future" Nesmith, Predator and Carlton Hines. Carlton had gotten a scholarship to Syracuse but passed instead for the streets. He had gotten arrested for striking someone with a bottle and bailed out of Rikers just in time for the Championship game. We won the "Chip" one year and were always in the playoffs and contending for the title otherwise.

The games were in such demand that the crowds would sometimes be crazy. This was all pre-security days, and before NYPD had a regular and heavy presence at the games. We policed ourselves. Based on our reps, a few crews, including mine, kept the order. If you knew what was best, you stayed in line, literally and figuratively. It was first come, first served to get in the park, and most of the time, it was orderly despite the large crowds. People knew to get there early, or they'd be watching the game from outside the fence, regulated to hearing the screams and shouts signaling a spectacular play because they couldn't get any closer to the action. These were the days when the overflow crowds still had people sitting in the trees surrounding the park or climbing up and hanging onto the fences.

Like The Rooftop, the top hustlers owned the sidewalks right in front of the park for our luxury cars and optimum frontin'. My entourage would jump out our vehicles, and the crowds would part upon our arrival into the park with cash conspicuously bulging throughout our sweatpants pockets, chains swinging, diamonds gleaming, commanding the full attention of all onlookers. We were the show...before the game.

Sponsoring teams and people had become a way of life, and on any given day, it was easy to spend at least $10,000, and that, of course, included on women… just because. The Rucker was almost an extension of 125th when it came to women knowing where to find guys gettin' money. It became a running joke about dudes forbidding their women from walking on the BOSS Emporium side of 125th Street. We didn't play fair. The continued joke was that we inflated the price of pussy because of how hard we went. Jokes or not, we didn't care. Girls and guys knew we had it and weren't afraid to spend it. Guys stood little chance of keeping their girls if they were not 100% faithful.

The games at 155th Street would get intense at times and the wagers crazy. I remember two instances that stood out. One was against AJ Lester's. They had a pretty good team coached by a guy named Chuck. He also happened to be the top salesperson in the store and was pretty popular with all the hustlers who shopped in AJ's. He was a very stylish guy, and the hustlers got with him for the fashion hookups. Albe always had a way of talking for both of us and in this instance, betting my money right along with his. Chuck and Albe got to going back and forth talking slick at one another. Chuck was getting a little beside himself talking beyond his wallet, so, at some point, I shut it all down by telling him to make it light on himself and bet whatever. In other words, put up what he could stand to bet or shut up.

The other instance was with Juan, the connect. Like myself, he talked it like he walked it. He had a team in the EBC called Flavor Unit. Jesus and I were together, and we had run into Juan and Alpo a couple of days before we were supposed to play them. We all got to popping shit about the game. So, by the time game day came, we were all in rare form. With the crowds as the backdrop egging us on, things always got crazy. I had my whole mob up there, and they were equally deep as well.

The crowd was such an integral part of the action that spectacular plays were often punctuated with them celebratory spilling onto the court. The crowds were also aware of the wagers, often in the tens of thousands. The money was usually on full display accompanied by shit-talking on a level only seen today by the likes of a Floyd "Money" Mayweather. I'm not sure what was more entertaining, us or the players on the court showing out. What I do recall is we won both of those particular games.

At this time, I found more joy on the sidelines being fly and talking shit than I did playing. Yet, I couldn't understand why in the world Alpo didn't feel the same. He would get out there on the court and play, although he was way out of his league. The one thing I can say about him is I don't believe he ever had any concerns about embarrassing himself. He was fearless in that regard.

Also, during this time in my old Highbridge neighborhood, the guys were starting a tournament called the Fojo Classic. Eddie "Fojo" Cusar died in his senior year on the court during a game at DeWitt Clinton High School from a brain aneurysm. He was a basketball phenomenon who we all felt was on track for the pros. Jeff to the Left, a guy who I had an earlier incident when he robbed one of my friends in my beginning hustling endeavors, had now changed his ways and was doing something positive in the community. He partnered his love of basketball with Mark Fielder, who, with Fojo, were my running partners coming up playing basketball. They reached out to me to sponsor the tournament. This was where I grew up and fell in love with the game of basketball and Fojo was one of my best friends as a kid, so it was a no-brainer to support this endeavor.

Basketball had been my first love. The good times I remember once we moved to Soundview were mostly spent playing basketball. I was already hustling, so the guys I did meet there were the local stars like Ed Pickney, who all played ball for their neighborhood school Adlai E Stevenson High School. I played with Ty Long, Slick Watts, Artie Green, and CeCe in Academy Park, the park located right outside the gates where I lived in Academy Gardens. During this same time, they had tournaments in Soundview Park across on Metcalf Avenue. Having me attached, besides the financial benefits, infused a different life and feeling to a local area and tournament that many of my guys were otherwise unfamiliar with. I brought my guys from uptown to play in both leagues. We made it bigger than a local tournament with a clear Harlem flair, which included the full production of entourages, cars, and women.

On one of the occasions, there was some gun exchange that interrupted the games. We would later find out that Henry, a guy known as Hen Dog, that was part of Fritz's crew, was killed up in that area. I knew Hen Dog from a situation that I had with him during my dealings with Fritz and Kenny. I wouldn't say we were friends, but the situation caused our paths to cross.

***

Mountains of cash and the outlaw lifestyle just lent itself to gambling. You heard about it all the time with Mafioso, and it was no different for us. Gambling was huge during the time and a part of the culture. Gambling had become Albe's thing, and he opened his own spot in the Bronx. He had won big several times racking upwards of six figures at times.

It was almost like peer pressure to gamble, just because you got it. I wasn't a big dice shooter, but I did go to the Zodiac or S&S, two legendary gambling spots owned by Willie. Willie was rumored to be an old school hustler, but most of us knew him to own real estate and businesses throughout Harlem.

He was the original owner of The Rooftop before Gusto taking over and of course, more well known for owning Willie Burgers, which S&S sat atop of, and the Zodiac was just through the light on 145th Street & 8th Avenue heading west housed in a walk-up building. Fortunes were won and lost on the regular, including with Albe. It was almost commonplace for guys to bet their pink slips and walk away some nights one car-less because the stakes stayed high. It only took 4 or 5 head-cracks, and you could easily be looking at a hundred thousand dollars. Luckily, I won more than I lost, but even when I won, I usually just gave the majority of the winnings, which could exceed twenty to thirty thousand dollars, away to whoever was with me. Street culture and cash are near as intertwined with gambling as it was with drugs. The yearly salaries of regular people were routinely wagered with the flick of a wrist, and the rush and even addiction that it held over so many always led to nightly spectacles within those scenes.

While dice wasn't my thing, I bet heavily and regularly against other crews. We bet on anything and everything, but most of the bets revolved around us competing against each other or our assembled teams in basketball. Gambling was analogous to hustling for me. While I knew I was risking my life with my hustle, I took a calculated risk on the players I surrounded myself with. I didn't just roll the figurative dice to things I had no control over. There were already so many factors I couldn't control in my situation. I wasn't ever going to let my fate be decided purely by chance.

I had too many responsibilities and people dependent on me than to "give" it all away by gambling. I could see how easy it was to get caught up in those moments. Big money wagering must have held an adrenaline or ego rush to many, but I hustled too hard to wage too much of it on games of chance, where I felt less in control of my odds. Plus, taking care of those close to me was more of a priority than the benefits I might receive from dice games.

My monthly family expenditures were significant. My family was never on a monthly allowance or stipend, but whenever they asked or needed, I gave. With Reika, there was never a set amount. If I brought home $280,000, I would round it off to $250,000 and give Reika the $30 thousand. She was expected to pay the mortgage and all the household expenses and dole out whatever anyone in the family needed if I wasn't readily available. She shopped as well, but Reika put much of it in her accounts. We established bank accounts for all of our kids, and she put a good chunk in each of their accounts as well.

Now, I just gave a sampling of what it was like to "ball" as a hustler with an almost unlimited budget. However, I need to keep it all the way real and admit that it was just a rudimentary sampling at best of what it was like to not only get money but also to spend money-- both for fun and the obligations for reaching the top. Unless you have had a certain kind of money, especially in cash, you do not fully comprehend how dependent you are on others to either help you hide and store your money, launder it or spend it. This is particularly true when you and those around you aren't really sophisticated in banking and financial affairs. I was not just the Ghetto Street Dream but even embodied the American Dream.

The more money you get, the more paranoid you get. Cash always has a way of spending itself. If I gave someone $250,000 to hold for me, when I came back for it, I would usually find it short. This was all with family or close friends, so you could imagine that the continually missing funds made it easy to lose faith.

There were no ledgers, but I knew, with certainty, what I left with people. It made me mistrust people, at least when it came to money. I am unsure if people thought I forgot what I left, but I always kept my drop-offs with clean round numbers. Maybe they took the money with plans to repay it. Or, maybe they just felt entitled to take a few dollars because they knew I had plenty more and would not figuratively miss it. What I do know for sure is that if you leave significant amounts of cash with people, some would be missing when you returned for it.

I had long accepted that I was the "hustle" for several people. In my prime, I knew that every day leaving the house I was going to spend minimally a few grand. This was money that I was not going to spend on myself. When you are on top, reasonably considered a good dude, and accessible, people have no qualms asking for money. Sometimes they ask because they want you to invest in them or their hustle. Sometimes they ask just because they know you have it. To be honest, the reasons mattered little to me, and I rarely made people go too deep in any of their explanations.

The amounts varied wildly, but many people had correctly figured out that there was a low probability of me saying no to them. Besides actually having it, I had to weigh the risks of creating enemies or people feeling slighted in some way because I didn't "help" them when I had the resources. It was easier and more prudent just to say yes when the money was rolling. Don't confuse this with me being a pushover or a walking ATM. I wasn't just giving money to strangers, and people couldn't easily approach me, but my circle was wide.

The expression "it costs to be the boss" is understated, and it's taxing when so many see you as their come up or at least their daily hustle. Giving is part of my nature, and I definitely enjoyed being able to help or put people on. I had it, so sharing my bounty came naturally. But, at some point, it became less about me giving and more about me somehow being obligated. Other than my family, I didn't owe anyone anything, yet I could see that people were starting to see it differently. People felt entitled to what I had.

11

THE STREETS ARE ALWAYS WATCHING

The streets are always watching... The streets are always talking... I had used this knowledge in my favor for the most part. I cemented a reputation and built a thriving business based on the street's rules of engagement. However, what is less known is that those same streets come filled with snakes lying in the tall grass that see your success and don't just hate you for it but want to take it from you as well.

People often say money changes people. I say money enhances the qualities of the person that has it. If you are a giving person, more money will just emphasize that point. If you were a selfish dude, to begin with, more money makes that more apparent. However, what money *does* change is the people around you. The more money you get, the more clearly you can see the looks in people's eyes and see the bullshit. I know this may sound weird coming from me, but money truly is the root of all evil. Of course, I loved money and what it was able to do for me and my mine, but beyond the fun, I started to look at it from a different point of view and the burden that came with it: more money, more problems.

"Keep your friends close and your enemies closer" becomes the rule to survive. At what point have you stacked enough? When does someone's knowledge of your wealth become the time they realize it is more in their best interest to kill you to take what's yours? A couple of years into it, I started realizing that I had taken on the responsibility of the well-being for so many; the enormity of such a task started to really hit me.

This feeling was punctuated by an increasingly brazen and violent mentality the era seemed to take on. In 1986, Larry Davis shot six cops blocks from where I grew up in the Bronx. In 1989, Howard "Pappy" Mason was convicted for the killing of rookie cop Edward Byrne in Queens. If cats didn't give a fuck about the cops, what do you think they cared about the average citizen or a drug dealer?

In the beginning, hustling was mostly fun. It was predominantly about getting money, girls, and partying. I had, of course, experienced some L's in the earlier days, like Chris's imprisonment, but three to four years in, those losses were becoming much more commonplace as more and more disturbing incidents started to take place mixed in amongst the fun.

I probably didn't give it any thought, but looking back, I can see that even fun activities had the capability of popping off into some BS with increasing regularity. On Christmas in 1988, I remember everyone was at the Apollo.

We often went to the Apollo Theater on Wednesday nights, which was Amateur Night. We went to support girls we knew that were often performing. This particular Christmas show featured Doug E Fresh, Big Daddy Kane, Slick Rick, and Nice & Smooth, to name a few. We came deep as a crew at least ten to fifteen of us on any given night. We usually occupied one of the hanging balconies that were on the left and right sides of the stage. Some other notable drug crew usually occupied the opposite side across from us. On a typical night, it was a friendly pissing contest between them and us, often leading to seeing who could throw the most money down on to the stage and garner the most attention from the girls and the people in attendance. This night, my guys were not necessarily all seated together, but many of the guys getting money throughout the city were there. I stepped in to say what's up to everyone but didn't stay the whole time. I was just coming off the road from out of town and wasn't up for the night's festivities, so I left early with Crusader Rob.

After the event, Billy Guy and Wise had a situation outside where a car came too close to Billy leading him to bang on it. The guy rolled down his window, and Billy and the dude had words where, at some point, someone from his entourage spit on dude. He got out the car, and Billy, Wise, and their crew proceeded to give the Uptown Stomp to the guy and his passenger until shots rang out and everyone dispersed. I don't recall hearing about anyone getting hit, but the hood newscasters remember the scene being so crazy, cops were running and ducking as bullets were heard hitting the storefront gates along 125th Street.

Once the streets got hold of the story, it was, "*Kev and them* had something to do with it." Ironically, one of the girls that worked at BOSS Sneakers happened to be dealing with the kid that got stomped out and said he wanted to speak with me. I was often sought out to mediate or intercede in situations, but I wasn't there when he stopped by, and our paths never subsequently crossed.

Two months later in February, Billy was celebrating his birthday. I had a tricked out 5 Series BMW that I only had about a month, which Billy borrowed for that weekend. That Saturday night, Billy and his man were idled in the car on 145th Street near Willie Burgers. He looked up and could see two guys aggressively approaching the car. Billy sensed something wasn't right and pulled off. They started shooting, and as he drove off ducking shots, he lost control, crashing the car into a parked *New York Daily News* delivery truck.

Artie, Doug, and Lamont were coming from the Rink, a skating rink in New Jersey, when they noticed my car on fire on 145th Street and paged me to check on my well-being. Billy's man in the passenger's side of the car got hit. Billy flagged a cab down and took him to Harlem Hospital. We later found out it was the dude that they had the incident with Christmas night at the Apollo that was the shooter. Billy didn't even know the individual that they had beef with. Yet another street irony is that you expend so much effort to get a rep, and one of the acute downsides is that everyone knows who you are while you may not necessarily know who you are dealing with. Dude immediately skipped town following the shooting.

***

Cars and bullshit were a recurring theme during these times. Within a couple of weeks of each other, both Billy Guy and Wise had both gotten their new cars confiscated by law enforcement.

Wise's BMW still had the temp tag hanging in the back window. There was an unmarked police car outside BOSS Sneakers, and officers were looking at the car. Upon exiting the store, Wise confronted the officers, and words were exchanged. I didn't witness the commotion, but the result was the police finding a way to confiscate the vehicle with the understanding he needed to come and retrieve the car with the rightful owner. Most of our cars were in someone's name that couldn't substantiate the purchase of the vehicle. Wise never attempted to retrieve the car, chalking the loss up to *The Game*.

Billy had just copped his new whip from Martin BMW on 11th Avenue in Midtown and stopped by BOSS to show off his new ride and chop it up. He had picked up a white 535i BMW with a white and black interior. We did our usual bullshitting, talking big money before he jumped in his joint and left. He pulled off busting a U-turn and made his way uptown going up 8th Avenue. When he got in front of Drew Hamilton Projects on 143rd Street, there was a housing cop double-parked and holding up traffic. Billy hit the horn attempting to get them to move out of his way. Billy got impatient and went around the police car, crossing over the double lines, proceeding to pass them. The patrol car immediately lit up with its siren howling and pulled him over. The exchange between Billy and the officers got heated, and he ended up getting arrested and taken into the housing office where they had a couple of holding cells within the housing projects.

They never actually stated why they had arrested him outside of the obvious. A couple of hours later, two White men dressed casually came in the area he was being held in, unlocked the cell, introduced themselves as DEA agents, and escorted him into a room. Right away, they started asking him about the car and who was the alleged owner. Billy replied who the owner was and asked what was all this about, stating all he did was move around a patrol car that was holding up traffic. They began asking him about the jewelry he had on and a bunch of things unrelated to the traffic stop.

The next thing Billy knew, they had the bill of sale for the purchase of the car in their hands. They pointed out that the car was paid for in cash. The questioning went on for about a half-hour before Billy asked whether he was under arrest, and if so, exactly what for? At some point, he got his answer, and it was no, but they said the car would be held until the owner of the vehicle contacted them. Billy asked if he could leave and they gestured that he was free to go. He would never go back or have anyone else make a claim on the car. Easy come and easy it went to easily come again because they both replaced their cars with new ones within days of their incidents.

Getting harassed by the police in our cars fell under occupational hazards. We fit every profile, and they hardly let any chances go by without testing how easy it was to violate our Fourth Amendment rights against illegal searches and seizures, regardless of whatever was or was not found. Take one night I was leaving Harlem with H. We were driving to check out Billy Guy. He was in his mother's neighborhood on Sedgwick Avenue. Billy had some money for me, so I stopped to get it. My mother's house was minutes from there, so I decided afterward to check in on her since I was so close. This was something I regularly did. I usually saw my mother a couple of times out the week when I was in town. If I didn't catch her at home, I would stop by her job to take her out to lunch or just drop in to say hello. Her job was actually within walking distance to her house. It took about 15 minutes going north to 195th Street and University Avenue, to reach my mother's.

As H and I got closer to the house, he noticed a blue and white patrol car in the rearview mirror that had seemingly started following us. I had placed the money Billy had given me on the floor in front of me. I wouldn't have normally ridden with the money so casually if I was going further, but I held onto it. There was about $100,000 in the knapsack.

When we got to the light directly in front of my mother's building, I told H to pull over so I could get out. Soon as we went through the light and they realized we reached our destination and turned on their lights. I grabbed the bag and exited the car. The officer that was driving asked me where I was going and I stated, "I'm going upstairs to my house, what's the problem?!" He responded that we had run a red light. It wasn't true, but in any event, it worked for me because I responded by saying, "OK, then give him a ticket... what has that got to do with me? I wasn't driving." I could tell I caught him off-guard by my response because he struggled to say something as I continued to walk off.

It just so happened that he was riding with a ranking captain. He paused his response looking for help or guidance to my retort. The captain pretty much gestured I was right and, as a passenger, had little to do with the traffic infraction. I walked right into the building and let myself in, shaking my head and saying to myself, *"You're a lucky motherfucker."*

If they would've stopped me, as was their usual routine, and looked in the bag, I would've had a tough time explaining the amount of money. Even if I could have used the store as an explanation, the real issue would have been trying to explain away the notes that Billy always left with his money. Billy would leave scriptures in coded gangster talk along with his money, sometimes even writing directly on the money. For example, he would write things like, "All for one and one for all" or "My brother's keeper," or "Bronx finest BG." Billy was different.

Not long after that incident, I was driving on 7th Avenue going uptown. This time, H was in the passenger's seat. I saw the plainclothes cops in a paddy wagon on the other side of the median headed downtown. I could see them looking in our direction. As we passed each other, our eyes met, and I knew what that meant.

I was looking in my rearview mirror, and I noticed them bust the U-turn, now coming in our direction and approaching fast. I knew if we got pulled over it wasn't going to end well because H had his gun on him. All we could have done was place it under the seat, knowing even with correct paperwork they were still going to find a way to pull us out the car, violate our rights and find it. They would have justified the search by lying in their reports. As they got closer, I made sure they were within a block of us before I made my move. If they were close, I knew they couldn't cut across the median and cut us off. I busted the U-turn and floored the pedal heading back downtown, giving us just enough room to get a block or so ahead of them so that when I made the first available right turn onto 121st Street out of their line of sight heading west, H could jump out of the car, and if nothing else, get rid of the weapon.

After H jumped out the car, I continued to 8th Avenue making the right heading uptown. I made it to 133rd Street before I was converged on. Guns were drawn. They demanded I turn the car off and step outside. It was early evening during the summer months, so there was plenty of activity on the streets and on a block on which I was well known. The cops were doing their typical yelling to startle you along with a bunch of rushed commands. I stepped outside the car already knowing the drill and put my hands on top of the car, all the while smiling. I got the "What the fuck are you smiling for? You think this is a game" remark. I simply looked at him, and my smile went to a smirk.

They aggressively searched me while other officers searched the car with all the doors open. The 130s on 8th Avenue was our area, so as people walked by, there was a chorus of "Kev, you alright?" Some people were even yelling things like, "Stop bothering him" and "All y'all do is harass people." Everything with the car was correct, so I wasn't concerned about that. This went on for about 20 minutes before they let me go. Honestly, being let go probably had more to do with the pressure the community put on in having so many vocal witnesses.

Partly why I made it as far as 133rd Street was because, unbeknownst to me, H and a few guys on 121st were harassed and searched after H jumped out of the car. He was able to toss the weapon into an abandoned lot on the block before the unmarked car made the turn and jumped out on them. They couldn't definitively place H in the car, which is why several other innocent bystanders got stopped as well. When nothing was found on any of them, they were all eventually released. This was just a day in the life of a drug dealer during the time.

***

The *Life* was always a balancing act, and right after Christmas, I was restless and looking to get into something fun. Mark and I got to talking about the great year we all had and looking to close it out with a bang. As the plan started to develop, we asked around about who was with Vegas for the New Year. No surprise, every woman we asked was with it. Most of the homies had their own situations with family or otherwise. Mark and I ended up in Vegas with three females we were both cool with and a guy named BoBo, who was one of the gay guys who was an associate of my store manager, Maurice. BoBo was probably the world's greatest thief or what was called a booster back then. We all dug him because he kept us all in the latest, fly-to-death fashion, especially our women. The women voted him in because of what he promised them he was going to do in Vegas, which was rob the town blind, and he didn't disappoint. The outlaw in all of us couldn't resist getting deals by hook or crook, regardless of how much money we were making.

We booked six first-class tickets a couple of days before the new year. When we arrived in Vegas, we went to Caesar's Palace and got two adjoining suites. We weren't sparing the cost of anything; it was New Year's in Vegas after all. We partied like rock stars for the next few days, truly bringing it in with a bang. The women shopped nonstop, and right along with them, BoBo stole everything that wasn't literally bolted to the ground. He procured furs, sequin gowns, and dresses for our women with designer outfits for us. You name it; he stole it. The champagne and the pleasantries were endless.

Unfortunately, this festiveness was not being enjoyed throughout Harlem as a shift was more noticeable. A madness had overtaken the less than four square miles that make up all of Harlem. The whole island of Manhattan is only 13.4 miles long and but 2.3 miles at its widest. The limited territory eventually led to battles over real estate. Cats getting money were increasingly having to defend themselves against stickup crews and kidnappers. This included some White guys who wore fake badges, pretending to be cops but specialized in robberies and kidnappings. Groups like Preacher's Crew, Young Guns and The Lynch Mob had a reputation within The Game for robbing, killing extorting as well as drug dealing. Those crews sometimes became targets, too.

Young Guns made their name extorting and robbing. One of their vics was a guy named Butch. He was an older guy who was selling weight, and after getting strong-armed, he reached out to a guy named Leon, who was the head of the Lynch Mob and someone he was hitting with work. Leon told Butch he could get it handled, but it would cost him. It came out in court documents that Butch paid $15k-a-head price tag on the Young Guns. The documents stated that Leon reached out to one of the members of the Young Guns and stated he wanted to talk to them about an issue that happened in hopes of resolving it. It was arranged for them to come uptown to meet about this. When three of the Young Guns came uptown to meet, they were slaughtered in an ambush. The wolves were susceptible to getting eaten by other wolves.

The increasingly violent environment effectively leads to a type of arms race where having the biggest and most guns, along with a big crew, was deemed to serve as a form of deterrence. We took arming ourselves to excessive heights. Our stash houses were stockpiled with so many weapons and body armor you might have thought we were a private militia training to overthrow a Central American nation. Every day, we prepared to fight. The enemy may have even been unknown, but the playing field had become so deadly and unpredictable that you were forced to adapt or fall prey to it.

However, once the violence started becoming a regular thing, me and my crew began not only carrying weapons at all times but wearing bulletproof vests and sometimes even bulletproof hats as well. Instead of changing our mindset and environment, we just adapted to the madness. We would rather have been caught with our weapons than without. There isn't the same finality in being judged by twelve versus being carried by six.

With my crew, there was a true structure with order and a hierarchy. We were a very tight, insulated group, and this is what increased our chances of staying safe from foes as well as law enforcement. There was a true bond, a real brotherhood. We were willing to give and risk our lives for one another, and I truly believe in the famous mantra because we were each "our brother's keeper."

There were a bunch of warring factions during this time as well. Many of those at war had one time been close friends and down with each other before beefing. The fallout and deaths from the various wars were contributors to the bleak landscape that the era encompassed.

One of the examples of this was the beef amongst Jason, Travis, and their crew versus T-Money. They had all been my guys, with Jason perhaps the closest, from the days of my first meeting and running around with Red. Jason and T-Money had once been good friends, and it is rumored that the initial beef may have started out over a girl. Whatever the reason, the situation soon escalated.

Jason got hit by someone on T-Money's side. In retaliation for his death, Rasheed, who was alleged to have killed Jason, was then murdered in broad daylight on 125th Street directly in front of the Mart and across the street from the Apollo, allegedly by Jason's younger brother, Ray Ray. Ray Ray was then alleged to have killed T-Money and Rodney in front of Rodney's video store on 7th Avenue. Rodney was a non-participant to the actual beefing, but as someone near T-Money, he was a casualty to it all. Shortly after that, someone shot Ray Ray. He was hospitalized and stable, but soon died following complications from one of his surgeries. Travis, Jason's friend, then got killed in broad daylight on 8th Avenue in the 140s. He was riding a custom, purple dune buggy, when a car pulled up at the light and blasted him with multiple shots. One of T-Money's people, Mike, was shot and killed while holding his baby daughter on 127th Street. This war lasted for six to seven months in 1988-89, and before its end, at least a dozen people had lost their lives, deaths that had derived from formerly close friendships.

Do Wop's beef with John John's crew was another example. These beefs also lead to a constant series of back and forth retaliations. As I understood, Do Wop and John John started out down with each other, no different than Red and I had. Yet, for reasons only they truly knew, they split and the fracture amongst the crew lead to deadly altercations. We were becoming unsure about everything, even the police.

Earlier, I mentioned a group of guys going around pretending to be police pulling drug dealers over in unmarked cars. They had the complete look with badges hanging from their necks as well as holstered guns. After pulling you over and out of your car, they would then handcuff you and throw you in the back of their car. Shortly after you were in their custody, you would be made aware of what the situation was. A couple of older cats had gotten ensnared in this caper leading to their family or crew paying ransoms. There was even an instance where things didn't go as planned, and the person kidnapped was killed even after the captors received the money.

Stories like this spread and all of the top hustlers essentially vowed we wouldn't pull over if something felt suspicious. Instead, we decided we would keep driving until we were on home territory or at least in front of a precinct. We'd rather deal with an irate police officer asking why we didn't pull over opposed to the other alternatives. It was understood that, even on foot, if you got approached and backed down, you wouldn't willingly get in an unmarked car because doing so could seal your fate.

So much of this shit was happening so regularly that details were less important. It had become my unfortunate new normal. To someone else, crazy scenarios like any of the ones just described might be ingrained into their minds, but for me, it was starting to be a regular Tuesday. There are literally dozens of similar stories. Unfortunately, one I do remember because it directly hit home, had 1989 starting on a particularly bad note.

Albe was living in the Parkchester section of the Bronx. He still served as a conduit between me and the connects for D.C., making his points, but his primary interests and hustle was the gambling spot he opened in the Bronx. It was on 167th Street and Clay Avenue, and it was called The Madhouse. Rob was in D.C., but he got the call before me telling me of the incident that had occurred.

Albe was living with his girlfriend. She was a Hispanic young lady, and they were always seemingly having issues with Albe consistently in the doghouse. What we were told was that Albe knocked on his apartment door instead of using his key. He told her it was alright, but it was clear he was in some type of distress. He had been hemmed up either in front of his building or the hallway inside the entrance. She stated that they were demanding money. She said he complied, but at some point, a struggle transpired, and he was shot. They then fled the apartment leaving her as a witness.

There was always speculation centered around her because she had a brother that had just gotten out of jail and because she was spared. It cast a shadow of doubt on her. His girl was light on details, including supposedly having no idea how much was taken. None of us ever had any personal relationship or direct dealings with her other than her being Albe's lady. She disappeared almost immediately after the incident, never to be heard from again.

There was no telling what the truth was behind his killing. He was my man, a good dude with a big heart and a great friend who was loyal to a fault. But he was sloppy when it came to his dealings with women (not so unlike the rest of us), and he stayed in all kinds of drama with them all the time. We never got to the bottom of his death.

We gave him the kind of send-off he deserved. We dressed him from head to toe in AJ Lester's, befitting his status in the game. His homecoming was held at Benta's Funeral Home on 141st Street and St. Nicholas Avenue. Benta's was the funeral home used by all the hustlers in the drug game during that time. It was the least I could do for my friend. I can remember my mother crying upon hearing the news of his death. She liked Al and knew we were close. I wasn't sure if her tears were all for Albe or her knowing any day they could be for me. It was all just another cruel reminder that more money really leads to more problems when your life was still tied heavily to the streets.

Unfortunately, Albe's death and the circumstances behind it were far becoming the norm. I first started hustling to help my mom and family. I felt like I was doing something positive for those close to me, with the irony of the potential negative effects that drugs can have on people lost on me when outweighed by the positivity I associated with my hustles. Of course, those hustles didn't even start out illegal. When I graduated to weed and coke, I still never made any real association with the destructive component of selling drugs. They were recreational, and party drugs and actual addictions to cocaine were rich people problems, not necessarily pervasive hood issues.

The advent of crack was a whole different story. Like heroin before it, the drug simultaneously made hood millionaires while having a lasting and profound effect on the community on multi-leveled layers. This is no justification, but partially an explanation, in that we all grew up with drugs being so commonplace where we lived. The users were already there. Our culpability wasn't in creating the demand or forcing people to do anything they weren't already doing but capitalizing on supplying to that existent demand.

The truth was when I graduated from just hustling to selling drugs, besides helping my family, I was in it for the money, broads, cars, jewelry, and clothes. The feeling I got from those initial Rooftop experiences embodied everything hustling was for me. I was addicted to the game, the status and, of course, the money and the perks that came with being a 20-something-year-old millionaire in the hood were unparalleled.

It was never all fun and games, but that original Rooftop atmosphere was real for so many of us. We made hustling a competition. We all wanted to be "that nigga." Years later, that whole sentiment had changed. The fun was minimized by the death and mass incarceration that permeated our world. While I came into the game with colorful characters who were true hustlers and some even stickup kids themselves, I quickly realized that for every dude that was about getting money within the code and framework of the game as I knew it, there were many others who had no respect for any of the principles we tried to apply to getting money.

The landscape was changing aggressively and fast in both New York as well as D.C. The Cocaine Cowboy outlaw landscape that allowed so many to get rich quick was now also breeding a generation of fakers who weren't hustlers but simply takers. Anyone who comes into lots of money can tell you, that dream can be a nightmare if the environment you are in still consists of lots of people who aren't sharing your good fortune.

This wasn't a new concept. The two always went together, but for us, we understood that money and violence didn't mix, so we avoided it at all cost. The reason we all got into the game was to get money in the first place. Me and my crew were far from perfect, but these other characters made for a ridiculously treacherous landscape in part because of their unpredictability. I feared no one, but the times had become so perilous, that jail was a true afterthought because the odds just seemed so much more likely for an early death with what our era had become. The takers didn't just want what you had financially; they seemed to have an actual disdain for your success, respect, and likability. We embodied everything they weren't, and it was clear that every day when I left the house, I prepared for war against unknown assailants that hated me because they weren't me. As you could imagine, that preparation alone could be exhausting. The darkness of the time is why I often say I was more prepared for death than incarceration. The expectation of one's own death is one thing, but there are others' that can never be prepared for.

12

DEAR MOMMA

Some days in your life you never forget. The birth of a child qualifies as one of them for positive reasons. Unfortunately, most other unforgettable days are asterisked and indelibly ingrained because of tragedy.

February 24, 1989 was a particularly cold NYC winter evening. It was a Friday night I recall in part because I was preparing to go to the movies with Mark, Troy, Kim, and Shayvon. If I was in town, I was relatively easy to find. I moved around, of course, in the city, but always made it a point to spend some time at BOSS Sneakers. It was easier to hold court there, with it being such a hub on 125th Street than having to make rounds to catch up to everyone all around.

This day was no different, and the five of us were preparing to leave the store as it closed to head over to the movies in Secaucus, New Jersey. I remember having to buy a scully from one of the outdoor vendors on the block. When we got to the theater in New Jersey, I bumped into Rich Porter who was there on a date with a girl named Landa. Rich had a condo in Secaucus he owned. We chopped it up for a few in the lobby before we headed inside to catch the flick.

I don't recall how long it was into the movie before my vibrating beeper wouldn't stop. I didn't recognize the city number, but the 911 code at the end made it imperative for me to get to a phone to see what was going on. We didn't play with 911 codes, and everyone knew only to use them in real emergencies. On the other end was Sarray's sister. I knew who Sarray was because she was Crusader Rob's woman, but I didn't know her sister at all, so her being on the other end of a frantic phone call with me only lead to more questions and suspicions than answers. She was emotional and might have even been crying. It was hard to clearly understand what she was saying and none of what I could understand made any sense.

What I did hear was that there was a shooting at my mom's house involving my mother, Sarray, and a woman named Rita, who I probably heard as Reika. I believe I stepped back into the theater only long enough to tell them I had to run, but the shock at that point made details and emotions hard to decipher.

Mark went ahead of me, and I made a beeline back over the George Washington Bridge. That trip from the movie theater to my mother's house may have normally taken a half-hour, but I probably made it over the bridge in nearly half of that time. At this point, nothing made any sense, and the randomness of the call with even Sarray being mentioned in the same breath as my mother seemed like it could be a potential setup. I frantically tried to reach Reika. I initially thought Sarray's sister said my mother and Reika. The similar names and the fact that I didn't even know a Rita made me fear that Reika was involved until I was finally able to reach her. She was nearby in Englewood at a friend's house, and I stopped by and picked her up on my way back into the city. No thoughts were clear, but I know I attempted to call my mother's house, with each unanswered ring increasing my frenetic need to get there. I then reached out to Aunt Diane, and though I woke her, she headed to my mother's as well, beating me there. I raced up the Major Deegan until I got to my mother's building, 95 West 195th Street, in the Kingsbridge section of the Bronx.

The otherwise quiet neighborhood was flooded with police activity, so as I got near, the reality that there was a problem came into sharper focus. I saw my aunt Diane and my cousins Lamont and Darnell downstairs in the lobby of the building. There was a heavy police presence in the lobby preventing access, but their inquiries were white noise, and I essentially ran past them as I attempted to make my way up to the 3rd floor of the building. As I neared her apartment, the police physically stopped me from going in. I remember my Aunt Diane yelling for them to leave me alone. They had a bunch of questions for me and I for them. When it was apparent, I wasn't getting enough answers beyond where everyone was taken. I had no more time to entertain them and headed back downstairs, past my aunt and toward the hospital.

The fury that had been bubbling upon taking the initial call and driving to the scene was now at a full boil once the police confirmed to me that my mother was one of two people deceased in the apartment. My mother, Barbara Chiles, Rita Faulk, and Sarray Watson were all tied and bound before being shot in the head. Sarray was the only survivor, and I rushed over to Jacobi Hospital, where she was taken.

I met up with Rob at the hospital and quickly caught up on details of the tragedy. He was there with a few of his guys, and several of mine met me there as well. This is what I was told and could gather: Sarray was visiting Rita Faulk in the Fordham Road section of the Bronx. She had a custom Mercedes 190E, and as she was coming out of a building, they were accosted and abducted by three guys with guns. They took them back into the building up to the roof and robbed them of all of their jewelry and whatever money they had on them. They were asking Sarray for money or something of that nature and telling her to take them to "Boss' house," and I am assuming that they were referencing me. It so happened that from where she was, my mother's house was less than ten minutes away. They piled into her car, and another car followed them. She then directed them to my mother's place. They waited for my mother to arrive home from work and once she did, they used Sarray to access my mother's apartment.

From these minimal facts, I had far more questions than answers. Why did Sarray bring them to my mother's house? She barely knew my mother, maybe seeing her on a few occasions. I know she knew where my mother lived because there were times when she might have been with Rob when he met up with me to discuss business or drop money off, and I just so happened to be visiting my mother. However, anyone that knew me knew that I never kept any money or drugs at my mother's house- NEVER. I have always questioned that if they wanted me, I was not hard to find. Any day I was in town, you could find me at some point on 125th Street at my store. The place was named BOSS Sneakers. Clearly, I wasn't hiding.

My mother was killed by cowards. I wasn't hard to catch. Instead, beautiful souls died, literally, for nothing. There was neither money nor drugs in the house. These cowards shot three women, murdering two in cold blood for nothing.

Maybe I had watched too many Mafia movies in my life, but civilians, women, children, and families were supposed to be left out of our affairs. Up until this point, though, I had seen too many other things that showed me otherwise, I still wanted to believe those unspoken rules applied to our lives as well. My mother's murder was another loud declaration that we were dealing with a different kind of savage in the Crack Era who followed no rules or code of ethics.

After meeting with Rob and my guys, it didn't take long to get a lead on the three cowards that took my mother's life. Between the information Sarray was able to give up and what the streets said, I had a good idea who the culprits were.

My emotions were overwhelming and contradictory. My sadness and my despair were being drowned out by rage, mixed in with guilt and remorse. I solely wore the responsibility of this occurring. I wanted blood on my hands, and I needed vengeance. I wasn't thinking rationally. I know I attended her wake, but I don't have any distinct memories of being there, talking to anyone or taking part in any of its planning. Revenge was the only planning I can even recall because otherwise, I was in a daze mixed with denial.

I was torn, but part of that thought process included feeling like my presence at her funeral would be an unnecessary distraction. My presence might take away from the mourning that my father, brother, and so many others that loved my mother so much deserved. For those reasons, I couldn't bring myself to attend my mother's funeral. I think I stayed in New Jersey with the kids, but I had little grasp of my emotions. Nobody else's mother had been killed at this time. I was having a hard time coming to grips with it all. So many years later these feelings haven't subsided. It still doesn't make any sense.

Clearly, I was the target and my name had to have come up. What was Sarray thinking or going through to bring people to my mother's home? I knew they knew where to find me if that's what they desired to do. I was hardly difficult to find. I kept saying that to myself repeatedly hoping at some point it would make sense and change things. If you wanted to follow me once I left BOSS Sneakers, it wouldn't have necessarily been easy, but they would have at least had a starting point. It is only Sarray and two other people who are alive today that know the truth for sure.

I reasonably knew who these individuals were out the gate. I remember having a conversation with Alpo about the situation. He knew a guy named Randy, who he thought might have run in the same circles with the guys who did it. I know for a fact that I put every single resource I had into locating these individuals. There was an instance or two when we got a lead on the jokers, but by the time me, Rob, and others got to a tipped location, there was no sign of them. They were aware of us being on their trail out the gate and got messages to us that they didn't have anything to do with what happened at my mother's house.

Unapologetically, I admit that the only satisfaction I ever could have gotten was to kill these individuals myself. I was made aware that one of them was killed while we were looking for them. I don't believe in karma, so chalking up his death to something else he may have done in the streets was little consolation for me. However, rather quickly, the trail went cold. It was soon apparent that they went on the run and most likely left the state. They had little other choice, because I would have never stopped looking for them.

These were some dirtbag dudes that I didn't know and had never heard of before this. They had no reputation or standing like some of the usual suspects I had come to know. My reach in the New York metropolitan area was extensive. The pressure I exerted to find them was real. If these dudes had shown up anywhere in the area, it would have gotten handled. Besides me personally addressing them, I had numerous dudes that would have taken great pleasure in doing it for me without ever taking my money.

I had never even heard of these creeps before the incident. I remember having a conversation with Billy Guy, where he explained having prior knowledge of them related to an earlier situation. I was in my feelings thinking that if they would have been properly dealt with, no harm would have come to my mother, Rita Faulk, and Sarray. Our relationship got a little strained, in part because of this. It probably wasn't rational, but in truth, I was a little different, and my relationships with everyone were strained for a while afterward.

Billy tried to make amends. One way included him getting a lead on one of the individuals early on. The lead put me onto the family home of one individual, where it was thought that he might either be hiding or make an appearance. One time, I was sitting in a car with a couple of guys outside one of the suspects' mother's house, a hit squad on deck. I saw one of the character's mother after she was pointed out. The car's near-consensus suggested we exact revenge upon his mother, but that just didn't sit right with me. I had to aggressively let others know that his mom was off limits. He did the dirt and ran leaving his mom and family open to retribution that was easy to exact, but this was just another distinction between myself and them. Just because we were dealing with cowards who didn't live by rules, was not an excuse to become less than the honorable man I always prided myself on being and professed to be.

I know this incident initially strained my relationship with Rob as well. I was angry, and a part of me would never be the same. Let me also state clearly, for any chatter that ever arose related to Rob and me. Never did I give any thought to the idea that Rob had anything to do with setting me up and hurting my mother. True, Rob had a reputation in his life for the *taking* game. However, my friendship with Rob was strong, and I trusted him. Yet, the most real thing I could say is that Rob knew where I had real money and product, and at any given time, Rob might owe hundreds of thousands on his end for consigned work over the years. We made millions together and never had one issue about or over money. It is ridiculous that I would ever have to clear that up, but you can never stop the streets from talking no matter how ridiculous the topic of conversation.

Not one day went by afterward in which I did not follow up or exhaust my resources in search of these guys, but as I mentioned, after several weeks, the leads grew cold. Probably six months after that, I got a phone call or page about the television show America's Most Wanted, producing a segment on my mom's murder. I had never spoken to the police at any point before or after my mom's passing. Several news outlets, including the *New York Times*, reported the double homicide as drug-related though there was no evidence of drugs, money or weapons found at the scene. I know this implication bothered my brother a lot, but I knew how lazy the police were. If a crime happened to minorities, it had to be drug-related. In my opinion, it was their way of minimizing Blacks and Hispanics when they were the victims of violent crimes. It wasn't that I just didn't talk to the police. I never made myself accessible to them or America's Most Wanted. As far as I know, the show never contacted anyone in my family. The show depicted a re-enactment of the event, presumably from statements by the one surviving witness to police. Shortly after the show aired, the two guys were apprehended, one in Detroit and the other in Massachusetts.

I found no relief in the news of their capture. Having them in police custody was far from what I wanted. Tom Cross and Felipe Conception were extradited to New York and housed on Rikers Island. There was only one-time Tom Cross and I ever had any engagement. He called BOSS Sneakers, not identifying himself. The phone was passed to me. When I got on the phone, he let me know it was him. He tried denying having anything to do with killing my mother while simultaneously trying to threaten me. He told me that I needed to call off the dudes I had getting at him on Rikers Island. He stated he had people in the street as well, and he would see to it that they'd equally get at me. Our conversation was brief with me pretty much telling him to go fuck himself.

A short time after this all happened, Rob was imprisoned on something unrelated to our drug organization, essentially leaving Sarray at 19, alone. She was the only actual witness in the case, and her testimony helped to convict the two, with the third already deceased.

I never set foot in the courtroom. Those dudes are strangers to me. February 2019 marked thirty years since this all happened. The two are still in prison. I have never physically seen either guy in my life, before or since. I told my story in *Don Diva,* and one of them sued me for misrepresenting the facts. He requested tapes or transcripts from my interview as proof or exculpatory evidence in his case. He claimed that my statement somehow contradicted Sarray's testimony. This is as stupid as it sounds since I wasn't there and never appeared at the trial as an observer, let alone a witness. My statements, fact, or opinion have nothing to do with his case at trial since I was not a part of his trial at all.

He later sued me again after doing an interview with another magazine professing to be a gangster and detailing some of his alleged street exploits. There was even an implication that my father snitched on him and was the only reason he was locked up in jail. I generally make it a rule not to acknowledge dumb shit, but I checked the dude in my next issue of Don Diva after his interview. Shortly after that, he sued me yet again for slander, stating what I said in the article put his life and safety at risk because people in jail don't take kindly to people that rob and hurt women and kids.

I hesitated in mentioning the names of these two fucking cowards. They don't deserve any recognition, fame or notoriety for their actions, especially since every time I do, one sues me. I realize my silence in naming them in the past has allowed them to try and rewrite history in telling tales of tough guy legacies in the streets. Nothing could be further from the truth. These weren't known, feared men. These were the snakes hiding in the bushes that knew to only prey on the weak and those that they knew couldn't defend themselves. They're fucking cowards.

Felipe Concepcion and Tom Cross were the ones who were convicted for killing my mother. Tom Cross is the clown who sued me. Tom Cross actually had a retort to my article throwing Felipe under the bus, saying he was the one who shot women and babies. I ignored all three lawsuits but ended up having to hire an attorney to reverse the summary judgment against me for ignoring the third suit. The first two were dismissed without me even having to acknowledge the dumb shit. I was able to use that reasoning as an explanation as to why I ignored the third as well.

Once the court heard my attorney, that summary judgment was reversed, the case is still in the courts, but beside it costing me money to fight the BS, I understand that any defense to slander is the truth.

After my mother's death, no one was allowed in the city-- not my girl or my kids. They didn't need to be subjected to this. I had signed up for this life; they hadn't. In the Italian Mafia movies, there seemed to be some rules. For Blacks and Hispanics in this Crack Era, it was becoming increasingly clear there were none. Unfortunately, this incident led me to be overly cautious. I became extremely protective of anyone I cared for. Reika was put on notice that if someone came to the house and I didn't call ahead to tell her they were coming, don't answer and call me. I didn't care how she knew them if they weren't family, they weren't to be let in the house.

My mother was the most precious thing in my life. Her loss made me a savage. I just got cold after that. The truth is, I have probably never had a real relationship with a woman after that in which I gave my whole heart. It's not an excuse as much as an explanation. I never could fully immerse myself emotionally, knowing in an instant it can be ripped from me. Having someone you love taken from you violently is even harder than other forms of death like disease, accident, etc. None of it is easy, but people taken from you prematurely and violently carries a different kind of burden and pain.

My zest for life was forever diminished. One silver lining occurred nearly a year later. My only daughter came into the world. She was named after my mother. This was a connection to her, as well as a reminder of what was missing. I miss the impact she didn't have on my children and even my grandchildren. I miss the lessons she taught me as well as the ones that never came. She didn't get a chance to see my brother's accomplishments or mine. She didn't get a chance to see how well we turned out as fathers, providers and the men she ultimately groomed and raised. I missed her tutelage, love and affection. All the women I have had relationships almost universally comment that I am a great provider, but cold and lacking in my willingness to fight to maintain our relationships. I effectively alienate myself from others, and

I am sure I have always given the distinct impression that leaving was a ready option to those unhappy with my efforts.

Losing my mother, the way I did, is probably the most ironic event in my life. The point of being a provider and safeguarding my family are probably the most important things to me, and this importance was built largely by watching my mother's experiences and struggles. In hindsight, I have come to realize how wonderful a woman she was. I understood and appreciated her while she was living, but slowing down my own lifestyle, and maturing has given me the perspective to see how amazing and beautiful a person she was. She uniquely had the ability to nurture and have relationships with three different personalities in her household that were distinctly different and had different needs.

My mother was everything to me. I could be having the worst day, but I would never want her to wear the burden of my issues when I was around her. This was the same as when I was a teenager into adulthood. I grew up faster in hiding my pain and troubles, much in the same way she tried. I was supposed to protect and guard her. Her death, and especially the way it happened, meant I failed. She wasn't a ghetto mom, running the streets and accessible to others. She didn't live in the middle of the hood. Not everyone knew she was my mother. What happened to her was almost unfathomable. She was never supposed to die that way when it was my job to protect her.

My mother lost her life due to the violation that occurred because they knew there could be no witnesses left behind. They knew that if the violation would've gotten back to me, there would have never been anything I wouldn't do to have exacted revenge. I understand the game. Part of it includes the kidnapping and extortion of drug dealers. Takers aren't hustlers, but opportunists. These were not even opportunists, just straight cowards that killed some women. They knew I would have never gone through the law, and it would have been between them and me. Instead, two women died, and they got nothing. There was no king's ransom-- nothing. There were no drugs or money in the house, and I have never been able to make any sense of it.

There is no silver lining that came from my mother's death. Yet, anyone that truly knows me knows that I consider her my guardian angel. There is no other explanation for my good fortune and even luck in avoiding so many of the traps that befell so many other hustlers.

My mother started as a teller before rising to run her own branch as manager. By working at the bank, she provided insight, regarding having credit and the federal deposit reporting laws, that I was unaware I even needed.

She took some of my money and bought me savings bonds. At the time, those bonds had interest rates of eight to ten percent. She purchased them in her name and mine. They varied but had 15 to 20-year maturity rates. She might have started purchasing these bonds from 1985 through 1989. They gained even more interest because they were kept in so many years longer at the significantly high-interest rates that are now unheard of. I looked at my mother as my angel during her lifetime. However, it rang even truer because I had a REALLY good piece of money when I got out of prison from the saving bonds alone that she had the foresight to purchase on my behalf.

Everything I learned about credit and purchasing properties in my name or with Reika was all because of my mother's guidance. By making large purchases in my name, the government couldn't convict me of money laundering (though they tried). I had great credit, reported income and paid taxes on significant income that could validate much of the documented spending.

Her guidance made a generational change. After the government tried to strip me of everything I had acquired, I still had money, legally, to start my new life strong — her guiding me to have legitimate businesses saved my life. Even the IRS had to testify that I had the legitimate income to support my lavish lifestyle.

My mother had an uncanny knack of understanding what each of us needed. My father and brother needed attention. She knew I needed guidance more than anything, and I never felt slighted. The guidance that my mother provided Reika and I has been monumental in changing and shaping the lives of my family. Reika and all my kids have near-perfect credit. Even after ten years in jail, I still have near-perfect credit all because of lessons instilled by my mother.

She is MY angel, but her help and presence have been generationally impactful, and in some small ways, I hope she may pass on some of that knowledge of foresight to some of you reading. No matter whatever your hustle is, if it is going well, spend money but take a few dollars and buy an IRA, saving bonds and insurance in your name, your spouse's and kids'. Let that money have impact and meaning beyond the immediate gratification of buying cars, tricking it off and having fun. Let that money help you in the future. I had no foresight on my own. I thought the money would never stop and if it did, it was going to be because I was dead. Yet, through her, it helped my second phase of life get off to a start that I know most people that do bids and ex-hustlers never get.

My mother's love and guidance may have also had another unintended benefit in sparing my life. I genuinely loved "My Guys," and it resonated with them. It is a large part of why no one from my original crew ever told on me. I bailed everyone out, regardless of whether I should have been responsible. No man was ever left behind. If someone got busted on a Friday, I got them out that night or by Saturday. I almost always paid for everyone's attorneys, as well.

If there was a beef, I stood right there with them. If they needed anything, I was there for them or their families. They all knew they could count on me, no matter the circumstance, without hesitation. I had their backs, and in turn, they had mine.

All of this ties back to my mother. One of the best things I, subconsciously, learned from her was how to genuinely manage people with love and care in the same way she did for me, my brother and father. If she was a less genuine, even more manipulative person, I might have done all these things to help people for the wrong reasons. Instead, it was pure, and my guys knew it, returned that love and remained loyal. Anything less from any of them would have resulted in certain lifetime imprisonment without parole, if not death, that often comes from street betrayals.

Yet again, one of the incredible gifts from my mother-- the only way I have ever been able to reconcile her death. The only way I could have it sit with me is that my mother's death occurred as some sacrifice for me to live and help my family and others. I wear her death… her sacrifice, knowing I have a greater purpose in large part for all she gave me.

13

LEVELS OF DARKNESS - THE KILLING GAME

This may come as a surprise to most of you, but nearly all of us have the capacity to take someone's life. Of course, most of those scenarios involve extreme measures of having to protect one's self or family. Nonetheless, that ability or even necessity to kill doesn't then make someone a killer.

Some people easily justify ending the lives of others for monetary gains, self-preservation, revenge, being slighted, etc. Yet, even with people that can kill outside of extreme emergencies, you should understand. All killers aren't created equally.

In the drug game, you must be willing to exterminate as an extreme measure because if you're not more than likely at some point, you will become a victim yourself. Violence is a necessary evil that comes with being in the drug game, but I was always measured and not one to abuse my power. I was in a position, during that time, to eliminate a person by just pointing in their direction. It was as simple as that.

At the peak of my run, I had so many guys, particularly the younger ones, who would have killed at the mere suggestion of me having an issue with someone. Some guys would have killed just to gain my attention or favor. I probably spent more time trying to talk these guys off the proverbial ledge because that was not the reason I got in the game, and the ability to trip wasn't going to change that.

That statement is as much a commentary on the level of power I possessed as it is on how little life was respected in the streets during the era. However, I got into the drug game to make money, and I was taught that money and violence didn't mix. I resorted to violence only in matters that were detrimental to me or my crew's wellbeing. Any threat to my life or anyone I had a love for would've been met with the full force of my resources. This was not just talk for me. I sometimes refer to hustling as the Game, but the reality is, once I got past my teens and started making real money, the Game became the Life because the stakes became so much more real. I embodied hustling to the fullest, and that included the good, the bad, and often, the extremely ugly.

I never pretended to be a super tough guy. Yet, I was far from a pushover, and my guys respected me because I was always ready, willing and able to put in work. That meant never asking anyone to do anything I wasn't ultimately willing to do myself. That said, I had some genuine, thorough guys in my crew. My strength was in numbers and alliances. With some notable exceptions, most of my crew and I were able to navigate and come out of an era that grew increasingly violent and reckless.

I have several friends who are true gangsters. I've lived most of my life around these kinds of individuals. Damn near every person I have some engagement with on a day-to-day basis has a felony. I'm sad to say this includes many of the women I know. We all did what we had to do to get by and back then, in many instances, it meant committing crimes

My comprehension and perspectives are ones only a few can relate to because of the level I played on. I had to walk way more than a mile in those shoes; it's been more like a marathon.

The good times, in the beginning, were eventually replaced by a backdrop more appropriately labeled "Hell Up in Harlem." The levels of death in the killing game had become all too real not only in Harlem but throughout New York and nationwide. I write this not as a passive reporter who was looking on from the outside, but as someone with more than 250 to 300 people whom I had personal relationships with who lost their lives during this time period.

In the height of the Crack Era, I had a store, centrally located in the heart of New York City in Harlem on 125th Street called BOSS Emporium.

The location alone gave me a 360 view of the *Life*. There wasn't anything that happened that I didn't hear about or directly know.

While there were many responsible for deaths during that time (including just random people and situations), I will use three notable organizations and figures during the time that operated in and around Harlem and D.C. during the '80s and '90s to highlight some of the different levels and motivations behind the era's killings: Preacher's Crew; the Lynch Mob; and Alpo and Wayne Perry. Preacher pled to 13 murders while the members of the Lynch Mob copped out to approximately 15 bodies. Alpo plead to 14, with Wayne being a part of many, and at least 8-9 others additionally he pled to.

All our paths crossed if for no other reason than us being in such close proximity of one another. I had direct, personal dealings with these individuals or their crews while I was on the street. I didn't have any specific interactions with Preacher, but I did with several of the guys that were a part of his organization. Crusader Rob did have a personal relationship with him. My perspective of these individuals and crews comes from a unique place. There aren't many who saw things the way I did because of my level of exposure.

Clarence "Preacher" Heatley was also known as "The Black Hand of Death." He had a crew led by former Housing Authority police officer John Cuff who had established quite a reputation for kidnappings and extortions. It was rumored that Preacher's Crew kidnapped entertainer Bobby Brown over an alleged drug debt and along with their uncle, were responsible for the kidnapping and killing of Rich Porter's brother, Donnell Porter.

Preacher was in the drug game, but I never considered him and his crew true drug dealers, and they definitely were not hustlers. Most of the drugs they got and then subsequently sold were the results of their extorting and robbing dealers throughout the Bronx and Harlem. They were primarily in the *taking* game, and Preacher was apparently charismatic enough to amass a crew that was devoted to the task.

I understand that "Takers" come with the Game and the *Life*. I have never particularly been a fan of them or their methods but understood they came with the territory. I loved hustling and making money with my guys. Matching violence with violence was a necessary evil, but for guys like Preacher and his crew, it was their chosen way.

While they targeted people of my stature, Preacher and his crew were never people I feared on any level. I was aware of their reputation and exploits, but they were equally aware of the reputations of the company I closely kept. Plus, with Rob and Preacher having some type of relationship that was marked by mutual respect and one of my cousins being part of the crew, I was essentially off-limits. I wasn't worried either way, but having the intertwined relationships kept the predatory nature of Preacher and his crew off my personal radar of issues to deal with.

However, other dealers in Harlem and the Bronx were not as fortunate. Preacher had a young, hungry crew, and as evidenced by Donnell's killing, they didn't have many limits to how they got down. They were committed to taking from others, and murder was probably less a necessity as it was something they possibly relished.

They had a building on the Grand Concourse in the Bronx, where they allegedly committed many of the murders. Before the killings, their victims were reportedly tortured before some of them were then dismembered to prepare for their disposal. He was the person who allegedly ordered the extortions, kidnappings, and killings implemented by John Cuff and others in his crew, and those orders did not spare members of his own crew that he was dissatisfied with. This included at least two of his crew being murdered and dismembered in the Bronx basement on his orders.

Many have tried to delve into the mentality of the likes of Preacher and his crew. That type of psychological evaluation is beyond my mentality, but I do know that some cats are just wired differently. Once you break that seal and take a life, it gets easier to do, especially if you are committed to the *taking* game.

What is interesting about Preacher is that as physically imposing as he may have been at 6'7" and nearly 300 pounds, the US Attorney never actually alleged that Preacher directly committed any of the murders himself. He became a bogeyman by name and reputation based on the acts of others under his direction. What is also interesting is that the man who extorted based on the killing and tough-guy reputation and easily ordered others to kill for his benefit cooperated and told on his crew to spare his own life once he got busted. No matter how many times I see that scenario play out, I still never understand how these killers are so willing to tell to save themselves by selling others out. That's not totally true. I do understand they're self-centered and just don't give a fuck. Yet, my other two examples play out that very same way.

The Lynch Mob was a more typical drug organization, most similar in structure to what I had going on. Their head was a guy named Leon. Their primary purpose was to make money, but Leon had a crew of guys willing to kill that was deeply loyal and efficient at protecting their interests, and that loyalty was often misused.

Lou Simms and Farris Phillips were just two in that crew that were about that gangster life. They were not pretending. Beyond doing extreme things asked by Leon to further their organization's interests, regulate violators, or exact revenge, members of the Lynch Mob were convicted of approximately 15 murders. It's alleged that there were more than 15. If you had beef or issues with the Lynch Mob, there was no guessing involved as to the stakes and potential consequences. For them, money and violence went together. Different leadership may have led to different outcomes, but under Leon, the crew seamlessly lived a "take no prisoners" existence, and that meant murders were always on the menu.

It's alleged that the Lynch Mob was so proficient at the murder game that they were sought after for contract killings outside of their organization's immediate interests. Their reputation quickly grew, and while their primary focus was on selling drugs, it was not out of bounds for them to commit robberies of hustlers when the vic just looked too tempting to pass up.

When the members of the crew got busted, I am sure the last thing that guys like Lou and Farris, whose outlook on the game centered on loyalty, expected was for members of their organization to start telling. The fact that the telling began at the top, with Leon, probably made their situations all the more difficult to take.

The third known figure during the era that I am using to help shine a light on the different levels of the murder game is Alberto "Alpo" Martinez. He was a charismatic and likable guy, but at some point, that all changed, and someone never really known for violence became synonymous with it to the general public.

Po was once a friend and someone I did business with. I give it up with no hidden agenda. Instead, I offer personal insight that can't be found in blogs, YouTube or other related content by outsiders weighing in on something and someone they really did not know.

I am not saying Alpo was any kind of punk, but I am saying that this false narrative of Po as someone known for gunplay and confrontation needs to be summarily dismissed. He copped to being involved in 14 murders, but this was no killer putting in work in the streets against adversaries. In almost all his copped cases, he admitted to basically killing friends.

If Alpo is described as a serial killer, then I would liken him to Ted Bundy. This is a guy that used his charm and looks to get close to his victims. He effectively killed them with kindness. Most of them, like Rich Porter and "Big Head" Gary, were people that he was able to get close to because they were friends, business associates, or just cool. He only seemed to kill once he gained your confidence and trust. His motives could be questioned, but in most of the cases, he killed his friends over money. It is partly why I always question, knowing what I know now if I could have been next.

Though I made Po pay for the vast majority of his work upfront, he had developed a pattern of killing friends and acquaintances whom he may have seen the opportunity to rob or avoid paying. Even then, those killings were executed by someone else. By Alpo's own admission, his man "Big Head" Gary from D.C., killed Rich to avoid Alpo from having to pay for consigned keys.

Gary also killed another D.C. dude named Andre for Alpo for $270,000, keeping the money and work they were supposed to be selling to Andre. That killing could have been as much about women as it was money. Gary was in his feelings, having found out Andre was messing with his woman. All the while, Alpo was messing with Andre's woman. It was like knocking out two issues at once.

Alpo then had one of Wayne Perry's henchmen kill Gary. They were making a move, according to Alpo, to cop $6 million in work in which they had to put up $2 million. Alpo was putting up $1.5 and Gary, $500k. Alpo alleges that he got word Gary was planning to set him up for his end and got him first. One of Wayne's guys killed Gary while Alpo drove. Alpo also had one of Wayne's people kill Domencio Benson in broad daylight at a basketball court after shaking hands with him.

Part of what may have changed Alpo from the person I knew well in New York to the person he seemed to morph into in D.C. was the fact that he was shot and nearly killed early in his D.C. stay. After he survived, he knew he needed protection in D.C. and hooked up with one of the area's most notorious figures, Wayne Perry. With that new muscle, Alpo changed, and his killing spree happened within about 18 months.

Alpo leaned hard on Wayne and others to carry out his agenda of needing to be protected and betrayal of those close to him. Yet, even Wayne was little more than a pawn to Alpo in his narcissistic game of self-preservation. Wayne appeared quite loyal to Po.

Tyrone LaSalle Price and Michael Anthony Jackson were D.C. dudes indicted on charges of killing nine people as part of a continuing campaign to protect and promote their drug organization from 1989 to 1991. The indictment contended that Perry was involved in eight of the drug gang's nine alleged homicides. Three of the victims were women; two believed to be cooperating with authorities investigating the organization while the other was Wayne Perry's child's mother. He was told by Michael Jackson that she was at Fray's funeral supposedly running her mouth, telling individuals that Wayne was the person who had killed Fray. Fray was a significant figure in D.C.'s drug landscape. Unbeknownst to Wayne, it was Michael Jackson himself who had actually committed the killing, leaving people to believe that Wayne had done it.

I spoke to Wayne. He was fresh out of ADX and a little guarded in his conversation, but appreciative for the platform *Don Diva* provides for individuals like himself to be heard. We both acknowledged that while we never personally met, we were certain our paths had to have crossed, and that we had mutual respect. In Wayne's own words, "As far as the Fray thing, I'm going to tell you about it. I wouldn't if it could get someone in trouble, but the rat already told it. Alpo set the whole thing up to look like I had murdered Fray," said Wayne, "Yes, I was after Fray because I had heard he had put out a hit on me. Alpo was scared of Fray, but I wasn't, and Alpo felt OK as long as he had me. Fray stated he had to get me out of the way so he could extort Alpo. I ended up finding out about the hit on me, and I got at those in Fray's crew who took the hit and let him know that he, Fray, was next. But I couldn't track him down. Alpo set it up with a dude who was my man as well as good friends with Fray. The dude who hit Fray then went and told all Fray's people that I did it, because he was close to me, too. The dude (Alpo) is a snake. All the time he (Alpo) was the one who had it done. One of my kids' mothers heard the whole lie about me killing Fray at Fray's funeral, where all the Michael Jackson and the dudes that got Fray were saying that I did it. At the time, I don't know all this and Michael Jackson, who did it, was my man. I didn't learn he did it until we got locked up. The dude knew my daughter's mother heard him at Fray's funeral, so he hurried up and came to me and tells me she was at the funeral telling people that I killed Fray. He knew I would believe him and ask no questions (and) just do what I do best, which I did. And that's my only regret. May she rest in peace. If I would have let her talk, she would have told me the truth. But I wouldn't have listened because I stand for loyalty, and my loyalty was with that dude, Alpo. That was my man, but he was a snake."

Over the years, *Don Diva* has done stories on the Lynch Mob as well as Wayne Perry. I'm friends with Lou Simms and Farris Phillips of the Lynch Mob and have spoken to Wayne Perry. They are the ones who have taken their punishment and are paying their debt to society, accepting responsibility for their actions. The ones who rolled over on them were once the ones who gave the orders and sent them out to do these deeds. Those people have dishonored themselves, and I have no interest in hearing what they have to say. Others are willing to hear their explanations and excuses for their betrayals of those they once lead.

What I do know is that historically, many of these so-called murderers and tough guys, whether in urban culture or even organized crime, end up telling on underlings and associates to save themselves. No matter what side of the fence you stand on, there can be no arguing in honor of those that essentially claim no responsibility for their choices.

Disclaimer: By honor, I specifically mean for those participating in this subculture and who live this Life. There are two understood value systems for those in the Life and that of those civilians outside of it. The mentalities are a stark difference from one another. Things that people did within the Game were acceptable to those who played, from law enforcement to our rivals. Never snitching, having a code of silence, and the violence that came along with this lifestyle was entirely different versus the expectations of civilians outside the scope of that lifestyle.

One thing that the streets and life, in general, has taught me: we ALL have a dark side. That fact by itself doesn't make us all bad. The continued long-term choices we make, for one reason or another, dictate what side of the darkness spectrum we ultimately fall on.

14

DOWN BUT NOT OUT

It would be an understatement to say that my mother's murder hit my whole family hard. She was close to her sisters, brother, Reika, and essentially everyone who she came in contact with. Her death was particularly impactful on my father and brother. My brother was at the end of his basketball season and just two months from graduating from college. I know it was difficult for him to even finish out the school year.

I dealt with her death in part by just not directly dealing with it on an emotional level. I refused to own it. I didn't know what else to do but stay busy trying to keep my mind off the reality. What I did do was look for her killers every waking moment, caring about little else besides vengeance.

I'm not sure how much my mother knew about my hustling or to what extent I had committed to the *Life*. I know, in a general sense, she was aware of what I was doing. I am pretty sure she didn't approve of it, but in all truthfulness, there was little she or anyone could have done to stop me. I was so confident in my hustle that my disposition screamed I was in total control and had it all figured out. I appeared safe and able to take care of myself and everything else for that matter. I had been making way for myself for so long I honestly believed my actions had just become understood and accepted.

I never wanted her to ever worry about me. I didn't want her to wear my stress or give her any. No matter how much I may have tried, I am sure she wore some of it, regardless of my outward performances, simply because she was a mother. I allowed myself to wonder if burying her wasn't somehow better. I'm not certain what her life would have been like if she would have buried me instead. She was so fragile in that regard to me. I wonder if she would have been able to move on. When you're searching for answers to the unimaginable, reaching becomes part of the process.

The dynamics between my crew and me was initially awkward because no one knew how to approach me or what to say. My life and world were upside down, but for them, things needed to find some order still. They all felt my pain and my enormous loss, but in a strange way, they were caught up in my madness. Things couldn't move forward for them without me because of the dynamic between us, with me being their source. At some point, I was confronted with that reality and attempted to get them back into position. I understood they had families to take care of besides being the ones holding me down and declaring vengeance with me in finding the cowards who had violated my family and me. I made attempts to get my head, somewhat, back into the game and back to business. Even in my greatest moments of despair and turmoil, I could never lose sight of the responsibilities that I had undertaken for so many.

Around this time, my situation in D.C. was fading due to all the turns of events, as well as personal and alliance changes. Business moving forward was less about making money just to make money as much as it was about ensuring I continued to take care of all of those I felt were dependent on me, both family and crew. Business also began serving as a distraction from my reality. Above all, I took on the extreme roll of protecting everyone I was close to. Life had become so much more precious. I refused to lose anyone else on my watch in this manner.

I was deep into reflection, trying to figure out how I'd gotten to this place in my life. What did I do wrong? What signs did I miss? What could I have done differently?

Though I am the firstborn, my brother, Tony, is named after my father. The fact that my brother is a junior could almost imply favoritism, but as an adult, I can see the irony because, in so many ways, they really are so similar. Somehow, it actually ended up making much more sense for my brother to end up as the junior. I believe I was named after an uncle on my mother's side. I never met the man and never really understood the significance or impact he had for me to be named after him.

My mother completed my father and my brother, and I know neither of them has ever fully recovered from her death. Hell, I have never recovered. My father was completely co-dependent on her, and even to this day, when anyone shows care for him, he will tell them they remind him of my mother. To a lesser extent, my brother shared a dependency on our mother, as well. I had always been a little more independent, perhaps because I was possibly more in-tune with her emotions and issues. Perhaps, because I was more cognizant of the stress she dealt with, I tried to be less of a burden to her.

I learned a lot from my father, and in many ways, those lessons were learned by default. I saw some of his actions and mistakes and used them as guides in what not to do or be. As a result, he caused me to be a better parent. We didn't have a healthy relationship when I was a kid by any stretch of the imagination. I nicknamed my father Mad Dog. He was being called this behind his back by me and my brother.

My brother and I sort of just stayed out of his way. He was like the bad, even angrier, James Evans from the classic television series of the '70s and in part, because of this, our family was short on "good times."

It was only when he started hustling and getting money that his disposition got better. I could gather that he began dabbling when I was in 11th or 12th grade. I was barely around the house during my latter years of high school. I didn't have to deal with him, so his problems didn't concern me as much. It's odd-looking back in that he never addressed, in any real way, what I was doing. I am talking about from my simple hustling to when I got really big. He just never addressed it.

Mad Dog clearly knew what I was doing at that point, and I had a good idea about what he was doing. Then, one day I randomly approached him and laid out what I was doing and offered that I might be able to help him. We talked a little, and it revealed what he was paying. I was able to give it to him much cheaper.

Even after we started doing business, when we saw each other, we just avoided any real subject matter. Our conversations were just sort of surface level and generic. It was almost like being introduced to the man for the first time, and because I was able to do something for him, the dynamics and control were gone as well as any fear or intimidation. We were even, if not more so, in my favor.

When my mother passed, my father was down South. He got the news and flew back the next morning. He and I had one of our most real and most difficult conversations we had ever had. The news was emotionally unfathomable to digest.

You choose to live your life a little different when something so tragic and violent occurs. Unfortunately, you can't change life with hindsight, so I put an emphasis on opening my third eye and developing even more foresight, especially as a means of protecting those that I loved. My brother was always the wildcard in this situation.

We are only fourteen months apart, but even as kids, I was tasked with the responsibility of having to look after my brother. At first, it was almost a burden to have to bring him everywhere with me. I was always moving fast and, who knows, my mother may have even looked at it as a strategy to hinder my antics. However, regardless of how it started, looking after him soon became the fabric of our dynamic.

I was the big brother — the protector. Just in the way I tried to address the stresses, my mother went through with my early hustles, my brother also received the benefits of not having to worry about not having. If I made some money, he had. I always made sure he had money to get food or gear. He didn't have to stress my parents by asking for things they might not have comfortably had to give. When my hustles increased, if I got a name chain and ring, his wasn't too far behind. However, he didn't have to hustle. My efforts allowed my brother to stay on the more natural course of being a kid and teen minus the distractions and deviations that come with trying to get money and taking on responsibility at an early age.

I may have naturally been the more talented basketball player amongst us, but when I traded my hoop dreams for bigger street dreams, consciously or unconsciously, it created an easier path for my brother to pursue his. He was able to focus solely on school and ball, which helped get him a scholarship to a prominent academic and basketball school like All Hallows. That uninterrupted focus then leads to college scholarships and a chance to play ball at an Ivy League school. My calling was hustling, while basketball may have been my brother's. He has been a college basketball coach for about 20 years. He not only never had to do street shit to survive or thrive, I made sure that was not part of his life, even as he was able to enjoy many of the spoils during the time.

Everyone who knew me and what I was doing also knew he was a civilian and not a part of any of my activities. However, my brother was in college in Manhattan. Columbia's campus is only blocks from the heart of Harlem, and he was always around.

Columbia University's extended campus, located between 110th and 120th Streets from Morningside Drive to Riverside Park, was one of New York City's safest areas, despite its proximity to a world-traveling so much faster and grimier than anything the shielded students would ever be exposed to. However, I still remember getting a page from my brother one Friday or Saturday evening. I could hear the concern in his voice when I returned the call. He was at a campus party, and a few guys he didn't recognize as students had been sizing him up. My brother never wore any jewelry on campus, so he wasn't sure why these particular guys seemed to be looking at him in that way.

I don't remember exactly where I was when I got the call, but I was there with the speed and quickness, the mob in tow, at the university's gates on 116th and Amsterdam. The guard stationed there was little match as we rushed through. He was less than a block away, at Hamilton Hall, and as the two guys saw us approaching, they fled. We caught up with them and gave them an old-fashioned ass-whooping. It was a true Bronx bombing accompanied with Louisville Sluggers.

On another occasion, my brother was on the Harlem side of Morningside Park with a young lady he had dated and known for years. Her ex somehow came upon them sitting in the park, taking issue with my brother and her conversing. The guy brandished a weapon and threatened him. One of the apartments I kept was literally on the other side of Columbia's campus across from the park. My brother came back to the apartment and told me the story. By the time I could come out and deal with it, the dude had taken off. I'm reasonably sure that neither of these incidents had anything to do with me. What I do know is that my brother was a potential target of sorts, in part, because of me. I could be reactionary in protecting him, but unlike Reika or my kids, I couldn't put the same restrictions on his life and movements. My brother was well-liked and known throughout Harlem. Nearly everyone that knew me knew him. This gave me some degree of comfort to know that others would look out for him as well. Yet, I also knew he was exposed in ways I could never fully protect or guard against.

***

The crack epidemic was dominating the news, and I recall a newspaper report that talked about the effects of relatively new legislation that was enacted in or around 1987, in what would become known as the "Crack Laws." It took a few years for those laws to take on any significance in our lives, but with the formation of multiple agency drug task forces, we finally began to be impacted by the overreaching harshness of the new laws. Possession or conspiracy to sell crack cocaine was now dealt with much harsher mandatory minimum sentences than for powder cocaine, even in large quantities. This was clearly targeting my demographic, and we were all forced to take notice as it was beginning to affect nearly everyone in the Game.

In part, because of the expanding laws, we avoided openly being a part of large, visible crews and taking the clichéd pictures together with our money or guns. We adjusted as laws changed or upon hearing about busts in the news. The RICO (Racketeer Influenced and Corrupt Organizations) Act began to be used to dismantle street crews. All we knew about the RICO Act was that the government used it to take down the Mafia, and conspiracy charges were hard as hell to fight under the vague connections that the RICO Act allowed to establish criminality and criminal enterprises.

Our mindsets didn't change as much as they should have, but we made adjustments and relationships changed in part because of this. My relationships in the streets never changed because of beef or money issues. They changed organically or just occurred because guys were going in different directions. You didn't need to be Nostradamus to see some futures, and I knew I didn't need to stand next to someone who was going in a wrong direction or one substantially different from where I thought I was headed.

Relationships continued to be redefined everywhere as much by default because of all the losses, guys going to jail, and casualties suffered in the Game. One of those evolved relationships included the one I had with Rich Porter.

I considered him more than a street associate, and over the years, we'd become good friends. We communicated regularly. We'd beep and call one another, making it a point just to chop it up and talk shop. Rich and I got close. I always dug his style, and up until then, we had never done any business but were super cool. During one of our casual conversations, he was complaining to me how he constantly had to carry most of his crew. Parts of his crew included Alpo and Black Jus from Queens. Rich was doing consignment with them on the joints, and he stated between those two alone, he had minimally 30/40 keys out on consignment at any given time. He complained that if he wasn't in pocket with the joints, he had to chase them down to get his money. Basically, as long as he had work, they were good, but the minute the connect had him on hold, getting his money from them was an issue. This basically meant a large part of his money was always in the street.

He told me he was trying to make a move and re-up, but he was short. He said that if I gave him the money, he needed I would, of course, get what I paid for but also have access to more if needed. I didn't actually need Rich to make this type of move, but in pooling our money, it kept the prices sweet, so it was not as if it was a bad move for me, and I got the additional benefit of the goodwill in helping him.

Rich and I started doing this on those occasions with the loads. I would move my end and still cop from my regular connects when needed. His price might have been about $500 better than what I was paying for a joint. That made sense when you're talking 40 or 50 joints. Those big loads may have only happened a few times a year, so I stayed with the different connects I had to maintain my steady flow. There was never one endless connect. Sometimes one connect was rocking when another wasn't and vice versa. In some instances, everyone was on at one time. There was no predicting it all, but that's just how it went.

On December 5, 1989, I was downtown shopping in the Fashion District for BOSS Sneakers, which also sold clothes. I remember getting a 911 page with Rich's code. I returned the page, and he informed me that something had happened to his little brother, Donnell. Rich told me he had not returned home from school and someone called him saying they had him. His mom and little brother lived on 132nd Street between 7th and Lenox Avenues. I had lots of dudes I fooled with on 131st Street between 7th and 8th Avenues in St. Nicholas Projects, so I met him on 131st Street, and he started telling me what he knew.

I knew Donnell well. He was a part of a clique of kids, Chris, Paul, and Ears, who played on one of my teams and frequently came by the store. I would hit them all off with a couple of dollars and sneakers whenever they came around, which happened to be often.

While together, Rich received a page from the kidnappers. When he returned the page, he had me listen in on the payphone and asked if I recognized the voice. The Hispanic accent didn't sound familiar as they demanded around a half a million for the safe return of Donnell. Most of the communication had been happening from his mother's house. So, I suggested he try my caller ID. Caller ID was a new technology. Rich never even heard of it. I explained how it worked and what could come from it. I had contacts in the police station that meant I could usually get a name and/or address with a license plate number or phone number.

I called Reika to bring me the caller ID box from my house in New Jersey. She came immediately and met me at the George Washington Bridge. Rich and I then went to his mother's house and hooked it up to his mom's phone. The technology was relatively new, and because the feature was not yet available throughout the region, the caller ID didn't work on their phone line in New York.

Rich had no intention of involving the police because doing so would only incriminate him and make matters worse. It just wasn't our way. We were drug dealers committing crimes and avoided contact with the police at all cost. It went further in that we had little-to-no respect for the police. We especially didn't believe they would actually help us. I sensed that my mother's situation was part of why Rich confided in me. He knew I understood his plight. I told him he was being given a chance to resolve his situation that I wasn't afforded and how I wished that I had the opportunity he was presented with to have Donnell returned. We then discussed various ways of paying the ransom.

The first few days of Donnell's kidnapping were frantic, but the main issue for Rich was collecting money that was owed to him in the streets. His guys, including Alpo, owed him well over half a million dollars collectively. The other issue was the logistics of getting them the money and being sure that Donnell was not only alive but would be returned unharmed.

Azie's situation then my mother's let everyone know these individuals didn't play fair or by any rules. Here was a kid being kidnapped. They didn't go after Rich or me directly but family members. If Donnell could ID the kidnappers, would they let him go? I knew Rich loved his brother and was trying to do anything and everything to have him returned safely, but we also knew the kinds of dudes that had Donnell weren't honorable and couldn't be taken at their word.

I was with Rich during most of that initial 24 hours, trying to strategize how to bring his brother back safely. All these contemplated options became even more complicated when the next day, on December 6th, the kidnappers called Rich and told him to check the bathroom of the 125th Street McDonald's. He found a finger and an audio cassette taped under the bathroom sink. The cassette contained Donnell's voice pleading for Rich's mom to give them the money saying he was hurt, needed help, and wanted to come home. The finger could also be identified as Donnell's because it included the name ring he wore.

The tape and finger were game-changers. Rich now definitely knew he was dealing with people that most likely would further harm Donnell.

His family heard the tape, and it caused his sister to reach out to the police. Shortly after, it might have made the news. Though the NYPD was contacted and immediately looked at this as a drug-related situation, all kidnappings are under the ultimate jurisdiction of the FBI, and they took the lead. Rich still attempted to deal with the situation directly, but the news of the police involvement spread to the kidnappers because they abruptly ceased all contact with Rich and his family.

I say spread to the kidnappers, because unbeknownst to everyone, Rich's uncle, Apple, was part of the kidnapping scheme. He was Rich's mother's brother and around the home when much of the planning and conversations were had about Donnell's return. He and his co-conspirators had not planned on Rich ever going to law enforcement, and when his sister did, it seemed to spook them enough that they effectively ceased all communication, especially now knowing the feds were on the case.

During all of this, Chris came home at the end of December. I was extremely conflicted. The joy in having my best friend return home from a four-year bid was muted with having another close friend dealing with something so horrific that was still ongoing. Chris didn't know Rich, but celebrating his return just wasn't something I could do with another friend immersed in so much pain.

Even with no communication from the kidnappers, and the FBI involved Rich, and I never stopped strategizing on getting Donnell back. I could see the pain in his eyes and the stress of the situation was probably wearing him down. He never gave up hope, but as each day passed, there was a greater reality of Donnell not returning. This was something Rich couldn't come to terms with even as they had not heard from the kidnappers since December 10th.

I spoke to Rich on January 4th, the day he got killed. This was nearly a month after Donnell had been abducted. He said he was going to meet Alpo, who was coming in from D.C. that night because he owed him like $300-$400k from fronted work. I didn't initially think Alpo had anything to do with Rich's death because Rich never told me they had any kind of real beef.

Rich's body was dumped not too far from Orchard Beach in the Bronx. A few weeks after Rich's death, Donnell's body was found in fields nearby on January 28th. His killers knew there was no chance of ever receiving any money after Rich's death, and now knowing that the uncle was involved, it seems clearer that Donnell had little chance of ever being returned home safely since he could identify one or more of his captors. The dumping of his body near where Rich was found was an obvious attempt by the kidnappers to try and tie Donnell's murder to whoever killed Rich.

My memory of all the details are somewhat fuzzy, but I do remember going to the florist and ordering a custom arrangement that said, "King Of New York, Rich Porter, rest in peace." There was plenty of discussion and concern about us believing that there was going to be a huge uniformed and undercover police presence at the funeral. We expected they'd be in the cut taking pictures

I remember me and a couple of my guys went. We parked a few blocks from the funeral home and walked. Honestly, if we wanted to park closer, it wouldn't have been possible. Rich was a beloved dude. As you can imagine, it felt like the whole of Harlem was there and truthfully, I believe it was. I wasn't trying to overly engage, avoiding the exposure due to the obvious reasons. I just wanted to pay my respects. I wasn't there long, just long enough to do exactly that.

Since Rich had paged me the night he died, my number was one of the last that appeared on his beeper, so it really shouldn't have surprised me when shortly after his death, I received a beep from the feds. I returned the call from a payphone in the bar next door to BOSS Sneakers on 125th Street called Spot Light. They identified themselves as FBI, and I immediately hung up. The very next day, two of them walked into the store. They walked right over to me, identified themselves and asked if they could have a word with me. There were several of us in the store, a couple of workers and a few of my guys, so I told them sure, go ahead. They said they were investigating the kidnapping of Rich's brother Donnell, who hadn't been found at that point, leaving it as an active kidnapping case.

They wanted to talk outside of the store and asked if I would come to the 24th Precinct on 135th Street between 8th & 7th Avenues to meet with them. This was an interesting dilemma I was being faced with. It was clear they weren't arresting me, but it also seemed clear that I didn't have much choice in not meeting with them about a kidnapping. They went on to say I could bring someone along since they just had a few questions for me. I reluctantly went with Breeze, only after I considered my options and decided it was in my best interest to go. I also considered that they stated that they weren't interested in my drug dealings and that they were quite familiar with who I was, but only cared about the kidnapping of Donnell Porter.

I had no information to offer them because I honestly had no idea who had kidnapped him. They left, giving me their card and saying to ask for them when I got there. Breeze and I jumped in the car and headed to the precinct a short time after they left the store. We mostly listened to their scenarios, very rarely speaking and not having anything to offer. Somehow, that brief conversation segued into them asking if I knew the specific details related to my mother's death. I only volunteered that I had an idea who did it as they handed me a folder with some information on her case, including the alleged suspects. I saw nothing I didn't already know.

There was some civility in the short convo and even a degree of mutual respect, like the De Niro vs. Pacino scene in "Heat." That respect was evidenced as I was leaving when one of the agents casually and cryptically told me I might want to stay out of D.C. He didn't elaborate any further, and I didn't need him to. Rayful Edmond had recently been busted and I knew D.C. had become hot as hell. We shook their hands, said thanks and left. No more information was given. None was needed. I had my stuff in D.C. packed up the next morning. I was already somewhat falling back from D.C. to a degree because of all the heat and violence that we had been dealing with recently. The fed's' statement just served as the last straw in knowing it was time to go.

The tip to stay out of D.C. probably kept me on the street four years longer. I will take my luck to another level and state that brief exchange might have spared me a life sentence from my being connected and indicted under the RICO statutes for my activities in D.C. Though I never set foot in D.C. again, I continued to service some of my crew. They, of course, did not make the abrupt stop that I did but as fate would have it, they all eventually came to the same conclusions about D.C. shortly after on their own. The tumultuousness and volatility eventually led to all my crew seeking greener and less treacherous pastures elsewhere. Ironically, Rich's death also indirectly brought me new D.C. business.

***

Alpo and I were always super cool, but up until then, we had never done any significant drug business. A few weeks after Rich got killed, he came to me to cop work. Before this, he was getting his work from Rich and before that Azie and others, I'm sure. We had just buried Rich, and even not knowing Alpo's role in his death, our world didn't make it seem callous that he would be looking for a new connect and to resume business after a tragedy. This applied to me as well. The game didn't stop for anyone or anything, and unless you were ready to get out, you understood, "The Game don't stop till your casket drops." It may not make any sense to many of you, but this was, in fact, our sad reality.

He had duffel bags of money for me, and while it may not have been an actual red flag, it did make me somewhat suspicious about his situation with Rich. From all the numerous conversations I had with Rich, I knew that paying upfront was not how Alpo normally moved.

***

Chris has always been someone I could count on and fully trust, so the least I could do was set him up with an apartment in New Jersey. I purchased a car for him and gave him some money. I had just recently hired someone to run BOSS Sneakers, but I put Chris in place to oversee the day to day operation of the store. He needed a legitimate job as a requirement of his probation. I was also trying to keep him out of the streets after his bid and hoped working in the store would keep him occupied. I wanted him to stay far away from drugs, and his being around and helping me at that moment was important.

The tragedies were piling up- first, Albe, my mother, Rich and then Donnell. Chris's return could not have occurred a moment too soon and neither could the addition of a baby girl. My daughter was born nearly a year to date after my mother's passing. My mother died on February 24, 1989, and Tiana was born on March 4, 1990, in Harlem Hospital, where Pop and Kevin had been born. She was named after my mother, Tiana Barbara Jean Carter. I had previously had all boys, and her birth helped me get through this time period because I saw some symbolism, her being my first and only daughter. I wasn't articulating or expressing any of my emotions during this time period, but Tiana's birth did contribute to a lot of reflection and introspection on both where my family life had started and what it had become.

Despite my best intentions, I was not able to keep Chris from wanting to get real money for too long. He had been away for four years and could see, similarly to when he got back from the Army, that I was so much bigger than when he had left. He wasn't content with just running BOSS Sneakers. So, within months, Chris was back hustling. He was initially still in the store as well, but hustling's appeal was winning over retail obligations. Yet, even once he returned, Chris's luck was soon put to the test.

Several months back home, Chris was by himself having just left the connect's house in Washington Heights. He was walking down the block, and some undercover police made eye contact with him. He was dirty, holding four keys, and still on supervised release, so he got in the car and pulled off to evade them. The undercover car busted a U and came following behind him. They eventually pulled him over. As soon as they got close to the car on foot, he burned out and pulled off. He was able to get a two-block lead before eventually seeing them closing in. Before they could get too close, still out of their direct line of vision, he threw the keys of cocaine out the window near the 155th Street Macombs Dam Bridge and continued towards the Bronx before he bailed out of the car. He got caught on foot in the Bronx. When he got caught, they questioned him as to why he ran since he didn't have anything on him. He claimed fear because of his probation. He was booked and went through the system. Ultimately, he ended up with a bunch of traffic tickets. Luckily, he didn't get violated for the offense of having had police contact... but someone ended up with over $100,000 in coke that was literally thrown onto the streets in 1990.

Run-ins with the police had become our norm. We dressed and acted the part and the police had no problem filling their stop and frisk quotas, no matter the occasion. Because of the continuous stops, we had all developed a "fuck the police" attitude. It was on full display during exchanges with the law. Anytime I got pulled over or was issued a ticket, we gave them the business. I understood they played a vital role in keeping order, but we viewed their overzealousness as totally unnecessary. I was an outlaw drug dealer, and that essentially made us naturally at odds if not enemies. It was a constant cat and mouse game, and though we may have been at the top of the hood's food chain, we were constantly on the defense with regards to law enforcement. We didn't necessarily fear street cops, but their presence could always make things uncomfortable.

One July night at the Apollo in 1990, H, Chris, and Mark pulled up in a Mazda MPV, as the show was letting out. As was the norm, H had a gun on him. He must have adjusted it in a somewhat conspicuous way because he got bum-rushed by the police that always maintained a strong presence during Apollo shows. He was searched and arrested. There are probably thousands of guys that caught gun possession charges during this time based on the police claiming probable cause for the search based on a "visible bulge" or a defendant "noticeably adjusting a firearm on his person." It was a numbers game for the police. They filled in the alleged lawful probable cause later. H ended up being another statistic because he got caught. There were countless others who were victimized by unlawful search and seizures, but their stories went unheard because they were completely innocent.

Because of H's two prior New Jersey cases, we were concerned he would not be able to get bail on this new case. However, lady luck was still riding with him, and I was able, after arraignment, to bail him out on a $3,000 cash bail. It seemed that New York and New Jersey were still not in sync enough to tie him to the earlier cases. While he served six months on the New York gun possession case, which was the mandatory minimum at the time, his Jersey situation never came to light. The trial

THE CRACK ERA

in NJ for the seven keys was going on while H was incarcerated in NY, and H wasn't going to volunteer where he was to New Jersey.

Everyone but H attended the trial for the case, and despite having private attorneys, everyone was convicted. H, of course, was convicted in absentia. I am unsure if H would have even attended this particular trial under a fake name, considering that he was sure they would have probably linked him to the other case, under his real name, he was still on the run for. Though it became evident at trial they still hadn't linked the two New Jersey cases with him absent, H had another more compelling reason for his absence from trial.

Even after Breeze, Walt, and Karen were found guilty. I was able to bail them out on appeal bond pending sentencing. They all then skipped out on the case. Everyone still got their convictions reaffirmed in their absences, with all of them getting fifteen years with a mandatory five required before the possibility of parole.

Karen was picked up first, years later, on a credit card case and did at least five years related to that Jersey case. Breeze and Walt got picked up afterward on separate matters and began doing time on the case. A year or two into those bids, they both got some relief from that sentence as the case was overturned related to larger I-95 profiling allegations against the police along that route that brought into question the legal probable cause for subsequent searches and seizures including the one Breeze and the others was part of.

***

Around this time, my uncle Fatman and Aunt Diane's relationship had run its course, and they got divorced. I had first started out mimicking my uncle. He was a mentor in so many ways, and while he was still hustling, I had outgrown Kid's stature in the streets. We were still tight and occasionally did some coke business, but the heroin business had died down as the landscape had changed so drastically in New York. It was the nature of the times and coke, and crack dominated over heroin use.

My uncle and I still maintained a good relationship, but of course, I was torn to a degree. My Aunt Diane was going through a tough time at home in addition to still coping with her sister's death. It was never something consciously said or done, but I just wanted to take care of my closest family in ways I knew I never could continue to do for my mother.

I was just shy of turning 24-years-old when I began looking for a new house in September of 1990 to accommodate my growing stature and, most importantly, my family. My aunt was used to the finer things in life, and she'd always looked out for me. I couldn't stand to see her going through her adjustments and having her as part of the process factored into my house search.

I initially had an African American realtor showing me properties, but her searches were limited to mostly segregated minority neighborhoods. I was a little offended at the stereotyped restrictions she was placing on me and my search. Perhaps those areas were the extent of her knowledge or comfort zone, but the limitation did not work for me, so I decided to use another realtor. I just randomly walked into another realtor's office. I was accompanied by Jeff. Jeff had become my go-to whenever I need to be accompanied by someone with a little more polish.

When I met Jeff some years earlier, he was working and doing whatever to make a buck legally. He reminded me of the Christopher Williams character from *New Jack City*. He was knowledgeable of the comings and goings-on in the hood. We had an apartment where the Rutledge Brothers were from in the 430 building of the Grant Houses on 125th street between Morningside and Amsterdam Avenues. Jeff was six to seven years older than me and lived in the building. He was somewhat of a heavy-set guy, very smart, and extremely resourceful. He was one of the few college-educated guys I knew. He was more refined, often wearing slacks, dress shirts and ties, which was different from any of the guys I was around regularly.

A gift I always had was understanding the mutual value in what people offered me and what I was able to offer in return. Everyone I knew had a different role or characteristic, and my team was unintentionally built on these principles. Jeff became an integral part of the organization. He started out driving and making runs because he didn't fit the profile of the usual suspect stereotyped and pulled over.

Later, on his own, he got involved in the credit card hustle game, and that lent to a lot of stuff we were doing. We could get a lot of things from him from clothes to plane tickets to whatever. Instead of spending $20k I could spend $10k with Jeff. He was personable, reliable and resourceful. He was well-spoken, and his disposition lent to his being able to navigate many situations the rest of us either could not or were less comfortable trying.

A good-natured, in-house joke was that Jeff was a big trick with the credit card game. He had the appearance of a drug dealer balling out of control, but that was the furthest thing from the truth. His fronts were exactly what they needed to be for the results he desired. Jeff may not have owned a car of his own but had access to all of mine and most of the crew's, because of the trade-offs and favors he was able to supply with his credit card access.

The new realtor was an older Caucasian woman. I have no idea what she initially made of Jeff and I, but after a brief conversation, she showed me a book (pre-Internet) with MLS listings, pictures, and descriptions. She did not automatically steer me in any particular direction and showed me a wide range of areas throughout Bergen County, New Jersey.

I was drawn to the houses she showed me in the Franklin Lakes area. They were like nothing I had ever seen before. Franklin Lakes was a very affluent neighborhood and home to many NFL and NBA players, as well as an enclave for corporate executives. It was a place filled with mansions on majestic lots. I knew Franklin Lakes would be perfect to raise my kids and keep my family safe. The realtor showed me several properties, all of which I liked, but it was a particular property that caught my attention. It was bank-owned, and she explained the foreclosure process, adding that it might be a great opportunity to get a deal. I always loved the art of the deal, and the idea of a mansion at a steal appealed to the hustler in me. I immediately knew it was the one.

The 8,000 square foot home had seven bedrooms with two master suites. The home was originally priced at $1.2 million before being reduced to $900k and then $850k. I got the bank to agree to a $700k sales price. My realtor put me with a mortgage broker. She had a relationship who claimed he could do a no income verification loan. I put down $400k. I could pay for the home in cash, but the money needed to come from bank accounts that were able to show its legitimacy. I had a childhood friend John Morton, who played in the NBA, write me a check for part of the money as a loan. The proceeds from the sale of my house in Hillsdale, which was probably close to debt-free, served as the most significant portion of my down payment. Though the mortgage broker sought a no income verification loan, I made the process even easier with the numerous legitimate businesses I owned which were doing relatively well and had money in their respective accounts.

I closed on the house sometime in November of 1990 and moved my immediate family of Reika and our three kids along with Aunt Diane, her two kids Nechelle and Lamont (both in their teens), Aunt Betty, and Darnell who was 15, and my brother, who occasionally stayed. The two master suites were on opposite ends of the house. Reika and I were on the right. I gave my Aunt Diane the other master.

I can't lie, the crib was straight out of an episode of *Lifestyles Of The Rich and Famous*. I didn't personally know anyone, definitely none of my peers, who were living in anything comparable to this. Thirty-foot vaulted ceilings, a huge chandelier was hanging in the entryway, a large sitting area, floor to ceiling windows with views of the backyard and porch, and a wet bar in the foyer, fireplaces in both master suites as well as the foyer. I went all out, and the house was fully laced with nothing but high-end furnishings, special ordered down to the carpets and hardwood flooring, all custom designed.

A left took you into the chef's kitchen and family room. There was a beauty parlor downstairs, and the basement had butler and maid suites. There were always minimally six cars in the driveway. My Aunt Diane had a BMW, Reika had a BMW station wagon, my brother had a 5 series BMW, and I had a Lexus and Tahoe.

I was still moving fast and hardly at home, but the Franklin Lakes residence provided a substantial peace of mind regarding my family's happiness, and well-being, and that fact alone was worth every penny spent on the crib. The house did not make me hustle harder, but everything after my mother's death made me start to think about hustling different.

As much as I loved the house in Franklin Lakes and what it meant for my family, I don't remember sitting back and enjoying it. I had made it a sanctuary for my family and built a full basketball court with fiberglass backboards. The kids had all the toys, dirt bikes, and actual arcade-sized games, but I was still living that lifestyle, and unfortunately, relaxing at home with my family was still not something I was able to do as much as I desired. I could never turn my life off, and the stresses and pressures of my life never allowed me to sit still long enough just to sit back and fully chill.

***

While home was good, it was not immune to the challenges from my life in the streets. The problems that come from getting fast money weren't just limited to the streets. I had my fair share of beautiful women, and while it was my unrepentant vice that everyone was aware of, it still does not mean that I was immune to dealing with the feelings of a strong woman who may have felt slighted.

Reika had probably run up on me a dozen times doing some BS with other women. The "honest asshole" was part of my shtick. Monogamy was just not something that I was coming to terms with or honestly considering. I lived on some "take it or leave it" shit. MOB (Money Over Broads), hell it was My Hustling Brothers Over Everything, and I was the poster child. I was entrenched in the streets, and with my homies, I risked my life and liberty with them, and the lifestyle was where I was consumed. We probably didn't have healthy enough relationships with the women in our lives to place the proper value on those relationships. I could count on my guys, and the perils that bound us were far deeper than relationships we had with our women and even some family members.

One time while I was out of town, I checked in on the crib, and it was clear Reika was upset about something. I told her I wasn't going to fuss with her and get thrown off my game while I was out there risking my life. A day or two passed, and when I didn't hear from her, I knew something wasn't right, but I didn't care enough to start arguing while away. Finally, after concluding my business, I called trying to reach her but was unable. I reached out to one of her girlfriends and, shortly after, finally reached her. She was on some bullshit, but I still didn't know the specific nature of her beef. She cryptically proclaimed, "If shit didn't matter to me, I would see when I returned." I wasn't sure exactly what she was talking about. My gut made me immediately call one of my younger cousins at the house and had him look in my closet. He couldn't see the disguised safe. I immediately called her, and she was like, "Now you want to talk?" I asked in a calm but stern voice if she had the safe and where it was.

The safe had to be approximately 200 pounds. She claimed to have gotten it out of the house by herself down the stairs on a comforter she dragged to the car, but there was no way. She had to get help to get that safe out of the house. When I got back to the airport in the city, I let her know that if the safe wasn't back by the time I landed, we were going to have a different kind of problem. I had at least a couple hundred thousand in emergency money in there. The safe was returned to its proper place when I got back. Reika stayed doing crazy shit. This was just one of the many over-the-top stunts she pulled. One of her ways of getting my attention.

15

CAN'T STOP THE HUSTLE

My overhead for bails, lawyers, and funerals were astronomical, and it became increasingly clear that my life was in shambles, and my business model was flawed. The losses were multiplying well before I realized and took stock of them. I chalked up the huge bail and attorney fees to the cost of doing business. I had it, so I didn't initially pay attention to the mounting costs. The amounts wildly varied, but bails would range anywhere from $5,000 to more than $100 thousand. Most of this money I never got back because more than not, guys usually skipped out on those cases. My known motto was no man is ever left behind, and you can't put a price on freedom. If they never received bail, they all needed lawyers, and I never got back any of those ridiculously costly retainers and charges.

Yet, later, I realized that not counting my own personal legal fees, I had spent millions (plural) on lost bails and attorney fees as well as subsequent appeal expenses. The structured organization of running a crew and being entrenched in a city made me plenty of money, but it was eventually totally replaced by my acting solely as a wholesale supplier. Besides reigning in many of the crazy expenses that come with heading a crew, the move to exclusively wholesale was also made to limit my accessibility and liability. I was supplying as far north as Boston and as far south as Atlanta. The only major city I managed to avoid in-between was Philly.

The times were changing, and I was changing with them. I was the head of a huge crew, and crews were getting busted. So, as individuals within my crew were being incarcerated for miscellaneous things, it ultimately forced me to change my business model and re-evaluate the need even to have such a noticeable presence. Heading a large crew represented a probability of having to answer for the actions of so many others directly and indirectly linked to me. I didn't stop hustling, but I wasn't going to allow my downfall to come solely at the hands of others' actions.

While I knew I needed to change, part of the change also took place organically as my crew grew and expanded into roles that I had once occupied in other states. As the fight for D.C. realty grew more strained and problematic, me and my guys branched out along with their crews as wholesalers in other places. I might have stayed as their main connect, but they oversaw the situations as I had once done on a day-to-day basis. The Rutledges had people in Richmond, Virginia, and John made that move first. Mark, Chris, and I also wound up in Norfolk and Virginia Beach. Robby was from our neighborhood in the Bronx, and he had relationships with some dudes named Terry and Lou, who had the town on lock. In the way Albe had introduced me to D.C., Robby made the intro. Truthfully, it was a move that he was unable to handle on his own, so Mark, Chris, and me just took it over from there. Terry and Lou had the demand that needed our supplying capabilities and infrastructure, and that was simply out of Robby's reach, so he made points. It was not as wide open as D.C. had been and knowing two key players made it easy. From there, they fed the town. Its proximity to D.C. also made it the most sensical move in many of the guys' progression.

I also looked at my legitimate businesses completely different. I initially did them just because it came easy to me, but now there was a greater sense to make them more successful because I knew if I didn't make a transition, it was going to be made for me. Selling drugs, for me, was a means to an end. I was still going out of town, but far less aggressively, so I was in NYC more often, and my efforts to engage in my legit businesses became my norm.

In 1990, we moved BOSS Sneakers from the corner of 125th Street and 8th Avenue to directly on 125th between 8th & 7th Avenues. The location was a couple of stores down from the world-famous Apollo Theater on the most prominent block in all of Harlem, and the space was easily four to five times larger than the original store. This move embodied my commitment and a step in the direction of ultimately becoming 100% legit.

When I opened the new store, I was still hustling, despite everything that had happened. Although it hadn't always been good to me, sometimes even tragic, it was in my blood. There still wasn't a close second to the feeling that hustling gave me. I also continued, in part, because I wasn't quite where I needed to be financially to retire and live comfortably on forever. I probably didn't have a clear idea of what that number was or should have been, but I just assumed I was not there. The reality is that number moves and changes as your lifestyle grows.

I renamed the store BOSS Emporium. The not-so-subtle name was the first but not sole element that made the store stand out. I stand corrected, the name Emporium came at the suggestion of one of my employees, Maurice Mann. BOSS Sneakers already had been in place. He stated that adding Emporium would signify we were a large retail store selling a wide variety of goods.

***

I was introduced to Maurice by Breeze Rutledge. He was a gay man from the neighborhood, flamboyant more by his style of dressing than necessarily his mannerisms. He wore high-end designer fashions from his hats down to his socks and shoes. He was about 6'3" and slim, with a stature reminiscent of a flamingo. He was someone who had fashion industry relationships with ties to and familiarity with the inner workings of the business.

When he came to me, he laid out all the things I was doing wrong and what he could do to take the store to the next level. I heard him out and quickly understood and agreed with his ideas and perspectives and welcomed him to the team. I had no issue with Maurice's sexuality, but that was not the case for Chris, who was quite homophobic. Chris was hardly alone in feeling this way during the times.

Homosexuality and gangster culture mixed about as well as oil and water. Chris was like a disgruntled co-worker in Maurice's presence in the store. He never outwardly said anything, but it was clear he was uncomfortable around Maurice and some of his friends. Chris's discomfort was a constant source of jokes amongst us. However, he never let any homophobic issues interfere with any task at hand. He was reliable and solid like that. Chris's issues with Maurice eventually dissipated as he came to understand and appreciate Maurice's value to the store, and the two became cool after a while.

Maurice was probably slightly ahead of the gentrification curve that Harlem is still undergoing. Despite the urban blight that existed, he saw Harlem as special and deserving of a clothing venue outside of simple urban gear uptown. Maurice initially set out to rearrange the store, so it flowed, giving the look and feel of a downtown boutique. He emphasized and implemented giving a different shopping experience to our consumers. He designed the front windows with seasonal displays. He did the same throughout the store, creating displays with mannequins, racks and such.

Maurice introduced us to many designers and retailers I was not otherwise familiar with. He then walked us through the process of trying to acquire new brands by going to showrooms and attending trade shows all around New York, Las Vegas, and elsewhere along the West Coast.

Although my mother tried to hip me to the concept of credit, it wasn't easily afforded to me in my initial legitimate business endeavors. I wasn't given net 30-60 days to pay for retail inventory, as most businesses get to float their inventory purchases. Instead, all of my inventory was always paid for with cash in advance. Add on to the store buildouts, and I was easily out of pocket for $200k plus for BOSS Emporium and its predecessor BOSS Sneakers.

One of the first things Maurice took on was trying to help us establish a credit line and rating through Dun & Bradstreet to do business with most of the higher-end brands because that's the way business on that level was done. He emphasized that we were not going to be able, with the high fashion brands, to just run up and make purchases with bags of money. Cash was normally king in my world, but the expansion of our store's fashions was going to require more finesse and planning. He let us know that appearances were everything when it came to be being recognized as a high-end fashion retailer. Whereas before I simply paid for anything I wanted, now we filled out credit applications detailing our store's square footage, location, and customer demographics. The retailer would then evaluate your application and decide if they wanted to allow you to carry their brands. Maurice walked their walk and talked their talk.

A bonus that came with dealing with Maurice was that he had a bunch of gay friends that happened to be some of the most notorious and prolific shoplifters in the city. They all wore nothing but exclusive, upscale fashions. Once they started coming into the store and felt accepted, they returned the love and quickly wanted us to be the flyest hustlers on the planet, and with their help, that's what we became. The fact that we were all comfortable in our masculinity and so accepting of the guys in an era and area where such acceptance was really hard to find helped us to gain new allies that minimally helped us stand out.

We had nothing but disposable income and were the perfect customers for them. Maurice and his crew acted as our personal stylist years before I had ever even heard the term. They boosted, in effect, to what they thought would specifically look good on us.

I cannot downplay what this did for the women we were dealing with both old and new. Maurice and his friends became their new best friends, dressing them in the latest designer fashions most of us couldn't even correctly pronounce. The new, gay best friends our women acquired alluded to having all the answers when it came to men and willingly hipped them to game. Between them and Jeff, with his credit cards, I literally could have several minks in my trunk at any given time. A new broad might get laced right away just because I had it like that. And the word of my generosity would always travel.

The actual design of BOSS Emporium was historic. I designed the store as an homage to the street's culture and the Game. I hired an architect along with carpenters and electricians, to bring my ideas to fruition. There was a mural painted on one full wall depicting 155th Street and Rucker Park. They positioned a fence in front, giving off the appearance of looking into the park. I had the floor painted black with two yellow parallel lines painted on it in the center accompanied by white lines at the top to create the street and crosswalk. Hanging directly above was a working traffic light that flashed from red to yellow to green. I had a sidewalk created representing the corner with a working payphone. I had monitors positioned on walls that played music videos and movies. The showstopper was the white 3 Series BMW convertible on display in the store right in the center tricked out with custom piping, seating, and rims with a spoiler kit, fog lights in the grill, and a wing on the trunk. Even when the store was closed, and you'd walk or drive by, it would be illuminated to show off the spectacle.

That was the Harlem way and vibe I'd come to live for, and no one did it on a sustained level as I did as a Boss. The who's who of our era patronized the store, including celebrities as well as street figures. Mike Tyson, Teddy Riley, LL Cool J came in regularly along with Tupac, Treach from Naughty by Nature, and countless others, too numerous to mention. Instead of posting taped pictures of these individuals to the brick facade walls, we let them tag the wall with their autographs graffiti style. It was all part of the marketing, and it worked, BOSS Emporium was the talk of Harlem.

I had created relationships out of town with different vendors, having initially been a customer. I did this to an extent with BOSS Sneakers, but with BOSS Emporium, I made these types of purchases on steroids. If something was hot in New York but not in other places, you could get that product better and easier out of town. Again, a D.C. store owner selling Sergio Tacchini, which wasn't popping in D.C. but was in NY, found it in his interest to do business with me. I would buy $40,000 to $50,000 worth of Sergio Tacchini from him and sell him the same in Fila apparel, which was super-hot in D.C. versus NYC.

There was a guy named Jeff Hamilton in LA that did custom leather jackets, including the one featured in *Martin*'s famous opening, that was one of a kind. I would buy wholesale from him and bring them back to NY. Before Karl Kani got big, my dude Lou Hobbs from Brooklyn introduced us, and I would do runs with Karl exclusively for BOSS Emporium early on before the brand was really introduced to the world. I clearly didn't need BOSS Emporium to be successful to live. However, the hustler in me needed to make it make sense. Unlike most, I never looked at the business as a front. I wanted all of my businesses to make a profit and gave it enough of my attention for it to do so. The branding and marketing that it provided was the icing on the cake.

Dapper Dan was located on 125th between 5th and Madison Avenues. It was a predecessor to BOSS Emporium to an extent because of the success he had in selling exclusives throughout NYC and beyond. Though, BOSS Emporium was much different. Dapper Dan's store had a feeling almost of an after-hours lounge more than a retail clothing store. A few big-time older hustlers hung out there, and there wasn't much off-the-rack merchandise available. Dapper Dan's niche was custom suits and jackets usually emblazoned with Gucci, Louis Vuitton and other luxury brand logos that cats would come in and order by design. I, along with my crew and most of the prominent hustlers of the time, supported Dap heavy. At some point, he was open 24 hours for orders. The infamous Mike Tyson and Mitch Green altercation, where the world heavyweight champ broke his hand on the jaw of a boxing contender, happened outside Dapper Dan at like 2 or 3 in the morning. That incident put a spotlight on the underground subculture and probably contributed to brands like Fendi and then US Attorney Sonia Sotomayor (current US Supreme Court Justice) initiating legal action that forced Dapper Dan to shut down in 1992. It took decades before Dap would rebound with a vengeance with a new store in Harlem on Lenox Avenue through a partnership with Gucci in 2018.

Similarly, with BOSS Sneakers before it, the irony is that I had so many guys that spent thousands at a time in places like BOSS Emporium, yet my friends weren't buying from me. That idea of their patronage was sound in principle but backfired. The only people that paid for anything were strangers. This isn't saying they didn't "shop" at the store, but they were mostly getting stuff on credit and leaving IOUs. The fact of the matter is the IOU's were in the tens of thousands, and none of them were getting paid. I guess they figured I had enough money already, and these items weren't going to hurt my bottom line. I still had to deal with the actual cost of the merchandise as well as my overhead and bills. They had to get paid by somebody, and that somebody was, of course, me.

Being able to do it and still wanting to do it are two different things. I was regularly carrying 30 to 40 people. These were the same guys going to Gucci, Louis Vuitton, Dapper Dan, and other luxury brands, throwing money down to pay with no haggling, but when it came to me, my dudes had deep pockets and short arms.

I could have forced the payments, but these were my friends, and the money didn't make or break me. I picked my battles with my friends, but it led to my frustrations, and it made the decision to eventually close the store easier. It was all part of getting a lower profile as well as lessening my stress.

BOSS Emporium was open from 1990 to 1994, and BOSS Sneakers preceded that from 1987 to 1990. Originally, we focused more on sneakers, and then we changed to almost exclusively clothes. BOSS Emporium closed, in part, because there was a huge rent increase on my store, and I couldn't make sense of it. I often wondered if the FBI had anything to do with the rent increase. I was being investigated, and I would later realize that they had a clandestine hand in a lot of things that went awry for me during that time.

***

During this time, my Aunt Diane and I purchased two laundromats in the Bronx on Laconia Avenue. One was adjacent to Edenwald Projects next to the 47th Police Precinct while the other was a few blocks south. I also opened a restaurant on the corner of the downtown side of 128th Street, at 321 Lenox Avenue. The restaurant came about by chance. A few years earlier, an older hustler had gone to jail and was a little uptight for money. He had the restaurant 80% complete but never opened, so I looked out for him and seized the opportunity. I knew nothing about restaurants other than ordering from the menu. My interest in opening it up was largely because of a woman named Gloria who worked in Lenox Lounge on 125th Street and Lenox Avenue. Gloria ran the restaurant, and she always took great care of us when we came in. We loved her food so much. I thought she would be perfect for my new spot. Getting such a good deal on the place that was near completion made sense, and I took the shot.

THE CRACK ERA

The whole situation and its potential to be profitable reminded me of Elise's restaurant in the Bronx. Elise's food spoke for itself. She was that figurative grandmother whose food we couldn't do without. It was a combination of soul and comfort food. She had a standard menu, but also customized plates for certain regulars. She ran a little restaurant on 163rd and Morris Ave on the east side of the Bronx. There wasn't anything special about the appearance of the place. It was a small, quaint place, and if you didn't know about it, you'd walk right past it and be none the wiser. I was originally introduced to it by my uncle when I was hanging out with him. The place was a known hangout for the older hustlers. I'm not certain what her connection was with them, but what I do know is that they all loved and supported her. It was one of those places that, no matter what it cost, all the hustlers left at least a $100 tip above the cost of the food.

Years later, this tradition carried over, and it was now a place the new school hustler from the Crack Era were patronizing. The relationship we developed with Elise was like the one we would later develop with Gloria. Some of her biggest customers were Billy Guy and his crew. He was introduced to the place as well by one of his elders. He and I would often meet there to kick it and grab something to eat. This all served as a perfect model to explain why I was so open to making the move to have a restaurant with someone like Gloria.

***

At this time, Hip-Hop as a business piqued my curiosity as well, so I started Boss Records along with a music management company called Take No Shorts Management. We signed local talents like Forbidden Fruit, King Sun, Okie Doke, and a kids' group called Uptown Kids. One of those kids later became a producer and rapper named Ron (Rondell) Browz. He was the producer for Big L's "Ebonics" and Nas' "Ether" and was a rapper on notable singles like "Pop Champagne" with Jim Jones and Juelz Santana, to name a few.

I began immersing myself in the music business and focused on it as I am prone to do. Many of the principals needed to succeed in the music business were similar to what it took to make it in the streets, particularly when it came to market the product. I am a hustler, and I could see the music business had the potential to be a lucrative hustle.

16

THE HITS KEEP COMING

The streets had changed; you could see and feel the difference. The Rooftop party atmosphere and a lot of the individuals I started out hustling with were now in the shadows, replaced by the tragedies and darkness of what the Crack Era came to embody. The landscape was completely changed, and I was beginning to feel like the last man standing out of my contemporaries. As a result, I knew I needed to stay under the radar, to a degree at least, when it came to hustling.

My name was great in the streets and with my connects. It would have been nothing to get 100 to possibly even 200 bricks on consignment. Yet, while this would have sounded good in a gangster documentary, there were real-life, logistical issues, and consequences that came with such moves that far outweighed any of the actual benefits at that time. I grew a little more cautious both because of the increasing volatility of the time as well as a natural instinct to try and minimize any potential losses versus only caring about maximizing profits.

I remember contemplating the issues with picking up work from my connect because the large quantity was what it was. I thought that I, or anyone making the move, couldn't afford to get caught with 50/100 keys at one time for several reasons. The most obvious was the loss I'd suffer from the second being the kind of time I'd get because of the number of joints. Becoming more cautious at this point with my connect made all the sense in the world to me. I was still making pretty good money, but mainly wholesaling. The thing that I contemplated was if I was to take a hit, the loss would easily be a million dollars or more. Having to make that up wouldn't easily be done because I was only making three to five points/thousands on a joint. A loss would mean I would have to hustle a lot more aggressively to make up for the money. Ideally, at this point, I wanted to coast in the middle lane going with the flow in no hurry to get anywhere.

I started breaking my moves up, picking up 25/30 keys as I needed them as opposed to taking them all at one time. This way, it limited any loss if it were to happen. Also, I wouldn't store everything in one place. Wherever the majority of the work was kept, it wasn't one of the places I frequented. It was only used as a stash house when necessary, and though my crew was tight, I limited who knew about these particular stash houses. I never kept ledgers but used a system that rounded things off in a way that I was able to memorize what was owed and what had been given out. The system wasn't necessarily perfect, but it worked for me.

Even though D.C. had been such a goldmine, I continued moving on and opening up more wholesale distribution networks. The branching out happened in large part because of necessity when one door closed another one opened. My stature, at this point, was larger than life, and I always had guys coming to me with different outlets all over the country, but mostly up and down the East Coast. Almost all African American New Yorkers were either originally from the South or still had large extended families there. The greater profit margins found in D.C. were easily found further down South as well. They weren't the natural distribution points for the product, but their user rates made it make sense. The demand way exceeded the natural supply, and I was opportunistic enough to offer my help. Somebody was going to capitalize on their desires and needs. Why not me?

The bigger I got, the less involved I wanted to be. You eventually learn all money isn't good money. I also wanted to be less involved as a means of limiting my exposure and accessibility that had, at one time, been my calling card and a key to my growth and expansion. Part of my niche, even as a wholesaler, was to deliver the goods to the respective cities and buyers. I always understood the more convenient I made it lessened the need for guys to have to look for other means or another connect.

Times began changing as well. The technology of using stash boxes, also known as traps, was innovative in 1990-91. The increasing technology and enterprise of traps in cars being built made it easier to move the product up and down the East Coast. We were simply ahead of the police, and they always had to play catch up. The government has far too many resources at its disposal and the ability to change the rules at any time so eventually, they win. However, I took advantage of the new technology and used it as a means of wholesale expansion, especially as airport rules were beginning to tighten on cash ticket purchases without identification and more and more people were getting busted couriering through the less and less friendly skies as well on trains and buses.

When I was put on to the technology, I looked at it as a clandestine adventure. The invention couldn't have happened soon enough. It was becoming more difficult to transport narcotics from one place to the other, especially because of the amount being moved. A regular traffic stop and search in those times could have cost hundreds of thousands of dollars if not in the millions if the load would've been in plain sight within a trunk or easily accessible door panels. The stash boxes also allowed you to carry your gun every single day without worrying about being pulled over and searched.

I remember having to talk with one of the guys I had putting traps in my cars. Gadget Mike was a friend of mine. He was a young dude like myself, who I gave a shot since he had a growing car installation business. He was one of a few people I knew that was doing it at the time. I got word he was casually talking about doing work on a car for me. I knew he didn't mean anything by it, but I had to strongly remind him that I didn't need anyone other than him knowing that he was doing any work on my cars. I immediately got rid of the car that he spoke about because it was not in my best interest for anyone in the streets to know about my trap cars, which they wouldn't otherwise recognize as belonging to me. I sold the car to an associate of mine who's profile wasn't as high as mine.

The traps with magnets were better than the ones with electronics though, admittedly, it wasn't until later that I understood why one won over the other. The police had developed technology where they'd open your hood and hook a device to your battery that would trip your traps dependent on electronics and cause them to pop open. What I do know is that they worked. I was in cars that got pulled over on several occasions with guns, cash and/or drugs, and nothing ever happened.

Eventually, the police in certain states learned that traps were being employed, and you began hearing about guys getting busted using them. Even that knowledge itself didn't necessarily make it easy for them to figure them out. My new way of operating involved having someone drive the trap car to a location in whatever state it needed to be in and just meeting them at the designated hotel. I would often fly in with a chick, meet up with the transporter and complete the sale myself. I'd usually hang out for a day or two just relaxing and enjoying my company. Most of the business was cash and carry or buy five and consign two to five, all depending on the individual. I'd have several individuals in the proximity of my drop off taking me to different parts of North Carolina, South Carolina, and Virginia.

I did it this way to ensure a degree of plausible denial. Nobody knew more than they needed to know. The guy driving never met the customer. The driver wouldn't even know how to access the box or specifically where the product or money was kept. I would then put the money back in the car and have the driver bring it back to NYC and park it in a garage or meet whomever I'd tell them to.

Additionally, I had a girlfriend housed in the cities I frequented and did business in. It was safer than hotels, and I got nothing but love since I was paying their bills. New Yorkers are known for our overwhelming personalities. Sometimes this has an appeal, but just as often it is a defensive turn off to those thinking you may be invading their territory. Incurring that love also helped diminish hard feelings amongst the locals, but more importantly, it kept you abreast of things. Having boots on the ground firmly on my side maintained, I always had eyes and ears in streets that were otherwise unfamiliar to me. This occurred all up and down the East Coast. I also made sure I had an ID from each state because if you got busted, you wanted the appearance of being a resident of that city. The lessons from Chris and others showed me that getting busted as a New Yorker out of town was a recipe for being considered a flight risk and never granted bail.

***

No two weeks were ever the same. It might be 25 keys wholesaling one week, 50 the next. I had a fleet of transport cars tricked out at that time. Everything from custom vans to Tahoes, BMWs, and a Lexus with the television systems and video games for comfort on our long road trips. The method I was using was similar to what BMF later became known to do, transport-wise, 15 years later, for their distribution networks.

This lack of a routine and not having a crew or spot any longer made me hard to clock. No more mills for preparing and packaging work, which was required for spots. I no longer had any routines outside of BOSS Emporium or my other legitimate businesses that could be surveilled and recorded showing me hustling.

The lack of a regular drug spot and crew ultimately helped in the police never had any real case on me. I lived the lifestyle of a drug dealer. Everything I did, the way I dressed, walked, talked, and spent money, screamed big-time drug dealer. However, my movements didn't necessarily say the same thing. I now made it difficult to catch me selling drugs and didn't have people answering to me the same way who were selling drugs. I took a bit of a pay cut but traded that for less aggravation and definitively less exposure.

***

My father, Mad Dog, was often on the road as well. He had been doing his thing DJing, and he often went back down South doing parties as well as in the city. Artie, my one-time store manager, shared his love of music and I introduced them on one of the times my father came by the store. They hit it off, and Artie eventually started going down South DJing with my father. Artie filled the void that my brother and I had once had as kids in playing for the younger generation while my father spun more for his generation.

In the course of going to Asheville, North Carolina, with my father, Artie got familiar with the locals and began realizing how crazy the drug culture was down there. It wasn't too long after that Artie got with me and asked if I'd give him something he could move while he was down there. Artie was no full-time hustler. He dabbled like most did during those times because there was such a demand, but upon learning he could easily move a key for minimally $30k wholesale and almost double if he broke it down, with the price I might give him at $25k, it was hard for him to resist the temptation.

Artie started making some moves in NC, and it didn't take long before my father was hearing the whispers about Artie's independence. Mad asked me what, if anything, I knew about Artie's hustling. I denied knowing anything and informed Artie whatever he was doing down there had come to Mad Dog's attention, and he needed to move differently.

As fate would have it, Mad Dog and Artie bumped into each other on a flight coming back from NC, unrelated to anything they were doing. Mad Dog told him he had been hearing about him and warned him that he didn't know the town as well as he thought he did. He told him, "Be careful, it's a small town. I was born and raised here and trust me, people run their mouths."

Artie didn't exactly take heed to Mad's advice, and on December 1, 1989, Artie and his female companion landed in Asheville. As they walked through the airport, they were approached by undercover agents and asked if they could have a word with them. They escorted them to a private area where they went through all the formalities which ultimately ended in finding them in possession of a kilo and a half of cocaine. They were both booked and charged with possession with intent to distribute. Artie attempted to take the weight for what was found, but because his female companion was the one carrying the drugs, it didn't work. Artie ultimately received 14 years while his companion got 7. They were required to do half of the time before being eligible for parole.

Six months later, in June of 1990, Mad Dog had a situation. A woman Mad Dog was in a personal relationship with got caught transporting his work. She got caught with two keys strapped to her in the Charlotte, NC airport attempting to make her connecting flight to Asheville.

After her arrest, she called him explaining what had happened and her situation. By this time, my brother and I were openly calling him Mad Dog to his face, and I remember telling him that her conversation just didn't sound right. I suggested we use an investigator I knew to investigate it first. However, he was impatient, in part due to the nature of their relationship, and wasn't listening to reason. He got aggravated and asked, "You going to help me or not?" Against my better judgment, I reluctantly sent Jeff, who had become my go-to guy in these types of matters.

In this case, Jeff met with the bail bondsman and made arrangements to get my father's friend released. Her bail was $100k cash.

Predictably, she had already told and was assisting law enforcement in setting him up though none of us knew for sure. He continued to trust and confide in her after the arrest. A couple of weeks later, Mad had her make his plane reservations coming back to New York from Asheville. Exiting the plane in Charlotte, he was approached by law enforcement and made aware he had a warrant lodged against him in Charlotte for his arrest for narcotics trafficking and distribution. When he was searched, he had $45k on him. They took the money and locked him up. He called me and made me aware of the situation. After his arraignment and bail hearing, I reached out to the same bail bondsman and sent Jeff back down to bail him out for $150k. I put up half the money in cash and half in jewelry just to try and offset it all being in cash.

Helping my father with his bail was, of course, a given. Helping any of my dudes when they were in need, regardless of whether I should have had to or not, had become an expectation bestowed upon me. I was considered a Boss and others placed duties on me regardless of the warranted circumstances. However, those times did sometimes serve as a reminder that my guys were not nearly as situated and comfortable as I imagined they should have been with all the money being made.

There were times throughout my getting money, where I had asked myself how much is enough. Honestly, I felt many times I had enough to be good, along with the businesses that I had created to live comfortably. In moments of drought or when the connect was on hold, I didn't go as hard because I didn't need to. I was good. Those moments, however, revealed how many of my guys weren't. I would state I'm taking it easy and let things play out, saying that these situations don't last long. In response, I would hear, "You're good, Kev, but I got bills to pay, and I've got to make a move." That let me know that they hadn't been putting money up planning for rainy days. Not having a cushion was very revealing.

I loved my guys, and knowing their situations always kept me in the game far longer than I should've been. I could name probably a hundred reasons I shouldn't have gone beyond the point that I continued to go.

Our first conversation when my father got out was an, "I told you so," which you could imagine he didn't want to hear. We hired a high-powered attorney from Charlotte to handle the case. I was told by my father not to go anywhere near the city because his female friend had mentioned my name as well and he wasn't certain of anything at this point. He had gone back and forth to court for several hearings and didn't have a good handle on his fate. A trial date was set for September 7, 1991. The trial started, and Mad's lady friend did testify against him, with my brother and Jeff in attendance. The trial lasted for a week before going to a jury who deliberated for a couple of days. The jury came back with a verdict of guilty on three counts of conspiracy to transport and distribute cocaine carrying 35 years for each count that ran consecutively. Mad Dog was sentenced to 105 years, with eligibility for parole only after doing half, which would be 57 and a half years. It was a definitive life sentence.

I immediately hired an attorney for his appeal. He charged me $35k for his initial retainer as my father headed to prison. I kept the condo he lived in part because I was hopeful and confident, he could beat the case one day. 1991 was the last time I saw my father for many years.

***

Not long after my father got busted, Billy got busted on September 13, 1990. It was a state case, but with heavy charges of trafficking in Baltimore, Maryland. In 1991, Charles "Billy" Guy became the first person and youngest person convicted under Maryland's newly enacted drug kingpin statute. The state statute was nearly two years in place though it had yet to be used prior to Billy and carried a mandatory prison term of 20 years without parole. Billy and I spoke regularly as I actively tried to help him with his appeal.

As we were making our names in the street, an already super charismatic Billy became known for being flashy and fly. Though his main hustle ended up being heroin in Baltimore, Billy became known throughout the Bronx and Harlem for always traveling with a caravan of cars. When he went to get a haircut or shopping, he would send someone ahead to announce, "B. G. was on the way." This would usually cause the barbershop and Harlem retail stores to shut their doors to everyone but Billy and his crew. He spent enough for those retailers to justify closing their doors to everyone else while he and his crew balled out. Billy would even have some of his people trumpet his arrival to BOSS Sneakers and Emporium, and we would just respectfully laugh at how extra Billy was. Everyone, especially my cousins, loved Billy stopping by the store because besides buying thousands of dollars' worth of goods, he would leave all his custom-made clothing and coats in the store after his new purchases.

Don't get me wrong, we all were getting wild money, but Billy stood out amongst the elite for being fly. His antics had a degree of showmanship that outshined others. While we all engraved our names into our furs and custom leathers, Billy would have whole gangster scriptures and quotes. He made a point to never leave the house in anything but designer fashion from head to toe. His low cut "fro" never had a hair out of place, in part because he got his haircut at least twice a week. His cars were always shining, and his rims gleamed just as much as the expensive jewelry he wore. Upon his arrest, even the papers in Baltimore commented on Billy's jewelry and how flamboyant he was. **The newspapers reported that the Great Billy Guy was arrested with** more than $50,000 worth of gold jewelry adorning his body, including a replica of Lazarus with diamond-studded eyes. "Hey, watch the jewelry," he reportedly told one of the arresting officers. "Give it to my girlfriend."

Besides coming from similar neighborhoods playing ball, a commonality we both shared is that we got our tutelage from the older hustlers before us. As youngsters, we hung around them and later would come to emulate their styles. Our rise in the game was happening simultaneously, as well. Early on, we'd catch ourselves on the same Trump shuttle flights out of New York, with me going to D.C. and Billy headed to Baltimore. Billy's thing was heroin whereas mines were coke and crack. I dabbled in heroin as well, no different than him dabbling in coke. The flexibility of our hustles and longstanding friendship would make it inevitable that he and I would do business.

Even after his conviction, while working on his appeal, Billy wanted to keep his operation going from jail. He was one of the few New York dudes that had ever established a heroin network on the ground in Baltimore. He stated how his blocks were goldmines, and he still had dudes on the outside in pocket and ready to go. He connected me with the people that he felt could help run his operation outside of his presence.

I put a crew together, along with the dudes Billy put me with. One of the first things I did was get an apartment out in the County. I was going to be down there for a minute and needed to be comfortable. I had done this a time or two before and knew exactly what was required to get a spot off the ground and running. It was that exact knowledge of all that was needed that probably made me initially reluctant to take on Baltimore. I had only recently left D.C. and was hesitant to amass another large crew and be tied down with the day-to-day operations, especially when my wholesaling was so profitable and less confining. However, partly as loyalty to Billy and keeping my guys busy and paid, I went ahead and got Baltimore going. Rob was just getting home from jail on another situation and was looking to jump right back into the swing of things, so he and Chris oversaw the Baltimore operation with the crew we had put together.

Dealing in heroin is far more complex than cocaine and requires a lot more effort. This probably contributed to the reason it never overly appealed to me. The upside was that you had the capability to make way more money selling heroin, especially if you had the right product along with the right mix.

There's a whole production that goes into rolling out heroin ready for the street. The first thing is you need a good product. Then, it all depends on what you plan on doing with it; going to the street or wholesaling. We intended to go to the street with our product, so that required us to get our mix right. We used quinine and menita (which is a baby laxative) to cut the heroin. Each ingredient has a purpose. Quinine caused the rush into the person system, and menita acted as a mixture increasing its volume. Menita came in bricks the size of a bar of soap that had to be put through a metal shifter into a fluffy powder substance that would then be mixed with the quinine along with the heroin. The ratio of heroin to the mixture all depended on how pure the heroin was. Particularly pure heroin could take anywhere from a two to five or even better. That means an ounce of heroin could take five or more ounces of the mixtures, thus exponentially increasing the amount of heroin and your profits.

The ability to increase volume also means that drug dealers would add other drugs or non-intoxicating substances to the drug so they could sell more of it at a less expense to themselves. It's a bit like watering down alcohol.

Fentanyl could be added, but it took a mastering of the right mix to make it work. Fentanyl is a synthetic opioid considered to be significantly more potent than heroin and, if not incorporated the right way, would lead to more bad than good at times, leading to casualties.

After all, that's figured out, you then need all the packaging products such as glassine bags, spoons, scotch tape, rubber bands, and probably the most important thing, a stamp used to name and identify your product. Your brand was everything, especially if your product was hitting. Dope fiends would travel from one side of town to the other if your product were making noise in the street for being the bomb. Good product sold itself.

Once processing and packaging were done, it was time to take samples to the block and get what's called a "reading." A reading would tell you where you were with your package. What you would do is pass out samples. Ideally, you want a fiend that you have a relationship with that knows his or her way around the area and whose opinions matter to the other fiends. It may seem like an oxymoron to some, but your sampler needed to be an honest fiend because the reading needed to hold true for the market. Either way, you gave out the samples and waited around for the response. The best way to do it was to watch a person shoot the dope in front of you and watch the reaction. Your dope is graded from a 1 to 10, 10 being the best. If you have an 8 or better, you have a product you can make money with. If it's less than that, it's back to the drawing board.

After all these things were worked out and moving along, you get your team out on the block and make it happen. One of our blocks was on 21st and Barclay. Of course, the details of shifts and hours depended on your science. There were times when we would be on the block at the top of the morning, finished by noon, and wouldn't do anything after that. Then, there were times when we may have worked through the whole day stopping for nothing unless it got hot. It just all depended.

"The Boy" was my Uncle Kid's thing, and coming up around it, I was quite familiar with the product. When you're a true hustler, you hustle selling pretty much whatever to make a profit, even if it's not your primary hustle. I had relationships across the board, and it wasn't too difficult to get my hands on pretty much anything, including a steady heroin connect.

There had been some defectors from Billy's organization that he felt should've held him down during this time. He openly expressed these sentiments to us all. It so happened that Rob came across a couple of them that at one point. Since Billy's incarceration, two guys named Mike and Sharrod had come up mostly on the strength of Billy's name and the reputation he had cemented in Baltimore. They were looking to cop two keys of coke, and Rob told them that he would get it for them, never having any intentions of doing so. For Rob, it was a return to old ways and free money. He already had certain feelings towards them from what Billy had stated about them. However, this all occurred unbeknownst to me.

Not long after Rob had taken their money for the two joints, Chris just happened to be driving through in his BMW in their neighborhood in the Bronx when he saw them. They flagged him down, and when he pulled over and got out to talk, they pulled guns out and told him they were taking the car due to the fact they were owed two keys by "us." They assumed because of our relationships, Rob was getting them from us, and that was the only reason that they would've done business with him. Chris told them he was unaware of any transaction between them and Rob, and he had nothing to do with it. They jumped in the car and left Chris stranded in the middle of the street on Sedgwick.

It didn't take long before my phone rang with an irate Chris detailing what had happened and how things were going to end. I told him I'd call Rob and see what was going on. Rob's attitude was basically, "Fuck 'em. I'll see them when I see them, 'cause they violated on some real shit." I totally got it, and honestly, had I known about it, then we all could have better dealt with it and been prepared. They got what their hands called for just on some real homie shit.

We recovered the car but hadn't crossed paths with Sharrod or Mike. Not long after, while Chris and H were in Baltimore, driving through and handling some business, they came upon Sharrod on one of the blocks. Sharrod didn't see them. H pulled over in the cut, and Chris reached for his gun in the stash box, then jumped out the car heading for Sharrod. When Sharrod looked up, he noticed Chris fast approaching. He took off running as Chris got to popping. God was with Sharrod that day because he escaped unharmed.

It would be a couple of months before the next time we'd run into him. We were outside on a block in Harlem. I was standing in the street in the middle of a one-way block. When I looked up, I could see Sharrod kind of stuck in traffic a couple of cars in front of me. Chris, H, and a few others all happened to be there. I stood in front of Sherrod's car and told him to get out of the car. As soon as he did, Chris immediately got to swinging on him, along with some of the others. I broke it up telling them to hold the fuck up. Sharrod tried to start explaining. I wasn't trying to hear it but did tell him, "The situation wasn't with Chris, so it should've been handled a different kind of way, and because of that, there isn't anything I can do for you now. You're going to have to take this one on the chin for the violation towards Chris." He didn't have a choice at the moment. Honestly, he never wanted that problem in the first place. He accepted his fate and got in his car. He went on his way with us, both knowing this could've ended way more tragically than it did. I considered him lucky, only having taken a beating. This turned out to be the best-case L for him under the circumstances. Every situation with Billy, even when he was in jail, always ended up interesting.

With Chris and Rob at the helm, we got Baltimore up and running somewhat consistently within three to six months of being down there. While the money was good, in all honesty, after leaving D.C., I looked at running spots as a step backward. I had no intention of having Baltimore consume my time and energy.

One of the guys we had brought in to help with Baltimore was Jack from our old block on Ogden Avenue. Once we got Baltimore up and running, we turned the spot over to Jack, and thru Chris or Rob, I continued to serve Baltimore.

In part because of our continuing business and helping him with his appeal (which he eventually did win after serving 11 years), Billy was one of the few people I regularly received messages from jail, talking to. I remember Billy and me having a conversation about him seeing a newspaper article about Alpo's arrest on November 8, 1991. Billy said the article described how Alpo was crying uncontrollably in court, and I was thrown by that, as wild and crazy as he was out in the streets. We discussed how we couldn't believe how they had broken him, and I particularly had concerns as to what this could potentially mean. We all had an impression of Alpo that this totally went against what we all proclaimed. We vowed never to fold in to "the man." It was always death before dishonor. That was the code we lived by.

There was no outright declaration of beef between Alpo and me, so when he got busted, I stayed on his list of people he was trying to contact. I remember not making myself overly available to speak with him while he was locked up. I was getting his messages and would reply to the person who was conveying his messages, but I mostly avoided the calls directly. My avoidance was not because I initially thought he was on some BS trying to line me up, but just out of being generally cautious about those types of jail calls from anyone. Alpo was a friend, but unlike Billy, he wasn't an intimate part of my organization and someone I was willing to bet on with these types of calls. I knew all these calls were recorded, and if I wasn't obviously on law enforcement's radar, I wasn't going to volunteer by putting my name and voice in their recorded thoughts unless unavoidable.

Alpo was an interesting guy. If he was cool with you and respected you, he was a good dude who was always doing something crazy. To many, he was intense and just straight over-the-top. I found most of his antics entertaining, and in the course of our friendly rivalry, he always minimally kept the competition interesting. He would pop shit about who had the baddest women or flyest cars. We would gamble on just about anything, be it baseball or basketball (1-on-1, 2-on-2, and, of course, 5-on-5) with Alpo always on the losing end.

He started copping minimally ten to fifteen keys at a time spending $300,000 to $400,000 each time. He would pay for them upfront, which I knew he hadn't done with Rich, and I would often give him additional keys on consignment. I was careful not to front him too much because one time he owed me some money and I found out he was in town and didn't come see me. I heard about him being around, and the fact that I had to find him didn't particularly sit too well with me. I got my money, but that one occurrence was enough to stop me from carrying him too far with any consignment, especially knowing his history with Rich.

Rich was killed on January 4, 1990. At that time, none of us knew it was Alpo. There was always some speculation, but it wasn't until he eventually confessed to Rich's murder years later after we all had been arrested and were doing time that it was confirmed. I never initially suspected Alpo. I knew him to be a bit over the top and at times out of control, but I assumed his friendship with Rich was true and genuine. And, to be real, he just didn't have a reputation at that time for being a killer, so that's why the talk and speculation about him killing Rich was so easy to dismiss. I know that Alpo claimed he killed Rich over business. He claimed Rich snaked him out of a situation they shared with a mutual connect. Only Alpo truly knows why he did what he did, but I suspect owing so much money, he used Donnell's situation knowing Rich was vulnerable to come up. Also, in hindsight, him doing the exact same thing to several other drug associates would lead me to question his explanation.

Alpo wasn't frequently seen in NYC after Rich's death. He had long set up camp and mostly stayed in D.C. He started going down there about 1988-89. Maybe it was his conscious that kept him away; maybe it was Fritz looking for him. I would only see him when we were doing business. He came in town to cop work and then he was out.

Fritz came looking for all the money Rich had owed him when he was killed. He started reaching out to Rich's known associates that would get work, and this included me and Alpo. He asked Rich's immediate crew, but much of the work gotten from Fritz had been out there on consignment. Fritz came uptown with his lieutenant Kenny who I already had a personal relationship and a business dealing with to talk to me. I had paid for everything I had gotten from Rich, but the way Fritz initially questioned me made me feel a kind of way about it. Thankfully, it didn't escalate in part because Rich had a guy that essentially kept a ledger of what was outstanding, and he was able to verify our arrangement and that I was good.

I told Alpo shortly after that that Fritz was looking for him. He didn't outwardly seem concerned, claiming he had paid Rich and dead men couldn't get paid twice.

Richard "Fritz" Simmons was one of the most interesting figures in our era. Fritz became known as the Consignment King. He was called the Consignment King partly as a reflection on how much work he was flooding the streets with when he had it. These occurrences may have only happened a couple of times a year. None of us knew exactly who his connect was, but we all assumed it was directly with a Colombian cartel. I didn't know anyone else who got it like Fritz did. He might have had between 500 to 1,000 keys at a time.

As you could imagine, when you are talking about mostly consigning 500 keys, Fritz surrounded himself with a significant enforcement crew. You had to estimate that Fritz had anywhere from $30 to $40 million owed at a given time. His crew was also in place to protect Fritz himself.

About two years before Rich was killed, there had been two kidnapping attempts on Fritz. It was a group known as the Wild Cowboys headed by Steven Palmer, from the Bronx. They were the ones posing as police officers equipped with badges and guns, staging fake arrests of drug dealers and holding them for ransom. Fritz himself escaped the crew's kidnapping attempts. His right-hand man and associate, Charles "Chucky" Caines wasn't so lucky and was killed as a warning to Fritz not to attempt to exact revenge.

I had stopped dealing with Alpo sometime in July of 1991. I remember because that was when I got the call from Brooklyn Lou Hobbs about Domencio. Domencio, like Lou, was a certified dude from Brooklyn that had also migrated to do business in D.C. I had become close with both, so when I got paged with a 911 from Lou's code, I hurriedly called him back from my burner phone. There was franticness in his voice. Lou's words were very rushed as he told me what had happened moments ago. He started out saying, "Sucker ass Po had Domenico shot in the park at the basketball court." I asked him where, and he said in D.C., I asked about Domencio's condition. I don't remember his exact response, but he was okay while Domencio was dead. The reason Lou called me was he knew I dealt with Po, and I believe to give me a heads up.

There had been a previous beef between Alpo and Domencio over Domencio supposedly slapping Alpo's wife. She was someone Domencio knew for years from Brooklyn and had a personal relationship with that extended beyond them just being exes. Lou stated that Alpo and Domencio had spoken, and the situation had supposedly been squashed. When Alpo came to give Domencio a pound on the court, they both were caught off-guard that the greeting's true purpose was to single Domencio out for the hit.

This didn't sit well with me, but being totally honest, I understood it. Domencio was my dude, but Po was a friend. Domencio and Alpo didn't have any kind of personal relationship. I was still unaware of Rich's situation, and if push came to shove, I probably would have sided with Po in this situation. He might not have handled it as I would have by rocking Domencio to sleep in believing their beef had been squashed, but I can understand his extreme reaction in feeling that someone had violated his wife. Anyone of us would have probably done the same thing. I surely would have spoken with Alpo about this situation, but we never saw each other again.

Looking back now, I can see Alpo was clearly in a downward spiral. What was so hard to grasp about Po, and what we later found out was that he was outwardly such a likable dude. However, that charm and charisma are what made him so treacherous. I didn't know any of this at the time, but he betrayed and killed friends in situations that allowed him to get close because the guys probably never saw it coming. The streets were speculating about several possible people being involved in Rich's death, including Po. But it was still just talk up to that point, and I never believed it, based on what I thought their friendship to be. Domencio's death was real and confirmed, and I'm sure with whatever he was internally struggling with regarding Rich, he knew Brooklyn dudes weren't going to let Domencio's death slide. He clearly changed in D.C., and the guy we knew in New York was a different person that emerged in his short run in the District. He adapted to the aggressiveness of the environment. The money was still great in D.C., but it was clear that visitors were no longer welcome, something we picked up on years later. Additionally, he still had that unresolved situation with Fritz, so I just never even knew him to return to New York before his arrest a few months later.

Though his initial reaction was cavalier, I know that Alpo actively avoided Fritz. I am not sure if they ever ran into each other because Rich was killed at the top of January 1990. In early 1991, Fritz became violently ill and was admitted to the hospital displaying several cold-related symptoms. A doctor confirmed he had pneumonia. He received a blood transfusion after being shot a couple of years earlier, and it was said his illness was related to that, while others speculated, he was poisoned. Fritz was in and out of the hospital dealing with his illness and died from it on August 16, 1991. Fritz's departure had a significant impact in Harlem alone because once he died, many cats lost their lives as his crew went on a mission for outstanding debts all around the city.

17

BIPOLAR STATE OF THE LIFE

I was not sure of anything at this point in my life. I had seen and experienced so much in such a short time. It made me question everything, from friends to family to all the women in my life. Money had changed us all to a certain extent. I was still fundamentally the same, but my mother and Rich's deaths showed me the full extent that others might go to get money. I could no longer be definitive when looking at anyone and what they would or wouldn't do for money, or even freedom. Everyone I had started in the game with was either dead, in jail, or out after doing a bid. While I never aggressively questioned the loyalty of those around me. I know that I was probably uneasy about completely putting my life or fate in anyone's hands.

Hustling truly embodies a lifestyle, and I was dedicated to that lifestyle regardless of the ups and downs that came with it. More accurately, I was becoming desensitized to tragedy and even growing numb to the pain that might ordinarily debilitate a sane or rational person. Death and seeing many around me going to jail had become an accepted consequence of the *Life*.

While my life was still in upheaval, I somehow understood that if I was going to stay the course, I needed to be seen living as I usually did. Anything else could be a weakness, and there were now too many out there looking to capitalize on anyone caught slipping. So, while I remained in the *Life*, I continued living as normal as I knew how. I still made the rounds and lived a hustler's life doing what hustlers did, including being social to an extent. Amidst the tragedy and drama, we still managed to entertain ourselves, and others.

I was living life in a constant manic/bipolar state. On a given day, I might regularly experience numerous highs and lows all within a matter of hours, if not minutes. I never knew exactly what to expect, but I always knew each day was going to be eventful. I always felt the pressure to soldier on for my family and hustling peers because I knew that so many were dependent on me to continue doing so. Even with all the obstacles, we all adjusted to our new normal. The *Life* didn't come with set rules, and the ones that we thought existed seemed to have flexible meanings for some. I can look back and see that we put up with so much because as young, Black men, we just assumed that's what we were supposed to do. Our people had never had it easy, and even as our enterprising spirits allowed us to improve our economic situations, it came with costs. Life was hard growing up. It was hard for our parents and their parents before them. I do not know if this serves as an explanation, but when you have never seen anyone with a simple, easy life, dealing with tragedies is expected, though I am sure we were even pushing the limits of those expectations.

Girls would want to come to the park when we played each other in basketball, and those games graduated to us renting out gyms. The gyms went from 500-person capacity at the Kennedy Center to 1,100 capacity at Gaucho's Gym to more than 2,000-person capacity at City College. We sold out all these venues. I never did it for the money, giving whatever money we made to my team and donating to some organization.

Part of that foray into Hip-Hop and entertainment probably initially started with basketball. It wasn't hard to put together a few of our mutual friends that we played with or grew up with to comprise teams that were usually unbeatable on this circuit. We had a couple of guys from my old neighborhood in the Bronx such as Spanish Chuck, a Division I player, and John Morton, that was a star on Seton Hall's Final Four team before turning pro. I had regularly taken Alpo and Azie's money over the years during these games. Rich wasn't much of a ballplayer and never played. Azie and Alpo were decent but not on the level of my squad and me. At $2,000 a game, up to $2,000 ahead, it was always an excellent payday for my team.

There were crews that were coming up that constantly wanted to challenge us hoping to make a name for themselves. There was Butt Naked, N.F.L. (Niggas for Life), No Fear, Slick, and The Family, and the X-Men, to name a few. Another was a loosely knit crew called Best Out. Two of the de facto leaders of the Best Out crew were Bob Burke and a guy named Terrell, who were both hustling. Two other members that later would become famous were Damon Dash and Kareem Burke, Bob's younger brother. They would go on to be ⅔ of Rocafella records along with Jay Z. They had a reputation for being above average basketball players and for throwing parties. They were a mix of a few cats hustling independently of one another that hung out with each other and formed a collective unit. They were the new up-and-coming crew. From talking shit, we ended up making a bet to play ball, Best Out vs. BOSS. They challenged us to a basketball game. We sold tickets to the game at BOSS Emporium, and word of mouth had such a buzz we easily sold out the Kennedy Center on 135th Street.

We had shirts and mismatched shorts and sneakers. Best Out had fully customized uniforms and matching sneakers. We had a reputation for getting money and didn't take it seriously while they were fully choreographed, including with the DJ's. The irony of that was that BOSS Emporium specialized in customized silk-screened t-shirts and uniforms. The game was close for the first half, and in the second half, they came out in different uniforms, all white with matching Jordans. I must admit it made an impression on me. To top it off, they won the game. They probably weren't as good as us, but we took them for granted, and they used the momentum from the crowd. We wanted get back, and the next game was to be held at the larger Gaucho's Gym right over the bridge in the Bronx.

The games were fun, but also a microcosm of how quickly things could potentially turn. Gaucho's Gym was in a more desolate warehouse district of the Bronx right under the Major Deegan Expressway. Mark was running a little late, and since the place was so packed, he was forced to park his BMW convertible down the block. A van pulled up, and three guys jumped out and tried to throw him in. He furiously fought the abduction. They were pulling him by his thick Cuban link chain that just wouldn't pop, and eventually, he was able to slip out the chain and run.

The chain was probably worth $15,000. Replacing the chain was the least of his concerns. The incident was an unnecessary reminder that stickup kids and the bullshit never take a day off.

We also started playing a group called Same Gang with Tab, Rick Dog, D. Ferg (father of the rapper now known as A$AP Ferg). D. Ferg was a dude getting money though not necessarily a committed hustler. D. Ferg, along with Mike Cock were talented artists who were into fashion and a lot of the exclusives t-shirt designs I bought for the store, they created and supplied. Puff (P. Diddy) loosely ran with the Same Gang when he was starting at Uptown Records and hanging in Harlem.

The games eventually got so big we moved them to City College's gym. They attracted lots of celebrities, including heavyweight champ Mike Tyson and the like. All those games sold out as well.

I really can't recall exactly how I met Bob and Terrell outside of the basketball games, but eventually, we got cool. They would go on to cop, a joint or two at a time, from me. At some point, Bob mentioned that he had family in the US Virgin Island of St. Thomas. He didn't bring up St. Thomas as a vacation destination but was told that his people there were in position because the island had recently become an outpost and pit stop for the importation of cocaine into the United States.

My business was still strong. I was making three to five points wholesaling without any headache. So, ten to twenty joints would still lead me to make $30,000 to $60,000 a week minimally. As a wholesaler, better connects and prices were always the goal, and my sense of adventure knew little bounds. Bob and I took the trip to St. Thomas to see how real the situation was.

We started out copping just four or five keys, in the beginning, to see how things would work on both sides. It quickly became clear that Bob's people had the right connections on the island. They had people at the airport and let our loaded bags slide through. This is prior to 9/11, so security screening was relaxed in general. Since St. Thomas was a US territory, there was no Customs for us there or upon returning. Our main concern was the airport security on the St. Thomas side, and we had that covered. I had to trust Bob, and his judgment and the relationships with people he trusted.

As we got more comfortable, our purchases got bigger. I started to get ten keys, plus. Then, at some point, the people in St. Thomas began to bring the work to us in New York. You pay a little more of a premium for delivery, but it was still worth it with the better prices minimally $5,000 cheaper per key. The biggest issue was getting the money to St. Thomas with just me and Bob. A hundred grand isn't necessarily a lot to carry, but $200,000 to $300,000 was more of an issue, even with our airport connects. The money transport was one of the reasons the government years later began putting the small metal strips in the US currency. Enough money would eventually set off the metal detectors.

Bob and I had a year or so run with St. Thomas. Bob came into the picture as much as a reaction to people getting busted as well as there being a conscious effort to change my business model. All these elements of change are probably what ultimately spared me from my own, more tragic fate. Bob became one of my nearest and dearest friends who I grew to trust, respect, and loved dearly.

***

When I first started getting real money back in '85/'86, I looked forward to counting every single dollar I made. I would make sure every bill was facing the same way and was right side up in sequence. Even before that, as a kid, I remember Ant-Man ironing his money, unfolding even the corners that had gotten bent because of the money being exchanged and spent in commerce.

I don't remember how I became aware that all denominations of paper currency weighed a gram. I know I saw someone early on weighing all the singles we had made during one of our shifts. As we began to make more money, we'd weigh the fives as well. A hundred singles were 100 grams, and that equaled $100. The same went for the fives. A hundred grams of fives was $500 and the same for ten-dollar bills. A hundred grams of tens was $1,000. I was getting so much money that it didn't matter if the count on those was off one way or another because truthfully, that money was what ended up being trick money for the many women I dealt with, or the daily shopping I did staying fresh; basically, pocket money.

For those I did business with on the regular, it was understood that I needed them to bring my money in a manner that made it easy on my end. The money needed to be in $5 and $10 thousand bands. A hundred hundreds was $10 grand. The fifties, twenties and tens could be banded together to make a $5 thousand stack. Packaging the money in this fashion allowed me to easily count it and keep it moving or in some instances, pass it on to a connect I needed to pay without having to recount it.

Then, there were those instances when someone I knew was a little shaky when I got the money from them, and I'd always ask if it was all there already knowing the answer was going to be, "Yeah, it's all there." I would keep it in the bag or whatever they gave it to me in and knew when I had the chance; I would have to count it. For those who I might have been doing business with for the first time, of course, I'd have to take the time out to count it and make sure it was all there when we met.

I had a money counting machine, but I rarely used it. In those instances, when a money machine was used, it had the dual benefit of detecting counterfeit money as well. Counterfeit money was an issue back then. I personally knew people who sold counterfeit money for 20 cents on the dollar. You could purchase $20,000 in counterfeit bills for $2,000. Now imagine someone spending $200,000 or $300,000 with you. It was easy to mix in $30,000 to $40,000 of some bullshit money.

It would be a whole production in the instances where it would be a new customer, and they bought ten or more joints. There would need to be some planning because a few things need to be considered, such as the moving of the money as well as the work on both our ends. Both parties needed to be comfortable with the arrangement. I'd move with my team, and usually, they would as well. The circumstances would determine how I moved. In most of those instances, I would be accompanied by Chris, Bob, or one of my closest confidants. I would have the building covered by my dudes on the outside, keeping us abreast of all things moving, including law enforcement or the potential cross. There would be a couple of cars positioned strategically, so when we exited, it would be all good.

***

Our games were quite the spectacle and created a buzz throughout Harlem. I was never interested in any money that the games potentially generated, but clearly, others took notice of our model. One of those people was Puff. Sean "Puffy" Combs was a young A&R executive for Uptown Records. His father had once been a hustler himself that ran with the likes of Nicky Barnes and such, and even as Puff moved to Mount Vernon and attended Howard University, he was drawn to the sights and sounds of Harlem and hustling culture.

We were the blueprint for every rap song and video that came after in the late 1980s and '90s. They rapped about what we drove, wore, and how we lived emulating the over-the-top personas that most of the top hustlers embodied. We provided the blueprint and soundtrack to what was hip and hot in the streets. Rappers were marketed on their street credibility. What could be more credible than affiliations with the guys running the streets?

I was starting in the music game, and I would see Puff around at various industry events. Puff knew how successful we had been in marketing and selling out the games at City College just out of BOSS Emporium. BOSS had become such a hub of activity in Harlem that word of mouth from the shop alone was enough to get people moving and excited. Puff was introduced to me by a girl named Tracey Waples, who at one time babysat my kids before later coming into prominence as a music industry executive with Def Jam and Bad Boy. He told me about an idea he had about a charity celebrity game he wanted to put on along with Heavy D. I liked Puff and did it for the relationship. Initially, the tickets were going to be sold at the Apollo, but they reneged, and BOSS ended up selling the tickets. Puff was just starting to make some traction with Uptown Records and making a name for himself.

From what I can recall, the game was nearly sold out in advance. Puff went on New York's biggest radio station at the time, 98.7 Kiss, and mentioned the event. On December 28, 1991, a few thousand people showed up to try and secure walk-up tickets for the otherwise sold-out event. There was a rush at the door towards the game already in progress, and unfortunately, nine people ended up losing their lives in the stampede.

The very next day after the tragedy, I avoided the store. Various news and print agencies were parked outside, and I remember seeing a sound bite with my brother being interviewed at the store. Tony said that he didn't deal with Puff and Heavy D and wasn't sure of the details. Puff and I had several conversations in length right after, and the tragedy sincerely and emotionally touched him. He wore that responsibility personally though he shouldn't have. It was an accident totally out of his control. The event was already underway, and crowd control generally isn't the responsibility of promoters. That was the responsibility of the NYPD and City College. Nonetheless, this impacted Puff immensely, and I did the little I could to hold him down. We both came out of it with even more mutual respect and admiration for each other.

That tragedy and the attention it brought along with the BMW parked in the center of the store, brought me a lot of heat. I was torn between feeling for the people that lost their lives in such a senseless manner, and knowing I was going to pay the price for something I had no real culpability in. I felt terrible for all those affected in such a tragedy, but I had little time to mourn or empathize with them when it soon became apparent as the primary venue selling the tickets, I was going to be brought into the mess. I got sued along with Puff, Heavy D, the X-Man security team, and City College. At the very least, I knew to have my name brought about in any investigation where nine people died was heat that no one wanted. As far as the civil lawsuits, whereas when the initial tragedy occurred, and I might have been a target, my eventual incarceration left them looking past me, especially as Puff's stature grew so significantly. I assumed that everything got settled without me.

***

I was still consumed in the moment. Everything after my mother's death was reactionary living. It was many years later that I was even able to reflect on how tumultuous a 24-month period was in my life from 1989-90. In January 1989, Albe was killed. On February 24th, 1989, my mother was killed. On December 1, 1989, Artie was arrested. December 4th, 1989, Rich's brother Donnell was kidnapped. On January 4th, 1990, Rich was killed. On January 28, 1990, Donnell's body was found. In June 1990, Mad Dog was arrested. In July 1990, H was arrested and incarcerated on the New York gun charge. On September 13, 1990, Billy Guy was arrested. Late 1990, John was acquitted but effectively dropped out of the Life. Late 1990, Crusader Rob was arrested. Unfortunately, these were just a sampling of the hits that just kept coming.

My new reality encompassed accepting the really good with the really bad. The hopes were probably just for the good to outweigh everything else. This was an acceptance of the *Life* and my reality. I can look back now and see that I lived in nearly a perpetual manic state. The incredible highs were always matched by the lows, and all of this could take place multiple times in a given day. This was the *Life... My Life*.

18

ARREST

November 1, 1994, started as any regular Tuesday in my post-hustling life. I checked into my office and hung out there for most of the day into the early evening. I had been trying to reach Chris and couldn't. His wife, Bunny, had reached out to me and was worried as well because she wasn't able to get him either.

We were all at BOSS Records' office earlier that day. He had left early that afternoon, and I told her that was the last time I saw or spoke to him. I assured her that he was OK, and if I heard from him before her, I'd have him call. I wasn't initially worried. I figured he was off messing around with some chick or some other nonsense. Later that evening, as I was in Harlem getting ready to go home, heading towards the West Side Highway, I noticed I was being followed by one of the cars I had become familiar with by this point. I got on the highway at 125th Street, heading home towards the George Washington Bridge and New Jersey. I called Reika at home from my burner cell phone. She immediately said something that irked me, and I quickly decided on a change of plans.

I noticed I was still being followed, so I started driving aggressively and was able to put some distance between me and my tail. I lost them at the juncture where you had to choose the upper or lower levels of the GWB bridge or continue north on the Henry Hudson. I made moves from the far right of the highway over to the far-left lane while moving at excessive speeds in traffic. I looped around the highway, and instead of continuing north on the Henry Hudson, I was now back around the juncture facing I-95 to New Jersey, and again, I kept straight and got onto the Cross Bronx Expressway. I exited the highway on Webster Avenue in the Bronx. I called Angie, a girl I had been dealing with who lived in the vicinity, to see if she wanted to go get something to eat. Angie lived in the Tremont section not far from my father's condo.

Angie came downstairs, and we went to get something to eat nearby. After we ate, I told her I was going to stop by and check on one of the producers working on some music. I noticed when I approached the building that the car that had been following me earlier, along with others, I was also familiar with at this point in different locations along the street. I parked, we got out the car, entered the building, got on the elevator and headed to the third floor. When I opened the door, Paul, the producer, turned the music down and let me know that I got a couple of calls on the landline. Someone stated that they were supposed to be meeting me and I stood them up and wanted to know if he knew where I was. I oddly looked at him and asked who called, but Paul didn't recognize the voice, and the caller didn't leave a name. Getting a call on the landline from unfamiliar people was unusual, and after seeing the cars upon entering the building and still no word from Chris, I became very concerned.

I hung out for a second, but the obvious was stirring in me, and I couldn't sit still. I told Angie, "Let's go. I'm going to drop you back off. I got some business to handle," and we exited the apartment. When I got downstairs, the cars were still there. At this point, being followed had become common and had long stopped alarming me, until now. We got in the car and headed north on the Grand Concourse. I noticed the cars pull out. I made the first U-turn possible and began heading south on the Grand Concourse. Angie lived only about ten minutes from where we were, but I decided against taking her home and told her I would take her downtown to her friend's house instead, and she could then take a cab back home. I played my mirrors all the way down the Grand Concourse. I reached 135th Street, made the right off the Concourse and went across the bridge into Harlem. After I crossed into Manhattan, I made the left onto 5th Avenue heading downtown. At this point, I could see a caravan of cars following.

This was different, and something was definitely wrong. As I got closer to where I was going to drop Angie off, I started to instruct her as to what I wanted her to do in the event I was to be arrested. A block away from the intended drop off at 118th and 5th Avenue, I started to pull over, and before I could come to a complete stop it felt like an entire police force converged on the car with assault weapons drawn demanding me to open the door. Immediately upon opening the door, we were both dragged out and shoved against the car, searched, handcuffed and thrown into different unmarked cars.

I arrived downtown at 26 Federal Plaza, entering from an underground entrance. They led me to an elevator, getting off on a floor and taking me into a room pre-designated for my interrogation. I passed a room with the door intentionally left open for me to see Chris sitting, handcuffed to a table, with two agents talking to him. They then brought me into a room, handcuffed one of my wrists, and sat me in front of a table with an array of surveillance pictures fully displayed. This was designed to scare me in that instance and serve as overwhelming proof of my guilt. Instead, it did the opposite. It just made me question what they had on me based on what was displayed. I didn't see any of the usual or real suspects in the pictures. All they showed me were miscellaneous people who I clearly knew but were insignificant about anything criminal or detrimental to me.

They were telling me I was looking at life in jail saying, "Chris is in the other room talking already. We've had him here all evening. Do you think he's going to do life for you? If you do, you're a fool. You better do what's in the best interest of you and your family." They were threatening that if I didn't make a decision immediately, they were going to execute warrants to arrest my whole family in the coming hours. I took their threat seriously, but I had no intention of ever cooperating under any circumstances. Their threat showed me how willing they were to play dirty and that was a real concern.

I had grown exhausted after many hours of interrogation that was filled with good agent/bad agent play. I couldn't make any sensible decisions. Nevertheless, I had no intention of talking to them and made my position clear by not even being willing to sign a paper stating I was who I was. I laid my head down on the table and closed my eyes, playing asleep just not to have to engage with them any further.

I had been locked up before on miscellaneous bullshit throughout my life. I had been processed and put through the system, then released. However, those cases were eventually dismissed after a few court dates, so this was new to me. My initial arrest complaint carried alleged offenses from 1987 to 1994 as the head of a large-scale drug organization. It seemed like it had any and everything that they had ever heard I had done or had something to do with from murders to dealing heroin and cocaine to money laundering. You name it. When it was all said and done, I realized that what they ultimately were doing was throwing a bunch of shit against the wall and just waiting to see what stuck.

The strategy was designed to overwhelm. It's not a coincidence that the federal government has a conviction rate between 97-98%. The long list of charges was designed to intimidate me, and everyone else locked up with me. It listed 21 co-defendants added to my case in which I was labeled a drug kingpin. However, at least 15 of those co-defendants had never been participants in selling any types of drugs with me. Their inclusion in my case confirmed my suspicions that the government's case was short on real facts or evidence and long on threats and intimidation.

The next morning, Chris and I were escorted out of 26 Federal Plaza in handcuffs made to do what's known as the "Perp Walk" for all the media and news agencies that had been made aware of our arrest. The government's initial complaint read in part:

"The investigation was conducted by the Federal Bureau of Investigation (FBI) Organized Crime Drug Enforcement Task Force, which is comprised of FBI Agents, Internal Revenue Service (IRS) Agents, and New York City Police Department (NYCPD) Detectives.

The case stems from a three-year investigation of Kevin Chiles and a number of his associates for distribution of narcotics and the laundering of the illegal proceeds of that distribution. On the onset of the investigation, the agents and detectives interviewed several confidential informants and cooperating witnesses, conducted surveillance, and obtained Court authorization for five separate wiretaps. The investigation culminated with the arrests, on November 2, 1994, of fifteen individuals suspected of being involved in the Chiles organization."

The press release read, in part: "'Major drug ring in Harlem busted' Federal authorities smashed a major Harlem drug ring yesterday that allegedly used a sneaker store and two music companies as fronts. Authorities said the ring ran a network that shipped hundreds of kilos of dope a year to cities up and down the East Coast.

The group's alleged leader, Kevin Chiles, described as one of the biggest Harlem Druglords since Leroy (Nicky) Barnes and 16 followers were charged with shipping cocaine and heroin to cities from Boston, New York, Baltimore, Washington, Norfolk, Va, Virginia Beach, Raleigh/Durham, N.C. Spartanburg, S.C., and Atlanta.

The 28- year-old kingpin maintained a lavish lifestyle that included the ownership of stately homes in New Jersey, luxury automobiles, front businesses, and stocks, according to a complaint filed in Manhattan Federal Court.

Authorities estimate that Chiles, who has no previous drug arrest, made $40 million in drug sales since starting his organization in 1987. The feds will seek to seize numerous homes and condominiums, including a 15-room mansion in Franklin Lakes, N.J."

When we got to the bullpen, I had already gotten brief glimpses of the complaint, so I was not surprised by who was there but seeing them reaffirmed my confusion as to why they would be. They all had little-to-nothing to do with me criminally, including my accountant Salvatore "Sal" D. Mercante. Acquittances Annon "Eric" Filippi, Lavell and another person associated with them were there. Eric had been renting an apartment I'd hooked him up with, but unbeknownst to me, they had about 20 lbs. of weed in their crib, a sawed-off shotgun, and a couple of handguns when the feds came calling.

I was introduced to Eric through Spanish Mike with whom I was doing business and was originally introduced to by my uncle Fat Man. The business with Spanish Mike was nothing too heavy, but occasionally, we hooked up. Eric started coming uptown in place of Mike just to hang out. He liked the vibe, and once he started coming up, he never left. He always paid his own way, so he was never a burden, and he was cool. He was different from most individuals I was dealing with, and he would always be in my ear about weed and it being the drug of the future. I wasn't interested. I didn't smoke it at all, and because of the bulkiness of it regarding having to transport it, it didn't seem overly profitable based on what I was already doing, so we never did any weed business.

Eric asked about getting an apartment and I hooked him up. Turns out the day I got arrested, the FBI kicked in his door, believing he had more to do with my organization than he did. That day in the bullpen, I was made aware that his name wasn't actually Eric but Amnon Filippi, and he was Jewish. I'd always assumed he was Puerto Rican or Dominican. I knew Eric and Lavell, but what they had going on had nothing to do with me.

Jose Marte, a dude we bought non-traceable, disposable, burner phones, was in there as well, along with a female associated with him when he was arrested. Besides Christian "Chris" Mack," Robert "Bob" Burke, and Jeffrey "Jeff" Parker, I was at a loss trying to figure what family members and friends, including Erika "Reika" Carter, Diane Brown (aunt), Darnell Duckett (cousin) Lamont Brown (cousin), Nechelle Brown (cousin) and acquittances like Harry Jerome Libby Louis, William House, Anthony "Ant-Man" Mack and Lance "Estos" Bradley, being locked up meant.

When I got arrested, they were all included as my co-D's though I had never hustled with any of them on any level. Their acquittal on the state gun charge was monumentally important. Besides them avoiding minimum state jail time of 1-3 years for the gun charge, a conviction would have had them potentially facing a minimum of ten years or more on any potential future federal cases due to having a prior conviction.

Glen Louis Brown (Uncle Fatman) and Lenue "Len" Moore, my uncle's associate and someone I considered an uncle as well, were also indicted separately but directly as a result of the investigation on me.

In the course of the feds surveilling me, my uncle's name had come up. We were still close but weren't doing any regular business at all during the investigation, so while he may have come up on the feds' radar; there was little related to me to substantiate their suspicions. It turns out an older hustler that owned a garage directly across the street from BOSS Records was already acting as a government informant. We often used his garage coming to the office, and I am sure the feds asked about his relationship with me. He stated he knew who I was, but in fact, had a relationship over the years being supplied heroin by my uncle.

Probably not comfortable with the totality of their case against me, the feds set up a controlled buy with my uncle and the garage owner a few days after my arrest. My uncle agreed to make the sale; however on the day, he had Len bring the package to the guy instead of coming himself. Len was busted and brought into MCC where he gave me the details and let me know I was clearly the bargaining chip he and my uncle were sacrificed for.

Len ended up getting sentenced to 12 years related to the case because he would never cooperate with them. My uncle went on the run, and they never actually caught up to him related to that case or mine. Fatman wouldn't actually get busted until nearly 16 years later for something totally unrelated, with the previous case seemingly forgotten about. However, the fact that he ended up later being sentenced to seven years for some relative nickel and dime shit may have been just as indicative of the government not having forgotten.

***

Once we all got processed, it was clear that they tried to put pressure on the people around me, including my accountant, Sal, to turn on me. We were all sent to the Metropolitan Correctional Center. MCC is a United States federal administrative prison in lower Manhattan that holds male and female prisoners of all security levels. It is operated by the Department of Justice's Federal Bureau of Prisons. The building has 11 floors, 9 of which house inmates with a north and south side starting from the 3rd floor going up the 11th. The 11th was supposedly where the most high-profile were held. My accountant and I ended up on the south side of the 11th-floor side which held some infamous defendants. In February 1993, there was an attempt by terrorists to blow up the World Trade Center's Twin Towers with the use of a truck bomb in the underground parking structure of the North Tower. The thirteen-hundred-pound urea nitrate-hydrogen gas enhanced bomb was intended to knock the North Tower into the South Tower, bringing both down. While over one thousand people received varying degrees of injuries, only six people died as a result of the bombing. I believe four of the six suspects, one being Omar Abdel - Rahman, the Blind Sheik, that would be convicted for the terrorist act, were housed on the 11th floor with me as well.

In addition to the first Trade Center Bombers, MCC was holding members of La Cosa Nostra and Eric Millan-Colon in a high-profile case where reportedly $40 million in real estate, used car businesses and merchandising companies were seized. Eric was the alleged head of a criminal organization that sold heroin labeled "Blue Thunder" as well as the exclusive licensing rights to sell Teenage Mutant Ninja Turtles merchandise in Argentina. Supreme's nephew Prince and other members of the Supreme Team were in there as well. Supreme was already incarcerated doing 12 years on a federal bid. Preacher and some members of his crew were in as well as Boy George, Lou Simms, Farris Phillips and other members of the Manhattan Lynch Mob. The Willis Avenue Lynch Mob crew from out of the Bronx and a host of other notable figures were there as well as in nearby MDC which held the likes of Peter Shue and others.

Sal was initially put with other Italians, and I was housed with guys I knew or knew of. They had already heard about my case from the news, so my arrival was expected. They gave me a care package for myself and Sal that consisted of the essentials, like shower shoes, toothbrushes, toothpaste, deodorant, and access to someone's locker for food to hold us over till we were able to get our own commissary items.

My immediate concern at the moment wasn't so much for myself as it was for Reika, my Aunt Diane, Nechelle, and my other cousins, not knowing their status. I needed to make a phone call and phone time was at a premium. There were four phones for about 150 people who were all basically in my same predicament of either recently arrested or awaiting trials. Phone slots and times were allocated, and I was given a few slot times by the powers-that-be. I called every number I knew but could not reach anyone initially. This was my first clue that the feds had followed through on the threats against my family. It was truly becoming solidified that I had been more prepared to die than I was to be incarcerated.

It was a Thursday and Aunt Betty made her way to the house to look after the kids. When I finally spoke to her, she informed me of what had happened and the current status of things. She said that she had spoken to them earlier that day. My aunt stated that they ransacked the house before taking Diane, Reika, and Nechelle to the federal building in Newark, NJ. From what she understood, they were going to be transported to New York to be arraigned at some point.

That following Monday afternoon, I was made aware that they had arrived in MCC and were being processed. I was able to make arrangements with the officer on my unit to call down to their unit so I could speak with them. I spoke to Reika and asked if they were alright. She said, "We're all fine under the circumstances. We're supposed to go to court tomorrow for something."

I answered, "Yes, to be arraigned on the charges. I have already reached out to some attorneys, and they will be there tomorrow to represent you guys. I will try and make this same kind of call tomorrow to see how things turned out." I said my goodbyes, told her I loved her and promised it was going to be alright.

I had already contacted Murray Richmond. He was a prominent attorney I had used many times before over the years for my guys that had caught cases. I made arrangements to get him a retainer to advise and represent Reika, Aunt Diane, and Nechelle. The lawyers hired were able to get them all released on what's called a signature bond. Essentially, what that means is someone who's gainfully employed and in good standing in the community signs it stating they're responsible for you and that you will return to court to face your charges. If not, they are on the hook for the bond amount.

They all were able to get bond, processed, and released from court that day. Their releases on $150,000 signature bonds were just further proof that the case against them wasn't supported by anything I deemed serious. Getting immediate bail in federal drug cases was rare, especially on the magnitude they were claiming my case was.

They watched me, and since there were no drugs, they tried to watch the money. I knew and interacted with a lot of people. They could see I tried to hide my money, residences, and whereabouts as much from the prying eyes of the authorities and from the vultures that the streets were now littered with.

Within that time frame, they knew exactly why I used outside addresses for my license and to register cars and that they belonged to civilians whose only guilt was their friendship and allegiance to me. The government knew there were no illegal activities attached to any of these people or addresses yet they put on the forceful display of essentially terrorizing these people for no real reason other than to intimidate them and possibly coerce them into making incriminating statements about me, though they had absolutely nothing to do with any illicit activities. In the same way that we could gather names and addresses of people from our contacts we had that worked in precincts, Chris and I went out of our way to never put ID or register cars at addresses where we laid our heads at night.

One of those people caught up in the sphere of the investigation targeting me included Chris's brother, Anthony. Along with the warrants they executed against my family and me, they also did the same with Chris, kicking in his house door along with several of his family members. Ant-Man still lived in the old neighborhood on Ogden Avenue in a high-rise, known as the White Building. Ant-Man had a nice little operation up in the Bronx dealing with a handful of people. So, when he was awakened by the banging on his door, he instinctively jumped out of bed in a rushed state and began attempting to flush narcotics down his toilet. Unbeknownst to him, the feds had turned his water off in anticipation of him doing exactly that.

ARREST

Ant was probably targeted because Chris and I would stop by his house when we were in the area. We were all close coming up together. Ant-Man was like a younger brother to me as well, but we didn't really include him in our business. The feds recovered a small amount of drugs, some cash, and a safe deposit box key in their search. They would later get a warrant for that box where they would find a couple hundred thousand dollars Chris had his brother stashing for him, incorrectly figuring he wouldn't be caught up in our situation.

While I may have been surprised by the collateral damage of those around me who were arrested or detained, I wasn't exactly caught off-guard by my arrest. The two years I was being investigated forced me to prepare. Looking back, I am unsure if I was preparing more for jail or even possibly going on the run. I had removed most of the money I kept in the house initially, but after some months went by with nothing seemingly happening, I got rocked to sleep, and I started bringing money back in the house. I wasn't hustling, so I wasn't worried about what they would find. So, when I got busted, they got a couple hundred thousand in cash from the house safes, as well as about $400,000 in jewelry between Reika and myself. Additionally, they found two handguns in the house.

***

I was handicapped initially after the arrest because all my personal and business accounts were frozen or seized. The fed strategy is to cripple you financially so you cannot secure competent legal representation. Everything, no matter how legitimate, was frozen.

When it became time to retain our legal team, the government made it all but impossible for myself and Chris to pay for our legal defense. I was fortunate to have other family members outside the scope of the ones being investigated who were financially able to contribute to our legal defense through legitimate means. The government wanted every dollar accounted for as a deterrent for those wanting to assist. I was blessed to have this scenario in place, having planned for this rainy day. Initially, when I started retaining counsel for my family, I was spending from an emotional place needing to get them all bailed out. I spent $20,000 to

$30,000 unnecessarily. They were all ultimately released on their own recognizance or the signature bonds.

Because of all the publicity from the newspapers and television, all the attorneys I talked to started at a $200k retainer just to take my case. I met with several and they all said the same thing. The magnitude of the case and all it entailed was the reason for the large retainer and if I decided to go to trial, then that was another monetary conversation. I wasn't overly concerned about the fee as much as I was concerned as to who to choose. After all, my life depended on my choice.

Initially, I didn't come to terms with the fact that I wasn't getting out. I was optimistic I was going to get out on bail since I thought the case against me was bullshit. Other inmates tried to pull my coat and tell me my case was too high-profile and letting me know I wasn't getting out if for no other reason than that. In my initial arraignment and bail hearing, I had assigned counsel and I was rejected for bail. It started to become clearer I wasn't getting out. So, I started interviewing different high-profile attorneys for the longer fight ahead. Some of those interviewed I had used in the past and a few others I was less familiar with but came recommended.

I had paid plenty of legal fees throughout the years for others, including drug charges and several murder cases with attorneys like Benjamin Brafman, David Breitbart, Mr. Semiels and Leon Port. Yet, I must admit to being taken aback by the amounts these attorneys were asking. Granted, it was a federal case, but it was definitely my first time dealing with attorneys throwing these numbers around to represent someone. Nothing before this for me was even was even close.

As fate would have it, the lawyer I ended up choosing came from an unlikely source. I had made a call checking on Tameka. She was a young lady who I was very fond of. We met years before on multiple occasions starting in 1988 but did not begin dating until the summer of 1990 and a relationship quickly developed.
She was from St. Nicholas projects a couple of blocks from BOSS Sneakers. She was really pretty, shy, sweet and naive, even innocent. She was nothing like all the women that had been in my life up until that

point. She didn't hang out at any of the usual spots everyone else did. I don't ever remember through the years seeing her any place I was ever at. All she did was go to school and from school to work to home. She was special. She was different. I remember her always questioning my whereabouts and asking me about other women she had heard I was dealing with from her friends that did hang out in some of my circles. I was always brushing it off as some gossip. I justified my lying to her to myself by saying she couldn't handle the truth, so I was protecting her feelings.

This was the first opportunity I had to update her on the phone and thank her for the money she sent me, since my situation occurred. Though I appreciated the gesture I let her know it was unnecessary. I was pretty much venting about everything going on. Tameka asked if I was OK and how was I making out. I told her I was alright, but having some issue choosing representation since I was not feeling any of the lawyers I had spoken to. She mentioned that her dad, who was a hustler, had a lawyer that he always used. They were personal friends as well and had grown up together in the same neighborhood. The lawyer happened to be experienced in defending state and federal criminal cases. I told her to give me his number and I'd give him a call because I had nothing to lose. She said his name was Mr. Anthony Ricco and she would call him as well, so he'd be expecting my call.

Mr. Ricco was an African American defense attorney from Harlem. When he came to see me, I got a good feeling from him right away. Mr. Ricco was a no-nonsense type. On sight, he conjured up images of Malcolm X with his bow tie and his mannerisms. He was a practitioner of Islam though he never really tried to force religion onto me or in our conversations. I questioned whether it would be a good decision choosing a Black attorney to fight against The Man's system. Would he be respected and viewed in the right light by both the judge and jury? I was literally fighting for my life, so every angle and issue had to be examined. I had never considered hiring an African American for those reasons in the past.

Once Mr. Ricco was retained, he consolidated the legal team for myself, my family and co-defendants. He basically handpicked Ed Wilfred as co-counsel and Frank Gonzales as a private investigator, with him as the lead. I felt strongly that he would truly fight for me as a real advocate. He laid it all out for me from the grandiosity of the courtrooms to the denouncement of The UNITED STATES of AMERICA vs. Kevin Chiles et al.

Once my legal team was in place, the uphill battle and my new reality began to settle in. On November 1, 1994, my life completely changed. Excuse the obviousness of the statement, but unless you have been arrested, with most of your family with the very real threat of incarceration for the rest of your life, just stating the arrest affected me and my family would be an understated disservice.

Prior to the arrest, I had anxiety and stress in part because I knew I was being watched and followed. The truth is I thought I could ride it out because I was not engaged in any present or continuing illegal activity. I naively assumed that they would let my past bad acts go or at least just hit me with an IRS penalty. By 1994, I was totally legit. My naiveté was quickly replaced by an introduction into systemic draconian authoritarianism.

***

The first few days I was incarcerated, it really didn't sink in and when it did, I was just drained. In a weird kind of way, when I was arrested, it was a sense of relief. I was exhausted from the hamster wheel of obligations and ripping and running in the streets. Initially it was surreal because I didn't have any phone, pagers or obligations to be somewhere for somebody. The relief also existed to a degree because I thought my initial situation was going to be temporary and I was going to get out on bail.

By default, the time was one for introspection. When I finally realized I was in "jail" and couldn't do what I wanted to do, things got different. I refused to initially eat that shit they called food, but after a few days hunger won over and further marked my reality. I had already taken pork out of my diet. I would eventually cut red meat out as well. This was an extreme measure for someone that literally ate out every day and night and many of those meals included the best cuts of steak.

In retrospect, when the reality of no granted bail hit, I probably became depressed. That depression didn't cripple me as it does for some, but it weighed heavily on my mind and spirit. The lack of liberty, food and inability to make calls regularly was real, but I had to always wear the mask of being strong for everyone else even when my world was in complete turmoil. The concern to not be burdensome to others takes a toll on you and some days it was unbearable.

The earlier months looked particularly bleak. The government tries to break you into thinking you couldn't win your case. I definitely had days where it looked like that might be my reality. Not being at important dates for my kids or being able to help them with any problems that arose was when it weighed most heavily. Being strip-searched was a close second. It's some degrading shit for a person and while you know it's coming, it's never something I could ever get used to.

I know that nearly every person that has ever been incarcerated proclaims some form of innocence. I'll spare those theatrics. However, the government had little in the form of any real evidence of any crimes that I may have committed in the last couple of years to warrant a major federal investigation and "kingpin" charges. There was no major money confiscated in the course of the investigation and no drugs ever seized. I mistakenly believed that because I had stopped and was laying low, they'd stop and go away ideally keeping me from going to jail. I also didn't know much of anything about the statute of limitations concerning my past acts.

I naively grew up believing that the government had to prove a case based on physical presented evidence and not just on theories or a stereotypical assumption of guilt. I quickly learned that not to be true and "innocent until proven guilty" never seems to apply to People of Color or the poor. You are assumed guilty until you have the audacity and resources to prove otherwise and the government knows most of us are short on both.
After my arrest, I went from a metaphorical Heaven to Hell. I was not worried about my fate so much but that of those around me. I had come to terms with the idea of the finality from the streets. I was much less prepared for the reality of lifelong incarceration. If you have not lived

your life in and out of the penal system, there really is no preparation for the mental element of enduring incarceration.

I was a boss on the street. I was an egomaniac, calling the shots for everyone in my sphere. In jail, I was now federal inmate 36481-054, someone having to strip, cough and bend over literally and figuratively at the direction of guards. Yet, the seemingly helplessness of my predicament only emphasized how much I needed to stay strong and fight. I had three kids with Reika at this time, my son with Gina and one on the way. Angie had recently told me she was pregnant.

Once most of my family was out on bail, I was able (to a degree) to regain my facilities to deal with the reality of my case. The only ones that wouldn't get bail were me, Chris, Bob and Eric. The feds bet the proverbial house on Chris flipping and if not, him then dangling my entire family before me. This was not personal to me, but indicative of their overwhelming track record in convincing countless others to roll over and cooperate. Cooperating was never something I ever considered. I wouldn't have been able to live with myself.

I was surrounded by the worst of the worst/best of the best criminals. This helped to create a volatile mix where the common area was often the center of disputes playing out along with the limitations of 2 microwaves, 4 phones and 4 televisions for 200 inmates.

One of the first disputes in jail I witnessed occurred in MCC 11 South by the pool tables. I don't know how it was initiated, but before I could figure out what was going on, I heard what sounded like rapid gunshots. It was pool balls being thrown missing their intended targets hitting against the walls. This was followed by people running out their cells with locks in their socks as weapons along with the pool sticks. I played the wall tight both to observe and make sure no one could come up behind me. Not long after, I heard the sound of the door into the unit popping and the guards rushing in screaming for everyone to get down on the ground. This was jail... and I was facing the possibility of life behind bars. It all served as an eye-opener that this was going to be my life and scenes such as this were little more than just another day in that life. Violence was commonplace for me in the streets, but on the inside, I had to adjust to the different cadences that set things off.

When it became obvious we weren't going to just flip and join team USA or plead out, the feds decided to move us from MCC in lower Manhattan to Otisville Prison. Otisville was a jail facility compound within a namesake village in Orange County, New York. Otisville was where the feds kept the overflow of MCC prisoners if their trials were still months away. We were also moved because part of the feds' strategy, especially prior to any disposition, is to move inmates around often and frequently. They don't want awaiting defendants to establish any normalcy or comfort prior to their convictions. The abilities to interact beyond just the wing of our floor also contributed to Otisville further cementing my new reality of incarceration. In Otisville, we were far less isolated and confined than in MCC. There, we were all able to meet up together in places like the library, walking the track, gym or mess hall for the first time since our arrests.

Once I was acclimated to MCC and then Otisville, where I had more liberties, I eventually got to talk to all the different guys that were there. Our alleged crimes ranged from everything from selling drugs to extortion to murder. Truthfully, on the street, I probably wouldn't have kept certain people's company because we didn't have anything in common or even possibly opposing interests. However, what happens in jail is all dudes that fight their cases and stand up tend to gravitate towards each other regardless of the differences we may have had in the streets. Even more so, we bonded against the dudes who ended up revealing themselves as rats. So, we ultimately unified as one. It was a weird occurrence when this happened, but when it did, all the things that had happened in the street were revealed; such as who did what to whom and why.

I had guys tell me how on the street they were plotting on me but never caught me slipping compared to all the individuals who they had caught. I found out how some got set up and who had something to do with it. So many things had happened on the street during my run. Some I knew what the deal was and others I assumed were at the hands of the usual suspects. I was now made aware of the facts and some included either new and/or surprising reveals. That theme was ongoing as everyone's paperwork was circulating. The truth eventually revealed itself with guys taking pleas and others cooperating.

MCC and Otisville brought to light how busy the feds were in locking people up in their war on drugs. From the Triads to the Mafia to noted street crews that I either knew personally or knew of, it became profoundly clear that the federal government was spending countless resources in both finances and manpower to dismantle drug organizations and their leaders. It slightly made more sense why they spent the type of resources that they did on me even when they could see I wasn't doing anything. Locking up people like me was their mandate and they were going to do anything and everything necessary to fulfill that mission. In 1984, the federal and state prison systems contained 446,108 inmates. By 1994, that number had reached 1,053,738. Those numbers would significantly continue to increase (today at over 2 million). This trend and the resources that the federal government would expend in its "War on Drugs" would continue until 9/11/2001, when those resources, at least, were redirected to the "War on Terrorism."

During the preliminary stages, the next federal tactic, when it became obvious, I was not going to cooperate, was to make it appear like I was cooperating. That led to the feds (prosecutors) essentially orchestrating a production in Otisville. About a month or so being in Otisville, the US Attorney called up to the prison and arranged for an emergency lockdown. The tactical goon squad came into my housing unit. The cells are all facing the common area, so they made a spectacle with everyone locked in them seeing me being escorted out. It was designed to make it appear as though I was being extracted from the compound to who knows where, or why. They moved me to the isolation block, known as the "SHU", which stands for Special Housing Unit. While in the SHU, you have to adhere to all the regulations in that housing unit. I was confined to my cell for 23 hours a day, with one hour for recreation and/or a shower. In the SHU, you're only allowed one phone call per month. My immediate concern was letting someone know what was going on so not to scare any of my co-defendants. My next court date wasn't for another several weeks till I would see them.

Luckily, Reika happened to be coming up that weekend, with Bob Burke's woman, Arianne. They had put me on separation from them, so I wasn't allowed to be in the visiting room at the same time as any of them. They split the visit between us even though they came together. I was able to meet with Reika briefly and tell her that I was good and that they were on some BS. I emphasized I needed her to call my lawyer as well as try and assure everyone that I hadn't done anything strange.

When our next scheduled court appearance happened, I was still separated from all my co-D's. They arranged to bring me to court in a van by myself with a Marshall escort, yet again attempting to create a perception. They loaded everyone else first in the regular transport bus and made my separate procession visible to everyone as my solo van then followed the bus heading down to MCC. Once unloaded, they kept me isolated from everyone else. In open court, I sat in the jury booth guarded by Marshalls while all my co-defendants sat at the defendants' table. My lawyer demonstrably spoke stating that there was no reason for me being separated from my co-defendants and asked the judge to remove the forced separation and that in effect let all of them know nothing had changed.

Thankfully, no one did anything strange in the interim till they were reassured there was no substance behind any of the inevitable rumors from the government's charade. The feds know it really doesn't take long for the rumors to start and people are quick to flip at even the slightest change and/or chance. It's understood that the first to flip gets the best deal. The feds are playing chess while the average defendant is playing checkers, and keep in mind, all the advantages favor them and their ability to change the rules as they choose.

***

Besides the realities of my criminal case, in the early stages of my arrest, I was still dealing with the many of the elements of my personal bullshit and as you could imagine, juggling those complex dynamics was much harder behind bars than in the streets, especially when added to by the dirty tactics that the feds were willing to employ to exploit my circumstances.

I needed Reika to go to the Bronx apartment and retrieve a few things. The feds still controlled the apartment, and my options were limited as it were. Pre-iCloud, Instagram and emails, you kept all your freaky video recordings, Polaroids and pictures in a box. When Reika got there, a female agent had all these pictures laid out in the bedroom.

Angie, who was with me the night I got arrested, had recently informed me that she was pregnant prior to my arrest and let me know she that she planned on keeping the baby. I had dealt with pregnancy scares from random women multiple times during my run, but Angie was different. She was a very attractive woman who could've dated any man she desired. She was an accomplished, independent woman with a good job doing well for herself. I respected her and who she was as a woman.

On our next visit Reika was furious. I'm not sure what had her madder, the fact that she knew many of the girls in the pictures or me expecting her to maintain some composure and not lose it under the circumstances. My immediate concern was to try and keep her calm. I tried to explain that they wanted her emotional and us at odds with each other. I implored her to stay focused and she could return to being mad at me later. She was still furious but held it together. I knew I needed to tell Reika about Angie before the feds did or it came out in any other way. The timing of all this couldn't have been any worse. A few weeks later I came clean about Angie. I told her I wasn't sure if I was the father, though in reality, I strongly believed it was mine. She lost it emotionally.

My shit was being held together by threads. I tried to genuinely apologize for hurting her, but not for me being flawed. I played Russian Roulette with my life on the daily in the streets, so the shit I was doing on the side was just that. I was a great provider, but she had long come to accept that I was a horrible companion who was emotionally flawed. The reality is that she had run up on me and women in the passenger seat of my car in the past and pulled them out of the car. So, none of this was really new, but the pressure of our cases, the feds baiting her, and then the news of Angie's pregnancy were a Molotov cocktail set to explode in my face.

I realized that being locked up was causing all sorts of issues in my life. Obviously losing my freedom was the biggest. Managing my life in the streets was difficult when I was free, but with my new reality, it was all but impossible. One day, I was free and then the next, I was locked up without being given an opportunity to get any of my affairs in order. Once in, I attempted to keep my life and affairs on track via the phone.

I was blessed in that I had women I was in relationships with all wanting to help. They felt the need to do whatever they were able to do, the very least of which was coming to visit me. Prior to my arrest, juggling the relationships was never easy, but not overly stressful. The loss of my freedom made managing my BS hectic, to say the least. I learned this lesson early on. From my recollection, MCC had a visiting schedule that included Monday evenings, Wednesday daytimes, Friday evenings and weekends. Reika wasn't always able to visit due to the kids and how far we lived, so I would attempt to juggle my visits. I was somewhat honest in stating to her that if she wasn't able to make it to let me know because I would have someone else come, without ever stating who the someone would be.

On one early evening, I arranged for Tameka to come visit after work. August 1995 would mark the first time I had seen her since my arrest, ten months earlier. We were speaking on the phone regularly and I assured her soon as I figured out how things worked, I would let her know and she could come visit. This particular day worked since Reika had told me in advance she couldn't make it.

MCC was in lower Manhattan on 150 Park Row. The way it works, as I understood, was visitors would enter the building in a lobby area downstairs, get a visiting form, fill it out and turn it in. It was a first come, first served kind of setup. The officers would take as many of the visitors that would fit on the elevator and bring them to the floor of the person they were visiting.

The officers in the lobby would call up to the unit and convey to the other officers' which inmates had visitors coming up. The inmate would be notified of his visitor and would wait for his name to be called before being searched in an area right outside the visiting area, then allowed access to your visitors beyond a locked door.

This day, after being told I had a visitor, I was waiting to be taken into visiting room. About five minutes later, the officer came up to me and said, "Chiles you have another visitor." I was expecting Tameka, but I had no idea who the other person was. I asked him if he could find out who it was. When he came back, he said, "There's two women out there not together. A Tameka Anderson and Ericka Carter, and they don't seem happy." I shook my head and said, "Damn," to myself. I wasn't expecting Reika and this didn't exactly qualify as a pleasant surprise. I contemplated what I was going to do and quickly decided it was in my best interest to deny the visits and not see either. I felt just like a sucker because I wasn't able to handle this as I once would've been able to do on the outside, especially without making a scene.

This wasn't the first time they had come into contact with each other. There was a time one night when I was in my father's condo that Reika came by unannounced and I had Tameka there with me. I hadn't been home in a couple of days, and she knew I was in town. We probably were having one of our many fights and I wasn't in the mood to be dealing with her. I had just arrived about a half hour prior, when there was someone at the door. I wasn't expecting any company, so I was surprised to hear the bell ring. The hardwood floors looked nice, but they were a low-level snitch, because I believe she could hear me approaching the door. So, before I could say anything she started saying, "Motherfucker I know you're in there with a bitch, so open up the door!" At first, I didn't say anything, considering my options. As I contemplated, she continued yelling all kinds of expletives in the hallway of this normally quiet building. "I see your car, so don't open this door and see!" I made the mistake of parking my custom BMW in front of the building, so she was pretty certain I was there.

I turned and walked over to Tameka and told her, "I'm gonna have to let her in because she's not going anywhere and I can't have her out there acting crazy." I kept a very low profile in the building with my comings and goings, so the last thing I needed was to bring unwanted attention to myself. I gave Tameka my car keys and told her, "I'm gonna let her in and when I do you, can just leave and take yourself home and I'll get with you later." I opened the door and Reika rushed in, straight towards Tameka acting a fool. I grabbed her and held her telling Tameka I would talk to her later. Tameka walked past us and left the apartment as Reika continued to act out.

So in MCC, here they were in the same place having not seen each other since that evening in the Bronx. When I decided it was in my best interest not to go out there, they were told of my decision, which neither was the least happy about. They were escorted back downstairs together. When they got downstairs, Tameka approached Reika, I guess calling herself getting to the bottom of things. They began to talk and Reika made it her business to inform her of all the things she didn't know and what she felt she should know since Tameka "thought" she knew Kevin. Reika told her about every woman she had ever heard of and anything I'd ever done. To top it off, she told her what I had just recently confessed to about Angie being pregnant and the child possibly being mine.

I had told Reika about Angie myself because that was the one thing I didn't want her to find out from someone else because of the sensitivity of our situation. She was my woman and co-defendant and the last thing I needed in the world would've been for her to find that out and lose it. I didn't need her super irrational, emotional and talking reckless or worse. The FBI wanted her to look for solace in them and they had attempted to do that with the pictures already. I felt it was in my best interest to tell her myself, praying she'd be able to handle it. As you could imagine, on the heels of that conversation, this wasn't something I needed to be happening. My shit was raggedy to say the very least.

Tameka was mature beyond her years. She and Reika ended up exchanging numbers claiming they would keep in touch. Tameka was very upset with me for not having told her of the potential pregnancy of another woman, but still had the uncanny ability to compartmentalize her emotions and deal with the immediacy of my situation. She understood Reika's point of view and sided with her in regard to what she said about me. The crazy thing about that night is that a truce was made. They both agreed they loved me and I was the biggest creep they knew, but they also agreed I didn't deserve the predicament I was currently in. While I was a good dude on the street, I was probably more delusional than I had admitted to myself in my dealings with women. I believed I was exempt from the rules of relationships as ordinary civilians maintained. Later that night, when I called them both, to my surprise, they had talked it out, and things weren't as fucked as I'd expected. Talk about being fucking lucky. I looked at that luck as a possible sign of things to come.

If nothing else, the episode gave me something additional to reflect on. My relationship with Reika was a whirlwind of dysfunction from the very beginning. I was probably too young to take on the responsibility I imposed on myself more so from a psychological place than actually being able to take care of and provide for her/them financially. She had so many issues herself including losing both her parents as a child. From there, she was effectively passed around amongst different family members, always lacking a sense of home and stability that was only compounded when she conceived at 14. Having to grow up so fast lent to an appearance of being way more mature than her age because life had left her no choice in that matter. Yet, ultimately, she still was only 15 years old.

However, almost ten years later, Reika was no longer that 15-year-old girl I'd met. I now felt I had robbed her of her innocence. In part because of my lifestyle, she had dealt with experiences and seen things a grown, middle-aged man, devoted to a life in the streets, wouldn't have been prepared to deal with. It left me feeling less than certain if I was the best thing for her looking back.

I genuinely got into her life to help her, and I desired to change it for the best. Examining it at that moment, I questioned would she have been better off never having met me. She was almost 25 and had three children that she now was totally responsible for. The prospects of their father looking at spending the rest of his natural life in prison was looming along with wondering how she was going to go on and make it. She had never worked a day in her life, and I realized I hadn't truly prepared her for this. Hindsight is truly 20/20. It was now clear that I had taken on more in my life than I was able or ready to handle.

I was a man-child, never really enjoying any part of my own childhood. At the age of 11/12, I was out the house making a way for myself, helping with small things around my house, and attempting to make a difference in our living conditions. By the time I met Reika, I felt as though I was grown and able to take care of her and the baby including protecting them from the world. I was but a child myself and, honestly, probably needed protection. Perhaps not physical protection as much as guidance. She was a Black girl lost and, I wasn't much more than a lost Black boy. With the best of intentions, we were the blind leading the blind.

As eye-opening as these moments of reflection may have been, the urgency of my situation left little time for them to be more than just moments. No matter what BS I interjected into my daily incarcerated life, the focus always quickly came back to trying to regain my freedom, and that meant the particulars of my case and trial.

My personal life and issues were daunting by themselves. When coupled with so many of my closest family members also serving as my co-defendants, the prospect of fighting the US government and its enormous resources was often overwhelming. Then you add to this fact that the federal government doesn't just try to prosecute you with their criminal cases and investigations. They engage in all-out psychological warfare in the process. They take no prisoners in the literal and figurative sense. If you are in their sights, they will do whatever it takes, and (even relatively) innocent people along the way are collateral damage that they willingly sacrifice to achieve their ultimate goal.

Except for my brother and Aunt Diane, who was initially arrested but not subsequently indicted, everyone in my family was fighting cases related to mine. They not only put pressure on my family to betray me. More than that, they dangled their potential long-term incarcerations as a tool to bring me to my knees and capitulate. My fight for my life and freedom had to account for the well-being of everyone I loved as well, if not first. In hindsight, if I understood what I do now (how dirty the government fights and how much the deck was really stacked against me), I might have taken a plea out the gate to spare my family the risks that we were thankfully able to escape. Unfortunately, I have heard too many other stories of other innocent family members who became casualties of the government's "win at all costs" strategy. It's easy to adopt a win at all cost strategy when you have unlimited resources. The process of going legit allowed them to freeze and/or seize anything in my name. I had stopped hustling for at least two years, and even being far from broke, the stress in trying to avoid a lifetime of incarceration, without parole, would push me to my emotional and financial limits.

I was a relatively fiscally-sound hustler. I paid for my work upfront. I always made sure I had the money upfront for 25, then eventually 50 keys. That was anywhere from $625k to $1.25 million in readied, working capital. I prided myself on having the ability to pay for my goods upfront and never having to owe anyone. I, of course, got work on consignment in addition to what I paid upfront for but made a point to get the connect's money immediately out the way. All of that contributed to me having a sizable cushion despite not hustling for two years before being arrested.

However, lower-to-no income and big hits along the way have a not so strange way of straining all that. When I got busted, they were only able to take about $500k, including only $200k in two safes in the Franklin Lakes house and another $30k in my father's condo apartment along with a couple of safe deposit boxes. Add my trial investigator, attorneys' fees, plus Reika and the family; it was upwards of a million dollars seized and lost related to my arrest. When you are more prepared to die than retire or walk away, the realities of how much is enough stacked to live or needed in case of being busted is something none of us, especially at our ages, were adequately prepared to assess.

My reality is that I probably should have bowed out the game earlier than I did and saved more in preparation for actually walking away. Violence during the time was so unreal and commonplace. Quitting flat out and moving away would have been rational much earlier than I did, but I was so indoctrinated in the Life that I just stayed the course. I know what Harlem represents to me, so even with gentrification, I don't see or romanticize today's Harlem like Caucasians or this newer generation. They don't have the history of blocks associated with death and tragedy. We strove to get out, not stay in our environment. While I love Harlem, I never viewed it as home sweet home.

Hustling embodied and breathed life into me even when it changed and represented death and dismay. We were just living until an expected death. No disrespect to veterans, but the constant tragedies and pressure from the lifestyle coupled with the environment was akin to suffering

PTSD. As such, we probably took unnecessary chances because there wasn't an expectation to live long. Statistically, at the time, one-quarter of Black males under the age of 24 were expected to be either killed or imprisoned. None of us had a long-term perspective on life. To say we were shortsighted would be an understatement.

The tragedies truly hit home with deaths like my mother's and Albe's, as well as the arrests of my best friends and father. Some of these more personal tragedies left me with a sense of hopelessness, but then as a matter of survival, you move on. The events always stayed in the back if not the forefront of my mind, but they also came with a more reckless credo moving forward: "I'm going to do this shit till my number comes up… death or jail… and if I'm going to do it, I might as well do the fuck out of this and be remembered in the process." I always made sure money was left in case something happened, but I was going to get rich or literally die trying. That all somehow made sense until the arrest came.

I previously mentioned personally knowing nearly 250 to 300 people that lost their lives during this time. The mention was made in such a cavalier way I know I need to further expound on such a statement. The first part of it is how not normal it is experiencing that magnitude of death outside of actual wartime.

The death, despair, and trauma had become such a common part of all our existences that it developed into our new normal. I could never identify any of this amid living through it. It was PTSD combined with a growing immunity from real feelings.

I did not have anyone to teach me any different. I am not even sure if I would have even been capable of hearing them while my life was so chaotic and fast-paced. That's the nature of the Game. It envelopes your psyche and blurs the lines of sensibility. What the circumstances keep you from understanding is "just because something has become our norm doesn't mean we have to accept it as such." Growth and reflection finally made me realize that those extremes should never be our new normal. It is a lesson I wish I would have learned earlier, but I am nonetheless grateful I came to understand at all.

Once you go to jail and people think you may never come home, it doesn't take long before everyone develops convenient amnesia about your generosity and their obligations to repay. This is just one of the many life lessons that came about from my arrest. While I had been on a path of change, losing my liberty and freedom put everything into greater perspective. While I still thought the government's case wasn't particularly strong, I knew I was still in danger of never returning home. I also knew that if I did get a second chance, I would have to adopt a mentality to be more self-centered moving forward. Life lessons finally understood once I began to contemplate life as a long-term game. Unfortunately, the lessons were not learned before my arrest, and once that occurred, the focus was initially less on reflection and more about doing what was necessary to fight a federal case at trial.

19

PREPARING FOR BATTLE

My charges on the eve of my first trial were all significantly different than what my initial complaint looked upon my arrest. At this point, there had been several superseding indictments, and there ended up being no murders or violent crimes listed amongst my charges. Nonetheless, I was still looking at life.

The Continuing Criminal Enterprise Statute (commonly referred to as CCE Statute or The Kingpin Statute) is a United States federal law that targets large-scale drug traffickers who are responsible for long-term and elaborate drug conspiracies. Unlike the RICO Act, which covers a wide range of organized crime enterprises, the CCE statute covers only major narcotics organizations. CCE is codified as Chapter 13 of Title 21 of the United States Code, 21 USC. § 848. The statute makes it a federal crime to commit or conspire to commit a continuing series of felony violations of the Comprehensive Drug Abuse Prevention and Control Act of 1970 when such acts are taken in concert with 5 or more other persons. For conviction under this statute, the offender must have been an organizer, manager, or supervisor of the continuing operation and have obtained substantial income or resources from the drug violations.

The sentence for a first CCE conviction is a mandatory minimum of 20 years' imprisonment (with a maximum of life imprisonment), a fine of not more than $2 million, and forfeiture of profits and any interest in the enterprise. Under the so-called "super kingpin" provision added as subsection (b) to the CCE statute in 1984, a person convicted of being a "principal" administrator, organizer, or leader of a criminal enterprise that either involves a large amount of narcotics (at least 300 times the quantity that would trigger a 5-year mandatory minimum sentence for possession), or generates a large amount of money (at least $10 million in gross receipts during a single year), must serve a mandatory life sentence without possibility of parole (sometimes referred to as a "living death" or "pine box" sentence, since the offender is strictly ineligible for release while alive).

There were two separate drug conspiracy charges (heroin and cocaine) that carried a minimum of 10 years to life sentence, which is what we all were charged with. In addition to the kingpin drug conspiracy charges, I was charged with money laundering that had a mandatory 20-year sentence. Additionally, I faced a consecutive five-year sentence for weapons possession in the commission of selling narcotics.

This is part of the prosecution play where they overcharge you. There are no restrictions on prohibiting them from being able to do this. The strategy is multi-layered. Of course, the first is to intimidate and overwhelm you into submitting to a guilty plea. If that doesn't work, the strategy plays on working at your trial. It's up to a defense to file countless motions to minimize charges, if even able to do so. They do this knowing the jury may not convict you of all charges or even the major ones, but still convict you on a seemingly lesser charge because they feel like you are not totally innocent, not realizing that the seemingly lesser charge could still get you 20 years to life.

When the government busted us, part of what they found during the searches was that Chris and I had phone scramblers. They were old but lent to suspicion and circumstantial evidence as to why we would even possess them if not engaged in criminal activities. However, in over 8,500 intercepted phone calls, there wasn't one recorded call that showed Chris or I ever using the scramblers. Their possession hurt and helped. My lawyer tried to explain it away by saying we had disposable income and did dumb shit with it, including owning a bunch of other counter-surveillance gadgets and bug detectors.

I spent tens of thousands of dollars on counter-surveillance equipment in my heyday, and some of that was introduced at trial. Many others they missed in plain sight at the house and apartments. Looking back, it seems crazy that they missed so much of that type of evidence out in the open, which could have only hurt me.

All the cars we drove had tracking devices placed on them by the feds. They installed surveillance cameras in the hallway exit signs of my father's condo, which only showed the musical groups coming in and out of the apartment along with my different female companions.

Knowing my propensity to seek pleasure, the government tried to use very attractive women to entrap me. In one instance, a beautiful woman showed up on a video set for one of my groups. The tactic might have otherwise worked, but the randomness of such an attractive woman on set at 7AM was a little too fortuitous even for my vanity. At Jack the Rapper, in Orlando, many of my dudes talked about all these women or producers stepping to them, and it was clear that they were feds or informants. The funny thing is there are several freak stories involving those women regardless of whether they were feds or informants.

The feds also tried to set me up to make drug sales, which I never did. When that didn't work, they tried to set me up with a guy named Richard Bailey, who I was initially introduced to by Chris. It turns out he was a confidential informant working for the government. He knew Chris when they were kids in their old neighborhood before Chris moved to my neighborhood in the Bronx. Ironically, unbeknownst to me, he was a second or third cousin of mine, a detail I didn't even realize until after my trials had begun. By design, Richard ran into Chris years later. He worked his way around to me, eventually approaching me to meet with some downtown bankers. They were all presumably undercover agents. A meeting occurred in which it was proposed for me to launder my money through their bank for a 5% fee. Thankfully, I never went for their program. The government still tried to hit me with a money laundering charge in my indictment that got dropped during the trial. My lawyer was able to show that I never tried to hide or conceal my ownership in any of my endeavors, which is a requirement to be charged with money laundering. I paid taxes, and my businesses and house were all in my name along with real and verifiable income from strictly legitimate businesses.

After we received our discovery, it was revealed that Chris and Chuck were the only people on any of the wiretaps or surveillance tapes. Unbeknownst to me, Chris had been set up by Richard Bailey. Richard

THE CRACK ERA

Bailey specifically asked for a key of crack-- not long after the laws had changed, making crack sales exponentially more heavily weighted with mandatory minimums versus powder cocaine at a rate of 100-1. Chris made the sale to him but balked at selling him crack and sold him powder instead. For some reason, Chris never fucked with the guy again despite knowing him. Chris never really told me exactly why he never continued to do business with dude, but it is reasonable to assert that if Chris would have continued with this informant, who knows how much more this could have impacted us. As it stood, that one kilogram of cocaine was the only actual drug sale recorded directly implicated against us. There would also be the testimony of an undercover cop stating he made a sale indirectly to me and Chuck's uncorroborated testimony, but Chris' interaction with Richard Bailey was the one direct drug sale they had against my "alleged" organization.

Ironically, even Chris's misfortune in working with the informant partly explains why I believe in a higher power. One kilo of cocaine may make you a drug dealer, but it doesn't make you a kingpin. If the feds had equipped Chris's informant differently, even with a higher initial sale order, the case against me would have been harder to fight. As it was, Chris had a prior felony conviction, and under the filing by the government of an 851 Federal Statute that the government threatened to pursue if he went to trial, his mandatory minimum would have doubled due to that conviction. So, the ten-year minimum was now twenty years, plus a consecutive five years for a gun found in his car. The 25 years was what he was minimally facing right out the gate.

The feds counted on that 25 years being enough time to flip Chris and make him give me up. This is why they arrested him first on November 1st. It wasn't a coincidence but a calculated action. If all had gone according to plan, they would have flipped Chris and re-released him back on the streets to set me up. They knew their case was weak without someone cooperating, and with Chris being the closest person to me, they knew his testimony would have had the same impact that Sammy "The Bull" Gravano's had against Gotti. Our close relationship was undeniable. Chris could have easily reduced his sentence, if not outright avoided jail time altogether, by telling on me. They wanted me, not him, and I am sure he was a tradeoff they would have been willing to make.

Truthfully, any testimony from him against me would have been virtually indefensible. However, Chris's love and loyalty toward me is indisputable. He has always been there for me-- no questions asked.

Snitching really is the prosecution's foundation for seeking a conviction in any major drug case. Their long witness list, trying to flip Chris and busting my cousins Lamont, Darnell, and Billy in the gun case were obvious strategies to try and intimidate me into submission. Had my cousins not beat the case a year earlier, it would have set them up for a minimum 20-year sentence and the pressure and incentive to turn on me.

There was a bunch of dudes who I had done business with in the past that were bought in from other jails during my trials on writs. A writ of habeas corpus (which means to "produce the body") is a court order to an agency holding someone in custody to deliver the imprisoned individual to the court issuing the order. Their presence wasn't a complete surprise since they were on my witness list, but unsettling nonetheless. This usually happens when these people are going to testify against you, and they have already been interviewed and are on stand-by until you go to trial. Then they are bought in to be prepared for trial prepped by the prosecutor, going over any prior statements they may have given and anticipated questions by the defense.

There were several instances where I was made aware of such individuals being in the building either by them getting a kite to me or arranged situations set up so that I'd see them. This was all done to intimidate me and make me aware that these individuals were actually there, ready and willing to testify against me.

However, except for Koran Winters and Chuck, who were not privy to or part of my actual organization, no one in the drug game that I actively did business with actually got on the stand to testify against me.

I am partially lucky and partially beyond blessed that others didn't trade their freedom, that was surely dangled in front of them, for mine. I was a drug dealer-- a criminal that had dealt with anyone that was someone during that time. I lived by very strict principles and always tried to do right by those I did business with. That may not hold much meaning to this generation but living by those principals effectively saved my life in the streets and surely my freedom. I established real and genuine relationships with people.

Fear only takes you so far. I played by not being greedy and a man of my word. When it came time for people to exploit me, I was by-in-large spared. Bernard could have done more damage. While I am no way giving him a pass, Alpo could have done more damage. There were many people on the government's list who chose not to tell on me that did tell on others. None of my original crew, many of whom were locked up on unrelated charges, could have easily presented me as their get out of jail free cards. Instead, my relationships held true, and I never look past those blessings, especially understanding how the government rewards snitching and the hard-on they had for me.

One example of the depth of my relationships beyond merely some street shit was Crusader Rob. He was one of over 100 people that ended up on the witness list provided by the government. That witness list included people I had some dealings with that would be mentioned in the course of the trial. I wasn't certain of the initial reason why Mr. Ricco asked me if I felt Rob would be of any concern. Part of the reason for his concern may have had something to do with him being incarcerated in the state doing time unrelated to me. His name may have come up in conversations with the government pertaining to our past and a bunch of speculation in my case.

Mr. Ricco knew all too well how they played and knew for sure they would offer him a deal for him to flip on me that included a get out of jail free card. His concern became obvious: did I feel he would take a deal? He mentioned the feds were going to see Rob, and he was planning to visit him as well. I expressed my feelings on how solid Rob was, but early on, I believe my lawyer thought I was overly optimistic and probably somewhat naive.

After returning from visiting Crusader Rob, Mr. Ricco was assured that we didn't have anything to worry about. I'm not certain of all the details of their meeting, but Mr. Ricco stated, "He's down for you, and I'm confident there's nothing we have to worry about."

They offered me 25 years, and even knowing the government's conviction rate, I couldn't bring myself to signing my name to a piece of paper accepting 25 years. I was either not man enough or not weak enough to voluntarily take that kind of time. They were going to have to impose that sentence on me.

I rolled the dice and went to trial based on my unique set of circumstances that I felt were favorable for me. Chris did take the plea offered him of 18 ½ years. He told me that 18 and ½ was a better deal than the 25 years he was otherwise facing minimally. Chris didn't initially tell me about his plan to take the plea. In part, I know this was because I'm sure he thought I would have tried to talk him out of it. I saw him the morning he did it in the holding cell. I thought we were going to the court to review the evidence in our case in preparation for trial. He never mentioned he was going to plea instead.

Leading up to the actual trial, there were several meetings where my co-defendants that were out on bail that hadn't pled out attended. This was a challenging task to arrange, but Mr. Ricco, along with the other trial attorneys, were able to pull it off. The meetings were designed for all of us to get on the same page and coordinate how we were all going to proceed collectively. Those of us that were inside had spent months with one another and were pretty much in-sync. We had taken on different responsibilities regarding our research efforts, compiling information, and sharing insight on anything we'd found in our discovery while preparing. These meetings were an important reminder that despite our innately personal interests, we all stood a better chance of fighting as a team. No one understands the concept of "divide and conquer" better than the United States government.

We were going back and forth to court all the time because we were one of the few crews to take our case to trial. One of the crews that did go to trial was right before ours. Erick Bozeman was the supplier out of California who shipped tons of cocaine by running a ring that hollowed out computers, filled them with the drugs, and shipped hem nationwide for sale. James "Blue" Piggot was the distributor and head of the organization on the New York side. We kept track of their case because it was before the same Judge Griesa, who was assigned to my case.

Additionally, Mr. Ricco was an attorney for one of the defendants. Though their case had nothing to do with ours, it wasn't exactly a good sign when all the defendants were found guilty after a trial. Bozeman and Piggot were both sentenced to life.

One actual upside of going back and forth to court so frequently was that we started to develop relationships and receive begrudging respect from the corrections officers. They even started getting us sandwiches from delis and giving us other extras when available. Outside food to an inmate was a pure luxury that most of us once took for granted.

***

The government's tactics and vindictiveness were eye-openers for me. I had been brought up and brainwashed to believe that federal law enforcement, such as the FBI were beyond ethical reproach. We are indoctrinated to believe that the FBI and federal government are righteous and operate within the strict guidelines of legalities. I had previously bought into this belief, but quickly and painfully learned what type of farce this is. They were supposed to be the good guys who tried to capture bad guys within the rules and with ethics. My naiveté is laughable now. While being investigated and before my arrest, I had no idea I was being pursued by wolves as treacherous as the ones I fought so hard to avoid in the streets.

As stated, there were over 8,500 taped recordings captured in my investigation. The calls were intercepted from many different locations and sources, including from many of our burner phones. Those 8,500 recorded calls were kept on cassette tapes. I know many of you reading this may not even know what cassettes are, but the task of listening to them was daunting, frustrating, and time-consuming. I have a unique ability to compartmentalize and focus, and that makes time go faster. However, beyond any inconvenience, carefully listening to every single second on those tapes was a necessity. I had to be 100% certain that there wasn't anything on those tapes that incriminated me. I was not only listening for myself, but for all my family and co-defendants. I know that none of them or their attorneys' were as meticulous or diligent in listening to these recordings, but because of the broadness of the conspiracy connections within the statutes I was being tried on, the evidence and outcome of their cases was as critical as the specifics of my own. Any convictions by my co-d's would be used against me, so I examined all the evidence within the various cases because it all ultimately affected me. Listening to every single word of the recordings was painstakingly my job and who better than me to take on the task since it was, figuratively and literally, my life on the line.

Unfortunately, I had the time, and at some point, listening to them all became a combination of comedy and reminiscing, with a large segment of my recordings covering the time between me and a bunch of broads. There wasn't one recorded call of me talking about any type of drug transaction.

The tapes helped Mr. Ricco, and I assess the government's case against me. However, as my attorney was also careful to point out, the massive volume of calls also signified the amount of money, agents, time, and resources that were spent investigating me for so long. And all that translated into-- someone had to go down for their efforts.

On television, every trial has some dramatic "aha" moment that miraculously proves someone's innocence or guilt. Real-life, of course, doesn't fit so nicely into that narrative for justice. Real-life trials include a series of ups and downs; some days, the prosecution has victories, other days, the defense does. Well, in my own trial, as Mr. Ricco and I made an initial assessment that the evidence and case against me weren't particularly strong, the arrest of Chuck Born in March 1995, nearly five months after everyone else, was a definite potential game-changer in my case.

***

Chuck came to be a part of my circle through a guy named Mike. Mike had come home from jail in 1990, weeks after Rich's murder. He was on Rich's block of 132nd Street and 7th Avenue talking with some of the locals. I was coming through the block from 8th Avenue and 132nd Street when I reached the red light. My peripheral caught someone running up on my car. I instinctively reached for my gun and had it in hand when this person called my name. I didn't know him. I rolled the window down just enough to hear him asking if he could have a word with me. I told him I was busy on the move, but for him to come by the store.

A little later that same day, he showed up at BOSS Emporium, asking for me. I was in the back office and was made aware that someone was looking for me. I came from the back and walked outside, and he followed. "What's up," I asked. He started by introducing himself as Mike, again telling me Rich was his man and that he just got home and was twisted. Now that his man was gone, he wasn't certain what he was going to do. He was looking for some help getting back on his feet and asked if I could do anything for him. We talked a bit, and he made me aware of the obvious, which was he didn't have any money, but he had a spot in Buffalo, NY, that was a potential goldmine. He asked if I could give him an eighth a key or two to start so he could prove himself and assured he would be grateful for the help. He was doing everything in his power to convince me that he was a good dude, name dropping Azie, Alpo, and a few others. I told him to come back in a couple of days, and I'll let him know something then.

Mike returned a couple of days later. I had asked around about him, and nothing came back sideways, so I entertained his conversation. The reality is that I was the last man standing. As many guys were coming home from bids upstate, it became a regular thing for me being sought out.

I told him I'd give him a shot and planned to get up with him later that day. We met up and handled the business, and things went as he stated they would. He soon came to be known as Buffalo Mike. A couple of weeks in, he introduced me to an individual named La Du out of Soundview. Mike said he was his partner in his Buffalo situation. He mentioned La Du would be coming in instances when he wasn't able. La Du's mannerisms and the conversation came off in a way I respected. As I got to know La Du, my instincts were proven right from the way he was handling his business. The money was always right. No games, all good business.

My relationship with Mike was developing as well, with no issues. During one of our conversations, he asked if I knew a dude named Chuck Born from Mount Vernon. I told him I knew of him, but not personally. Chuck used to run with Azie and Rich as well. I mentioned I knew his woman and baby mother, Tanya pretty well, and she and I were cool. Tanya was in the finesse game and I had copped things from her from time to time. He went on to say that Chuck was his man, and they were up north together. He said Chuck was home, and he told him he was rolling with me now, and Chuck wanted to meet me personally. I told Mike to tell the homie to come by. I knew of him in passing though we had never connected; he had a good name in the streets.

Chuck showed up at BOSS Emporium within days of the conversation with Mike. When Chuck came around, I no longer had a crew, just independent distributors. The discussion was different than the initial one I had with Mike because there was a degree of familiarity with Chuck. The code of the street back then was when a good dude came home; it was your duty as a top hustler to help a person get on their feet if you were in position.

There were several incidents that defined my relationship with Chuck. They made me believe he would never betray me. I was willing to bet my life on it. However, Chuck would prove to be one of the few times my instincts concerning the streets were dead wrong.

Right out the gate, I handled his probation situation and gave him a job at the store, a new Nissan Pathfinder, and a means to make money again. Early on in our relationship, Tanya got locked up for credit card scams, and her bail was five thousand dollars. He didn't have the money to bail her out, so I gave it to him, no questions or hesitation.

A second instance was sometime later when we had been rocking for a minute. Chuck came to me about someone wanting to buy three keys of crack at premium points *above* what they were going for. This was suspicious to me, but his greed blinded him, and he was pressing me to make it happen for him. I let him know he needed to get the money upfront if I was even going to consider making it happen for the simple reason that once it was cooked, I wasn't going to deal with the possibility they no longer wanted it. Plus, the specificity of their request didn't feel right considering the new sentencing guidelines.

He couldn't get them to give him the money, so he tried to move past me to make it happen. However, he couldn't get it done, and they found someone else he knew to do it. His replacement was taken down in the DEA sting. Remember, crack now had a 100- to-1 ratio versus powder cocaine, which means those guys got charged for 300 keys of cocaine and a mandatory life sentence.

Chuck had a friend he brought to me to buy two keys on a couple of occasions. I made the sales, and Chuck made his points on the deals. It turns out his man was under the protection of another crew in Harlem who I happened to have been cool with. One of the principals reached out and got in contact with me, asking, "What's up with your man Chuck?" I asked what they were talking about, and he continued, "He's running with my little homie who I've been holding down, and I eat off him and your man getting in between that, and that's an issue. We're going to get at them soon as we catch up with them, but the only reason you're getting this courtesy call is out of respect because we fuck with you." I assured them that Chuck was my man, and I would holla at him and appreciated the heads up.

I hit Chuck up and told him to push back because his man had a serious problem on his hands. Within days of my warning, his man was murdered on the Eastside of Harlem. Chuck called me in a panicked state immediately after hearing what had happened to his man and asked me if he was good. I assured him he no longer had anything to worry about.

Needless to say, that crew went down around the same time I did in 1995, and members of that organization flipped and told on my dude who had reached out to me on the Chuck situation about the many murders that occurred in and around Harlem that they had committed. He ended up taking a plea of almost 30 years to avoid a life sentence in prison.
Chuck was the only one of my 21 co-defendants who was not arrested on November 1st or 2nd. He was fortunate to not be in their sights and avoided being arrested and went on the run for nearly five months. I remember hoping that they wouldn't catch up with Chuck. Even if they

did, I felt that because I had saved his life on those two occasions and looked out for him in so many other instances that he would be indebted enough to stand up and not do anything crazy.

Chuck had reached out to my brother Tony while he was on the run. My brother said he didn't know what was going on, but that essentially the case against everyone was BS and to hold tight. When they finally caught up to him, in Raleigh, NC, in March of 1995, he began telling as soon as he got arrested without even seeing where the case was. When he got busted, Chuck was literally telling upon being handcuffed by the regular cops in North Carolina even before the feds flew down there and had a chance to talk to him. Later, I would find out he had official government documents pertaining to the case, passed on to him from Alpo, who at this time was known to be hot and in the witness protection program. Alpo sent these documents to Azie, who, in turn, made arrangements to give them to Chuck while he was on the lam.

When he was caught, he was detained briefly in North Carolina and then expedited back to New York for arraignment on our indictment, making a court appearance with the rest of us. This would be our first time seeing each other or talking since the last time seeing one another before my arrest. He seemed regular. There was no funny vibe, and he told me stories about what was going on while he was on the run. I was telling him that the case was good and that we could probably beat it. We just had to stay the course and hold tight. I let him know that I had some pull with the COs in receiving and discharge and could have him moved to my housing unit, and he seemed good with the idea. The rest of my co-defendants weren't as optimistic as I was that he'd stand tall. I banked on our past and felt he wouldn't betray me, if nobody else, because of our history.

I then went and asked that he be reassigned to my unit, and they agreed. Three hours later, when Chuck didn't make it up to my unit, one of the guards let me know Chuck wasn't coming. I started inquiring as to his whereabouts and soon found out that he was on separation from the rest of us. I was blindsided. I immediately knew what time it was, and my lawyer quickly verified it.

Otisville was a compound with a mess hall, with food way better than at MCC, a full gym, track, and most importantly, being able to look up and see the sky during the day and the stars at night. Being housed in MCC, none of this was an option. These were simple pleasures we had all previously taken for granted in the free world.

After that day in court, they sent Chuck up to Otisville. There was a separation order put in place, keeping us from being in the same place at the same time as him. This meant if he was there, we weren't allowed to move freely because of the separation. We were more restricted because of the steps used to protect him, and that meant less library and outdoor time for us.

This now left us all being housed back in MCC on separate floors throughout the building. I was able to get my own cell with my own TV, one of only five on the unit. One night, around 1 AM, I heard keys and my cell door opening, and I was pissed because they knew I didn't want a celly. The person came in and turned on the light. Before I could check whoever, it was, I realized it was my dude, Lou, from the 142nd Street Lynch Mob. He was down from Otisville because he had to go to court that morning. I told him we were on restrictions because of Chuck, and he was surprised because he had no idea. He said Chuck was on the compound fronting, acting like everything was all good with me and all my co-D's.

Lou went to court, and when he returned that afternoon, they packed him back out to return to Otisville for the next day. As soon as Lou was sent to general population, he stepped to Chuck and exposed him. Shortly after that, they robbed Chuck, and he checked in to protective custody and was quickly moved from the compound.

Jail was volatile like that. You had unresolved outside beefs on the street that could easily set things off. In turn, friends could quickly become foes if they were enticed by the government to save themselves. We all thought our crews and friendships were immune to the treachery but quickly found out weak links were pervasive amongst us all. All this tension led to fights and stabbings and besides being common, often happened with little warning. Once we heard Chuck was gone, we asked to be sent back to Otisville and eventually were. Chuck ended up being sent to Valhalla, another facility that held federal inmates. Eventually, as the trial got closer, I knew the star team USA member was moved back to MCC on the south side of the 9th floor, which had a special housing unit for individuals like him.

After Chuck was caught, he started proffering with the prosecutor and the agents. They reissued their search warrants on all our cars based on information provided by him. One of the few useful pieces of information Chuck was able to feed them was about our use of traps. Chuck knew and was friends with the guy we got the traps from. While he didn't know all the specifics as to where they were or how to operate them in our vehicles, he gave them enough info for them to revisit their searches for the impounded vehicles and that is when they were able to find guns in every car and a key of coke in Chris's car. It was the first drugs, besides Eric's weed, they found for the entire case, and this was nearly six months after our initial arrests.

I knew he was telling, but the level of activity in his actions was deflating enough to really make me come to terms that Chuck was a game-changer for my case. I had a relationship with him, but fortunately, he didn't know enough to bury me. I always kept people at a distance to a degree for "plausible denial" purposes, so I didn't randomly have conversations about my past or present. Chuck didn't have any evidence even to substantiate our conversations. Nothing personal with him was taped since he didn't start cooperating until after he got busted. Yet, Mr. Ricco and I knew that Chuck and Bernard knew enough of the people that I knew to at least pose a challenge to me during the trial. Thankfully, I had an attorney up to the daunting challenge.

20

FIRST TRIAL

I couldn't stop shaking my head. Sitting at the defense table, defending myself against my charges wasn't far-fetched, but having to defend myself against them with my children's mother, Reika, cousin Nechelle, and others who had no roles in drug dealing of any kind, was surreal, to say the least. I hated myself for putting them in this situation. I had become the patriarch-- my family's protector and provider, yet here so many of them were in harm's way directly related to my doings.

I wasn't sure how or what the government was going to do to find them guilty. However, one thing was becoming abundantly clear: their convictions were going to have to be manufactured.

The government had actually begun with the intimidation tactic that may not have worked on me but had worked on others out of my presence. The government was relentless in their pursuit to intimidate my less culpable defendants, knowing they were susceptible to their propaganda. The closer it came to trial, the more pressure was applied.

Before the first trial, after Chuck had switched teams, ten of my co-defendants decided against going further and took pleas. While I might have recommended for some of them to fight on, they were afraid of the significant time they were threatened with. I am sure they rationalized accepting the various pleas versus the outcomes presented. There were still eight of us at the defense table going to trial: myself, Reika, Nechelle, Eric, Bob, Libby, Estos, and Sal. Part of the picture they even tried to paint by the ten taking pleas was that they were all now admitted criminals and, therefore, part of my criminal organizations that lent to the rest of our guilt, and the simple facts were they were all pawns in a much bigger play.

Remember, most of them were out on bail and meeting with their lawyers unbeknownst to me. I had little-to-no control or influence over their chooses or how they were being advised. Our communication was minimal at best. I'm not sure of what they knew about my mental state or how competent I might have been to face the weight of the trial. I do know that they were being given the "save yourself because it's in your best interest" speech. I'm lucky that all they did was take pleas knowing the government's persuasive threats and aggressive tactics. Though the reality is they shouldn't have. All their cases were winnable since they had little, if anything, to do with me other than just being around. As the trial played out with my remaining defendants, it took on a circus atmosphere.

In my trial, the government's star witnesses were supposed to be Bernard Thomas. He and I spent a lot of time together from 1992-1994 when my primary focus and energies were increasingly devoted to the music business, and Bernard was central to those pursuits. Despite us being at odds on several issues, his handling of our distribution situation stood out the most. At no point did I have any idea that Bernard was an actual informant for the government until after my arrest. I thought our relationship was real, and you can only imagine the disappointment I felt to learn that Bernard's undermining efforts were purposeful.

Bernard introduced me to an individual, a friend of his, early on in our relationship who wanted to cop drugs, and he asked could I obtain them for him. The guy tried to step to me, but I pretty much ignored the conversation he was trying to have with me in the office and went about my business. During my trial, they wanted to claim I sold an eighth of a key to this friend who turned out to be an undercover detective. The assertion was that Bernard brought him a bag that had drugs in it to the office that he supposedly got from me. The detective's testimony never said he directly received any drugs from me, but that I had supplied them to Bernard, who gave them to him. Though I was under constant surveillance and Bernard had his office equipped with listening devices, the undercover officer testified that there was no available surveillance or recording of that day or the alleged transaction.

Bernard had a private office within the record company's office. I remember him putting a lock on his office and making a big deal about no one going in when he was not present. It turns out that's where multiple microphones were hidden. The location of the hidden microphones in the office proved ineffective and ironic since he never really had any conversations with me in that specific room. It came out in the trial that he was paid by the government a couple of hundred thousand dollars for his work as an informant for the two-plus years he was assigned to me in addition to what I was paying him.

Bernard was with me on an occasion when I met with Sam, an old connect/friend in Miami. It turns out that Bernard knew Sam as well from the music business. However, he always conveniently and purposefully excused himself when I was with Sam.

Over the two-plus years he worked for me, we developed a real bond. At some point, he became an extension of my family. Evidently, it became harder for him to do what the government was asking him to do. He was between a rock and a hard place. His eventual actions at trial in serving to sabotage the government's case just fell short of him pulling me to the side and secretly telling me about the investigation.

Though he was supposed to be a key informant and witness for the prosecution, Bernard would eventually deny remembering or even saying what the agents said he had told them in their debriefing sessions. I suspect Bernard flipped on the government because we indeed became cool along the way. He ended up undermining their case, becoming a de facto ally, and a hostile witness for the government. His denials and contradictions throughout his intended testimony damaged their case against me. Even within my disappointment, many of Bernard's actions were finally more understandable. As much as he undermined our efforts, he also was more distant at the end and not around, giving them less information to feed against me. He came with a purpose, but our bond was real enough to curtail those efforts against me.

With dirty tactics, informants like Bernard and the undercover officer not really working out as they hoped, I knew that much of the government's case rested on the testimony of Charles Allen Brown, a.k.a. "Chuck Born."

Once the trust and resources the government placed in Bernard backfired, Chuck was effectively brought in off the bench and groomed to be Team USA's next star. He was always scheduled to be a key for them, but Bernard's total turn against them made Chuck's testimony much more vital than I am sure they initially intended it to be.

The actual day that Chuck was scheduled to testify against us was a sort of judgment day. I had no idea what to expect, and while his testimony affected us all, its level of importance was focused more on me since I was the only one with any relationship with him. Others knew him, but I was the only one who directly dealt with him and effectively the only reason anyone else knew him.

After changing into our suits, Bob, Eric, and I were all handcuffed and escorted by the Marshalls toward the bullpens of the federal courthouse at 500 Pearl Street. As we were walking through the halls, we could hear footsteps and the metal shackles of someone else ahead, around a corner, headed in our direction. Right before our eyes, there was Chuck. When he noticed us, he got startled and jumped back, trying to getaway. His assigned Marshalls quickly ushered him into a nearby room. We were held at bay and then continued past the room he was placed.

His reaction was kind of funny because under the circumstances, there is little we could have done since we were all handcuffed. That moment in the hallway was the first time any of us had laid eyes on Chuck since we last saw him in court shortly after he was apprehended and indicted with us.

About ten minutes after we were placed into a holding cell, we could hear a door pop. It was the Marshalls bringing Chuck into a nearby holding pen. He was a few cells down from us, but we couldn't visibly see one another. Once the Marshalls exited the holding cell area, I shouted out to Chuck, "Homie, I can't believe how you are doing me.

You're going out like a real sucker." He responded by saying, "I was facing life on this case and lifetime parole on the back of my state case. I had no choice." I immediately replied, "You can't do life, but I can?"

Before the conversation could go any further, we heard the door pop again and the Marshalls returning. I am not sure if they could hear our conversation or just realized how close they had left him next to us, but they quickly removed Chuck. This was the last time he and I ever spoke.

Chuck didn't come into my circle until after Rich was killed and Alpo had gotten locked up in January of 1990. They were all counterparts in the street. He had already been in jail, so he missed all of DC and my true organization days. I was strictly wholesaling when we were introduced officially, so he only actually met people through me from being around the store. All he knew about was the trap cars and the type of cars he might have seen me in or around. Some of the vehicles he described we might not have had at the time of the arrest, so he was describing what he thought we did versus what he actually knew. He was able to tell anything he and I personally did, which in of itself was bad enough. It was more than what the FBI had at that point on their own. He did know Gadget Mike, the guy who outfitted the traps and was able to testify that he got drugs from me directly, though none of that testimony was able to be substantiated by anyone else or the government itself.

Ironically, guys he knew from his earlier state bid up north had warned me about how he carried himself on the inside. They had commented to me how much of a chump Chuck was in that he didn't handle his business in prison. One day in the store, La Du crossed paths with Chuck and told me he didn't care for dude. He told me that Chuck had got violated in the joint when they were together and how they took some of his personal effects along with some pictures, including some of his women, and passed them around. He stated Chuck didn't handle the situation even though he knew who did it. I listened but shrugged it off. I didn't need Chuck to be a tough guy. Those positions were already filled. Chuck, on multiple occasions, had matter-of-factly stated he wasn't going back to jail but never said what he'd do if caught committing another crime. Of course, after the fact, I questioned whether I should have taken heed of the multiple examples I had been shown and given of the weakness of his character.

***

The majority of Chuck's testimony made me realize how lax federal rules of trial procedure are, relative to most state procedural rules. As defined by Black's Law Dictionary, hearsay "is a term applied to that species of testimony given by a witness who relates, not what he knows personally, but what others have told him, or what he has heard said by others. Hearsay evidence is that which does not derive its value solely from the credit of the witness but rests mainly on the veracity and competency of other persons. The very nature of the evidence shows its weakness, and it is admitted only in specified cases from necessity". In most cases, what someone else heard from another person is designated as hearsay and inadmissible. However, in the federal system, it is much easier to let hearsay in as evidence, and in most federal instances, it is allowed, specifically in RICO and conspiracy related cases.

"Federal Rule of Evidence 801(d)(2)(E) is the modern codification of the co-conspirator exception to the hearsay rule. For a statement, otherwise, hearsay, to be admissible under the exception, the statement must be offered against a party and ... [be] a statement [made] by a co-conspirator of a party during the course and in furtherance of the conspiracy."' (by- David Calabrese, Federal Rule of Evidence 801(d)(2)(E): Admissibility of Statements from an Uncharged Conspiracy That Does Not Underlie the Substantive Charge, 52 Fordham L. Rev. 933 (1984)

So, what someone says someone else told them occurred is allowed as evidence against you, and as you can imagine, this type of hearsay is troublesome to defend. However, during the trial, when my lawyer cross-examined Chuck, his firsthand knowledge of many of the incidents he was describing became questionable. Frank Gonzalez, my investigator, discovered that Chuck had received this paperwork where we could see he was effectively reading experiences from confidential government documents supplied first from an incarcerated Alpo who mailed the documents from jail where they ended up with Azie who made arrangements to get them to Chuck.

I was able to hip my lawyer to the fact that stuff Chuck was testifying to were things that I had done prior to even meeting him or conversations with Alpo directly. Alpo was a cooperating government witness, but as it turned out, not a testifying witness to my case. It also seems apparent that before being shot, Azie was also being targeted and set up by Bernard Thomas.

We all pretty much knew the same people in the street; after all, Harlem and the drug selling culture were a relatively small clique on the bigger levels. So, I disseminated info to people stating what Chuck was doing before him testifying in my case in hopes that this would maybe deter him or change his mind knowing that his betrayal would go beyond the courtroom, and he'd be exposed for the rat he was. I even reached out to his woman, Tanya, and told her what he was doing. She seemed surprised. He had told her he had just taken a plea to get out of the way and denied cooperating. I told her to come to see for herself. The prosecution did make noise about the "community" being so prevalent as observers during his testimony, but the judge didn't remove anyone. I wanted him to be uncomfortable, and she did end up attending my trial during his testimony. The prosecution took notice and made it seem like he was brave and noble in testifying while members of the community were present.

***

In my trial, the government highlighted my lifestyle. It was a full production of trying to show the mansion, cars, clothes, and documented spending. Frankly, they attempted to overwhelm the jury with otherwise underwhelming evidence. The trial took nearly three months. Mentally and physically, it was exhausting. Coming to court every day was a production. They got me, Bob and Eric up super early every day to make the short transit from MCC even though it was connected to 500 Pearl Street via tunnels. They justified waking us up and having us in the court's bullpen so early to give us time to prepare with our lawyers. We had become aware it was a fed tactic. The mental exhaustion and anxiety were real to go along with the ups and downs of the day's events, which was part of that psychological warfare. Some days, it seems we made progress; sometimes, it seems they had. Either way, we'd have to go back, review that day's events, and prepare yet again for the coming day's events by going over testimony, evidence, and getting prepared for the following day in court.

The picture they painted of me, specifically to a jury, initially only revolved around my wealth and lifestyle. In 1994-95 there were no images of young Black entrepreneurs, such as music moguls like Jay Z and Puffy, as we know them today. So, with no one on television or the media as a baseline, I was just living a lifestyle and with assets that made no sense for people's expectations of what a young Black male from Harlem and the Bronx should ever expect to attain. I had mostly white jurors who weren't a jury of my peers and were likely resentful of the opulent lifestyle. Forget evidence or drugs; I was being tried for being young, Black, and rich, having a lifestyle, money, and assets that jurors couldn't comprehend that weren't gained by illicit means.

Testimony that undoubtedly hurt me came from a variety of sources: the mortgage broker for my Franklin Lakes house, American Express, various car dealers, random jewelers, the brokerage firm I bought approximately $100,000 in stocks, and various pictures of furs and jewelry on my family and me.

In the apartment that I converted into a studio, I had most of my groups come in, and many of them often spent the night. The government used surveillance pictures and videos of them coming in and out with overnight and grocery bags to imply to the courts that drugs may have been in them. This false information had been used to continually substantiate and renew wiretaps and surveillance warrants throughout their investigation. They knew very well that drugs were never in any of those bags, and my cousins were just teens themselves and my group members as young as 12 and 13-years-old. They knew none of them ever hustled on any level. They used these blatantly false assertions to secure warrants, wiretaps and pen registers. A pen register allows law enforcement to see one phone's contacts to another phone to see what numbers I was calling and receiving calls from during wiretaps. There was a mountain of recorded evidence used against me, and the basis of securing most of that evidence was done on false pretenses. Nonetheless, once admitted, it was my burden to minimize and defend against the government's case.

The feds play as dirty as the alleged criminals they chase. They manufactured, manipulated, and withheld so much evidence on me those tactics eventually became what would later inspire the creation of *Don Diva Magazine*. Someone needed to be a voice for the otherwise voiceless. The government was unethical with their tactics at trial. They had all those hours of recorded phone conversations that showed little more than my basic engagement and my day-to-day comings and goings with those I interacted with. They still introduced taped phone conversations from people like Libby.

Libby was just a teenager, around my cousins' age. I was cool with his older brother, Jeff, who I used to hit off with work. I'm not sure what his exact circumstances during that time were at home, but I took to him and often let him hang around the office and studio, even allowing him to stay there at times. Like my cousins, he didn't hustle in any shape or form. Libby had no capabilities of selling weight but would occasionally be talking drug prices on the office or studio phone for no real reason at all. Oddly, this was just the culture in the hood. They played that tape dozens of times at my trial though there was no connection to Libby, me, and drugs. Yet, the phone conversations alone, with no evidence of Libby selling any types of drugs ever, was enough to have him arrested as one of my co-defendants in a federal drug conspiracy trial.

Much of the testimony was about other co-conspirators who weren't at the defense table and had already taken pleas or weren't even indicted. They were attempting to connect me to Chris. This wasn't hard to do since we knew each other since childhood. So, despite his plea, they tried to use his recorded conversations during the government's two-plus year investigation against me. Their theory was that I was the head of an organization, and Chris was my second-in-charge, getting his direct orders from me. They alleged the fact that I was never caught speaking about or handling any type of drugs was because I was too smart to put myself in such a predicament. The totality of the underwhelming evidence against me was supposed to show just that. This may all have been factual at one time pertaining to me, but none of the actual evidence against me supported those facts.

It got so ridiculous that, at one point, all my co-defendants and their respective lawyers were just sitting there listening to countless hours of testimony, no different than the jury, waiting for their clients' names to even be mentioned detailing their specific roles in this supposed large scale drug organization. Every now and then, one of the lawyers would, on the cross, ask a prosecution witness if their client was present during a situation or if they even knew him/her. In almost every instance, the answer was no. The tactic was employed to remind the jury of the lack of involvement of their particular client.

Bernard and Chuck's testimonies may have been the only times when any of the remaining co-D's names were even mentioned. Even then, it was hardly a smoking gun against them. It was more to the effect of the prosecutor asking Chuck when he would bring Kevin drug monies, where was it, and who would he give it to. Chuck partly testified to bringing alleged drug proceeds owed to me to the store and occasionally giving it to Reika or one of my cousins. When Chuck was asked whether any of them knew what the money was for, Chuck would respond they did, because since he was an admitted drug dealer, why else would he be bringing me money? This was purely fabricated testimony against Reika and my cousins, but in a drug conspiracy trial, hard evidence of a crime isn't always offered. This was absurd to me. The idea that someone could potentially get sentenced to ten years in prison on such flimsy evidence, for activities that they actually didn't participate in, should sit poorly with everyone reading this. It really has happened to countless people serving federal sentences.

Unfortunately, my trial is indelibly embedded in my mind, but one particularly memorable part of my first trial was the use or, should I say, misuse of a picture by the government. The surveillance photo of me was exaggeratedly blown up beyond life-sized dimensions. They were trying to paint a picture of the violent nature of my organization, and then the agents would testify and show the guns recovered. One particular image they wanted to show was me with my hands inside my waistband alluding to that I was most likely adjusting or reaching for my gun.

My lawyer tried to clarify to the jury that the fact that all FBI agents were titled special agents meant, in fact, not one of them was, in fact, "special." Titles matter to a jury and civilians. As far as the picture in question, my lawyer cross-examined the FBI agent, who acknowledged there were more pictures of this day. The next day, the prosecution gave the whole picture roll to my lawyer and showed the picture 62 of me looking menacing, apparently reaching for a gun. However, once pictures 59, 60, 61, and 63 were displayed with 62, it simply showed me coming out of the office and just zipping my coat on a cold day. There was no menacing beyond being cold. There was no gun coming out. It was pictures of nothing.

This type of cross-examination was at the heart of the rigorous defense Mr. Ricco lead on my behalf. The IRS was supposed to be a key witness for the prosecution, but Mr. Ricco was able to cross-examine agent Alan Love in a way that his testimony also became key to my defense. He acknowledged that all my legitimate businesses were profitable. This contradicted the image that was painted of the "drug dealer only" lifestyle when, in fact, I had businesses that made money and could have theoretically supported the lavish lifestyle of a drug dealer that had been painted.

Aside from the cross-examination tactics he employed against adversarial government witnesses, Mr. Ricco employed a vigorous defense on my behalf. Puff offered to testify as a character witness during my criminal trials, but Hip-Hop still had such an overall negative perception at the time that my lawyer chose not to use him.

There was never a plan for me to testify. I am sure I was willing, but Mr. Ricco had the foresight and experience to understand that innate prejudices some jury members may have had would have not been swayed by anything I had to say. After weeks of the government impugning my character, Mr. Ricco put several people on the stand to cast me in a more positive light. No one was more effective than Maurice.

Maurice was colorful, charismatic, and articulate. Gay Black men were often cast in Harlem's shadows, particularly within the hustling subculture. Our acceptance of Maurice and his friends and his employment were eye-opening to some of the jury members. The minimizing of the stereotypical tough guy, gangster prejudices against people that were different than us, with no sexual innuendos implied, was enough to make people look at us in a different and positive light. Maurice was compelling. He was sincere. He let the jury know I was essentially a good dude despite the characterization of me as a violent drug kingpin. Maurice did an excellent job of humanizing me to the jury as well as countering Chuck's testimony of the store as serving as some type of drug front. It was a testament to me always trying to treat people right, no matter who they were.

I was blessed to have many others testify on my behalf. Everything helped to try and counterbalance the government's negative portrayal. The government could see the effectiveness of the testimonials, and besides their cross-examination, they did everything they could to limit the jury seeing me in a non-stereotypical and positive light.

It was known that my brother was never part of my illicit activities. He had been on an exemplary path and would have served as a great witness in my case. He would not only have been a potential character witness, but his aptitude, character, and success as a productive model citizen could have been used to dismiss the stereotypes placed on me as an uneducated Harlem drug lord and thug.

His testimony could have been used to paint a very different picture of my capabilities to succeed as a legitimate businessman. He could have been vital in exposing how I could be a successful entrepreneur because I had the intellectual capacity to make money beyond illegal means. The presentation of a high school valedictorian and Ivy League graduate raised in the same household by the same parents would have been a comparative analysis hard for any jury to ignore. In the early 1990s, if you weren't an athlete (rappers weren't that wealthy at the time), it was assumed the only way a young Black man could acquire the assets I had attained was solely through illegal means.

They held the possibility of arresting him in my case as a threat or incentive. So, the feds made a deal with my lawyer that my brother couldn't testify for me, and he'd never be arrested as a part of my case. They did the same with my Aunt Diane.

After her divorce from my Uncle Fatman, Aunt Diane had enough money and real estate assets to show my family's financial situation in a different light. The government knew her assets could help to offset many of the lifestyle attacks directed at me, including the purchase of the Franklin Lakes home. Instead, the government excluded her from my defense in the same way they did with my brother.

The trial took approximately two months to complete. Television and the movies do little to capture the stress and anxiety that defendants face every minute that a jury is out deciding their fate. I was in jail for over a year before the first date of the trial even began on November 27, 1995, lasting until January 16, 1996.

Earlier in the trial, before deliberations, we had to deal with a hearing about alleged jury tampering. It turns out one of the members of my jury lived in Harlem, and it was said that a person related to the defendants recognized him as someone in their neighborhood. Without our knowledge, allegedly, someone approached the guy in the neighborhood and mentioned they knew he was on the jury, and to take into consideration, I was a good dude. The jury member did not express that he was threatened in any way, but clearly, dude was shook. The judge didn't declare a mistrial or declare any wrongdoing on anyone's part, but he did dismiss that particular juror. In the back of my mind, I wondered if this had any effect on the jury's decision-making process at all.

That stress was magnified each time the Marshalls would come into the bullpens we were being held in stating there was a note from the jury. Bob, Eric, and I would all have to be handcuffed and escorted back up to the courtroom. In my case, there were at least three or four instances throughout the deliberations where the jury had a question for the judge wanting clarification or reading back specific testimony. Each time the paper came in, our nerves were on edge because we assumed it was a verdict. Finding out it wasn't was not much relief because then the focus quickly shifted in trying to decipher the significance of the jury's request/question and whether it was something potentially positive or detrimental to our fate.

There were moments during the deliberations when Bob, Eric, and I would sit in the bullpen without a word being spoken. We all sat in silence in what felt like prayerful reflection. I've never been overly religious. Quite frankly, the most time I spent in my life in or around a church was when I was a kid and made to go. There's an irony in those moments when your life is in turmoil, and we begin calling on a higher power to spare us, particularly when we never made deposits in a spiritual bank, but desire to now make a withdrawal. Ironies aside, when the turmoil is deep enough, we all make that call.

After eight days, the jury came back to the judge and declared that they were hopelessly deadlocked in being able to reach a consensus decision. The final standing was 8 in favor of my acquittal, 4 for my conviction. The judge then declared a mistrial because of the hung jury, and as expected, the prosecution was quick to refile charges.

After my hung jury and eventually declared a mistrial, there was a disposition on all my co-defendants. They were either given time served or negotiated plea agreements. I was the only one left whose fate hadn't been decided. It started with 21 of us. Now, it was down to just me; the United States of America versus Kevin Chiles.

21

2ND TRIAL & PLEAS

Before my second trial, everyone (with my blessings) took pleas and resolved their situations. Most, except for Chris Mack, received time served with the others receiving minimal additional years above that. They knew Reika didn't do anything, but since the Franklin Lakes house was in her name too, they needed a conviction. They made her voluntarily conceding her interests in the property part of her plea. They probably wouldn't have had enough to seize the house without her signing her interest over. Nechelle was the same. They found about $100,000 in a safe deposit in her name, and they wanted her to forfeit it as part of her plea agreement. Legally, they needed a conviction on her to be able to do that. The money, house, and cars were the motivating factors for them being arrested as co-defendants. Some of the dispositions were as follows:

Chris Mack - pled guilty to one count of conspiracy to violate federal narcotics laws and one count of criminal forfeiture. He was sentenced to 18.5 years in part because of his prior felony conviction.

Robert Burke - after a hung jury in his initial trial, pled guilty to one count of possession of a firearm by a convicted felon and sentenced to time served after over 18 months of incarceration.

Amnon "Eric" Fillipi - pled guilty to one count of possession with intent to distribute marijuana. He was sentenced to 18 months imprisonment (time already served), followed by three years of supervised release.

Erica "Reika" Nicole Carter - pled guilty to one count of possession of cocaine. She was sentenced to two years' probation.

Anthony Mack - pled guilty to one count of possession with intent to distribute quantities of mixtures and substances containing detectable amounts of controlled substances. He was sentenced to 36 months.

Jeffrey "Jeff" Parker - pled guilty to one count of conspiracy to distribute and possess with intent to distribute 500 grams and more of cocaine. He was sentenced to 63-months imprisonment, followed by four years of supervised release.

Lance Bradley - pled guilty to one count of Possession of a Stolen Firearm. He was sentenced to five months of imprisonment to be followed by three years of supervised release, with a special condition of five months of home detention.

Salvatore D. Mercante - pled guilty to one count of wire fraud. He was sentenced to five years' probation to include six months of home detention and a $3,000.00 fine.

Nechelle Brown (Cousin) - pled guilty to one count of wire fraud. She was sentenced to three years' probation with a special condition of six months of home detention.

Lamont Brown (Cousin) -pled guilty to one count of conspiracy to violate federal narcotics laws. He was sentenced to 21 months of imprisonment to be followed by three years of supervised release.

Harry Jerome Louis - pled guilty to one count of conspiracy to violate federal narcotics laws. He was sentenced to 21 months of imprisonment to be followed by six years of supervised release.

Before my second trial, there were some unresolved issues concerning testimony given by an undercover officer in the first trial about a controlled buy orchestrated by the government. The government finally came clean after it had come out during cross of a government agent that there was, in fact, surveillance of the controlled buy and that there was an audiotape pertaining to the purchased drugs from Bernard that were supposedly supplied by me. They had denied the existence of the specific audiotape in the first trial. When that tape was "miraculously" found, they tried to explain its absence from the first trial as purely accidental because of so many other hours of recorded evidence it was simply overlooked. The tape itself clearly revealed that I had no participation whatsoever in selling drugs to the undercover officer or supplying drugs to Bernard in any way as the officer, under oath, had testified.

My lawyer submitted a motion, stating a Brady violation had occurred and to have all the charges dismissed stemming from the withheld, critical, and key evidence which amounted to clear government misconduct. A Brady motion is a defendant's request for evidence concerning a material witness that is favorable to the defense and to which the defense may be entitled. Favorable evidence includes not only evidence that tends to exculpate the accused, but also evidence that may impeach the credibility of a government witness. A Brady violation occurs where the failure to disclose evidence to the defense deprives the defendant of a fair trial. It is all derived from a 1963 Supreme Court ruling that stipulates that prior to trial, the prosecution must turn over all exculpatory evidence to the defense in a criminal case. Exculpatory evidence is evidence that might exonerate the defendant.

While the granting of the pretrial Brady motion would not have dismissed every count in my indictment, it still would have likely lead to my overall acquittal instead of a mistrial. The government's only credible (non-criminal) witness was this particular undercover officer. When the recording was played, it showed Bernard made the sale directly to the undercover without me having any interaction or being mentioned to the undercover.

Despite compelling evidence of the government's misconduct, the judge chose not to grant our Brady motion. It was hardly a "harmless error" by the prosecution as the judged ruled, and the dismissal of the motion showed the judge's bias against me. In all reality, the ruling itself would have probably been enough to overturn any conviction on appeal. Even with the denial of the motion, the introduction of the "new" recording evidence effectively eliminated the strongest part of the government's case with the alleged sale to the undercover that, in fact, never occurred.
'

***

With every one of my initial co-defendants having taken pleas prior to my second trial, the government was still looking to prosecute me as a major drug kingpin minus any other defendants at the table. Of course, I expected them to use all their pleas against me, but I am sure they were worried about the optics of me sitting at a defense table alone as the leader of an alleged organization. That strategy may work for the Mafia because everyone is familiar with the organization's existence. No one had ever heard of the Chiles Organization outside of the hustling community and me alone at the defense table could have caused more harm than good.

So, for my second trial, they picked up H (born Robert Lee Jones) based on Chuck's testimony in the first trial. Chuck originally testified that a guy named "S" was the drug transporter but now recanted and said it was H instead of S. Estos actually ended up getting arrested and was an initial defendant because the government believed Estos was the "S" Chuck was referring to, though he was not.

H not being a defendant from the onset, was clearly a huge oversight by the government. I suspect that once they regrouped for the second trial, they must have found early surveillance photos, showed them to Chuck, and he was able to identify H as the transporter he was referring to. This is why the feds went and attempted to find H by leaving a card at his mother's house. He voluntarily turned himself in and was arrested before my second trial.

Prior to H turning himself in, he went to a public advocate's office directly across the street from the federal building to seek some legal counsel. The person he spoke to in the office said he wasn't able to represent him because of a conflict in having represented someone else related to our case. H was adamant that he did not want to turn himself in unrepresented, and the attorney agreed to sit with him during his initial processing. H simply tried to avoid even being isolated by the agents or prosecutors. When the case agent Timothy Cole came in and asked if there was anything he wanted to say, H said no, and since he could see he was already represented, any possible further questioning ended before it could even start.

H is a G. He had a literal "get out of jail free card" in the face of really significant time, and he wouldn't give them the satisfaction of even making him an offer.

I am actually understating how vital H could have been to the prosecution's case had he flipped. The prosecution surely did not realize how valuable a potential asset H was to their case against me and possibly against so many others, including the true members of my organization. H was there from nearly the beginning. He knew everyone and was probably personally responsible for transporting over a ton of cocaine during our run. H could have buried me and so many others. Unlike Chuck, who lacked details and had conflicting information that made it clear to a jury he did not have the intimate knowledge of my doings, H did. Thankfully, the government lacked a similar understanding of precisely who H was.

He had dodged numerous bullets in the past, including Chuck initially confusing him with an unknown S. H was able to get out within a few days on $50,000 bail. I never even saw him before he secured bail. He was put on a different floor in MCC, and I got a kite he was in the building. He was out before I could try and maneuver for him to join my floor. I can't lie, H's arrest and subsequent quick release initially might have made me nervous. I didn't know any details of what had taken place and probably had not spoken to H in at least a year to 18 months. I knew how solid H was, but so much time had passed I was just unsure of anything at this point with the stakes being so high.

I didn't see H for a month or so until our next court date. After the pretrial proceedings, he was remanded by the feds who had finally linked him on the first Jersey case that was in his name. The case was old, and I am not even sure that the statute of limitations was not up, but it was enough to use to revoke his bail as a flight risk. Ironically, they still did not link him to the Jersey case that he had been convicted on, under an alias. Once we were finally able to talk, H left no doubt that he was as willing to battle the feds as I was.

H was probably facing as much time as I was for the trafficking charges as part of my case combined with the Jersey case and his felony gun

2ND TRIAL & PLEAS

conviction. H is truly his brother's keeper. He was my only actual Co-D for the second trial.

H was given a lawyer, Valerie Amsterdam, who was appointed by the courts. Unlike all my previous co-D's whom Mr. Ricco and I directly or indirectly hired their lawyers to work in conjunction, Mrs. Amsterdam seemingly was not a fan of my lawyer and wouldn't cooperate with him. She was continually trying to throw me under the bus to defend her client. H often told her he wasn't pleased with how she was going about defending him. They had open disputes to the point H asked to address the court directly regarding his defense.

My charges were still the same, and the government was vigorously pursuing a conviction. The second trial was much shorter than my first. It lasted just over two weeks from May 7th thru May 22nd of 1996. Instead of a dozen defendants, there were only two, and now we knew the strengths and weaknesses of their case. The government streamlined their case with the focus being almost solely on me, limiting some of it because they also were aware of weaknesses. They were able to use technology and phone towers to place H at scenes, but even this was problematic because, in those cases, H was more linked to Chris's phone and not me. Chris and I having those scramblers, was somewhat questionable and how they, in part, tried to tie us together. The fact that they didn't have any actual calls with us using the scramblers was surely a saving grace. The fact that virtually none of the government's case was new made it easier for Mr. Ricco to negate some of the government's witnesses' testimony, especially Chuck's.

***

My lawyer, on cross, asked Chuck if he was friends with Azie and Alpo. He said yes. He was further asked if Azie provided him with any documentation on my case, and he said yes and then added he knew that Azie received the documents from Alpo, although he didn't know how Alpo received the documents. Mr. Ricco then asked Chuck if he was testifying based on information he had firsthand knowledge of or if it was from a script (documents) that had been provided by Alpo and Azie, backed up by discrepancies that made it clear Chuck was not there or physically present for some of the things he was testifying about. Mr. Ricco, perhaps in an attempt to flush out a broader conspiracy, further crossed FBI agent Tim Cole, who confirmed in open court that Alpo was a government cooperating witness and that Azie Faison was a target apart from my case. Ultimately, no further explanation was given by the FBI agent as to either's involvement in my case because the judge always made my attorney move on when he attempted to further inquiry.

Let me state my feelings about Azie being a target apart of my case. When the initial arrest indictment was served, Azie's name was at the top of the investigation instead of mine. I do not know definitively why that was the case, but it is nonetheless a fact. I do not personally know of any instances in which Azie testified against someone in open court beside the trial against the individuals who attempted to kill him.

However, what has always been offensive is why Azie, if he was aware of Bernard Thomas' informing, would not directly tell me when there was ample opportunity to do so as well as why he would have my paperwork concerning my case. In his own book, Game Over (pages 151-158), Azie admitted to having received paperwork concerning my case from Alpo in 1992, and in his own words, this paperwork was received prior to my being arrested in 1994. Why didn't he warn me directly when he said in his book he attempted to do so through Chuck? In truth, as per his own testimony, Chuck didn't get the paperwork until 1995 when he was on the run. He referenced Chuck as my man when, in truth, Chuck had a relationship with Rich, Alpo, and Azie first. And again, based on his timeline in his own book-- why would he give this paperwork to Chuck instead of me directly? I never knew of this "paperwork" while I was out and only found out through the extensive workings of my private investigator who realized this all took place months after I was arrested. Any explanation Azie gave in his book contradicted the factual account of this subject and was self-servingly inaccurate.

***

The government's approach in the second trial was not much different than it was in the first. The main difference being there were fewer defendants at the table. Perhaps they surmised, in hindsight, too many defendants were probably a distraction to the jury.

Chuck was used to show an inside view of my organization as a self-professed member. His task was to explain who everyone was and what roles they played as well as providing explanations to phone conversations by breaking down what they called coded discussions between criminals. He emphasized how I stressed never talking on landlines or the burners we used, opting instead for payphones and how surveillance conscientious I was. The government explained and justified using someone with Chuck's questionable character by stating to catch criminals they had to use criminals, adding how vital his testimony was to shed light on the organization he was allegedly a part of.

From a purely evidentiary standpoint, most could see that there was hardly overwhelming evidence to support the magnitude of the charges against me. There were guns recovered from all of us at our arrests. There were several specifically attached to me. Two were recovered in Franklin Lakes house and two in the Bronx condo I occupied. However, there were no drugs attributable to me. There were no sales except two Chris had made, which all recordings showed I had no affiliation with as well as Chuck's that clearly were in no way affiliated with me. There was no self-incrimination or any incrimination by any others of me on all the recorded calls, even suggesting I was selling drugs. I had one co-defendant caught with 20 pounds of weed. The only real value Chuck's snitching gave the feds was when he walked them through where some of the traps in the cars were, and they finally found a kilo in one of Chris's cars along with guns in all the cars. Otherwise, there was no evidence of any actual drug sales in the course of their two-year investigation.

I had two trials that took nearly thirty months to complete, and after both resulted in mistrials leaning in my favor. The government weighed the possibility that I might be acquitted. The first was 8-4 in my favor the second 10 to acquit, 2 to convict.

By this time, Ed Wilfred and Mr. Ricco had become more than just my lawyers and defenders. More so, Mr. Ricco and I had developed a personal relationship. I considered him a life coach because all the lessons and insight he'd shared along the way came as a free bonus to his legal counsel. I had grown and evolved into a different person altogether by then. I had been through quite a bit since my arrest from family, friends, and dealing with betrayal.

We were discussing my options for a third trial. Mr. Rico stated that he had some discussions with the government at the judge's behest. Judge Griesa told Mr. Tempkins, the government prosecutor, and Mr. Ricco to iron it out because he thought it was in the government's best interest at this point. Mr. Ricco felt I was in an excellent position to be offered a decent plea. We went back and forth, and I told him I thought we had a great chance to win in our third trial. My position was we now knew everything they were going to be presenting, and based on how we had fared thus far, it was favorable for me to get acquitted. Mr. Ricco stated that that was a possibility, but what if 12 jurors came in the courtroom and didn't see things the way we desired? Could I live with a natural life sentence? He said, "You'd hate me. You'd have to hate me to have a chance ever to get your conviction overturned, possibly. You'd have to file a motion for ineffective assistance of counsel and say all the things I had done wrong. And, even then, who's to say you'd get any relief?" He went on to say it wasn't about the money; he didn't feel it was in my best interest. At that moment, I felt let down. I wanted to fight further. I wanted to be acquitted and go home. The prospect seemed obtainable to me. I was asking myself if he was selling me out, and I'm sure my deposition lent itself to those conflicting emotions. We ended our discussion that day on that note. He told me to sleep on it and that we'd get together in the next coming days. As far as I was concerned, there was nothing to sleep on. I wanted out, and I was ready to go.

The government was now offering me ten years, and Mr. Ricco thought that was a much better alternative than the continued possibility of a life sentence. I was dead set on going to trial and asked that he at least try and get me out on bail to get my affairs in order. When the judge shot down the bail motion, it knocked the wind out of me a little. The fact that they still refused to grant me any bail after two mistrials is almost unheard of, especially considering I wasn't actually on trial for any violent crimes and didn't have a record of anything significant. Understand, John Gotti's brother Gene was out on bail for his major heroin trafficking trial and even maintained bond after his conviction. John Gotti himself received bail for two of his trials, even when implicated for murder and jury tampering. I was not being tried for any violent offenses. Here I was facing life and unable to secure bail though I had significant and strong family ties. It was a further indicator of how rigged the game is, especially against defendants of color. Who looks more guilty: someone coming through a side door accompanied by Marshalls or a defendant walking through the public doors with his family and counsel, on his own accord?

Still unconvinced, I said I would be willing to take five years. I figured since I had been in almost three years at this point, that would be tolerable. Mr. Ricco told me they weren't willing to go below the mandatory minimum of the conspiracy of ten years. Looking back, I can see the ten years he and the government came up with was around the time they knew it would take for me to minimally serve even if I was to win a probable appeal because of the denied Brady motion.

In the upcoming week, there was a scheduled conference to discuss the disposition of the case. On the morning of the status hearing, Mr. Ricco came into the back room outside the courtroom, where I was in a cell waiting. Mr. Ricco mentioned again that he had been in talks with Mr. Temkin, the prosecutor, and Judge Griesa. Mr. Ricco stated that before we went out into the courtroom that he had arranged a meeting between me, the judge, and him. The judge asked if he could talk with me and I said I didn't have a problem with it.

I was escorted into the judge's chambers along with my attorney. I sat down in a chair in front of the judge's desk, and my lawyer sat to my right. Judge Griesa started by saying, "Good morning, Mr. Chiles. Mr. Ricco and I, as well as Mr. Temkin, the prosecutor, have been discussing your case. I have watched you throughout the two trails, and you have conducted yourself accordingly as a gentleman in my courtroom." He said he didn't give me bail, in part, because he couldn't assess my temperament or intentions. He said that he felt I didn't deserve a life sentence, but if I got a conviction, it was out of his hands and that the statute calls for a mandatory life sentence. He thought the government's offer of ten years was fair.

While I knew much of what he said was right, I was inwardly upset. I also felt like I might not get a more vigorous defense from my attorney, especially after the judge tipped his hand that he was never going to rule for me. The judge's denial of the previous Brady motion was a strong enough indicator that I was not going to get any favorable rulings in his court no matter how much of a gentleman he may have viewed me as. I believed Mr. Ricco's energy was going to be different moving forward if I didn't take the plea since he felt like he did all he could up to this point, and I went against his better judgment and what he clearly thought was in my best interest. Nobody wants to represent a fool. I saw the writing on the wall.

My lawyer and I were non-aggressively at odds. I said the only other thing that bothered me was Chris had copped out to 18 and ½ years, taking a plea to protect me. I wasn't good with the idea of me getting less time than him with me as the principal and leader. Mr. Ricco gave me a speech that he did what he did as a man, and I had to do what I needed to as a man for my family. I said I couldn't in good conscience take a plea less than Chris's knowing I wouldn't have gotten to this place had he flipped on me. Mr. Ricco went back to the government with my sentiments and came back saying the government agreed to let him get the same as me, but they wouldn't give him less because he had a prior federal conviction. I spoke to Chris, and he said the ten years beat the 18, and he was good with everything.

I then had to have a conversation with H about our current situation and what I'd come to feel was in our best interest. H wasn't trying to hear what I was saying at first. Keep in mind; he had all but gotten away with two trafficking charges. One he was convicted of had just never been caught again after, and another he got caught in another name and just never returned after being bailed out. He went to jail on the gun charge outside the Apollo and felt that they didn't know a whole lot about him because they still weren't using the one Jersey conviction against him. I felt, in part, what he was saying was true, but I also knew that those two cases could still be brought up, especially the one he was already convicted on.

H hadn't been in that long before we went to trial, so he didn't fully understand things as I had come to learn. They were not going to just let any of us walk away unscathed. I explained to him how bad I would feel if he decided to go on and ended up getting convicted and serving way more time than me just due to his jacket. He finally came to terms with the real prospects of his circumstances, and reluctantly agreed that it was a safer play to accept a plea in this instance.

Robert Lee Jones (H) - pled guilty to a one-count Information charging him with using a communications facility in connection with the distribution and possession with intent to possess cocaine. He received a 48-month sentence (The charge carried 0 to 48 months, and he was sentenced to the high end because he was on probation during the time the offenses occurred).

I plead to something, not on my original indictment. I plead down from kingpin to sale and possession of between 6.45 and 7.45 keys. Mr. Ricco made sure the language to my plea was very specific. "The defendant denies all charges in the underlying indictment, denies being a leader of any organization and denies participating in a continuing criminal enterprise. The defendant also denies involvement with any other co-defendants or co-conspirators other than Koran Winters." The plea of 6.5-7.5 kilos brought me to 10 years since it was over 5 kilos. However, the specific language of the plea, along with the fact that my conviction was to a non-violent offense, meant that instead of going to a maximum-security penitentiary, I was now eligible for a low-security prison. My life is filled with ironies, but another one is the fact that the specifics of my plea and criminal admissions revolved around someone who was absolutely otherwise insignificant in my hustling exploits.

Koran Winters testified in both trials that "in the spring of 1992 he was introduced to Kevin Chiles in BOSS Emporium by his father William Winters, where Kevin sold him 500 grams of cocaine for $11,500 which Koran Winters took to Virginia, converted to crack and sold."

"Winters further testified he bought cocaine from Kevin Chiles on 5 or 6 more occasions in quantities ranging from 600 grams to 2.3 kilograms. The second transaction that took place, Winters sent tow wires to Chiles. One in the amount of $4,500 to Nechelle Brown and another in the amount of $6,200 to Jeffrey Parker."

"On August 24th, 1992, Winters was arrested in Washington, D.C., attempting to sell 125 grams of crack to an undercover officer and a confidential informant. At the time of his arrest, Winters had in his possession a receipt reflecting the Western Union money transfer to Parker as well as a personal address book that had a listing for 'Kevin' along with a number for Boss Emporium."

Though Koran was a cooperating government witness in both of my trials, Mr. Ricco was relatively easily able to impugn his credibility because of so many inconsistencies and misstatements in his testimony. I knew Koran's uncle and father. We all came out of the Bronx and migrated to Washington, D.C., and set up shop during my run there. I had done some business with them. I barely knew the younger Koran, and anything I did with him was almost like a favor that I let others help him out with instead of ever really dealing with him directly.

When it was all said and done, I was sentenced to 120 months. As much as I was reluctant to take the plea for ten years, I must admit that once it was done, I felt relieved. The plea wasn't the resolution I had hoped for, but it at least meant the uncertainty was over.

I had grown and become wiser throughout the process. I could never be the old me. I had gotten a front-row seat to racism and classism and how power affects policy and all our lives. Systemic injustices aren't just catchphrases used by civil rights leaders and militants; they are part of the everyday fabric for People Of Color and one we lack a full and true understanding of how pervasive and diabolic it really is from the powers-that-be that work every day to change and make up laws that contribute to widespread oppression.

My arrest and enduring incarceration made me realize how shaky the foundation was for all I had set up. I was now 30 and realized no one had been tested to face long-term adversity. I wrongly assumed everyone else had those abilities to maintain things even though the reality was that I had taken care of everything for everybody up to that point. The situation had taken a toll on everyone associated with it. The government engaged in propaganda spreading lies that I had AIDS and was going to die in jail. This got to some in my family, and many had given up on me. They didn't think I was coming home, and everybody stopped thinking like family, and things fell apart. "You cut off the head, and the body will fall" isn't just a saying. All of the things that I thought they should have been capable of handling in my absence were not.

It was clear to me, and everyone at this point, the government didn't play fair, so by taking pleas, most of which were misdemeanors, it allowed the government to seize and forfeit the money, stocks, insurance policies, jewelry, cars, and my house, that they wouldn't have otherwise been able. It was clear all the government wanted were convictions cause on the original indictments, everyone was facing a mandatory minimum of at least ten years.

They couldn't seize the house outright but put a lien on it, so I wasn't able to sell it. My accounts, as well as Reika's, continued to be frozen. However, we still had resources and could have possibly maintained paying the mortgage. They wanted Reika to sign over her rights to the house as part of her plea of no jail time. We could have fought for it, but at this point, with all the stress in the house, it was easier to let it go rather than fight for it. Everyone had been dragged through the wringer and was spiritually and emotionally bankrupt, me included.

My kids had accounts that the Feds didn't seem to know about and thankfully never found that money. Besides being able to keep her jewelry, it was the only thing they didn't take. They didn't freeze my Aunt Diane's account, and the Laundromats were in her name. My brother also didn't have his account frozen. The restaurant and laundromats were self-sustaining and could have been maintained and saved. I was handicapped but not crippled. They may have gotten over $300,000 during the searches, but I know that didn't satisfy them because Reika and my brother both said they were still being followed years after my initial arrest. I know they were still looking for the money.

The reality is that things could have been maintained till I got out. However, a more realistic fact is that most of my immediate family were relatively young and immature. Facing the full weight, resources, and threats of the United States isn't easy for anyone to handle. Sometimes people panic under duress, and in hindsight, I don't blame them. Dealing with the federal government, being intimidated, and working on the businesses weren't ultimately a priority for people under indictment. For the few who weren't indicted, their deals to not indict always felt easily breakable by the government if "they" felt like it was a means to gain further leverage against me. The pressure was enough to kill anyone's drive.

I may have been initially disappointed with many in my family for not stepping up further in relation to maintaining the household and businesses, but in retrospect, their actions were more easily understood and justified. With a little time, I understood that they gave 100% of themselves, with a deck stacked against them and having to ride out my two mistrials that ended up taking just over three years to resolve.

The government works in a heavy-handed manner. They effectively seized my father's condo though they had no legal right to do so. It was in no way ever proven to be part of any criminal or illicit activities. My father's apartment and some vehicles that were seized were never given back. Nor was a claim made for them, so inevitably, they were lost. The overreaching seizures were all part of the government's plan in indicting nearly all my family.

Ironically, the one co-defendant that pled out to the most and most severe charges, of course, received the most lenient treatment of everyone. As Team USA's #1 draft pick, Charles "Chuck" Allen Brown - pled guilty to one count of conspiracy to violate federal narcotics laws, one count of use of a firearm in connection with a drug trafficking crime, one count of money laundering and one count of felon in possession of a firearm and one count of criminal forfeiture. He received time served on December 20th, 1996, after my second trial, as a reward for his cooperation.

An unexpected occurrence took place after I formally went in and accepted my plea. When I returned to the bullpen leading back to MCC, I received an ovation of sorts. By the time I was re-processed and made it up to the 11th floor, the news had beat my arrival, and cheers continued.

I hardly felt victorious. I was not leaving jail, and it was all too raw to accept any moral or comparative victory. However, I understood and appreciated where the sentiment came from. Most guys in the fed system did not take their case to jury decisions, let alone twice. Guys had witnessed me fighting the government for nearly three years, and with that came a degree of respect.

My case was not just noteworthy amongst inmates. Besides family and supporters that regularly attended my trials, the large courtroom, that could hold over a hundred spectators, was always packed. This included both uninvolved prosecutors and defense attorneys. Peter Shue, staying in MDC, was going through a similar battle, and our multiple hung juries supplied actual courtroom drama that most only saw on television.

For the inmates, who had still not settled their fate or taken pleas, we supplied a degree of hope, especially in light of the increasing jury counts in our favor. My plea signaled the end of my fight, but the applause was indicative of the respect guys had for my battle. While I still had to digest taking a plea, most guys seemed to understand better than I did. My plea was still a victory, of sorts, in comparison to serving life in prison. Getting a number always beats receiving letters.

22

PRISON

After I got sentenced, my mentality changed. The first three years had been all about fighting my case. I read and continuously researched. I was surprised by how many other cats in my situation didn't put any real effort into fighting their cases. Instead, they watched TV and played cards. In retrospect, I realize that many of those guys may have either been illiterate or not educationally capable of really comprehending legal case law and documents. In all reality, they hoped that if they didn't directly deal with it, it would all work itself out.

I had looked through thousands of pages of case law and transcripts. No one, including my lawyer, was going to fight harder for my freedom than me. After my plea, I sent most of my case documents home and only kept my Pre-Sentencing Investigations (PSI), which could also serve as documentation as to whether you were a rat or not.

Think about it. I was facing life and ended up with ten years. The cynical prison mentality was that anyone with my type of original charges shouldn't have gotten my sentence or placement in a low-level prison facility. I always kept my PSI handy. I understood that unfounded rumors always occurred behind bars. While no one I knew ever questioned my ethics, the paperwork was still readily available to dismiss inevitable rumors and hate. There was never any physical threat, but I understood cats that heard of me and didn't know my situation entirely could have questioned how I ended up in the facilities with the five-plus years I had left. These institutions typically housed snitches and less culpable people in most instances.

The higher the security level of prison you were housed, the higher the level of respect is demanded and given throughout. The stakes are different. More serious individuals were housed throughout the higher security level prisons, so people gave respect and minded their manners. It's not called "jail culture" for no reason, and the expectations to abide by the culture came with real-life consequences. Nearly all my peers and counterparts were in the medium and maximum level pens.

Mr. Ricco, unbeknownst to me, made sure that part of my plea included a lower custody level. He understood how my plea and PSI report needed to be designed because it affected the level of custody and where I would be housed. He made sure my plea was written specific enough to allow for the lower custody level designation. Before my sentencing, I was labeled a high-security inmate where I was placed in administrative custody with the likes of the first World Trade Center bombers, mob figures and a bunch of street gangs.

The Federal Bureau of Prisons gives inmates custody rankings to designate the type of security risk and corresponding facility an inmate should be placed in based on the ranking. They go from an offense level high of 43 to 1 and across to category 1 to 6. There's a bunch of determining factors that go into calculating a sentence and an inmate's security risk, from prior criminal history, violence, victims, etc. My initial ranking, when arrested, was on the high side of 43 because of the associated life sentence as part of my original charges. I was dropped down more than 12 points to a level 31 category 1, with 120 months; with three-quarters of that remaining, my ranking was reduced, putting me in a much lower level security facility. A sentence of more than ten years would have increased the security level of the facility; I would have been allowed to be housed.

By happenstance, on the day leaving Otisville, Lynch Mob Lou and I rode on the same bus in transit to our new destinations. In the federal system, inmates never really know where they are being moved to. Though Mr. Ricco had made arguments to have me placed in lower-level institutions, I do not think I fully grasped its significance or what to truly expect. I got dropped off first and arrived at the Federal Correctional Institution at Allenwood Low in PA. Lou continued and ended up in the maximum-security United States Penitentiary in Lewisburg.

Though I was initially labeled a "kingpin" with 21 others, I ended up simply pleading out to possession and the sale of seven kilos of coke with no co-defendants. (ten or more keys would have affected my security custody classification). The additional significance of not having any co-defendants was that I would have no "management variable." No one wants the management variable because it labels you a leader and organizer of criminal activities, which also affects the security custody classification.

The outcome of my trials wasn't what I wanted. I fought two cases to mistrials that were increasingly in my favor. I wanted to be acquitted. But never once have I ever stopped counting my blessings in understanding that I had a lawyer that continued to really fight for me even after my plea.

I had no knowledge or perspective of any of this, but his fighting made jail far more tolerable. I am who I am, and I would have stood up to my bid in any facility. While jail is jail, not all prisons are created equal. The less restrictive facilities that I stayed made doing my sentence undoubtedly more tolerable than had I gone to the maximum facility they intended for me to live the remainder of my life.

Approximately a year or so after my plea, my points continued to drop, and I went from a low-security facility to a federal camp. My time in the low-security facility was mostly uneventful. I had the goal of making it to the camp, and that kept me focused and under the radar. However, when they sent me to the camp, it was like putting a fox in the chicken coop. The camp had so few restrictions it opened up a whole new set of issues for me because it clearly was my nature to exploit these circumstances fully.

The lower the prison level, the lower the level of danger and threats of physical violence in a facility. Part of it is that the lower levels weren't so much filled with street guys, and another part is guys generally had shorter sentences. Getting out was the foreseeable goal, not establishing prison as a permanent home or an ingrained part of your culture. The most striking element of the minimum-security facilities wasn't the fewer restrictions, but in noticing the type of people and their attitudes toward being in jail. The lower level guys didn't always mind their manners because you were dealing with white-collar felons, scam artists, embezzlers and others who honestly didn't know or understand jail culture. They were not used to street codes that often resulted in people being physically checked for their disrespect and indiscretions.

In the lows and the camps, people also had more of a sense of entitlement versus people in the higher-level facilities who implicitly understood boundaries and perimeters. These understandings are part cultural and partly born from necessity.

I've often been asked about rape/homosexuality in prison. Homosexuality of varying levels goes on in every prison. That's a fact. While rape is different, I know it happens in some facilities. I never saw and only heard about one guy getting turned out in any of the jails I was in. That instance was of a guy allegedly turned out by Preacher.

It was rumored in jails as well as in the streets that Preacher went that way as far as the late '70s from a previous state bid in Green Haven he had served years before his 1996 arrest. This individual and I were in the hole together in Otisville during the time I had been placed there due to my forced separation. He was a shooter for a crew out of Brooklyn, and though he was in his early twenties, he had several bodies he was being charged with.

I could tell from our conversations he wasn't really about that life, but he had found himself out in the streets doing whatever he felt he needed to do to garner acceptance. It was clear he was being used. He told me he just had a kid, and he was in love with his girl, but she was telling him she wasn't doing the bid with him. It was typical of things you go through when you're in our predicament. Nonetheless, he wasn't handling it well, and I was trying to help him keep it together.

At some point, I left the hole after having a court date in Manhattan where my forced segregation got resolved. I came to understand after I left the hole, Preacher was placed in the hole, and they ended up being cellies where whatever happened is supposed to have occurred. When the kid was finally released to the compound some months later, he was visibly different.

While I may not have been personally aware of much of this behavior, talk of it was prevalent. I paid little mind to most of it, but one pervasive rumor going around in the federal prison system was that guys from D.C. had a strong rep for entertaining homosexual behavior. This isn't me saying this because I have anything against dudes from D.C. I'm super-cool with a lot of dudes out of D.C., but they have that tag on them. This was never something obvious in all the time I spent in D.C. But it made me think because most of the women I messed with in D.C. had men from there.

There was a lot of consensual homosexual activity going on regularly. A few of the guys were openly homosexual. However, most of the guys participating in these activities were doing so on the down-low. These guys outwardly acted hetero but were doing what they were doing. I never saw any of this personally, but it was known throughout the compound. I would see the girlfriends of some of these rumored down low guys and remember thinking many of them were attractive women. It was another real eye-opener because I could see how AIDS and other diseases were so easily passed in the streets since these were women I would definitely have dealt with.

I got in trouble within my first month at the camp because the rules were just too loose. I don't remember the actual infraction I was charged with. I believe it was a shot for being out of bounds, which meant I was somewhere doing something I had no business doing. I was sent to the hole for a little over a month. Eventually, the infraction got thrown out for a lack of actual evidence. Unlike most, I didn't tell on or incriminate myself. Once the shot was dismissed, I was sent back to the camp.

In all honesty, I wasn't ready for the camp nor did I ever become ready. I had a callous attitude that lead to some reckless behavior. I had been carrying around a ton of anger and resentment throughout this whole ordeal. I was angry at the government related to all that had been done to me and, more specifically, my family. I lamented all the things that I'd lost along the way and what I was enduring. Rationally or not, I was full of resentment and that lead to me just not giving a fuck toward respecting rules or authority while locked up.

One of the downsides to the lower-level facilities and camps was that snitching was rather common. A large segment of the lower-level facilities' guys told all the time. Many were already rats, which is why they were in the lower-level facilities. They continued telling every chance they got, especially if they felt someone was interfering with their quality of life. These were mostly guys who had that strong sense of entitlement.

Don't get me wrong. There were some good dudes at the camp that, like me, slipped through the cracks and caught a lucky break. So, I wasn't totally on an island by myself.

At the camp, I encountered all kinds of people, but what I quickly realized was that white privilege had its place even in the criminal justice system. Many in real estate, banking, and Wall Street were there for financial crimes such as embezzling tens of millions of dollars, and in a few instances, hundreds of millions, doing minimal time.

The extremes were unimaginable in the inequity of time versus crime. Because on the one hand, you had strictly minority individuals doing more time for small amounts of crack. Sixty-two grams or half of an eighth of a kilo, which cost approximately $1,200 during that time, positioned people to receive a mandatory minimum ten-year sentence. These were just the people in the camp. There were many others in higher facilities with not much more significant amounts doing similar or more considerable time. The disparity was utterly ridiculous, and it highlights the racism and classism that lawmakers used in punishing minorities versus everyone else.

I was able to have conversations with some stand-up guys. From those conversations, I realized I had been doing it all wrong out in the streets. I risked my life every day while they were doing gas tax and other scams netting millions without so much as lifting a finger, let alone a gun. Their experiences made me realize how limited we were in some of our thinking and hustling options. Nonetheless, I held my own, giving them a different perspective of a drug dealer because of my own life experiences. I was able to speak on a lifestyle that was identifiable and not come across like a peasant. Despite our apparent differences, we shared many commonalities. We talked about business and real estate holdings, homes, cars, and vacations, etc. I spoke their language from a monetary and lifestyle standpoint.

What was so revealing was, even in committing serious crimes, when it was all said and done, they had an unfair advantage in the time received. I also was made aware that they didn't seemingly lose everything they had worked for, acquired, or stolen. They still had their homes, boats, stocks, etc. It seemed the most they had to deal with, besides relatively short prison sentences, were fines and restitution. They were given payment options that they could take the rest of their lives to pay back. My woman was followed for two years and arrested as a strong-arm tactic. Their women were treated with white gloves and seldom ended up as co-defendants. Black and Latin mothers, daughters, sisters, and spouses were treated much differently.

***

In Allenwood, my daily focus and energies were no longer fighting my case. Visits had been a priority during the trial process as well, but with the resolution, I settled into my "new normal," which, of course, was far from normal. Much of the quality of life, particularly for those in the lower-level facilities and camps, centered on the sustained interaction we had with our families and the outside world.

Tameka and I were still pretty cool, and she stayed supportive by visiting me in MCC and Otisville and attending both trials. I felt bad for having her going through all this and told her I thought it was in her best interest to move on with her life. Tameka never agreed with my sentiments, but I realized I broke her heart. She eventually moved away to ensure distance from a situation she was never deserving of, to begin with.

After Reika's case was resolved, our relationship started to change. The emotions related to my infidelities were still unresolved and started to fester. By the time I took my plea and was finally sentenced, my relationship with Reika was at a low point. She had been holding so much in over the years regarding my bullshit, as my trials wore on, her support was definitely not as strong as it had always been. Angie was still in my life, so Reika and I were at extreme odds. Angie didn't disappear during my trials and even got embraced by my family. Jarrett Dwayne Chiles was born on May 14, 1995, and his addition brought her closer and more involved with the rest of the family.

Angie took up the slack in coming to visit and holding me down. Going into my third year, and by the time I got sentenced, Reika was seeing me much less. If Reika didn't commit to visiting me, I had someone else come in her place. As you could imagine, this only added to our issues. Between the stresses of our situation, along with what was going on with her and my family, it was more than she could bear. She moved out of the house and got a one-bedroom apartment in the Bronx. I'm not sure what her motivation was. Doing something, so rash under the circumstances wasn't what I'd desired, but things had gotten to that place with us.

I don't fault her by any means. However, my emotional bankruptcy, which only multiplied after my mother's death, was equally challenged by my pride. I let her know that because I was in this predicament, I wasn't going to take being handled any kind of way. I felt Reika was being way more breezy in some of the things she was saying that I know wouldn't have come out of her mouth had I been home. When I wasn't getting certain kinds of things from Reika, instead of groveling or even displaying contriteness, since in fact, I had been in the wrong, I simply sought it from someone else who was more accepting of me and my circumstances.

So, I wasn't surprised when I got word from my people that Reika was messing with another hustler. I knew of him when I was home. He was getting money, but he wasn't by any means on my level. I wasn't surprised or bothered by the fact that she was seeing someone because that was to be expected at some point. The specific issue I had with it was that I had become aware this individual was setting people up. Guys I was with on the inside had provided me documentation on these incidents.

I reached out to Reika out of concern to let her know what I had been made aware of. We were calmly talking at first, though she was evasive, blowing me off and not acknowledging that she was even talking to the dude. I told her, "Listen, whatever you're doing is for you to do. I'm not trying to police your pussy from here. I couldn't do that when I was in the street, and I'm not trying to do it from here. All I want you to know is that the dude you're fooling with is a rat, and he's out there setting people up, and it's known. I don't want you or our kids getting caught up in the crossfire of someone gunning for him, and you happen to have them with you around that character!" She became defensive and started saying, "When you were out here showing your ass, then it was all good. Now you're in your situation all up in mines..." I responded saying something someone of my stature would've: "I don't give a fuck what you do with your pussy, let's be clear."

As the conversation started getting nasty, the dude seemingly entered the house unannounced. I would have to assume he had keys. Suddenly, she started to get extra and out of character, evident she was performing for him. "I don't know why you are saying all this about him, tell him yourself." She then puts the dude on the phone, and he's like, "My dude, what's good?" This was all laughable to me at the moment because if I were home, this character wouldn't have even looked in my direction.

Nonetheless, this was my reality, and I was dealing with it accordingly. I told dude what I knew and that these were facts that he and I knew to be true. All the while, I hear her in the background carrying on for him, having him believe it's them against me, and she knows I'm on some bullshit. I finally had had enough, and I banged the phone on them. It would be over two years before the next time I would see or even speak to Reika.

Prior to my incarceration, guys would shoot their shots at Reika. That was a common thing that goes on in that lifestyle. Dudes took the shot hoping to come-up on a dude's woman on some ego shit. I'm guilty of this myself. Not so much targeting the woman of someone specific, but not giving a damn, nonetheless. My truth was if she's your broad, then she can't be gotten or swayed by the like. I understood the rules of engagement: don't hate the player, hate the game. Many have lost their lives or liberty playing that game. Nicky Barnes snitched on Guy Fisher and the other members of "The Council" because of ego and jealousy.

Reika was a very attractive girl. She received compliments on the daily, and it didn't hurt that she was always doing the most. She heard it all-- how they were willing to take care of her and do all these fantastic things for her, all while she was my woman if she just chose them.

Now she had her freedom. She was able to take up all those suitors who had pursued her for years. I had often told her these dudes only wanted to fuck her to have a one up on me. Besides, they didn't want the cost that went along with maintaining her lifestyle. Those conversations we had during those times were starting to resonate as she was getting a real reality check. The reality check was that as desirable as she was to men, those particular suitors were more interested in the clout chasing of the conquest than they were in the day-to-day sustainability of loving her, taking care of her children and keeping her maintained in the lifestyle she had been accustomed to for years now.

Once the breakdown in communication with Reika came to a head, I still had to deal with the issue of being able to see my kids. Eventually, I would speak to my family and have them ask Reika if she'd let someone else who was coming bring the kids. Reika didn't initially go for this, but eventually, those dysfunctional dynamics became part of our reality. In the facilities I was in, you got visits Thursday through Sunday. Angie would come and stay for the weekends after getting off work on Friday, and at some point, many of those visits from Angie included bringing my children.

The camp was about as good as it got as far as jail goes. The officers were mostly laid back. Most of the camp consisted of open dorms with two bunk beds, two lockers, and open space. In an honor dorm, there might be eight people with just single beds and no one on top of you, located closer to the bathroom and showers.

There were no lights out or required wake-up times. As in all facilities, you're required to keep your area and contents in order. You could go to the microwave or television room within the dorm without any restrictions.

The psychology of jail and being institutionalized was something I fought every day. I never wanted to get comfortable with the idea of being in prison and always reminded myself that the shit was just temporary. Guys would be in there waxing their cells and tailoring their visiting clothes. Dudes were in there acting like they were Dapper Con. Don't get me wrong, I was neat and clean, but I couldn't make this my reality and normalize it. Some guys needed their cell to be their home or space. I felt like that normalization was a contributor to so many having a difficult transition back to reality if they were fortunate to return to it. My cell was never going to be my home.

I saw the landscape in camp and quickly surmised what was what. Early on, one of the guys cut into me and told me about a hotel two miles away. He told me that he got there by jogging. That was all I needed to really know, and it didn't take me long after that to start getting my work out on.

I was shown the route how to get to the hotel, and it only took one time to get it down. The next step was explaining to Angie the preciseness needed for the mission possible. I would designate a landmark that I would be at a specific time. I gave her a two-minute window where I would allow myself to be visible and knew that she couldn't have a car ahead or behind coming in either direction before pulling over, and I'd jump in the car.

Once I was made aware, I could see that there was so much opportunity to hustle in the camp, and I had the heart to go get it. I was dealing with cats who were accustomed to privilege. I wasn't going to let a big thing like prison stop me from being who I fundamentally was a hustler. Supplying hair and muscle supplements like Rogaine and Creatine were gold in camp along with special seasonings for the Italian dudes who liked to cook.

When you are at higher-level institutions, they have clocked movements and regular counts of inmates. Some inmates are restricted to 23 hours of confinement and 1 hour of recreation. At the camp, you could move whenever you wanted. The camp wasn't walled or fenced, and no one was checking for you for lunch or dinner. There were two counts during the day at 4 PM, 10 PM or 11 PM, and one in the AM. I usually made the runs between 4 PM -10 PM and still did the earlier visits to sometimes play it off.

I couldn't be seen in or out of a car. Eventually, I got it down to a science. At some point, I got walkie talkies. I knew I had 20-minutes to get back to the compound if there was an emergency count, and the walkie talkies would give me a fighting chance to get notice and back.

Although the hotel was only less than two miles from the camp, it was considered no small feat to get there. Most of the trips were made in densely wooded areas at night with virtually no light, except a cooperating moon. My folks may have been from the country, but I was a city kid, and running through the labyrinth obstacle courses from housing projects, and tenements was far different than backwoods in the dead of night.

I literally saw it as freedom. Nothing was going to stop me short of them chopping off my foot to prevent me from running. I remember having to dive down and lay in the ground to escape detection from the random prison patrolling lights. My punishment wouldn't have been as severe as being given lashes from a whip, a chopped off foot, or being hung by a tree as an example to prevent others from attempting the same thing. However, the reality is, if caught, I could have been removed from the camp and given additional time for trying to escape.

Nonetheless, the reward felt far greater in those moments and well worth the risk. It wasn't the smartest move, but I still had that outlaw mentality, and I couldn't just succumb to the overseers' rules. And, did I mention you couldn't put a price on pleasure?

Those weekends had dual motivation. I would go to the hotel and pick up enough goods to bring back to camp to sell, regularly making $500 to up to $2,000 for some weeks. This was enough to initially pay for Angie's expenses, including my son's private school, put money towards

THE CRACK ERA

my father's appeal, and have some left over. I was paying down another $30,000 on my father's appeal. He was sentenced to 105 years and parole eligibility only after 52 ½ years. All that effort would be rewarded because the appeal eventually worked. He ended up doing 13 years. I didn't see my father from 1990 -2004, so the ability to pay the appellate lawyers was essential in my father returning home and us re-establishing a relationship as well as his with his grandkids and even great-grandkids.

When I first got to the compound, they had vending machines that took money, and you were only allowed to have up to $30 in change. Cash still ruled in the camp between commerce and gambling, so while it wasn't allowed, guys had people smuggling it in, and I was only so happy to help them spend it. It was a free market, and if someone was willing to pay for it, they could eventually find it. I may have had $1,500 in actual cash because of all the business I was doing. I had to smuggle money out of the facility to Angie regularly.

Food in the camp was one of the biggest vices, and lots of stuff was smuggled for those purposes. One time, some Italian guys asked for 100 pounds of pasta, which was like 100 boxes of spaghetti. I was benching 250 pounds plus so I figured 100 pounds would be easy to carry. It was a fiasco just unloading and delivering the boxes. This wasn't a simple scheduled delivery, but me trying to secretly smuggle 100 pounds covertly into camp after carrying it through the woods for over a mile. I charged $10 a pop for boxes that cost $1, but trust me; it was the hardest thousand dollars I ever made.

The spaghetti capers aside, when the opportunity presented itself to make a buck, I took it. I didn't want to be a burden, and I still saw myself as a provider. Not only did no one ever have to put money on my books. Ten years is a long time, and I knew I was far from comfortable.

The bid was initially sweet, and probably the reason I was able to hustle so hard was that others weren't willing to take risks. I was used to not only paying my way but everyone else's. If I called someone, it wasn't a burden to them to come to see me, and in many ways, it was an opportunity. I always paid their gas and hotels and, in some cases, gave them bill money.

***

My brother and I spoke regularly on the phone. On one of these occasions, he delivered some news he had received from one of our mutual friends. Steve Burtt had been a star at Iona College with Jeff Ruland. He was drafted by the Golden State Warriors and played in the league for several years before maintaining a long professional career overseas. It was never my brother's style, nor Steve's, to start shit, so I took the info he was passing along seriously.

I could hear him almost reluctant to say the words but compelled to inform me of something he felt I should know. I cannot recall Steve's specific source, but my brother told me that Angie had some dealings with a dude that played in the NFL, during the time I was with her, and there was a possibility that Jarrett was not my son.

The news was initially a lot to digest. Jarrett was nearly three at this point, and never once had I questioned his paternity. On Angie's next visit, I brought up what I was told. Angie denied everything, maintaining that there wasn't even a possibility there was someone else who could be our son's father. I struggled with her all-out denials because I respected the source of the info being my brother and Steve. Nonetheless, Angie wouldn't own up to anything, and this is what I was having a problem with.

I wasn't mad at the possibility that she could have been with someone else. How could I be? However, not giving me the option of understanding that there was a possibility, the child might not be mine, led to a domino effect that could have been deadly for me. I am far from one to overdramatize my life or any situation, but the decision to tell Reika I was having a baby in the midst of both of our arrests carried risks on many levels

Despite her adamance, things got a little different between Angie and me after that visit. Angie had been handling all my affairs up to this point, including my father's appeal and all the contraband pickups and deliveries. She was holding all the money I had been making on the compound up to this point. This initially continued, but nearly a month or so went by before Angie would return to see me. Coincidentally, this is also the time when Tiffany came back into my life.

***

I initially met Tiffany in the summer of 1991. She was in front of the Apollo with two of her friends on 125th street near my store, Boss Emporium. I happened to be outside, and she came up to me and asked me if she could use the bathroom. I had seen her in passing before at the skating rink in New Jersey, but this would be the first time we interacted. I remember casually hitting on her telling her she could use the bathroom but asking her if she needed my help. Her shock at my directness was amusing. Tiffany was from New Jersey, but she knew who I was. She and her friends from high school hung out with my brother and Mark Riley. I would end up giving Tiffany my beeper number, and we casually hung out. She had a boyfriend and I ended up messing around with some of her girlfriends. I garnered the reputation of being "community property." Needless to say, I was more than amenable to being passed around.

In 1992, Tiff got her real estate license, and I would refer my friends and associates. In 1993, She put Chris Mack in a 3-bedroom luxury condo in Edgewater. After our arrests, the FBI went to her grandmother's house to question her about the transaction.

By this time, Tiff had moved to Virginia Beach. Concerned they would harass her grandparents, she called FBI Agent Love to see what they wanted. Agent Love asked if she sold Chris the apartment in Edgewater and if the transaction was in cash. She simply replied that she did, knowing they already had that information. The FBI didn't really have much need for her or reason to question her about us beyond that.

I didn't hear from Tiffany again until she bought a house and moved to Atlanta in 1996. Tiff stayed in touch with my brother. Ironically, on the day he told me about the situation with Angie, he mentioned Tiff asking for an address to write to me. Most of this initial correspondence was via mail because I only had 300 minutes a month and used that mostly to speak to my kids.

At some point, Tiff mentioned that she was coming to New York and wanted to visit me. It had been at least four years since I had previously seen her. She was just about to start working with Dee Dean from Ruff Ryder. Ruff Ryders was coming off their success with DMX and starting their own label with Interscope Records. Tiff's new role required her to spend a lot of time in New York.

Eventually, when Tiff wasn't traveling for work, she would visit Thursday and Friday regularly. She would soon relocate back to New York, and our visits started to extend to Saturdays.

These initial visits with Tiff occurred while things were getting funny with Angie and me. I probably hadn't spoken to Angie in two weeks and didn't anticipate her coming to visit. So, I was caught off guard when Angie walked in the visiting room while I was sitting there with Tiff one weekend. I was already in the midst of the visit when the guard came up and asked me if there was going to be a problem. He knew who Angie was from previous visits. I told him there wouldn't be any issues. It was weird with way more awkward silences than actual conversations.

Angie had come on the visit with my cousin Nechelle, and the awkwardness eventually resulted in them choosing to leave. Angie and I never had an actual full-blown argument. We continued speaking, and she would still occasionally come up to visit me in the camp. I would eventually transition from her handling all of my affairs to Tiff, but I would continue giving her money when asked.

As Tiff started coming on the visits regularly, I started seeing her in a different light. The young girl I once only knew as pretty and a suburban square now took on a different perspective for me. When I met her initially, she was young. She was a college graduate now, more mature, with a lot of substance.

A year into working at Ruff Ryders, Tiffany was offered a job at an independent reggae label. The label was interested in breaking into the American hip-hop market and offered her double her salary. Tiffany was only at her new job about a month when the person hired to run the hip hop side of the label was fired. Tiffany was asked to step in until they figured things out. Suddenly, she wasn't just responsible for running the business; she was responsible for breaking the label's newly signed artist— a stripper turned rapper, Bonnie Clyde. Tiff hired her friend Susan Hampstead, a publicist and a few other associates from the music industry, to assist her.

In one of her letters, Tiffany talked about preparing to take Bonnie with her new single, "Strippin' Ain't Eazy," to the How Can I Be Down Music Conference in Florida. She was having some DVD's pressed, but she needed a marketing idea.

I had obviously been out of the music game for a minute, but the principles of marketing remained the same. Breaking a female rap artist without a crew or male counterpart was going to be challenging. She needed to create a buzz.

At this point in my bid, I was living vicariously through the letters and especially the photos that friends and family would send. My pictures were probably the most important items I had as they marked time and moments. When you're doing time, all you have is your memories, and they're sacred.

My concept developed into her creating a free promotional picture book like a yearbook. The booklet featured old school hustlers, my peers, and other street legends. Most people had heard these individuals' names in rap songs but didn't know what most of them looked like. The only words in the book would be ads for Bonnie Clyde. This was pre-social media and a time when certain individuals stayed away from taking photos. The only way to get these photos was to start making phone calls to personal friends and reaching out to Alex, the Photographer.

Tiffany would need assistance getting the images from Alex as well as others. I introduced her to Jule and Troy Rutledge. They agreed to help her get the photos and hold her down as she moved around.

Don Diva presents the "Past, Present and Future" was completed in October 1999. Tiff printed 3000 copies and started to give them away as a promotional item with Bonnie's single. Tiff told me she was hearing about people she gave them to actually selling them for 20 bucks a pop. I told her to stop giving them away and sell the remainder. They made a net profit of like $5,000 by accident.

We had no idea we had just printed the premier issue of what would soon be known as Don Diva Magazine, *the original street bible*. Soon after the booklet hit the streets, Tiff started getting letters asking when the next issue was coming out and how could they get a subscription?

On my recommendation, she went back to the guy whose label she was running, to see if he wanted to partner and run the "magazine" as a separate business. The guy wasn't interested. This was clearly a no-brainer for me. I had Jule and Troy come up with Tiff and asked them if they would help me with this new venture. They agreed, more so, as a favor to me.

In all actuality, neither Jule nor Troy had time to run around with Tiff. They had their own lucrative businesses to tend. At some point, Tiff had to rely on her friend, Susan, Reika, and Cavario, a dude she dated while she was in college, to get the project finished and distributed. My relationships in the street, as well as in the federal prison system, would set the tone for them to move easily through the street, entertainment industry, and secure stories in the future.

Aside from Tiffany and I starting to build Don Diva together, our romance and bond grew organically. Tiff was now meeting me for my hotel and contraband runs, so it was no surprise when she told me she was pregnant.

In between the conception of our child and *Don Diva,* I got really hot in the camp for the commissary contraband. Tiffany eventually parted ways with the guy with the startup and she moved from working in New Rochelle to a space in Harlem that Jule owned. She went on and incorporated *Don Diva* Entertainment. In some paperwork she had mailed me, it had me listed me as the co-owner. We had never had that conversation, so I was totally caught off-guard when I saw this.

I really started out just to help her, but the gesture made me look at her in a different light. It's one thing for people to romanticize the *ride or die* chick. It's easy and colorful to say, but experiencing it speaks volumes. I had always done so much for so many, never really asking for anything in return besides loyalty. The gesture from Tiff went a long way in letting me know who she was as a person. Character is who you are and what you really show to people. Reflecting on it, I can truly say that I believe her doing that may have been the one single thing that saved my life because I surely had other plans to get my life back on track, and it had nothing to do with running a magazine.

Don Diva may have started as something to help Tiff and even distract me from my imprisonment, but it quickly grew to embody so much more for me. I have always taken my participation in the *Life* very seriously. The Game, as it's been labeled by many, is the furthest thing from one and had dealt me some serious blows, yet I never forgot that I was a willing participant. That is why I have never understood or accepted others that willingly played the Game who could not abide by even the most minimal codes of honor.

"Death Before Dishonor" is more than a catchy slogan to me. I live, breathe, and abide by such principals always and not just when it's convenient. I have often heard the clichéd expression about not understanding someone or their circumstances unless you have walked a mile in their shoes. I've run a lifelong marathon in shoes that hurt my feet, but when it comes to honor, there is no grey area, and this is something that I think society has gotten twisted.

We glorify all these so-called "gangsters." We see them on TV and in documentaries and movies and talk about all the money they made and bodies they bagged accepting, beyond their criminality, that most of them became snitches. There is nothing more cowardly than telling to serve your own purpose. Today, guys and the public can come up with any justification to explain their actions, but as someone who has been on the side in which people were willing to (and did) tell on me to save their own ass as well as a candidate to save myself if I told, I can categorically tell you there is never a justification to dishonor yourself by telling. Definitely not for me. I made these life choices. We all knew the risks that come in search of the rewards. When shit doesn't work out, you take your L like a man. Anyone that tells you any different is full of shit and someone trying to justify why telling works for them.

Don Diva came to embody a platform to both expose those fake gangsters and acknowledge those that stood tall through it all. It was also intended to serve as a deterrent to those who were considering entering the Life. You rarely hear about those people because they usually are buried deep in prisons, serving long sentences while the rats get to tell and exploit their stories, hoping to re-write history in the process in a favorable light to their betrayals.

After a while, I knew that my hotel missions and contraband hustlin' were not going unnoticed by other inmates. I was very careful in my movements and only confided in a couple of people who had a vested interest in my moves as well. Even as careful as I was, some hating undoubtedly led to the guards paying closer attention to my movements and activities. It probably had a little to do with the fact I all had the latest kicks and wore more stylish GAP sweatsuits etc.

For two-plus years, the guards were mostly lenient until they started fucking with me and going through my stuff regularly. Eventually, someone began telling on me and all the hustling I was doing out of the camp. I may have had an inkling, but the reality is it could have been nearly anyone because there really were so many likely candidates. After a while, a few of the guards developed a hard-on for me, and it made my time at the camp more and more intolerable.

In the low-security facilities, strip-searching happened but less regularly. In the camp, strip searches were allowed but highly uncommon. When they started fucking with me, strip searches became the new norm and occurred every time Tiff visited. I had a cush job in the laundry which gave me access to the kitchen. I could make money in the laundry as well with supplying extra, new socks, t-shirts, or things for guys and have them put it on my commissary. Once they were fucking with me, they stripped me of the laundry job and tried to make me manually mow lawns. I wasn't having it.

THE CRACK ERA

Eventually, I filed a grievance because they were harassing Tiff at every visit with the go-to being that her clothing was somehow inappropriate. They were also constantly shaking down my cubicle and changed my relatively sweet job in the laundry to mowing using a manual lawnmower, which I just wouldn't do, so I ended up working directly for the lieutenant assuring they'd be able to keep an eye on me. Every federal inmate in the prison system is required to work unless they have been designated with a medical exemption. The irony of forced labor for outlaws, many whom have never worked real jobs on the outside, for pay ranging from twelve to forty cents per hour or ten to twenty-five dollars per month, was lost on no one.

When I started doing *Don Diva,* and it generated money, I didn't feel the need to do the other, risky jail hustles because I knew that Tiff was comfortable. The visits had become hot, and it was becoming burdensome for her. *Don Diva* made money from the first issue, and by issue eight, eighteen months later, we were starting to receive sizeable sponsorship checks from the likes of Def Jam.

On top of all of that, I knew Tiff's pregnancy was not going to be a good look, so I put in a transfer request to be a cadre in MDC Brooklyn. Most people would not think about voluntarily returning to a high-security building from a camp, but I requested to return to MDC. My shit was hot, and Tiff's situation was only going to make it more complicated. I was on the back end of my bid with a little less than three years left, and MDC in Brooklyn was a far easier trip for Tiff than traveling to Allenwood FPC in PA. More importantly, moving meant I wouldn't have to explain how my woman was five to six months pregnant to guards who knew she wasn't pregnant prior to her visits to a facility with no walls or fences.

23

HOME SWEET HOME - SORTA

As it turns out, leaving Allenwood was bittersweet. Besides the supposed leniency of a camp, I was leaving behind a handful of guys with whom I had developed a strong bond. The Millers had all gotten busted together. They were from Patterson, NJ. I knew Mr. Miller from the streets as he used to cop from Kid. I got particularly close to his son Jas, who I worked out with every day, and I became cool with his brother, Travis, as well. I also hit it off with Bryce, a real sharp dude out of Philly, who was well respected there as well as a guy named Dunn, out of the Bronx, and Deon from Buffalo. Deon worked in the kitchen, and I worked in the laundry. The two areas shared a back door, and with all the bullshit I was doing, we ended up becoming tight.

Additionally, there was my guy Artie. After he finished his state case in North Carolina, he ended up catching a fed case a few years after I was in, and we ended up back together in the compound. All of them were short, meaning they were likely going home in the next 12 to 18 months. They all eased the burden of bidding. Things were sweet while they lasted, and they all understood that my leaving was in my best interest.

I remember being relieved when the transfer went through. It took a couple of weeks for the transport to follow. I stayed low until that time neared. When that day arrived, I came alive as we got closer to the city. Seeing all the familiar signs on the highway reminded me it had been some time. I'd almost forgotten what it felt like to be home. As we approached the Lincoln Tunnel, I could feel the excitement building in me. Man, I missed New York.

THE CRACK ERA

The Bureau of Prisons typically houses inmates in facilities within 300 miles of their home. Of course, if you are deemed a security threat, then they have no issue shipping you to the other side of the country. Voluntarily returning to a maximum-security facility versus a camp was unorthodox, but at least I was closer to family.

Once through the Lincoln Tunnel, the Metropolitan Detention Center in Brooklyn was only 15 to 20 minutes further. The bus was full of inmates from the Northeast corridor. Some were destined for MDC while others were only housed there, awaiting transport to their final destination. MDC was a drop-off hub or hold-over facility.

We all went through the same processing. However, I wasn't a hold-over. I was intended to finish my remaining time at MDC. I was designated a cadre, which is the name of the program in which inmates are brought in to work around the prison grounds.

The cadre was needed in jails because our low-level security status meant we could work in and outside the building, providing no-cost maintenance. We did everything from delivering commissary throughout the building to working in the kitchen preparing meals, to keeping the building clean to maintaining the facility. We essentially did whatever was required.

There were two buildings: one described as the old building and the newly constructed building. Both were housed on the same city block alongside one another.

After getting processed in Receiving and Discharge (R & D), I was escorted to my unit. The cadre units were in the old building. Once I reached my unit, I was assigned a bed, unpacked and got situated. When I was done, I went to the common area.

The unit was set up with dorm-style bunk beds and two rows of lockers. The common area was more to the front where there were TVs and a kitchen area. There were two cadre units on the floor I was placed; the north and south side. I am guessing there might have been a hundred or so of us. It was early, and from what I could gather, most were already doing their assigned tasks. I just hung out, getting myself acclimated to my new surroundings.

Later that day, I was sitting at one of the tables in the common area, and on the other side was a dude who kept staring at me. It wasn't menacing, but it was clear he wanted to say something. This didn't go on for long before I asked, "What's up?" He responded, with a smirk, "You really don't know me?" I said, "Yeah, you look familiar, but I can't place your face."

I honestly didn't recognize him. He responded and said, "I'm Phil from Brooklyn. Lou Hobbs and Domenico's man." At that moment, it became clear. "Oh yea, now I remember you." It had been a minute since we'd seen one another. He had braids now, and it gave him somewhat of a different appearance. Even prior, we had only been in each other's company at outings such as the fights or All-Star Weekend.

As he was talking to me, everything from the last several years started coming back. I recalled that it was said Phil was hot and had told on Lou or had something to do with his situation in a negative way. He also supposedly had something to do with the dude, Jimmy Henchmen, from Brooklyn's case in North Carolina. Jimmy allegedly was giving work to Phil in North Carolina when they were both busted. Jimmy somehow got out of it, taking a plea on a related gun case out of either New York or California while Phil took a plea in the case, which landed him in MDC.

I recalled having mixed feeling running into Phil, based on things I had heard. I had been carrying that rat thing hard all through my bid. I straight despised all of them, and as a matter of principle, I didn't talk to or have anything whatsoever to do with them in any shape, form, or fashion. However, I wasn't 100% certain of my information, so in this instance, I maintained neutrality outwardly, not knowing what the actual deal was.

Immediately, I asked about Lou. I wanted to see Phil's reaction and response. Whatever he said didn't matter because I was going to get to the bottom of it, since I was in regular contact with Lou. Phil and I talked about catching up and filling in the gaps since we last met. That night, I wrote Lou asking what was up with his man.

During those initial days, several guys approached me, exchanging pleasantries and introducing themselves. They knew who I was and mentioned it was a pleasure meeting. In these situations, pleasantries are easily exchanged. I got cool with a couple of guys early on who hipped me to the comings and goings.

A week or so later, I was assigned a job as an orderly at Dayton Manor. It was a 116-unit apartment building in Brooklyn owned by the Bureau of Prisons. Everyone that lived in the building was employed by the BOP. I was introduced to a guy named Emmanuel, who I was assigned to work with. Manny was a Colombian guy who turned out to be a good dude. He was well connected on the outside, and we got along with pretty well.

A crew of about ten of us were primarily responsible for keeping the building clean. That mostly consisted of mopping, waxing the floors, and apartment repairs. There was even some painting when someone moved out to prepare the apartment for any new tenant.

The reason I transferred to Brooklyn was making more sense with each passing day. It was as if I had just started my bid in MDC. I wasn't familiar with any of the guards or staff, so my introductions started with a clean slate.

I no longer had any anxiety about having a pregnant woman and watching her stomach expand with every passing month. For all the guards in the visiting room knew, I just had come to jail. It was above their pay grade to question or investigate otherwise. In short, there was no obvious history for anyone to question. Tiff was now able to get to Brooklyn in about a half-hour from Bergen County, New Jersey opposed to the three-plus hours it took to get to Pennsylvania. Our routine picked right back up, with her spending her weekends with me in Brooklyn. She rarely, if ever missed a visit-- even after our son was born.

Chance Christian Chiles was born on March 31, 2001. He was named after my best friend and co-defendant, Christian Mack, and the *chance* we took to have him.

***

A couple of weeks after writing Lou, I got a response from him regarding Phil. Lou stated that he had love for Phil, and they were good. Lou was already serving an unrelated life sentence. I respected what he stated and accepted his explanation.

A couple of months into the job, Manny hipped me to his play. He had his wife meet him in the BOP apartment building we were assigned to clean/repair. They were spending days in the vacant apartments. Things were just getting better by the day. I don't even have to say, but this became part of my regular program. Despite being owned by the BOP, it was a regular building with the comings and goings of its tenants. Having a visitor could be as simple as having them access the building by one of the several entrances we could leave open. We didn't abuse it, but those clandestine visits were always something to look forward to.

As Manny and I got more familiar with one another, things revealed themselves. We were both in jail for drugs and could potentially do big things together on the outside. I wasn't sure what the future held, but it was looking brighter.

I must be honest. I hadn't grown beyond my past. I had a chip on my shoulder about how things had turned out. While my legal disposition was favorable, under the circumstances, my resentment fed into my plans to get back on top by any means necessary. That was my truth, at that moment. So, having a new Colombian connect was something worth cultivating.

The clock was ticking, and time behind bars was doing as it does. I had been in Brooklyn close to a year, and I was up for a furlough. The BOP had a furlough program at certain institutions that allowed for a defined, excused absence from the prison. It was only attainable for inmates of a specific security level, and those in the cadre were usually eligible.

Your first furlough is for 12-hours. Then, six months later, you're eligible for a 24-hour leave. Six months after that, a 3-day pass. This could potentially occur again in six months, up until you're out the door. I was looking forward to spending some time outside of prison. The excursions outside the camp and my cadre job allowed me outside of prison walls (both proverbial and real), but a furlough meant the chance to get out and pretty much whatever I wanted.

The granting of furloughs was hardly a given under any circumstance. The sun, moon, and stars all needed to be aligned. I had been doing all I was supposed to be doing and then some. By now, anyone reading this has ascertained I try and leave as little to fate or chance as possible. I was going to earn a furlough-- by any means necessary. I had been properly toeing the line in my cadre duties. Of course, "proper" was a complete misnomer, but in the eyes of the guards, I was doing everything asked of me.

After a few incidents of contraband being found on the job and in the prison, some whispering started as to who was responsible. Consequently, we all got reassigned to new posts.

I was assigned to work under the direct supervision of the deputy warden. I was placed along with a guy named Andre "Dre" Hudson. I had been in Brooklyn for over a year now, and I already knew Dre. We were really cool, so I wasn't bothered by the job change. The new assignment probably did me a favor, eliminating any further temptation. I had been pushing my luck throughout my incarceration, including at the manor.

Plus, other than the warden, who would have more say in the granting of extended privileges, including furloughs? It was fortuitous to be placed under someone so potentially influential, and I was willing to do anything to secure favor.

Oh, I have failed to mention a couple of essential details related to my new job assignment. The deputy warden was a beautiful, mature woman, with an even more stunning secretary. The secretary was in her mid-to-late twenties, with a fit, curvaceous body that couldn't be hidden or denied even in relatively conservative work attire. She appeared to be a mix of Black and Asian, with a personality as sweet as her perfume. The deputy warden was an African American woman in her early forties. The years had been kind to her, and while she may not have had the more youthful athletic figure of her secretary, she was voluptuous, fitting for anyone who preferred their women a little thicker than Victoria Secret models.

Now, there was fucking going on in MDC, but I could not treat these two like correction officers. The CO's were literally women from around the way, and no different than in the streets, they were not immune to the charms and status of guys on the inside. Some of these relationships even resulted in these women losing their jobs. Talking slick comes second nature, but I tried to watch my tongue as much as possible not to offend two women who could potentially affect my privileges.

My main goal was to garner favor, but I would have hardly been mad if anything additional had transpired. Tiff was my co-conspirator, seeing the bigger picture. I anonymously sent flowers and/or gifts like perfume to both women in the office. I am unsure if the gestures would have warranted disciplinary actions, but it surely could have moved me out of the detail if either had been offended or uncomfortable.

While I never directly took responsibility for the gifts, I would allude to my role. I am sure they figured it was me, but because I never pushed it with sexual innuendos or asking for any type of favoritism, it was left unspoken, if not accepted. While I was not directly asking for favor, I was trying to push every button to ensure that I was seen in the most favorable light.

Everything seemed to indicate my plans were working, and I was comfortable that the deputy warden was sufficiently on my side. When I was eligible, I put in for my first furlough when I was just shy of 24 months. As I had hoped, I was approved.

24

FOLLOW THE LEADER

Despite the continued turmoil all around me, I forged on almost mechanically. You find things to keep you distracted and justify the crazy. I managed to try and enjoy life with my guys. This included going to all the major prize fights and sporting events. I never went with less than ten people. Ringside and courtside seats cost $500 apiece; the $5,000 for the tickets was only the start. Once you factor in the first-class flights, hotels, and meals, I was spending a small fortune. During this time, All-Star Weekend and championship fights were spectacles that indeed highlighted this new era of young Blacks getting big money.

All-Star Weekend had been on the East Coast for three years in a row: 1990 in Miami, Florida, 1991 in Charlotte, North Carolina, and 1992 in Orlando, Florida. Attending these events had become our norm, so piling in our cars or jumping on a plane was almost mandatory because we were going to be in the building. The one in Orlando, I remember it was myself, Chris, Bob, Kid, Tone Wop, Kev Simmons, my cousin Lamont, his partner Doug and a couple of my out of town dudes. Jesus, Roy, and his entourage that consisted of three others. Black Mark and his crew met us down there as well.

The reason I specifically remember this was because I spent $6,000 buying tickets from one of my friends that scalped tickets from my days back at Yankee Stadium. He had stepped his game up and was now traveling all over the country, scalping tickets to these big events. However, what stood out in my memory was that Lou Hobbs, my dude from Brooklyn who was also a business associate, had a bunch of tickets to the weekend's event. Lou called me and asked if I had tickets, and I told him I did. He said, "Kev, get your money back. I got you." I ended up getting back with my dude who took them back from me, then resold them and I got my money back. The game was also noteworthy because it was the last of Magic Johnson's career after he had retired once he was diagnosed with HIV.

These trips on the East Coast were great for me because they served a dual purpose. I had situations all up and down the coast, so I'd stop either on the way down or the way back up to drop off or collect my money. In those instances, I'd invite my dudes from these cities to join us in getting up and having a good time. These instances were few and far between, but when the opportunity presented itself, we enjoyed balling out. The festivities during All-Star were legendary, with everyone wanting to be part of the parties thrown by Michael Jordan and Magic.

***

All these circumstances that ended 1991 probably made it not so coincidental that the government put a plan in place to bring down my organization. With all these things taking place, I had had a long run, and it was inevitable for my number to come up. This was not exactly a surprise, but the truth is, I had envisioned the circumstances of my death much more vividly. Being followed and investigated was more of an unknown and uncertainty.

Around 1992, I started seeing agents following me. I always played my mirrors and was accustomed to watching who could be following me. I was essentially groomed to watch my own back. Once I realized something different was going on, I started using unorthodox driving maneuvers. The windows of the tail car were deeply tinted, and that could only mean either stickup dudes or law enforcement.

I had become paranoid about being followed or investigated, but this new development made me change my program even more. This led to me limiting my exposure to certain things and events. I was one who enjoyed the company of a beautiful woman or two, so falling back publicly worked since I preferred to spend my time in this manner. It would usually take for my guys to corral me to attend one of the typical street events. I had already grown weary of being on the scene in the company of or in pictures with other hustlers. It was always understood that those certain kinds of crew pics would come back to haunt you, so they were to be avoided. That explains why there aren't many of these pictures of us floating around. Honestly, I don't have a recollection of any.

I had always been very disciplined in my day-to-day communications. I never used landline phones or even the burner phones for anything that wasn't above board. Burner phones were phones with stolen or chipped accounts, and the numbers were "cloned" while the authorized user would be unaware until their next billing cycle hit. Most people did not have cell phones at this time, and the bills would routinely be several thousand a month. We would pay $200 for the phones and have unlimited access and calls, including international. We never knew how long the phones would last, anywhere from 10-30 days. I used them for convenience to call family and my girlfriends, but never to do business. I made a point of telling everyone I did business with to do the same and to make no exceptions to that rule. I would use payphones and not the same ones regularly to do business. I remember when I would get a beep, and I was home in Franklin Lakes, NJ. I would get in my car and drive to a payphone (the closest one about a half-mile away) to have a conversation and even in those not being overly descriptive. Payphones only allowed for local calls unless you had a ton of change, but in urban areas, they were widely available on corners. We used to have these calling card numbers and pins that allowed us to make long-distance calls for free. I always kept several of these pins with me on pieces of paper. These numbers would last for a week then burned out, so I'd go on to the next one. I provided these pins to all my guys, so they had no excuses for doing anything other than following this protocol.

I also made it a point to never talk in rooms or cars. If I had to speak in a room or car, I always made a point to have some background noise, so even if something was heard, it wouldn't be audible.

My paranoia was not unwarranted. Around the same time, Reika and everyone else in my Franklin Lakes house started noticing they were also being followed. They saw the surveillance because the suburban landscape in New Jersey made it easier to spot cars following them. Initially, I asked if the person following them was being aggressive thinking that they might be kidnappers, but eventually realized they were the police.

I was able to confirm this when I managed to get the plate numbers. I had a family friend who worked at a local police department run the plates and verified the cars' government vehicles. This was the first of several defining incidents that occurred in a manner of a few weeks that ultimately made me make lifestyle changes that were probably a long time coming.

I had a friend from the Bronx who I had scalped tickets whose wife worked for the FBI, though I am uncertain in what capacity. He got in touch with me and let me know that my name was being mentioned and may have even come across memos in the office. Shortly after, but unrelated, someone who went to college with my brother and worked in some capacity in law enforcement called him to say that he had heard my name come up in regard to being investigated. They also didn't have any specific details, but I knew I had a problem.

The most defining situation occurred with a tip I got from my guy, Jesus. He and I had a business relationship that extended to a more personal one that included hanging out and doing the various out of town sporting events like All-Star and the fights. Sometime in 1992, Jesus got arrested in North Carolina before being released on bail. (I'm a little sketchy on the details.)

Once back in New York, he reached out to me and said he needed to get up with me. We met at a club downtown. I don't remember what club it was, but I had someone in the car as I pulled up and double-parked in front. I hit him on his phone, and he came to the door. As I approached the bouncers, they allowed me to pass, and I walked in. We proceeded downstairs to a basement area where it immediately became clear this was not a regular business or social call. Jesus was acting strange; in a manner, I couldn't quickly identify other than to know something was up.

He didn't keep me in suspense for long. He told me about getting picked up in North Carolina. He was less focused on the details of his case and more on how my name came up during the fed's interrogation. He let me know that they were quite familiar with our relationship, and they were pressing him crazy about my organization. He stated that he didn't tell them anything other than we were just friends, but he said it was clear that the feds had a real hard-on for me.

He told me that he was going to lay low and stay out of the way. He asked if I could look out and give him some scratch to hold him over until he figured out his next move. I told him to come by the office, and I'd give him whatever. He looked at me as crazy as if I'd asked to borrow his wife. He stated that I was on fire, and he wasn't coming anywhere near the store or office. He was sure someone around me was talking and giving it up. We talked a little longer before I dapped him up and told him I would get at him for what he asked for.

I got back in the car and immediately hit Chris up to tell him I needed to rap with him about something. This warning was the final straw that broke the proverbial camel's back. After Chris, I began calling other individual meetings to get with my guys and tell them that I was hot. I was short on exact details, but I knew I had an issue. I told them I needed to fall back until I was able to figure out what's what. I let them know we wouldn't be seen together because I didn't want them caught up in my BS.

I abruptly shut down some of the apartments I was keeping from Baltimore to North Carolina. I had to literally clean house(s) to remove any signs of drug dealing. I recall even putting some of the apartments' furnishings in storage.

As I began to evaluate my predicament, I thought about all the things that had recently taken place, trying to figure out where my issues were coming from. As far as my inner circle, none of them had been busted on anything, as far as I knew. I must use that qualifier because what often happens is someone gets busted without your knowledge, gets flipped, and returns to the streets before you even become aware. None of what I could figure made sense other than Alpo. He was not part of my immediate circle, and I didn't have direct knowledge of his status, but I had gotten word that he had gone bad. Still, nothing made sense to me because Reika and my cousins were also being followed, and they had nothing whatsoever to do with my drug organization. I was getting pulled over more frequently in what were supposed to be random traffic stops. The reality is my issue could have been coming from anywhere. I was on an eight-year, uninterrupted run, and it stood to reason it was my time.

The timing just didn't make any sense to me because I had slowed my business down significantly. With all the recent arrests, I was being cautious and had been moving completely different. I went to the extremes of hiring a company to sweep my houses and cars for anything out of the ordinary. I spent thousands of dollars on counter-surveillance devices so that I could sweep my surroundings daily myself. I bought call scramblers, which had to be attached to the phone you were using as well as the one you were calling. The device would distort your conversation so that even if law enforcement was tapping your calls, they wouldn't get anything audible. I didn't talk on phones anyway, but in an extreme situation, I'd resort to using this device within my increasingly smaller circle.

The bug detectors were devices that looked somewhat like a beeper with an antenna that you'd pull out and point in the direction or area you were scanning. It had earplugs directly into the device, and if you talked and were able to hear yourself, then there was a bug in the area you were scanning. The bug detector picked up on anything sending signals on that frequency.

I was essentially the last man standing within my generation, and this was now not going unnoticed. I can't say the heat I was getting was totally a surprise, so laying low meant the minimal hustling I had been doing went to nearly zero. I was already more immersed in my legitimate businesses. Knowing the FBI was investigating me made me focus on making these legal hustles work. The music business was where I then put most of my energy.

Once I made that decision, I employed all the people around me to help in the pursuit. This mostly consisted of family members. By this time, my younger cousins and some of their friends had all come of age and were more capable. I looked to them to assist in bringing some of my ideas to fruition. They had all been fixtures around the store just hanging out. They had all lived a carefree existence where money seemed to fall out of the sky.

My cousin, Nechelle, had worked in the store at one point along with my brother, Tony. My cousin, Lamont, and his friend, Doug, ran errands and supported them in whatever capacity was needed. My cousin, Darnell, was the youngest and closer in age to one of my groups, Uptown Kidz, signed to BOSS Records. He worked closely with them, helping develop their confidence and stage presence. Libby, a neighborhood kid who had issues at home and nowhere to stay at times, was someone I'd met through my cousins. I took a liking to him and took on the responsibility to look out for him. Then there was Billy House. He was Chris' younger brother-in-law, who had hooked up with them and became part of this group. I pretty much put everybody that was around me to work, finding things for all of them to do. They had all had long, free rides, and now it was time for them to pull their weight and toe the line.

Taking on these new tasks put them in the position to move around quite a bit, which meant they had even greater access to all the cars that were around. They had all the perks to maximize their frontin'. I quickly began to see some of the benefits they'd saw for themselves when lots of girls from the neighborhood started hanging around the office.

Their coming of age and added responsibility came with a hefty price. They all collectively would go on to cost me quite a bit of money from the many cars they crashed and their juvenile antics. They were just young guys being young, but this came with a consistent price tag for me.

***

I started a record company with little-to-no knowledge of the inner workings of the business side of the music industry. I grew up loving music, but that in and of itself wasn't going to be enough. I initially hired Eric Alvarado, a childhood friend who went to high school with my brother, to run the day-to-day operation of all the groups. Eric had been working in the industry on the production and editing side of big-budget music videos. He approached me to help me make music videos and cut the costs. If he was a part of a big-budget video that had filmed over Thursday, Friday, and Saturday that cost $150,000 or better, I might get use of all of their equipment that didn't have to be returned until Monday along with a scaled-down version of their crew. While it still might cost me $35,000 - $40,000, my videos looked every bit the part of the big record company videos. Eventually, he came to play a more significant role on a day-to-day basis. Eric and I discussed all the things we needed to get the company up and running. We knew we lacked certain experience, but that didn't stop us from working towards figuring it out. Eric did a great job, but after some time, I knew we needed further help. Seemingly out of nowhere, a guy named Bernard Thomas showed up with a wealth of knowledge and experience within the music industry. Hindsight has made it clear that Bernard's arrival in my life was neither luck nor coincidence.

I was standing in front of BOSS Emporium one day talking to rapper Eric B. when Bernard Thomas just happened to walk down the street. Eric and Bernard warmly greeted each other. Bernard had previously worked for a guy named Robert Hill at Zakia Records. Eric B and Rakim, along with Kingsun, were the label's marquee acts. Robert Hill, like me and many others, had allegedly started his record label with street money. Besides the music, one of Bernard's jobs for Robert Hill was going back and forth, bringing money to the Bahamas. On one of these trips, he got arrested and flipped, becoming a confidential informant for the government. I never knew of Robert Hill going to jail, so I'm not sure what his story was.

Bernard Thomas came to me with strong credentials and affiliations within the music business at a time when I needed someone more experienced to help take BOSS Records to the next level. I don't recall exactly where he was from, but I know he had strong family ties in both Boston and Florida. He mentioned working with New Edition and Maurice Starr, who also founded New Kids on The Block, before working with Robert Hill and Zakia Records.

Bernard then went on to work for David Hyatt out of Miami. David Hyatt was a big-time drug dealer, credited with discovering R. Kelly. He signed R. Kelly to his Miami-based label Tavdash Records before being instrumental in Kelly signing with Jive Records. Four years later, he was arrested and sentenced to Life in prison under the kingpin statute. After Miami, Bernard migrated up north and started working, for a short time, with Joe and Sylvia Robinson at Sugar Hill Records. I had a personal and working relationship with their son Leland, so it was easy to verify Bernard's role there and at Zakia.

After Sugar Hill Records, Bernard went on to work with Azie Faison. He had an independent group and label called Mob Style. They were like a pre-NWA, but instead of talking about gang culture, they focused on drug culture. They put out a few videos and singles and had some mild success. One of the individuals who helped Azie achieve music success was Bernard Thomas.

Azie was part of that original Rooftop class. He was getting money primarily from two spots. One was on 145th Street between 7th and 8th Avenue called the Jukebox. The other was on 7th Avenue & 132nd Street, a little storefront closer to 7th Avenue that was putting out work at a steady clip. I don't remember how Azie and I initially met. I just remember knowing of him.

The first time I remember for sure we had a personal interaction was the spring of 1987. Rob and I were driving around Dyckman, the most northern part of Manhattan. We were coming from visiting the connect, when I noticed Reika's car double-parked. I saw her and Azie talking, standing outside their vehicles. We immediately jumped out, and our energy spoke more than any words. At this time, we weren't friends but knew of one another. They both quickly said that nothing was going on, but I had little time or patience for explanations. Azie was with another guy, but it was clear neither was trying to match our energy. Reika quickly got the picture, jumped in her car, and left.

Our paths subsequently crossed, and there was no real acrimony or beef. Weeks later, I was in front of the Rutledges' building in the Grant Houses on 125th Street with Shavar. Azie pulled up and jumped out of the car with another person. He was with an older hustler that had just gotten out of jail and wanted to talk to me. He introduced the guy, and we acknowledge one another. He began by asking if I knew his wife, Angie. I replied I knew a few Angies, which was indicative of being dismissive to any line of questioning. He didn't really push and said Angie was his wife and asked if I wouldn't see her anymore. I simply told him that was a conversation he needed to have with his wife, whoever she was.

The situation never got aggressive or took on a tone I was uncomfortable with, but it still left a bad taste in my mouth. I had to calm Shavar down constantly. Shavar was a different kind of dude, and any perceived aggression or even slight directed toward me would not go unanswered. I wasn't sure what Azie's thinking was. Maybe he called himself just trying to act in the role of peacekeeper, but if I had been power-tripping, it could have ended in a very different manner.

A couple of months later, on August 22nd, 1987, Azie was involved in a drug-related robbery in the South Bronx at 1295 Grand Concourse, near East 169th Street in the Morrisania section. It took place in a third-floor apartment described as one of his stash houses. Six people were shot in the head at close range. Three died immediately, but three others were found alive, Azie was one of the survivors.

After his situation, he recovered and was laying low, virtually out of the game on any significant level. Throughout the years, I would still see him regularly, and we were cool. He came to the store on 125th on several occasions. Outside of that, the only other times we'd be in each other's company was when we played basketball games, betting against one another, my squad versus his.

Azie wrote a book titled Game Over and in his 2007 book, he alluded that he tried to warn me about Bernard Thomas by stating he told Gangster Lou, a Mob Style member and personal friend of his, to give me a heads up about Bernard while on our way to Jack the Rapper, a music conference in Orlando, Florida. I never got any message. I ran into Azie regularly before the conference and after. At this point, we had a personal relationship he could've easily told me himself. Bernard had been around me for over two years since leaving Azie and that Mob Style situation. Az came into the store from time to time, but never once did he personally warn me about Bernard. Or anyone else for that matter. He had plenty of opportunities to pull my coat.

***

BOSS Records' office was initially in the BOSS Emporium basement. It was the size of the store and functioned as a full-service office. I was also operating a silk-screening business down there. As it became clear that it was a real and growing business, I moved it to a ground-level office on 121st Street and St. Nicholas.

The label was beginning to flourish. Uptown Kidz was being compared to Kris Kross and the Youngsters, both receiving national acclaim. I had groups that hosted and were featured on several video platforms and routinely getting videos played on Rap City and In the Basement with Big Tigger on BET. As the label grew, so did my relationship with Bernard.

Bernard came to me as a stranger, but over time he could see how dedicated I was to grow the label and just as importantly how dedicated I was to my family. I was surrounded by family and close friends every day. Eventually, Bernard took on the role of an uncle figure. We were spending quite a bit of time in each other's company. There were several holidays like Thanksgiving, Christmas, birthdays, and several music conferences that we attended together. I was his employer, but more than that, I was someone who he came to know he could depend on in his times of need, like when his wife got sick. Overall, we became relatively close over the nearly two-plus years we worked together.

I had heeded the warnings I was given, and I virtually stopped hustling during this time. My days consisted of being in BOSS Emporium, BOSS Records, or one of my other businesses. For the world, I couldn't figure out why I was being followed every day for months on end. This one day, I grew tired of being followed, and against anyone's better judgment, I started following one of the cars that had been following me. I was in the car with The Uptown Kidz on my way to the studio. The gesture went unappreciated and led to the vehicle aggressively trying to get away from me. It didn't take long for several cars with dark tinted windows to converge on me at an intersection. No one got out, but their move was intended to be a message and show of force.

Throughout their investigation, I would talk to Reika and different family members, who informed me they were still being followed as well. They were following Reika to insignificant places like the grocery store. Chris also made me aware that he was being followed, as well.

At some point, it didn't make sense to me, so I figured maybe they were monitoring my spending to come at me with a tax problem. So, I went to see my accountant, Sal Marranti, to make sure everything was right.

I had not always been this thorough or responsible related to long-term planning. The last thing I had previously been concerned about was jail. I always thought my participation in the *Life* would lead to death. As the Crack Era grew in infamy, the increasing commonality of death somehow seemed more realistic. If not in a morbid way, a better alternative than being locked up in a cage for life.

I made sure my family was good with the amount I gave them to stash. My brother had graduated from Columbia University and was selling life insurance, so I had multiple policies making sure, in addition to the cash and businesses I had, my family would be well provided for in the event of my death.

While some adjustments were made, the reality is that I still lived and maintained a lavish lifestyle despite no longer hustling on any significant level. This included several monthly, continuous nuts. BOSS Emporium's rent was $6,000. The leases for both the laundromats in the Bronx was about $3,500-$4,000 a month each. The restaurant's rent on 128th & Lenox Ave was $2,500 and approximately $2,000 for the record company, which didn't include the miscellaneous expenses of studio time, maintaining the groups, and music videos, which could easily run into the tens of thousands a month initially without immediate recoupment. The nearly $15,000 a month in business rents did not include any of the myriads of other expenses and fees associated with running businesses like employees' pay and all utilities and insurances to cover them. In my case, these businesses were not just fronts, but entities intended to hold their own. Luckily, they did more than that, and besides the initial startup costs, the businesses took care of themselves and even made profits.

However, my personal monthly fixed expenditures had no recoupment besides my continuing to make money hustling. My main Franklin Lakes house mortgage was approximately $6,000. The condo I kept in the Bronx on Grand Concourse was roughly $2,000 a month. I had at least five other apartments that I kept women in that I paid rent every month for years. Because these were all apartments, I personally spent time in, they were all in luxury buildings or gated communities to ensure my safety and comfort. The rents were minimally $1,500 to $2,500 a month.

The more than $20,000 a month in fixed housing mortgages and rents did not include the various expenses that come with running all of these households, such as taxes, insurance, landscaping, and maintenance costs. All the properties had utility expenses, which were easily over $5,000 a month cumulatively. That's more than $35,000 in fixed housing costs alone. However, as I started to run around less, I began to downsize many of those side expenses. Once I wasn't doing business a certain way, these expenses, like extra rents, were less necessary, especially out of town.

My homes and apartments all had bulk expenses like the custom furnishings that each held as well as being equipped with whatever was the latest and greatest in technology. I paid the premium in large part to keep the women playing their position with as little complaining and disruption of my program as possible. It allowed them to feel special even when they knew they were not my only woman or main-woman. In addition to those costs, all my women had allowances for food, shopping, and just general living in addition to the cars they all got. As much as there was a personal relationship to these situations, there was also an obvious business component to it as well. It was always my goal to make all my relationships mutually beneficial, and this was no different.

My initial methods of hustling were a means to an end, not the goal. Don't get me wrong; the rush and adrenaline that came with being a hustler became addictive, an addiction I quickly had to deal with. I was never naïve enough to believe that there was any long-term future in drug dealing. The streets didn't easily allow for a comfortable retirement with a pension plan.

With all that was going on, I began stressing to everyone around me to stay away from all the things that at any other time I would've overlooked. They were told not to bring anything into the office that didn't belong in there-- meaning drugs, guns, and people who may have had their issues.

This mandate all came about because one day, I came into the office and found a package of crack stashed in one of the drawers. I don't remember what explanation I was given, but I flipped and went ballistic on everyone that was in the office. It was mostly my younger cousins and their friends who hung around in the office who I needed to direct this to. My counterparts knew the severity of this without me having to tell them.

***

I kept and maintained my father's condo in the Bronx. Besides being hopeful of his appeal, I turned the space into a full-fledged pre-production studio for my groups. It was routine for the place to be full of activity between my groups, my cousins, and my lady friends coming in and out of the spot. The condo/studio was devoid of any illegal activities, but it didn't stop the authorities from surveilling everyone that came in and out. With all my stresses and not really hustling, it may have only enhanced my drive-in spending time doing the one thing that truly let me escape the BS. Others got high to escape the stress and anxiety.

I was self-indulgent when it came to women. I was anxious and had more time on my hands than I was used to. Instead of seeking therapy or prescription medication, I self-medicated with the pleasure of women. My pleasure-seeking knew few limitations, and I've had many, very fulfilling, and satisfying experiences with women as a result. My lust became so crazy my women would bring me other women almost like a bounty knowing they would be rewarded for them presenting it to me. Our sex play was such we'd literally playfully fight over the women.

Some of them seemed to love women as much I did, if that was at all possible.

One day, I received a call from a girlfriend, and she asked me whether I was in town or not. I mentioned I was at one of the apartments she was familiar with, and she asked if I wanted company. I stated I wasn't in the middle of anything overly important, and that would be cool. When she showed up, she was with one of her friends that I happened to have been dealing with as well. It was supposed to be a "Gotcha, you're busted, nigga" moment. Instead, I just smirked and invited them in. We had a wonderful afternoon. By this time, my reputation had preceded me, and this kind of behavior had become the expected norm amongst the women I was dealing with.

I remember another instance where yet another one of my women called me late one night. We often played together, and she intimately knew my ways and had adopted some of them herself. I answered, thinking it was potentially going to be a booty call, but it turns out that she called to let me know she ran into one of the women we had played with that had been introduced to her by me, and she knew I was fond of. She playfully and competitively let me know she booked her and that she was now hers. She put her on the phone, and she told me, "Baby, I wish you were here, but oh well," and the phone hung up. All I could do was smile to myself. These were precisely the type of late-night calls and distractions I welcomed.

Most times, my road trips involved females. They served the dual purpose of keeping me company and limiting police profiling. They were also my playmates. My philosophy was I worked hard and played harder. There is never any robbery in a fair exchange. For them, the perks were fine dining and shopping till they dropped along with traveling to all different parts of the country and in some instances, the world. For me, if you can imagine, some of the best freak sessions legally permissible.

***

My cousins had to be entertaining to follow, but it would only take minutes to ascertain; they were not engaged in any illegal activity. Once they came of age and had full access to my cars, they clearly maximized their fronts. They went from being flies on the wall, present at so many eventful moments (good and bad) throughout Harlem, to acting like privileged heirs with little cares. There were quite a few girls left in their wake who gave them play based on what they thought they had going on versus the actual reality.

One day in June or July of 1993, my cousins, Lamont, Darnell, and Billy, were up in the Bronx with Chris's brother Ant-Man at his house on Ogden Avenue and 166th Street When they left, they jumped in a taxi heading back to Manhattan. The taxi crossed over into Harlem and a short time after it was pulled over on 127th and 7th Avenue. Upon searching the car, a gun was discovered under the front passenger seat of the cab. They were all arrested. These types of situations were not just random or coincidental. They had started to become the norm. Their case went on for about a year, with several hearings before leading to them taking it to trial. They all ultimately beat the case when a jury acquitted them.

***

Amidst the never-ending drama and ongoing investigation, business was moving positively along. In late August of 1994, we all went down to Jack the Rapper. This was the year Puff showcased Bad Boy being on Arista Records and premiered Craig Mack and the Notorious BIG. Death Row, newly signed to Interscope Records, also had a big presence with upcoming albums for Dr. Dre and Snoop Dogg. In effect, I made sure it was going to be BOSS Record's national launch party as well. I chartered a bus to take people from Harlem to work and support our movement down in Orlando. This event was major for the industry with a virtual who's who in Hip-Hop present. I marketed and promoted my label independently. The guerilla marketing technique of having 60-70 people all wearing the same t-shirts, bandanas, etc., with a glow in the dark "BOSS Records" emblazoned on them was far more effective than anything I could have envisioned. Our presence was so loud and impactful it was clear all we were missing was a major distribution deal. Shortly after the conference, I was entertaining distribution talks with major record labels, including Relativity and Universal. It was just a matter of time. Our self-sufficiency and marketing prowess made us a hot commodity. However, Bernard and I were majorly bumping heads because he had a problem with me signing any deal. It's the music business, and 95% of the deals suck, but Bernard's objections to any steps forward made no sense.

There is no telling how many calls Bernard was probably getting and not telling me about. We were taking a lot of record distribution meetings, and Bernard would shoot every deal down, saying they weren't good. We showed our resourcefulness and that we meant business and had lots of suitors. Less than 60 days later, I was in jail. The timing, I would say, was far from coincidental. In hindsight, I realize he was there to derail all those deals. I already had the money but securing a real distribution deal would have made me totally legit and possibly untouchable to the government. So, Bernard was doing what he was put in place to do.

The record business has historically been financed or backed by criminal elements. However, with some exceptions like the prosecution for payola in the 1950s that included Dick Clark, the industry and government have largely ignored the criminality by the various Caucasian ethnicities that controlled the music business. The Crack Era and the evolution of Hip-Hop were a totally different story.

The government pulled out all the stops to make sure that Black men that may have started in the streets did not gain any legitimate wealth through the music industry. It was bad enough they couldn't catch us, but the feds pulled out all of the stops to derail legitimate music businesses because of the affiliations that these Hip-Hop labels may have had with the streets. It happened before me, and it continued to happen after me. You don't believe me, ask, Suge Knight, Irv Gotti, or Tekashi 6ix9ine. If you came from the streets, the government was more relentless in trying to prosecute you, by any means necessary, before they allowed you to have continued and legitimate success within the music industry. Part of it is the government's vindictiveness, and part of it is their war on the influence that the streets have on the culture.

The government knew they didn't have me on drugs. They were simply late to the game. I'm sure that perhaps if I were still doing drug transactions, they would have had him in to see or feed information. When it was clear that I wasn't going for that, he was there to sabotage my record company. The only thing worse than a successful Black drug dealer was a reformed drug dealer with the ability to influence the culture and make money legitimately. They wanted to stop that rise for sure.

25

STILL DODGING BULLETS

September 11, 2001, started as a typical day. That particular morning, they had me doing some clean up in front of the building, sweeping the block, and then cleaning the building lobby where visitors enter. I got downstairs at about 8 AM and hadn't been working more than a half-hour before I heard a blaring siren. The guards started ushering us back in the building in a panicked state. At first, I wasn't aware of what was going on, but I was quickly able to figure out what was happening. That realization instantly turned into the surreal.

You could see one of the World Trade Center towers on fire from MDC. It was hard to believe what I was witnessing. I had been a New Yorker for most of my life, and I had never seen anything like what I was witnessing. Despite the bombing of the north tower's garage in 1993 in an attempt to bring both towers down, I still couldn't even fathom anything like this, and I am sure that nearly all New Yorkers had shared the sentiment.

Officials put the prison on lockdown. We were all confined to our cells. From my window, I was able to continue to watch the destruction of the World Trade Center, including the moments the second plane hit the south tower. Nearly 90 minutes later, both towers came down in their entirety.

We were locked down for that entire day. I wasn't sure of any exact details until the next day when we were allowed out to watch the news. Out of concern, all the inmates called home checking on loved ones who were as worried about us as we were them. A handful of us were assigned to go outside and clean in front of the building. MDC is approximately 4.5 miles across the Hudson from where the World Trade Center once stood, and there actually was debris from the towers that littered the street in front of the building. This would go down as one of the saddest days in New York's (if not America's) history.

A week or so went by, and things were back in some order at MDC. Inmates returned to doing their jobs, and the institution re-implemented visitations. My furlough had been approved around this same time but was on hold because of the attacks. As you can imagine, I was upset but understood at the same time. The first chance I got, I spoke with the case manager, and she assured me that as soon as it was possible, she would give me a date. About a week later, I received a furlough date. I let Tiff and my family know that it was confirmed. The night before my furlough, I couldn't sleep at all.

For people that work a 9-5, 12 hours almost seem like an eternity. For my first taste of real freedom in years, it went by in a blink. I wanted to see every person I knew-- my kids, family, and friends. I wanted to eat in my favorite restaurants and re-visit a life I once had. Though I didn't sleep the night before, I never even thought about shutting my eyes. From the time they let me out till the time I got back, I didn't stop moving. The mix of anxiety, desire, and freedom kept me high the entire time out.

Returning to MDC was probably one of the most depressing moments I had experienced in a while. As great as getting out of jail was, returning was one of the hardest things I had to do. It was such a tease. At that point, I'd been locked up for about six and a half years. I had never done a stretch before this bid and truly didn't have a concept of time on the inside. In hindsight, I realize anyone who's done or doing time knows how precious time is and that it's never to be taken for granted. All I could do was get my head back into the bid and look forward to the next furlough in six months.

My time at MDC was fair. I didn't have any real complaints because being in jail was what it was. However, I was getting closer to regaining my freedom. At about this same time, they moved the cadre unit into the new building in MDC. One morning, without explanation, an announcement was made, and we were told that we were moving. They provided instructions as to how it was going to be done. It took most of the day, but by its end, we were officially in the new building on the fifth floor.

We were no longer in the dorm-style housing of the old building. The new building consisted of two-person cells. I kept the same bunkmate, Chewy, who was a Hispanic kid from Rhode Island. He didn't have much money or a lot of family and rarely got visitors. He was in there for some drug shit, but nothing significant. He was at least seven or eight years younger than me. I took care of him as best I could, and without it ever being said or asked, he cleaned the cell, mopped, and cooked his ass off. It was a sign of his loyalty and gratitude, and I, in turn, appreciated him for it.

As time went on, tension arose somewhat based on geography, with Brooklyn and Queens looking to Phil, and Manhattan and the Bronx more entrenched with me. It wasn't anything overt on either of our ends, but nonetheless, it was there.

Prior to my arrival, Phil was the guy everyone looked up to. He had gotten money when we were all in the streets, and he often reminded people of his status through conversations, supported by his pictures. So, when I got there, I believe he felt his status was threatened. Honestly, this was the furthest thing I was thinking about, personally. But over time, the situation started forming itself around this energy.

There was Inch, Artie, Quan, and a hand full of others that ran with Phil. Then, there was Stafa, Troy (a good dude from the south side of Queens), Tate from Harlem, Chewy, Gus from the Bronx, and a few others whose names slip my mind that rode hard with me. This, for the most part, was our core group. The division was primarily the Bronx and Manhattan guys versus Brooklyn and Queens. Troy, like many others, had initially been with Phil, but over time he got closer to me. I was made the leader by proxy, because of my known status in the streets.

I had no desire whatsoever to assume that role. I was short on my remaining time, and all I saw was getting on the other side of the door. Immersing myself in jail politics was the furthest thing from my mind.

The guys we ran with were all cordial towards one another, but it was understood we didn't care for each other. Quan was different. He was from Brooklyn and knew Phil from the street. Though he was cool with him, Quan and I use to rap all the time. He was a smooth dude, especially with the ladies. Quan almost came off like a conman, but not in an offensive way, if that makes any sense. He had several children by a few different women and always was in some shit attempting to juggle his visits and relationships.

Quan was from the Brevoort projects in Bed Stuy. He was tight with notable rappers from his neighborhood, such as Fabolous and Paul Cane. They would come to visit him, and on one of those occasions, he'd introduce us. *Don Diva* was popping in the streets. The magazine had only been in existence for about two years, and we had already been featured on several news shows and were often shouted out on New York's hottest radio station, Hot 97, by the likes of Funkmaster Flex and Kay Slay. Besides my rep from the streets, *Don Diva* made me a celebrity in the joint along with Michael Lohan (Lindsay's father).

Quan was short, having only several months left on his sentence. If I had to guess, he saw the value in developing a relationship with me, realizing I would be home shortly after. I only had about 18 months left on my sentence. All I could think about was going home getting back to my life, so I immersed myself into my *Don Diva* business and looking forward to my weekend visits.

I had another furlough coming up, and because I was working directly for the deputy warden, I was confident in my prospects for approval. The warden has to sign off on all furloughs after the case manager makes the request. I was going beyond what was required of me, ensuring a great impression. The warden signed off, and I was set to have my overnight furlough. My excitement and anticipation were similar to the first. I enjoyed my family and had an opportunity to catch up with a friend or two. No different than my first furlough, it was bittersweet, and returning to jail was difficult. While the day was great, I realize, even subconsciously, I may have tempered my enthusiasm, understanding how difficult the transition was in returning.

I reverted back to my routine, which pretty much consisted of going to work and developing different concepts for *Don Diva*. I just tried doing everything within my means to contribute where I was situated. Usually, on Tiff's visits, we would discuss what went on during that week and what we need to be working on moving forward. I had a lot of friends that I reached out to in prisons all over the country. I wrote letters to them, asking them for their support. They lent a hand in assisting us by either being featured in the magazine or contacting me with someone who we wanted to featured. We were getting very positive feedback in the jails as well in the street, and guys in MDC, surprisingly, were well aware of the strides we were making and the feedback we were getting.

I wasn't overly present in my immediate circumstances, choosing instead to focus on my future and impending release. Working in the commissary, Gus overheard a conversation with Phil and a few dudes from Brooklyn about some issues they had with Peter Shue. In 1994, Peter and I had been battling our cases nearly simultaneously. He also had two hung juries. He was offered five years after his second trial. Instead, he took his case to a third trial and was given a 25-year sentence after a subsequent conviction. He went to a maximum-security facility, and Peter and I had not seen each other since the streets. He was a recent arrival to MDC because of a writ subpoena to testify on behalf of Darryl "D Nice" Taylor from Brooklyn.

I am not clear why, but Phil or one of his guys had an issue with Shue, which may have been an unresolved street situation. While in MDC, Peter was frequenting the law library in the building. As cadres, we were able to move around the building pretty freely. We had access to all the floors that housed inmates. I was cool with most of the CO's, but with most being from Brooklyn, Phil garnered additional favor. It wouldn't have been difficult for either of us to get to anyone in the building. When I got wind of the plot by Phil and his dude, I sent a kite to Shue, giving him a heads up on the scheme. Whatever was supposed to take place never happened.

A couple of days later, as soon as the doors opened at 6 AM, Troy came into my cell and made me aware of an incident that took place late, the evening before, with Gus. He told me that Gus and a couple of dudes from Brooklyn were in the TV room, where cadres were allowed out all night on the weekends. An altercation took place, in which Phil swung on him. It was some real jail shit. Gus was sent out to the infirmary, where he received stitches in his chin and had a bandage on his face.

The CO that was on duty must've reported it as only an accident because no one was locked up for the incident. In any event, Troy was worked up and wanted to handle the situation. I got dressed a little earlier than usual and headed to the common area. Typically, this early, there would only be a handful of individuals that worked the early morning shift. Yet when I walked into the common area, I saw about 15 to 20 people already up and dressed who wouldn't usually be up. It was clear that there was an issue.

Phil and his group of guys were on one side, and the guys that sided with me were on the other. We all just sort of stared across at each other in awkward silence. We were all pretty cool with the CO that was on overnight when the incident occurred. He knew there was an issue and called Phil and me in his cubicle and said it was apparent there was tension. He suggested letting Phil and Gus alone in the TV room to handle their business. Once done, they should shake hands and squash the beef and move on with it. Phil agreed, and all we could hear was a bunch of commotion in the TV room.

The rest of us were still in the common area when Inch began starring over in our direction, and it was clear he was holding a knife. Troy jumped off the table and set it off. After that, everything just erupted. The fight ensued with mop sticks, wringers, makeshift knives, and whatever else could be used as weapons. We were getting it on, and at some point, Phil and I were going at it head-to-head. A couple of minutes went by, and before we knew it, we heard the doors popping, and CO's came rushing in. Everyone dropped whatever weapon they had, and we all headed to our cell.

The CO's locked down the unit and secured the common area. From our cells, we could see a lieutenant called to the floor with a team of investigative officers. They began to open each cell, asking us to step out so they could evaluate us. We were required to remove our shirts and pants to be inspected for cuts and bruises that would potentially indicate having something to do with the incident. Pictures were taken.

As individuals were discovered with signs of fresh injuries, they were immediately escorted from the unit and placed in the Special Housing Unit known as the SHU. I gave myself the once over before they got to my cell. I had some abrasions on my chest, but nothing I didn't believe I couldn't explain or attribute to working out. When my cell was opened, they asked Chewy and me to step out. We both did what was requested. I was cool with the CO that was evaluating us. He pretty much looked us over and put us back in our cell, moving on to the next. I figured we had made it through, and we were good while I continued seeing them escort guys out the unit to the SHU.

The guys from my work crew were called out as this was all going on. My door was opened, and I stepped out, heading down to go to work. Procedurally, you have to show your inmate ID before leaving the unit. I realized I didn't have mine and went back to my cell to retrieve it. Once inside, I noticed it wasn't where it would generally be. I checked a couple of places, but quickly realized I didn't have it. Then, it hit me. It must've fallen out of my pocket during the melee. I went back downstairs and stated I couldn't find it. Damn near in that exact moment, the lieutenant called me over, and I could see he had my ID in his hand. I was handcuffed and escorted to the SHU.

The officers that escorted me upstairs asked, "Chiles, what happened?" I just shook my head and said I had no idea. Their looks of disbelief said enough. This was early enough that technology was still not my enemy. Closed-circuit cameras, as we know them were not as developed, and other than a few strategic areas of the facility, surveillance was not widespread throughout the jail. Since they were unsure as to what happened, we were all placed in individual cells. Before it was all said and done, they had rounded up everyone involved as well as a few people who actually didn't have anything to do with the incident.

I wasn't in the hole an hour when I got a message from the orderly working in the SHU. Peter Shue was there as well and told the orderly to tell me to come out in the morning for rec where he'd meet me. That morning I came out in what is nothing more than a large dog kennel for humans. It's fenced from the floor all the way to the roof, where you're able to see the sky. They only allowed us to come to rec in intervals of half-hours, preventing any of us from interacting with one another.

Shue and I finally got to talk through the fence across from one another. He first told me why he was back at MDC. He explained the situation with D Nice and how he was here to hopefully help him in his case by testifying on his behalf, supporting or providing an alibi for Nice. We then discussed my current situation and it having something to do with that issue with him but not necessarily totally about him. He told me about his relationship or lack thereof when it came to all them dudes.

We were all issued shots. The most serious of the charges were 100 series, which are a loss of good time and a certain amount of time to spend in the SHU. As the days played out, a few people were sent back down to the unit. I already knew a few of those dudes who ran with Phil were hot. So, when the SIS interrogated them, I felt it was only a matter of time before they told what happened. Special Investigative Services - is simply the BOP's version of the police.

We each met with SIS, and everyone's experience was going to be different. Of course, if you help them with their investigation, you were promised it would be taken into consideration. Those that chose not to cooperate were told that no leniency would be considered when it came time for punishment. When my time came to be questioned, I was pretty much told that I was responsible for what had taken place. I was threatened with outside charges being brought and receiving an additional sentence that would begin after my present sentence ended.

They let me know they knew about *Don Diva Magazine* and its (my) aggressive anti-snitch position. I was reminded that I had less than a year to go, and I should consider that more than anything. I didn't waste the person's time going back and forth. I simply said I didn't have anything to say about the incident. They were going to have to prove their case, and I wasn't going to help them.

The SIS investigation went on for several weeks. While in the SHU, you're only allowed one phone call a month, and all visitation was suspended. Each day, you're permitted either an hour of rec or a shower. The choice is yours. About two months in, things started to happen. None of the guys on my side told anything. Honestly, it didn't seem like the other side had told much of anything flat out that I could directly put my finger on. Close to the three months while making a tour of the SHU, the deputy warden was passing by, and she looked in my cell, and I jumped up to talk to her. She said, "Chiles, I'm really disappointed in you. I was surprised when I heard you were in the middle of this." I told her she shouldn't believe everything she heard. I asked what was going on with whatever they were going to do. I said I've been here fighting these charges and hadn't heard much from the Discipline Hearing Officer (DHO). She said that the shots were going to be thrown out, but we were all being transferred to other jails. They weren't going to allow us back in the building.

About a week later, we were officially informed of the dropped charges and transfers. The moves, however, could take weeks. In the interim, our visits were given back. We just weren't allowed to have them in the regular visiting rooms. They took place in the SHU, which was a whole production.

Tiff had to be escorted to the top floor where I was being housed, and my visit was confined to the area in the SHU assigned to attorneys meeting their clients. Tiff gave me the business. She couldn't believe that I would risk my liberty over some jail bullshit. I agreed with her but explained that it wouldn't have mattered if I had one day, I would never allow anybody to disrespect. I assured her the last thing I was trying to do was be in the middle of some nonsense. Not long after our visit, I was told that I was being transferred to the Metropolitan Correctional Center (MCC).

Life is funny; is all I could say to myself. MCC is where this whole nightmare started, and it was where it would end. I now had five months left on my sentence. Once in MCC, my security clearance was lost, and I wasn't allowed to do much of anything. I was good with that. I was more than ready to go and did everything in my control to stay out of the way. I did odd jobs for my last couple of months, nothing worth talking about.

The one thing that did leave an impression on me was meeting some younger dudes from my old Soundview neighborhood in the Bronx. A crew called Sex, Money, Murder had been taken down, and a few members were around in the building. Their presence highlighted the growing presence and impact of gangs in New York.

I knew LA and Chicago guys, so I understood how deep and pervasive gang culture was in places like that. However, I honestly didn't understand it in New York. Yes, we always had gangs, but I always looked at New Yorkers as crewing up for strength in numbers, centered on getting money, not just some set shit.

Their prevalence began in prisons. Hispanics, with The Latin Kings, Netas, and such had unified in places like Rikers to combat safety issues from Blacks and others. Blacks were mostly just unified by neighborhoods and street connections. O.G. Mack was from the Bronx and is universally credited with founding the United Blood Nation in NY. I didn't know Mack, but it turns out he and I had some very interesting connections.

Billy knew his older brother, OG Ty. Ty was one of the people that knew Tom Cross and helped us get info on him right out the box after my mother's death. At some point, Tom supposedly got word of this. Ty was killed, and years later, when Mack was in jail and had founded the Bloods, and Tom was in, there was a directive by the Bloods to get at Tom "on sight." Between Mack's instruction and cats vying to get at Tom to win my favor, Tom endured multiple stabbings. Circumstances, including Mack being found to have testified against someone else when he was 16, and my own arrest and incarceration, ultimately took some of the pressure off dude.

I knew Sex, Money, Murder's de facto leader, Pistol Pete when he was just a kid, and I was a teenager. I knew of his pops, Pete Sr., his mother, and family from the neighborhood. However, Pete wasn't in the building.

He had already been convicted and moved to the federal supermax facility, where he could have virtually no contact with anyone.

Kevin "Bemo" Aller approached me one of those times I was in his unit helping deliver commissary. He introduced himself and stated he already knew who I was and that we were from the same hood. I let him know I had heard about them and all their exploits. We rapped on a few different occasions, but the moment that stood out was when he pulled out his photo album and showed me how he had been living.

Specifically, what stood out was how young he and his experiences were, and now all his positive memories would be frozen in time. Bemo had received a 50-year sentence and was just in his 20's. All I saw was that 40-plus years later, these would be the experiences that he would have to hold on to if he wasn't lucky enough to get relief. It made me think of myself and my co-defendants and the further realization of how fortunate we all were. I was deep in reflection and sad at the same time, for him. I kept a straight face and sincerely told him that I hoped he caught a break. We exchanged info and have been in touch well over 15 years since.

That interaction reflected the crossroads I was at in my life. I was still angry from my own experiences. I was still an outlaw at heart and hadn't lost my edge. I had made connections inside, and many others I had done business with were still on the outside. I couldn't wait to get out, hustle, and get back on top.

However, I was also not the same person. I had experienced a loss of liberty and could see its effects on my family and myself. I wasn't trying to go back to jail, and my interaction with Bemo was another stark reminder of the stakes at play. I was more mature and smarter, but also well aware that the government had a hard-on for me. They were not going to let me escape if there was a next time.

I embodied the dichotomy that often comes with growth and knowledge. This was my conflicted mindset as I prepared to embark on my next chapter. I was filled with as much hope, as I was uncertainty. The only consistent, clear thought was I could not wait to be home.

I knew that day was real when my clothes were received. I was made aware that they were in receiving and discharge. The feelings that I had the morning I was called down to R & D were indescribable. I dapped up the handful of dudes I fooled with and rolled out. I was taken downstairs where I was put in a room and given my clothes. None of that overly mattered to me because I had been on two furloughs, so I had gotten past having street clothes on. I needed the doors to swing open to free me.

As the doors popped one after another, I was that much closer to the beginning of the rest of my life. It was time to fulfill the promises I made to myself, Tiff, and my family. I knew it was game time. I walked out in January 2004, nearly eight and a half years after I was arrested. Right there waiting with open arms was Tiff, the person who held me down for what felt like forever. She jumped into my arms, and I told her I got it from here.

I recall looking to the left and the right: the proverbial crossroads, and to be honest, I could see merits in going in either direction.

EPILOGUE

Anyone that knows me knows I don't seek publicity or fame. Twenty plus years later, I still don't have my name on the masthead of *Don Diva*. Nor do I have any personal social media accounts. I do what I do to give a platform to the voiceless and share my perspective. I do this so that some may not have to walk through the fires I did to realize they will get burned. I do it for the love of the Game and all that is wrong with it.

The hardest thing about writing this book was trying to be the young Kevin Chiles. Channeling the energy to give an authentic experience was very difficult. I wanted my words to come off rhythmic, for the reader to be able to feel my excitement, my energy, and my pain in the sincerity of my words.

When I first started, the landscape was full of naive, youthful, men believing we were the solutions for our families and even our communities. In hindsight, I now realize we were more the problem. Thirty-plus years later, here I am writing about my life and all it entailed, the highs and the lows. Most of the individuals I started with are dead or in jail, and the few that aren't, at the very least, have spent significant time behind bars.

I have evolved so much that reliving some of these things; I find myself reflecting in disbelief at some of my antics. Some were utterly ridiculous and others unbelievable. It also was very revealing and therapeutic. This experience enabled me to reflect on individual relationships in a specific light, and in others, I found a resolution. I've never really been in touch with my emotions or my reality. Writing this book has been the closest I've come to anything so revealing regarding providing insight into my life.

Even as I am writing these words, I am shaking my head. I do not know why I didn't stop hustling. Reflecting on it now seems like madness. I don't know the young Kevin. I wrote certain aspects of my life in my youthful egotistical mindset and others with the temperament of an older wiser man. Hindsight is truly 20/20. I do not know where I had the energy to get out of bed and deal with the negativity and danger voluntarily. I had no spiritual awakening or incredible epiphany. Jail, of course, forced a change of lifestyle, but I was starting to come to that realization already. I can recall the addictive draw of the money and The Life. We lacked guidance and understanding. We had the balls to take the chances, but not the foresight and wisdom to comprehend the dangers and long-term detriment that those chances entailed. That is all part of the psychosis of life in the streets.

I am unabashedly someone who disdains people who lack loyalty. Does this include rats? Yes, but it is so much more than that. It is about people who treat integrity as disposable. Friendships and relationships mean so much more to me than that. I started *Don Diva*, in part, to call out those that had no honor and shed light on those that played the Game out until the end as we all knew it should. I am no old, washed-up, bitter dude. I am smart enough to know that most millennials don't give a fuck about these morals and principles to which I refer. Millennials reward fame and money regardless of how it is gained. However, I keep *Don Diva* going to provide a different perspective to many of you that only know what you do because of who was able to shape the narrative first.

When it comes to these gangster tales, based on true stories, it is no coincidence that the ones who generally get to narrate history are the ones who sold out and told. They are able to tell stories of crimes freely because their cooperation agreements often include immunity.

I've stood the test of time. I've been stabbed, been on both ends of a gun. I have been incarcerated and am now free. I've made millions, lost millions, and saw and endured things unimaginable to the average person. It was not easy for me to tell my story. Instead, as someone beyond blessed, with the benefit of time, hindsight, and growth, I thought it would be selfish not to share some of the knowledge that longevity has given me.

Many truisms govern America. One in particular that stands out for me is that "if the government hates you enough, they will make up or find laws to throw your ass in jail." Who does America hate more than drug dealers or, more specifically, young black and brown men making more money in a year than most could ever imagine in their lifetimes? If you don't think the system is rigged against you. Think again. I am not standing on a pulpit preaching. But I do hope you let my life and mistakes serve as a cautionary tale.

America is a sociologist's dream/nightmare. America has an Urban Underclass that is mired in a perpetual cycle. Urban Underclass is given insufficient resources to survive and compete on its own. Educational resources are lacking— systemic racism, injustices, and mass incarcerations that become its own self-fulfilling prophecy run rampant. Social services and resources are limited, and when people who are in need ask, they are belittled and made to feel ashamed. When those entrapped in these urban wastelands show any entrepreneurial spirit, they are pursued and punished with the full weight and resources of the US Government.

This isn't a justification for selling drugs or illegal hustles as much as an understanding of its partial cause and effect. And before some of you ride off on your moral high horse, understand that one of the major elements to that cause and effect is the US population's overwhelming desire to get high. You can condemn that on any level you choose, but in doing so, be cognizant of the US government's duplicity in legalizing, sanctioning and profiting through allowing tobacco, alcohol and pharmaceutical companies, through the dispensing of opiates and stimulants, toward contributing to America's appetite to get high. And let's not forget the US government's role in crack distribution with the Iran-Contra affair. It's only apparently a problem when inner-city youth within that Urban Underclass change their economic circumstances through those same means.

Sharing my story has been a delicate balance between glamorizing a time and lifestyle that had devastating effects on multiple generations for a multitude of reason versus becoming too preachy in serving as a cautionary tale to the youth of "don't do what I did." I have been asked, would I do it all over again. My answer may surprise and even confuse you.

I would not change anything about my life or my path, except for my mother's passing. Everything that I did saw and experienced made me the man who I am today, and for the most part, I am happy with that person. That said, if I were advising my younger self, as I have tried to do with my sons, I would strongly let him know what the distinctions are between being a hustler and playing in those murky waters of "illegal hustles." Don't just take my word. Statistics show how disproportionately imprisoned and harshly sentenced Black and Latino youth are for crimes versus the rest of the populace.

This brings me to sharing something I once read, written by a good friend of mine. There is much we do not know when we are young or merely un-educated to the more significant nuances of life. However, do not mistake what you do not know as an excuse for willfully choosing not to educate yourself.

IGNORANCE VS. LACK OF KNOWLEDGE

A definition of 'ignorance" is a lack of knowledge or information. While I am not Merriam-Webster, I do think there is a distinct difference between ignorance and lack of knowledge.

I am formally educated and went to a great high school. I was privileged to attend one of the world's best and most recognized Universities. I went to law school and subsequently passed the bar. Yet, what I do not know, far surpasses anything I would claim to know by such a vast margin it would be laughable.

An education, even coupled with a wealth of significant life experiences, still leaves most of us on the deficit side of knowledgeable. It is okay not to know everything. There are many sides to issues that there is no real expectation that we should be knowledgeable about all (but that isn't an excuse to know nothing).

Ignorance, however, is the pervasive and persistent continuation of a lack of knowledge and information when you have the ability and resources to change that course.

Ignorance is a refusal to learn. Ignorance is a refusal to try and understand viewpoints other than your own. It is one thing to simply not know something and, it is entirely plausible that you do not understand what knowledge or information you are lacking. However, when it has been brought to your attention, refusal to investigate something or otherwise further educate yourself, then transfers from a lack of knowledge to ignorance.

I am sure this falls within semantics, but lack of knowledge or information is a state of being. It may occur naturally. Ignorance is a proactive occurrence and one that takes place by choice. Technology may come with downsides, but one of the absolute positives is that information is literally at our fingertips.

So much of what I learned in school had little to do with the subject matter itself and more to do with the ability to learn. Pre-Google, I had to research topics, fact check, and cite sources to substantiate my thesis or arguments. I had to go to libraries and find books or microfilm. The process was time-consuming, and in no way do I miss it.

That type of research to learn basic information on subjects is unnecessary today. The real task is in trying to disseminate amidst all of the information that comes up at the touch of an icon. Too much information may be a challenge, but it cannot serve as an excuse for not putting in the time to educate oneself.

The time excuse also holds little weight. I understand time is a valuable commodity in all of our lives, but taking the time to educate yourself better has to fall within the priority section of our lives. I am super busy, yet I learn something every day because it is so evident that there are so many subjects, I NEED to understand better.

We all lack knowledge to a degree. Those of us who continue, by choice, to stay uneducated and uninformed are the problem. That is ignorance - a proactive choice that should never be made, especially with the wealth of resources available to us all.

Made in the USA
Middletown, DE
28 March 2021